W9-BED-162

THE

Reader's Digest
TREASURY OF
MODERN
QUOTATIONS

THE

Reader's Digest
TREASURY OF
MODERN
QUOTATIONS

Selected by the Editors of
Reader's Digest

Line Drawings by Jerome Snyder

Reader's Digest Press

DISTRIBUTED BY

THOMAS Y. CROWELL COMPANY

NEW YORK

1975

Manufactured in the United States of America

Library of Congress Cataloging in Publication Data
Main entry under title:

The Reader's digest treasury of modern quotations.

  1. Quotations, English. I. The Reader's digest.
II. Title. Treasury of modern quotations.
PN6081.R43   828′.02   75–12867
ISBN 0–88349–027–7

---

10 9 8 7 6 5 4 3 2 1

Grateful acknowledgment is made to the following organizations and individuals for permission to reprint material from the indicated sources:

Arlington House for QUOTATIONS FROM CHAIRMAN BILL, by William F. Buckley, copyright © 1970 by Arlington House, New Rochelle, New York. All rights reserved, used with permission; Atheneum Publishers for THE MAKING OF THE PRESIDENT 1972 by Theodore H. White. Copyright © 1973 by Theodore H. White, reprinted by permission of the publishers; THE PERSECUTION AND ASSASSINATION OF JEAN-PAUL MARAT AS PERFORMED BY THE INMATES OF THE ASYLUM OF CHARENTON UNDER THE DIRECTION OF THE MARQUIS DE SADE by Peter Weiss, copyright © 1965 by John Calder Ltd. English Version by Geoffrey Skelton. Verse adaptation by Adrian Mitchell. Reprinted by permission of Atheneum Publishers, New York and in Great Britain by Calder & Boyars Ltd; Coward, McCann & Geoghegan, Inc. for THE FRAIL OCEAN by Wesley Marx, copyright © 1967 by Wesley Marx, reprinted by permission of Coward, McCann & Geoghegan, Inc. and Mary Yost Associates; Thomas Y. Crowell for LAST SURVIVORS by Noel M. Simon and Paul Geroudet, reprinted by permission of Thomas Y. Crowell for the U.S. and Canada; MARK TWAIN HIMSELF by Milton Meltzer, copyright © 1960 by Milton Meltzer, reprinted with the permission of the Thomas Y. Crowell Company, Inc.; Crown Publishers, Inc. for THE JOY OF SEX by Alex Comfort, M.B., Ph. D., © Modsets Securities Ltd. 1972, used by permission of Crown Publishers, Inc., New York; MEN AT WAR edited by Ernest Hemingway, copyright 1942 by Crown Publishers, used by permission of Crown Publishers, Inc., New York; Dial Press for THE FIRE NEXT TIME by James Baldwin, copyright © 1962, 1963 by James Baldwin, reprinted by arrangement with The Dial Press; Harper & Row, Publishers for excerpt from p. 116 "Poetry" in ONE MAN'S MEAT by E. B. White, copyright 1940 by E. B. White; excerpt from WHY JOHNNY CAN'T READ by Rudolf Flesch, 1955; excerpt from MALABAR FARM by Louis Bromfield, 1948; excerpt from ON ACTIVE SERVICE IN PEACE AND WAR by Henry L. Stimson and McGeorge Bundy, 1948; excerpt from p. 157 in JESTING PILATE by Aldous Huxley, 1926. Reprinted by permission of Harper & Row and in Great Britain by Mrs. Laura Huxley and Chatto & Windus Ltd.; David Higham Associates and Ann Watkins, Inc., for UNPOPULAR OPINIONS by Dorothy L. Sayers, published by Victor Gollancz, copyright 1947, Dorothy L. Sayers, renewed 1973 by Anthony Fleming; Holt, Rinehart and Winston, Inc. for "The laws of God, the laws of man," from THE COLLECTED POEMS OF A. E. HOUSMAN, copyright 1922 by Holt, Rinehart and Winston, Inc. Copyright 1950 by Barclays Bank Ltd. Reprinted by permission of Holt, Rinehart and Winston, Publishers and in Great Britain by the Society of Authors; THE QUIET CRISIS by Stewart L. Udall, THE SQUIRREL CAGE by Dorothy Canfield Fisher, THE OUTERMOST HOUSE by Henry Beston; Indiana University Press for THE MORAL DECISION by Edmond Cahn, copyright © 1955 by Indiana University Press, Bloomington.

CONTENTS

ix

The Working World

Education

Health

History and Civilization

Law and Justice

THE ARTS

The Arts and Artists

Living is a form of not being sure, not knowing what next or how. The moment you know how, you begin to die a little. The artist never entirely knows. We guess. We may be wrong, but we take leap after leap in the dark.

Agnes De Mille, as quoted in *Life*, November 15,
1963

Is adversity in the arts ennobling? I doubt it. I struggled 15 years before I made any success. It didn't make me a better person, it just made me hungry. Whatever moral character you're ever going to have you pretty well have by the time you're 20. Repeated failures don't help.

Agnes De Mille, as quoted in *Life*, November 15, 1963

What is the public responsibility to the arts? You have to distinguish good from bad, support the good and write your congressman. He may not be able to read your letters, but he can count them.

Agnes De Mille, as quoted in *Life*, November 15, 1963

Art flourishes where there is a sense of adventure, a sense of nothing having been done before, of complete freedom to experiment; but when caution comes in you get repetition and repetition is the death of art.

Alfred North Whitehead, *Dialogues of Alfred North
Whitehead*

The arts cannot thrive except where men are free to be themselves and to be in charge of the discipline of their own energies and ardors. The conditions for democracy and for art are one and the same. What we call liberty in politics results in freedom of the arts. There can be no vitality in the works gathered in a museum unless there exists the right of spontaneous life in the society in which the arts are nourished.

Franklin D. Roosevelt, on the dedication of the Museum of
Modern Art, New York, May 10, 1939

We must never forget that art is not a form of propaganda, it is a form of truth. And as Mr. [Archibald] MacLeish once remarked of poets, "There is nothing worse for our trade than to be in style." In free society art is not a weapon and it does not belong to the sphere of polemics and ideology. Artists are not engineers of the soul.

John F. Kennedy, address at Amherst College, October 26,
1963

If art is to nourish the roots of our culture, society must set the artist free to follow his vision wherever it takes him.

John F. Kennedy, address at Amherst College, October 26,
1963

4

Art-speech is the only truth. An artist is usually a damned liar, but his art, if it be art, will tell you the truth of his day. And that is all that matters. Away with eternal truth. Truth lives from day to day, and the marvellous Plato of yesterday is chiefly bosh today.

D. H. Lawrence, Studies in Classic American Literature

America has not always been kind to its artists and scholars. Somehow the scientists always seem to get the penthouse while the arts and humanities get the basement.

Lyndon B. Johnson, speech upon signing the Arts and
Humanities Act of 1965, September 29, 1965

All art is based on non-conformity.

Ben Shahn, as quoted in the Atlantic Monthly, September
1957

At one time a famous state undertook to resolve the problem of the arts by getting along without them. The venture did not succeed. Sparta is today an undistinguished valley visited by tourists who remember something about a boy with a fox in his shirt. At other times and in other places governments have gone at the trouble the other way around: they have attempted to domesticate the arts by supporting the artists. This method has sometimes worked as, for example, in Florence during the years when the Princes were artists themselves, and in France when the French were Parisians. Elsewhere its success has been dubious. In Russia, where artists are rewarded with the best apartments and the prettiest dachas, works of art are rare.

Archibald MacLeish, statement marking the fiftieth
anniversary of the American Society of Composers,
Authors and Publishers (ASCAP), February 13, 1964

Art is reaching out into the ugliness of the world for vagrant beauty and the imprisoning of it in a tangible dream.

George Jean Nathan, The Critic and the Drama　5

Criticism is the art wherewith a critic tries to guess himself into a share of the artist's fame.

George Jean Nathan, *The House of Satan*

What was any art but a mould in which to imprison for a moment the shining elusive element which is life itself—life hurrying past us and running away, too strong to stop, too sweet to lose.

Willa Cather, *The Song of the Lark*

An artist's saddest secrets are those that have to do with his artistry.

Willa Cather, *Youth and the Bright Medusa*

Art, it seems to me, should simplify.

Willa Cather, *On the Art of Fiction*

Nothing can come out of an artist that is not in the man.

H. L. Mencken, *Prejudices: Fifth Series*

Nine times out of ten, in the arts as in life, there is actually no truth to be discovered; there is only error to be exposed.

H. L. Mencken, *Prejudices: First Series*

The impulse to create beauty is rather rare in literary men. . . . Far ahead of it comes the yearning to make money. And after the yearning to make money comes the yearning to make a noise.

H. L. Mencken, *Prejudices: Fifth Series*

Art is the stored honey of the human soul, gathered on wings of misery and travail.

Theodore Dreiser, *Life, Art, and America*

Art is the mold of feeling as language is the mold of thought.

Susanne K. Langer, as quoted in *Who Designs America*

There is nothing but art. Art is living. To attempt to give an object of art life by dwelling on its historical, cultural, or archaeological associations is senseless.

W. Somerset Maugham, *The Summing Up*

Art, if it is to be reckoned as one of the great values of life, must teach men humility, tolerance, wisdom and magnanimity. The value of art is not beauty, but right action.

W. Somerset Maugham, *A Writer's Notebook*

Art is the difference between seeing and just identifying.

Jean Mary Norman, *Art: Of Wonder and the World*

Except for the American woman, nothing interests the eye of the American man more than the automobile, or seems so important to him as an object of aesthetic appreciation.

Alfred H. Barr, opening a 1963 exhibit at the Museum of Modern Art, New York, displaying "pop art" that incorporated pieces of old cars

If art can reveal the truth, art can also lie. An artist can be not only divinely inspired, but diabolically inspired.

George Bernard Shaw, as quoted in the *Christian Commonwealth*, October 14, 1908

Today, in a secular world, it is almost wholly through the arts that we have a living reminder of the terror and nobility of what we are.

J. Robert Oppenheimer, speech in New York, March 1963   7

An artist is always alone—if he *is* an artist . . . the artist needs loneliness.

Henry Miller, Tropic of Cancer

I have a feeling that people who go in for involved, unexpected super-original—if I may coin that word—forms of art ought to have credentials.

Sir Winston Churchill, as quoted in The New York Times,
May 1, 1954

Without tradition, art is a flock of sheep without a shepherd. Without innovation, it is a corpse.

Sir Winston Churchill, address to the Royal Academy of
Arts, as quoted in Time, May 11, 1953

The famous "modern break with tradition" has lasted long enough to have produced its own tradition.

Harold Rosenberg, Tradition of the New

Criticism clearly recognizes in every work of art an organism governed by its own law.

Joel E. Spingarn, as quoted in New Criticism, March 9,
1940

Any great work of art is great because it creates a special world of its own. It revives and readapts time and space, and the measure of its success is the extent to which it makes you an inhabitant of the world—the extent to which it invites you in and lets you breathe its strange, special air.

Leonard Bernstein, as quoted in Vogue, December 1958

Art must unquestionably have a social value; that is, as potential means of communication it must be addressed, and in comprehensible terms, to the understanding of mankind.

Rockwell Kent, It's Me O Lord: The Autobiography of
Rockwell Kent

8

The finest works of art are precious, among other reasons, because they make it possible for us to know, if only imperfectly and for a little while, what it actually feels like to think subtly and feel nobly.

Aldous Huxley, *Ends and Means*

Nothing is so poor and melancholy as art that is interested in itself and not in its subject.

George Santayana, *The Life of Reason*

Immature artists imitate. Mature artists steal.

Lionel Trilling, as quoted in *Esquire*, March 31, 1962

In art economy is always beauty.

Henry James, *The Altar of the Dead*

The true artist sees the harmony, the wholeness, the tendencies toward perfection in things everywhere.

Richard Guggenheimer, *Creative Vision*

The artist of today says to the public: If you don't understand this you are dumb. I maintain that you are not. If you have to go the whole way to meet the artist, it's his fault.

Marya Mannes, as quoted in *Life*, June 12, 1964

The artist, like the God of the creation, remains within or behind or beyond or above his handiwork, invisible, refined out of existence, indifferent, paring his fingernails.

James Joyce, *Portrait of the Artist as a Young Man*

It is for artists to remind humanity of the unconquerable and to assert the eternity of ideas.

John Oliver Hobbes, *The Dream of Business*   9

Art is the terms of armistice signed with fate.

Bernard De Voto, *Mark Twain at Work*

An artist is anyone who glorifies his occupation.

Bliss Carman, *The Making of Personality*

Despite the triumph of scientific technology, the modern world still derives its color from art, music and poetry, and its catchwords from history and fiction. People could reject science more readily than singing, dancing and storytelling.

René Dubos, as quoted in *Reader's Digest*, January 1973

Eccentricity is not a proof of genius, and even an artist should remember that originality consists not only in doing things differently, but also in "doing things better."

Edmund Clarence Steadman, *Victorian Poets*

My reply to the superior critic has always been—forgive me—damn you, do it better.

H. G. Wells, *World Brain*

Accuracy is not just a matter of facts; it is also correct spelling, punctuation, grammar, measurement, context, relevance—in a word, precision. I learned this from my first city editor, who taught me that a door is not a doorway; that "no injuries were reported" does not mean "there were no injuries"; that a man *charged* with burglary is not necessarily a burglar. . . .

At its best, accuracy is a painstaking, caring, patient and reasonable faculty of mind. And ultimately it is creative, too. For it not only looks up facts, it discovers them in the first place.

 Evan Hill, as quoted in *Reader's Digest*, October 1973

Creativeness often consists of merely turning up what is already there. Did you know that right and left shoes were thought up only a little more than a century ago?

Bernice Fitz-Gibbon, Macy's, Gimbels and Me

A painter must have his canvas. A musician must have his instrument. But to take the invisible stuff of life and mold it so as to awaken another's awareness, strengthen another's faith, deepen another's love, steel another's courage—this, too, is artistry.

Jean Bell Mosley, as quoted in Reader's Digest, November
1973

A guidance counselor who has made a fetish of security, or who has unwittingly surrendered his thinking to economic determinism, may steer a youth away from his dream of becoming a poet, an artist, a musician, or any other of thousands of things, because it offers no security, it does not pay well, there are no vacancies, it has no "future." Among all the tragic consequences of depression and war, this suppression of personal self-expression through one's life work is among the most poignant.

Henry M. Wriston, as quoted in the Wall Street Journal,
June 1, 1960

The art of our era is not art, but technology. Today Rembrandt is painting automobiles; Shakespeare is writing research reports; Michelangelo is designing more efficient bank lobbies.

Howard Sparks, The Petrified Truth

You can't get high aesthetic tastes, like trousers, ready made.

W. S. Gilbert, Patience

The art of showmanship is to give the public what it wants just before it knows what it wants.

David Belasco, as quoted in Reader's Digest, July 1970   11

An artist cannot speak about his art any more than a plant can discuss horticulture.

Jean Cocteau, as quoted in Newsweek, May 16, 1955

The sartorial artist no less than the sculptor, the painter and the musician dreams of creations that will awaken a response in the soul of the world.

Lady Duff-Gordon, as quoted in Reader's Digest, February
1947

The origin of art: the discrepancy between physical fact and psychic effect. The content of art: visual formulation of our reaction to life. The measure of art: the ratio of effort to effect. The aim of art: revelation and evocation of vision.

Josef Albers, as quoted in Abstract Art Since 1945

I have always believed and still believe that artists who live and work with spiritual values cannot and should not remain indifferent to a conflict in which the highest values of humanity and civilization are at stake.

Pablo Picasso, in 1937, while director of the Prado
Museum, Madrid, as quoted in Picasso on Art

The more perfect the artist, the more completely separate in him will be the man who suffers and the mind which creates; the more perfectly will the mind digest and translate the passions which are its material.

T. S. Eliot, as quoted in "Tradition and the Individual
Talent"

All in all, the creative act is not performed by the artist alone; the spectator brings the work in contact with the external world by deciphering and interpreting its inner qualifications and thus adds his contribution to the creative act.

Marcel Duchamp, as quoted in New Art

Everything is already in art—like a big bowl of soup.

Willem de Kooning, as quoted in *Abstract Art Since 1945*

Today the artist is no longer constrained by the limitation that all of man's experience is expressed by his outward appearance. . . . The whole of man's experience becomes his model, and in that sense it can be said that all of art is a portrait of an idea.

Mark Rothko, as quoted in his Pratt Lecture, 1958

Today when our aspirations have been reduced to a desperate attempt to escape from evil, and times are out of joint, our obsessive, subterranean and pictographic images are the expression of the neurosis which is our reality.

Adolph Gottlieb, as quoted in *Abstract Art Since 1945*

Art is much less important than life, but what a poor life without it!

Robert Motherwell, as quoted in a letter to Frank O'Hara, 1965

What I dream of is an art of balance, of purity and serenity, devoid of troubling or depressing subject matter, an art which could be for every mental worker, for the businessman as well as the man of letters, for 13 example, a soothing calming influence on the mind, something which provides relaxation from fatigue and toil.

Henri Matisse, as quoted in Matisse on Art

The artist who sets about making a critique of social ills is bound to play the role of utopian: one who cannot, like the academic sociologist, allow the grim tyranny of established fact to monopolize the discussion of human potentialities.

Theodore Roszak, The Making of a Counter Culture

Painting, Sculpture, Photography

Modern paintings are like women. You'll never enjoy them if you try to understand them.

Harold Coffin, as quoted in Reader's Digest, December 1960

There is nothing more difficult for a truly creative painter than to paint a rose, because before he can do so he has first to forget all the roses that were ever painted.

Henri Matisse, comment recalled in obituaries reporting his death, as quoted in news summaries of November 5, 1954

Colors have the inherent power of affecting the feelings of those who look at them.

Henri Matisse, as quoted in Abstract Art Since 1945

At its best, photography can be an extra sense, or a reservoir for the senses. Even when you don't press the trigger, the exercise of focusing through a camera can make you better remember thereafter a person or a moment. Photography can teach people to look, to feel, to remember in a way that they didn't know they could.

14

Edwin Land, as quoted in Reader's Digest, January 1974

Some pictures are in the gallery because they belong to humanity and others because they belong to the United States.

André Malraux, visiting the National Gallery of Art in Washington as French Minister of Culture, as quoted in the New York *Herald Tribune*, May 12, 1962

A greater sculptor than a Rodin or a Michelangelo is Thought. What a man thinks in his heart he advertises with his face.

Thomas Dreier, as quoted in *Reader's Digest*, July 1951

Art does not reproduce the visible; rather, it makes visible.

Paul Klee, as quoted in *The Inward Vision*

Art, like morality, consists in drawing the line somewhere.

G. K. Chesterton, as quoted in *Reader's Digest*, October 1939

If only we could pull out our brain and use only our eyes.

Pablo Picasso, on painting objectively, as quoted in *Saturday Review*, September 1, 1956

Art is a lie that makes us realize the truth.

Pablo Picasso, as quoted in *Quote*, September 21, 1958

Not only did we try to displace reality; reality was no longer in the object. Reality was in the painting. When the Cubist painter said to himself, "I will paint a bowl," he set out with the full realization that a bowl in a painting has nothing to do with a bowl in real life. We no longer wanted to fool the eye; we wanted to fool the mind.

Pablo Picasso, as quoted in *Reader's Digest*, July 1972

Cubism is no different from any other school of painting. . . . The fact that for a long time cubism has not been understood and that even 15 today there are people who cannot see anything in it means nothing. I do not read English. . . . This does not mean that the English language does not exist, and why should I blame anybody else but myself if I cannot understand what I know nothing about?

Pablo Picasso, in 1923, as quoted in Picasso: 50 Years of His Art, by Alfred H. Barr, Jr.

Rembrandt painted about 700 pictures—of these 3000 are in existence.

Wilhelm Bode, as quoted in Reader's Digest, October 1927

For me, painting is a way to forget life. It is a cry in the night, a strangled laugh.

Georges Rouault, as quoted in Look, April 15, 1958

There are three kinds of people in the world: those who can't stand Picasso, those who can't stand Raphael and those who've never heard of either of them.

John White, as quoted in Reader's Digest, May 1960

When I am finishing a picture I hold some God-made object up to it—a rock, a flower, the branch of a tree or my hand—as a kind of final test. If the painting stands up beside a thing man cannot make, the painting is authentic. If there's a clash between the two, it is bad art.

Marc Chagall, as quoted in the Saturday Evening Post, December 2, 1962

Compared to Velasquez I am nothing, but compared to contemporary painters, I am the most big genius of modern time . . . but modesty is not my specialty.

Salvador Dali, as quoted in the New York Herald Tribune, January 13, 1960

Unless a picture shocks, it is nothing.

Marcel Duchamp, as quoted in Life, January 2, 1950

If a man takes 50 Campbell soup cans and puts them on a canvas, it is not the retinal image which concerns us. What interests us is the concept that wants to put 50 Campbell soup cans on a canvas.

> Marcel Duchamp on the paintings of Andy Warhol, as quoted in *The New Art*

My aim in painting has always been the most exact transcription possible of my most intimate impression of nature.

> Edward Hopper, as quoted in *Life*, April 17, 1950

I paint the women slimmer than they are and their jewels fatter.

> Cornelius van Dongen, as quoted in *Reader's Digest*, February 1954

Being present at your own exhibit is like being called out of rank during an Army physical inspection. It's embarrassing.

> Ludwig Bemelman, as quoted in *Time*, March 31, 1952

[Abstract art is] a product of the untalented, sold by the unprincipled to the utterly bewildered.

> Al Capp, as quoted in the *National Observer*, July 1, 1963

Too many of today's artists have persuaded themselves that the grotesque is more expressive than the higher grace. It is always easier to caricature than to reveal, to shout than to sing, to pretend than to be true.

Richard Guggenheimer, Creative Vision

My ideal of a picture is that every part of it should oblige the looker-on who has any real sense for a whole to see the rest.

Leo Stein, Journey into the Self

Painting is the art of protecting flat surfaces from the weather and exposing them to the critic.

Ambrose Bierce, as quoted in Reader's Digest, February 1968

Paintin's not important. The important thing is keeping busy. If you know somethin' well, you can always paint it . . . people would be better off buyin' chickens.

Grandma Moses, as quoted in Life, September 19, 1960

We all cry and laugh but never at the same time or for the same reason. It is up to the photographer to catch the instant that is the reality of the person or of the moment.

Edward Steichen, as quoted in Time, April 7, 1961

One of the finest designs in all industry was the Coca-Cola bottle. It fitted the hand, enhanced the quality of the contents, felt good when cool, and was less breakable than an ordinary bottle. I wish I could do as well with some of my ideas.

Paolo Lomazzi, creator of the inflatable armchair, as quoted in Reader's Digest, September 1969

If my husband would ever meet a woman on the street who looked like the women in his paintings, he would fall over in a dead faint.

Mrs. Pablo Picasso, as quoted in Quote, July 3, 1955

18

Looking at sculpture teaches people to use their inborn sense of form, to improve their own surroundings, to make life marvelous! . . .

You know, there's an artist hidden in every human being. A few years ago, I took on a hired man who had no use for sculpture. Then he watched me work. After a while, he started bringing in some pebbles he'd found. Well, they were beautiful. That's just what happens: people begin to look!

Henry Moore, as quoted in *Reader's Digest*, April 1970

Within every man and woman a secret is hidden, and as a photographer it is my task to reveal it if I can. The revelation, if it comes at all, will come in a small fraction of a second with an unconscious gesture, a gleam of the eye, a brief lifting of the mask that all humans wear to conceal their innermost selves from the world. In that fleeting interval of opportunity the photographer must act or lose his prize.

Yousuf Karsh, as quoted in *Reader's Digest*, January 1973

Consider the drama of Van Gogh: zealous preacher turns clumsy artist, paints crawling landscapes which nobody buys, finally commits suicide.

Consider his historical impact: the art establishment of his time failed to recognize him, but almost everything he did has been recognized since, and his works have probably been reproduced more often than those of any other artist. In sum, we realize now that his pictures are as exciting as his life—and so spontaneously painted that the magnitude of his personality is immediately felt.

Thomas S. Buechner, as quoted in *Reader's Digest*, January 1972

I am just making the last painting which anyone can make.

Ad Reinhardt, on his all-black paintings, as quoted in *Abstract Art Since 1945*

The truly modern artist *consciously* perceives the abstractness of the emotion of beauty: he *consciously* recognizes aesthetic emotion as cosmic, universal. This conscious recognition results in an abstract creation, directs him toward the purely universal.

Piet Mondrian, as quoted in *Abstract Art Since 1945*

For painter Henri Matisse, art was a kind of pilgrimage. "It is like taking a train to Marseille," he once explained. "Each painting completed is like a station—just so much nearer the goal. The time comes when the painter is apt to feel he has at last arrived. Then, if he is honest, he realizes one of two things—either he has not arrived, after all, or Marseille is not where he wanted to go anyway, and he must push farther on."

> Melvin Maddocks, as quoted in *Reader's Digest*, September 1973

I want to literally be in the painting.

> Jackson Pollock, as quoted in *Abstract Art Since 1945*

It is to devoted Christian artists like Raphael and Botticelli that we owe our own workaday image of an angel. Arrayed in brilliant garb, the airy messengers are poised in flight or busy ministering to Christ and the Madonna. Their wings, however, are shown to be mere symbols— too small to carry them, by all rules of flight. (And how, quibblers might ask, does an angel get into his tunic?)

> Ernest O. Hauser, as quoted in *Reader's Digest*, December 1972

The emergence of abstract art is one sign that there are still men able to assert feeling in the world. Men who know how to respect and follow their inner feelings, no matter how irrational or absurd they may first appear. From their perspective, it is the social world that tends to appear irrational and absurd.

> Robert Motherwell, as quoted in "What Abstract Art Means to Me," *Bulletin of the Museum of Modern Art*, Spring 1951

Architecture

I venture to predict that long after the public has wearied of Frank Lloyd Wright's inverted oatmeal dish and silo with their awkward cantilevering, their jaundiced skin and the ingenious spiral ramp leading down past the abstractions which mirror the tortured maladjustments of our time, the Metropolitan will still wear well.

Robert Moses, on the Guggenheim Museum, New York, as
quoted in The New York Times, May 21, 1959

Always design a thing by considering it in its next larger context—a chair in a room, a room in a house, a house in an environment, an environment in a city plan.

Eliel Saarinen, as quoted in Time, July 2, 1956

We shape our buildings; thereafter they shape us.

Sir Winston Churchill, as quoted in Time, August 8, 1954

We live in the time of the colossal upright oblong. We are meeting in the city where the skyscraper was born.

Carl Sandburg, address to the Chicago Dynamic
Committee, as quoted in Life, November 4, 1957

I tell you, again, the need of the hour is for Men! Be a man! And, in the manliness of your own soul, impart virility to your art! When you shall carefully have studied the forms and the spirit of these historic structures, you will realize the more and the more impressively as you grow older, that the civilizations which produced them are definitely of the past—and that the ways thereof are not your ways.

The more deeply this truth sinks into your consciousness, the stronger will grow your conviction that never can you use these forms as they, who made them, used them. For the peculiar, characteristic subjectivity which animated these men, and which they infused into their works, has vanished with the physical presence of these men, their day and their generation.

Louis Henri Sullivan, Kindergarten Chats

Architecture is the will of an epoch translated into space.

. . . creative work has only a single goal: to create order out of the desperate confusion of our time.

21

A chair is a very difficult object. A skyscraper is almost easier. That is why Chippendale is famous.

Ludwig Mies van der Rohe, as quoted in *Time*, February 18, 1957

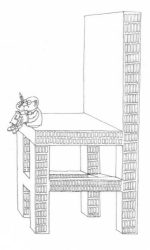

Less is more.

Ludwig Mies van der Rohe, as quoted in the New York *Herald Tribune*, June 28, 1959

I know that the White House was designed by Hoban, a noted Irish-American architect, and I have no doubt that he believed by incorporating several features of the Dublin style he would make it more home-like for any President of Irish descent. It was a long wait, but I appreciate his efforts.

John F. Kennedy, addressing the Irish Parliament, assembled in a Georgian mansion that was once the seat of the Fitzgerald clan, as quoted in *The New York Times*, June 29, 1963

A new space-concept is needed. . . . A definite phase of this new ideal comes in what we call organic architecture—the natural architecture of the democratic spirit in this age of the machine.

Frank Lloyd Wright, *The Living City*

A doctor can bury his mistakes, but an architect can only advise his clients to plant vines.

Frank Lloyd Wright, as quoted in *Reader's Digest*, January 1955

Architecture is a cultural instrument. Man wants to express something that he sees in his mind or feels in his soul, but few men get the chance—especially college students. But every time a college student walks past a really urgent, expressive piece of architecture that belongs to his college, it can help reassure him that he does have that mind, does have that soul.

Louis I. Kahn, first American architect to achieve fame for college buildings, as quoted in *Fortune*, May 1963

The emotion that possessed me was one of great elation, that my life's wish had been granted; but with it came a strange humility, the awful feeling that the finger had pointed at me; and that I was not worthy or able.

Sir Basil Spence, on learning that he had won the architectural design competition for the new Coventry Cathedral, as quoted in *Phoenix at Coventry*

Architecture, like government, is about as good as a community deserves. The shell which we create for ourselves marks our spiritual development as plainly as that of a snail denotes its species.

Lewis Mumford, as quoted in *Reader's Digest*, March 1962

The tendency to make the capital a catch-all for a variety of monuments to honor the immortals, the not-so-immortals, the greats, the near-greats, and the not-so-greats must stop. We must be on our guard lest the nation's capital come to resemble an unplanned cemetery.

Senator Hugh Scott, as quoted in *The New York Times*, September 11, 1960

23

A modest structure would have provided durable and hygienic protection for the mortal remains of Mumtaz Mahal and Shah Jahan. But by spending more—by some estimates, about $8 million—Shah Jahan got the Taj Mahal. It has rejoiced the whole world ever since. Surely this was sound economy. Our test should be similar: the most economical building is the one that promises to give the greatest total pleasure for the price.

> John Kenneth Galbraith, as quoted in *Reader's Digest*,
> August 1972

I prefer drawing to talking. Drawing is faster, and allows less room for lies.

> Le Corbusier, as quoted in *Time*, May 5, 1961

A house is a machine for living.

> Le Corbusier, as quoted in *Le Corbusier*

When I am working on a problem, I never think about beauty. I think only of how to solve the problem. But when I have finished, if the solution is not beautiful, I know it is wrong.

> Buckminster Fuller, as quoted in *Reader's Digest*, October
> 1971

Architecture is preeminently the art of significant forms in space—that is, forms significant of their functions.

> Claude Bragdon, in *Outlook*, May 27, 1931

Music and Dance

The opera always loses money. That's as it should be. Opera has no business making money.

> Rudolf Bing, former General Manager of the Metropolitan
> Opera, as quoted in *The New York Times*, November 15,
> 1959

Composers should write tunes that chauffeurs and errand boys can whistle.

> Sir Thomas Beecham, conductor, as quoted in *The New York Times*, March 9, 1961

Most of them [sopranos] sound like they live on seaweed.

> Sir Thomas Beecham, conductor, as quoted in *Newsweek*, April 30, 1956

[Good music] penetrates the ear with facility and quits the memory with difficulty.

> Sir Thomas Beecham, conductor, as quoted in *The New York Times*, March 9, 1961

Tenors are noble, pure and heroic and get the soprano, if she has not tragically expired before the final curtain. But baritones are born villains in opera. Always the heavy and never the hero—that's me.

> Leonard Warren, baritone, as quoted in the New York *World-Telegram and Sun*, March 13, 1957

Music with dinner is an insult both to the cook and violinist.

> G. K. Chesterton, as quoted in *The New York Times*, November 16, 1967

Music and religion are as intimately related as poetry and love; the deepest emotions require for their civilized expression the most emotional of arts.

> Will Durant, *The Story of Civilization*

Music was as vital as the church edifice itself, more deeply stirring than all the glory of glass or stone. Many a stoic soul, doubtful of the creed, was melted by the music, and fell on his knees before the mystery that no words could speak.

> Will Durant, *The Story of Civilization*   25

Music is indivisible. The dualism of feeling and thinking must be resolved to a state of unity in which one thinks with the heart and feels with the brain.

George Szell, conductor, as quoted in *Time*, February 22, 1963

Conductors must give unmistakable and suggestive signals to the orchestra—not choreography to the audience.

George Szell, as quoted in *Newsweek*, January 28, 1963

Genius is an overused word. The world has known only about a half dozen geniuses. I have achieved only a medium approach to my ideal in music. I got only fairly near.

Fritz Kreisler, violinist, comment to reporters on the eve of his eightieth birthday, February 2, 1955

You do what you do because you must do it at that instant in time. If it lives, it is because posterity demands it.

Martha Graham, dancer, as quoted in *Newsweek*, November 15, 1963

Success can corrupt; usefulness can only exalt.

Dimitri Mitropoulos, conductor, as quoted in *Hi-Fi Music at Home*, May–June 1956

26

Even before the music begins there is that bored look on people's faces. A polite form of self-imposed torture, the concert.

Henry Miller, *Tropic of Cancer*

Don't tell Mr. Hurok, but I love playing the piano so much I would do it for nothing.

Arthur Rubinstein, as quoted in *The New York Times Magazine*, January 26, 1964

I cannot tell you how much I love to play for people. Would you believe it? Sometimes when I sit down to practice and there is no one else in the room, I have to stifle an impulse to ring for the elevator man and offer him money to come in and hear me.

Arthur Rubinstein, as quoted in *Reader's Digest*, March 1971

Competitions are for horses, not artists.

Béla Bartók, composer, as quoted in *Saturday Review*, August 25, 1962

Bach opens a vista to the universe. After experiencing him, people feel there is meaning to life after all.

Helmut Walcha, organist, as quoted in *Reader's Digest*, January 1970

If you think you've hit a false note, sing loud. When in doubt, sing loud.

Robert Merrill, baritone, as quoted in the *Saturday Evening Post*, October 26, 1957

Now that John Cage's most successful opus is 4′ 33″—four minutes and 33 seconds of silence—we may expect his example to be followed by more and more silent pieces by younger composers, who will   27 produce their silences with more and more varied and beguiling combinations. I only hope they turn out to be works of major length.

Igor Stravinsky, composer, as quoted in *Reader's Digest*, May 1970

Music is as well or better able to praise [God] than the building of the church and all its decorations: it is the Church's greatest ornament . . . religious music without religion is almost always vulgar.

Igor Stravinsky, *Conversations with Stravinsky*

It is the interaction of his personality and period that results in the formation of a composer's style.

Aaron Copland, composer, *What to Listen For in Music*

The opera is like a husband with a foreign title: expensive to support, hard to understand, and therefore a supreme social challenge.

Cleveland Amory, comment on NBC-TV, April 6, 1962

One of the major differences between Beethoven and all other musicians before him was that Beethoven looked upon himself as an artist, and he insisted on his rights as an artist. Composers before him thought of themselves as skilled craftsmen who supplied a commodity, and the notion of writing for posterity did not enter into their thinking. But Beethoven was of a special breed and he knew it. He was a creator and, as such, superior to kings and princes.

Harold C. Schoenberg, as quoted in *Reader's Digest*, June 1970

Music being the universal expression of the mysterious and supernatural, the best that man has ever attained to, it is capable of uniting in common devotion minds that are only separated by creeds, and it comforts our hopes with a brighter promise of unity than any logic offers.

Robert Bridges, *Collected Essays*

What I am interested in doing is finding and expressing a new form of life. The Greeks lived. People do not live nowadays—they get about ten percent cut of life.

Isadora Duncan, dancer, as quoted in *This Quarter*, Paris, 1929

Playing "bop" is like playing "scrabble" with all the vowels missing.

Duke Ellington, as quoted in the New York *Herald Tribune*, July 9, 1961

I have my own particular sorrows, loves, delights; and you have yours. But sorrow, gladness, yearning, hope, love, belong to all of us, in all times and in all places. Music is the only means whereby we feel these emotions in their universality.

Harry Overstreet, as quoted in *Reader's Digest*, May 1939

Our appreciation of dancing, poetry and jazz music is due to the metabolic rhythm inherited from our flagellate (jellyfish) forefathers, and shows that we are still flagellates at heart.

Dr. G. P. Bidder, as quoted in *Reader's Digest*, January 1928

It got to a point where I had to get a haircut or a violin.

Franklin D. Roosevelt, as quoted in *Reader's Digest*, May 1938

Singers' husbands! Find me stones heavy enough to place around their necks and drown them all! In all my 35 years of managing artists, I never quite got used to the sharp little men who tell me where Madame is to be booked, what fee she is to be paid, who is to sing with her and what the critics will have to write. Somewhere in the brain of every prima donna there is a deep craving for security and comfort, linked with a fear of old age. This causes her to pick a man who is prepared to act as a permanent wet nurse.

André Mertens, as quoted in *Time*, August 1, 1960

To play great music, you must keep your eyes on a distant star.

Yehudi Menuhin, violinist, as quoted in *Reader's Digest*,
December 1953

Dance is the only art of which we ourselves are the stuff of which it is made.

Ted Shawn, as quoted in *Time*, July 25, 1955

The greatest American music of the future will be a music to which America will listen and respond. But it will not be the music of Sitting Bull or Booker T. Washington—or even George. It will belong to us, because one of us made it; but it will, like all great music, belong to the world. And the world will not be curious regarding the name and address of the composer.

Deems Taylor, *Of Men and Music*

All you have to do to write music is to remember a tune that's never been written.

Deems Taylor, as quoted in *Reader's Digest*, November
1927

I play a musical instrument some, but only for my own amazement.

Fred Allen, as quoted in *Reader's Digest*, March 1936

The word "Soul" comes out of the church, of course, but jazz and blues brought it out into the non-black world. Soul music embraces a wide variety, but it all has that distinct feeling. For the brother, this is important. He can be moved by Soul music for days. At a theater where, say, Soul Brother No. 1, rhythm-and-blues singer James Brown, is into his act, performer and audience are not separate. They feel as one, and the music is made up to fit the mood then and there. You know this moment will never again happen. . . . Soul music is relevant to this time, and these people. It is a gift from our culture to all of America.

Adrian Dove, as quoted in *The New York Times Magazine*,
December 8, 1968

Music is the only language in which you cannot say a mean or sarcastic thing.

John Erskine, as quoted in *Reader's Digest*, April 1934

I'm a guy who likes to keep score. With ballet I can't tell who's ahead.

Fiorello La Guardia, as quoted in *Reader's Digest*, June 1969

I can't tell you what a good time I have onstage. Everything sparkles; I glow. I love being able to sing well, to have it just pour out of me. I'm greedy for those three hours onstage. They're hours of pure joy. People should go to the opera and have a good time. I do.

Beverly Sills, soprano, as quoted in *Newsweek*, April 21,
1969

Jazz will endure just as long as people hear it through their feet instead of their brains.

John Philip Sousa, as quoted in *Reader's Digest*, May 1933

If you are happy you can always learn to dance.

Balinese saying, quoted by Santha Rama Rau in *East of Home*

The notes I handle no better than many pianists. But the pauses between the notes—ah, that is where the art resides.

Artur Schnabel, as quoted in the Chicago *Daily News*, June 11, 1958

Music is not a drug, but a diet.

Sir Henry Hadow, as quoted in *Reader's Digest*, October 1927

The universe lies before you on the floor, in the air, in the mysterious bodies of your dancers, in your mind. From this voyage no one returns poor or weary.

Agnes De Mille, *To a Young Dancer*

If I was a good trumpet player I wouldn't be here. I got desperate. I hadda look for a job. I went in the union business.

James C. Petrillo, former president of the American Federation of Musicians, as quoted in *The New York Times*, June 14, 1956

I didn't wish for anything I couldn't get, and I got pretty near everything I wanted. They're going to enjoy blowing over me—cats will be coming from everywhere to play. Be good if I get to the Pearly Gates. I'll play a duet with Gabriel. Yeah. We'll play "Sleepy Time Down South."

Louis Armstrong, as quoted in *Reader's Digest*, December 1971

Life can't be all bad when for ten dollars you can buy all the Beethoven sonatas and listen to them for ten years.

William F. Buckley, Jr., as quoted in *Reader's Digest*, August 1971

If a guy's got it, let him give it. I'm selling music, not prejudice.

Benny Goodman, as quoted in the *Saturday Evening Post*, December 18, 1954

Every child can learn to play music well enough to enjoy it, just as any boy can learn to play football well enough to get fun out of it. As working musicians know, about 90 percent of music is dedication and practice; talent only makes it easier. There is fun in playing in a rock group or in the high-school band. And everybody who plays an instrument, even a little, understands music in a different way from somebody who has never felt the thrill of making music himself.

James Lincoln Collier, as quoted in *Reader's Digest*, August 1973

No good opera plot can be sensible, for people do not sing when they are feeling sensible.

W. H. Auden, as quoted in *Time*, December 29, 1961

Teaching music is not my main purpose. I want to make good citizens. If a child hears fine music from the day of his birth, and learns to play it himself, he develops sensitivity, discipline and endurance. He gets a beautiful heart.

Shinichi Suzuki, as quoted in *Reader's Digest*, November 1973

One of the current hazards of organ-building is that after you've designed and placed an organ as well as you possibly can, some well-meaning lady is able to ruin the whole thing by donating memorial carpeting to the church.

Robert Baker, organist, Fifth Avenue Presbyterian Church, New York, as quoted in *The New Yorker*, December 23, 1961

Nowhere else in the world has such an audience survived. It is one of the great charms of New York that at the Met one may still see bejeweled Grandes Dames, rouged like crazy, wearing what at first appear to be black fur stoles, but then turn out to be their enervated sons slung across their mamas' magnificent shoulders; one may still see Elderly Patricians hanging from boxes by the heels, with their opera glasses pointing like guns right *down* the decolletage of a huge soprano;

one may still see swarms of Liveried Chauffeurs waiting to escort their Employers to their cars, to place fur wraps about their aged shanks, to touch their caps respectfully at the words, "Home, James, and don't spare the Rolls."

Tyrone Guthrie, as quoted in *The New York Times*,
January 5, 1958

Literature

A great book should leave you with many experiences, and slightly exhausted at the end. You live several lives while reading it.

William Styron, as quoted in *Writers at Work*

What I like in a good author is not what he says, but what he whispers. Every author, however modest, keeps a most outrageous vanity chained like a madman in the padded cell of his breast.

Logan Pearsall Smith, *Afterthoughts*

No man understands a deep book until he has seen and lived at least part of its contents.

Ezra Pound, *The ABC of Reading*

Literature is news that stays news.

Ezra Pound, *How to Read*

Every fine story must leave in the mind of the sensitive reader an intangible residuum of pleasure, a cadence, a quality of voice that is exclusively the writer's own, individual, unique.

Willa Cather, *Not Under Forty*   35

When you reread a classic, you do not see more in the book than you did before; you see more in *you* than there was before.

Clifton Fadiman, *Any Number Can Play*

Years ago, to say you were a writer was not the highest recommendation to your landlord. Today, he at least hesitates before he refuses to rent you the apartment—for all he knows you may be rich.

Arthur Miller, as quoted in *The New York Times*, July 6, 1965

About the writer's craft: It has always been much like writing a check. . . . It is easy to write a check if you have enough money in the bank, and writing comes more easily if you have something to say.

Sholem Asch, as quoted in the New York *Herald Tribune*, November 6, 1955

A publisher lives by what he feels. Authors do too, but authors are blind moles working their solitary way along their individual tunnels; the publisher is like the Pied Piper of Hamelin, piping his way along a path he wants them to follow.

Lovat Dickson, *The House of Words*

Books won't stay banned. They won't burn. Ideas won't go to jail.

A. Whitney Griswold, *Essays on Education*

Censorship, like charity, should begin at home; but unlike charity, it should end there.

Clare Boothe Luce, *Nuggets*

I've always believed in writing without a collaborator, because where two people are writing the same book, each believes he gets all the worries and only half the royalties.

Agatha Christie, as quoted in the *Times Literary Supplement*, London, March 15, 1955

A writer's problem does not change. He himself changes and the world he lives in changes but his problem remains the same. It is always how to write truly and, having found what is true, to project it in such a way that it becomes a part of the experience of the person who reads it.

Ernest Hemingway, *Men at War*

All our words from loose using have lost their edge.

Ernest Hemingway, *Death in the Afternoon*

Writing, at its best, is a lonely life. Organizations for writers palliate the writer's loneliness, but I doubt if they improve his writing. He grows in public stature as he sheds his loneliness and after his work deteriorates. For he does his work alone and if he is a good enough writer he must face eternity, or that lack of it, each day.

Ernest Hemingway, accepting the Nobel Prize for
literature, as quoted in news reports of December 11, 1954

Child! Do not throw this book about;
Refrain from the unholy pleasure of cutting
　　all the pictures out!
Preserve it as your chiefest treasure.

Hilaire Belloc, *The Bad Child's Book of Beasts*

Words are, of course, the most powerful drug used by mankind.

Rudyard Kipling, speech, February 14, 1923

Writers write for themselves and not for their readers. Art has nothing to do with communication between person and person, only with communication between different parts of a person's mind.

Rebecca West, as quoted in *Vogue*, November 1, 1952

Through books . . . ideas find their way to the human brains, and ideals to human hearts and souls.

Dorothy Canfield Fisher, as quoted in *The Christian
Leader's Golden Treasury*　37

Writing a book is an adventure; to begin with it is a toy, then an amusement, then it becomes a mistress, and then it becomes a master, and then it becomes a tyrant, and the last phase is that just as you are about to be reconciled to your servitude you kill the monster and strew him about to the public.

> Sir Winston Churchill, as quoted in *The New York Times
> Magazine*, November 13, 1949

I am proud but also, I must admit, awe-struck at your decision to include me. I do hope you are right. I feel we are both running a considerable risk and that I do not deserve it. But I shall have no misgivings if you have none.

> Sir Winston Churchill, accepting the Nobel Prize for
> literature, recalled in news reports on his eightieth birthday,
> November 30, 1954

The profession of book-writing makes horse racing seem like a solid, stable business.

> John Steinbeck, speech upon accepting the 1962 Nobel
> Prize for literature

A bad book is as much of a labor to write as a good one, it comes as sincerely from the author's soul.

> Aldous Huxley, as quoted in *Newsweek*, January 2, 1956

A word is not a crystal, transparent and unchanging, it is the skin of a living thought and may vary greatly in color and content according to the circumstances and time in which it is used.

> Justice Oliver Wendell Holmes, Jr., opinion in *Towne* v.
> *Eisner* (1918)

Great writers leave us not just their works, but a way of looking at things.

> Elizabeth Janeway, as quoted in *The New York Times
> Book Review*, January 31, 1965

Mostly, we authors must repeat ourselves—that's the truth. We have two or three great moving experiences in our lives—experiences so great and moving that it doesn't seem at the time that anyone else has been caught up and pounded and dazzled and astonished and beaten and broken and rescued and illuminated and rewarded and humbled in just that way ever before.

F. Scott Fitzgerald, *Afternoon of an Author: A Selection of
Uncollected Stories and Essays*

The novel remains for me one of the few forms where we can record man's complexity and the strength of decency of his longings; where we can describe, step by step, minute by minute, our not altogether unpleasant struggle to put ourselves into a viable and devout relationship to our beloved and mistaken world.

John Cheever, accepting the National Book Award, as
quoted in *The Writer*, September 1958

[A book is] a single minded attempt to render the highest kind of justice to the visible universe, by bringing to light the truth, manifold and one, underlying its aspect.

Joseph Conrad, *The Nigger of the Narcissus*

I get up in the morning, torture a typewriter until it screams, then stop.

Clarence Budington Kelland, as quoted in the New York
Herald Tribune, February 20, 1964

If the writing is honest it cannot be separated from the man who wrote it. It isn't so much his mirror as it is the distillation, the essence, or what is strongest and purest in his nature, whether that be gentleness or anger, serenity or torment, light or dark. This makes it deeper than the surface likeness of a mirror and that much more truthful.

Tennessee Williams, introduction to William Inge's play
The Dark at the Top of the Stairs 39

Failure is very difficult for a writer to bear, but very few can manage the shock of early success.

Maurice Valency, as quoted in *The New York Times Book Review*, May 23, 1965

Fiction reveals truths that reality obscures.

Jessamyn West, as quoted in *Reader's Digest*, April 1973

. . . existentialists declare
That they are in complete despair,
Yet they go on writing.

W. H. Auden, as quoted in *Fear of Flying* by Erica Jong

A poet is, before anything else, a person who is passionately in love with language.

W. H. Auden, as quoted in *The New York Times*, October 9, 1960

I divide all readers into two classes: those who read to remember and those who read to forget.

William Lyon Phelps, as quoted in *Reader's Digest*, December 1940

Its [poetry's] essential character lies in its bold flouting of what every reflective adult knows to be the truth.

H. L. Mencken, as quoted in *The Smart Set*, June 1920

All the best stories in the world are but one story in reality—the story of an escape. It is the only thing which interests us all and at all times—how to escape.

A. C. Benson, as quoted in *Reader's Digest*, August 1935

Poetry is the language in which man explores his own amazement.

Christopher Fry, as quoted in *Reader's Digest*, April 1970

A true sonnet goes eight lines and then takes a turn for better or worse and goes six or eight lines more.

Robert Frost, as quoted in news summaries of March 29, 1954

Poetry is a way of taking life by the throat.

Robert Frost, as quoted in *Reader's Digest*, February 1961

Poets aren't very useful,
Because they aren't consumeful or very produceful.

Ogden Nash, as quoted in *Reader's Digest*, July 1952

A greater poetry is a flowing in of light from the source of all light, from that King from whom comes our knowledge of the kingly, in whose wisdom we advance, under whose majesty we move, and in whose beauty, if we have cared for beauty, we may come to dwell.

John Masefield, address, London, 1931

The real purpose of books is to trap the mind into doing its own thinking.

Christopher Morley, as quoted in *Reader's Digest*, July 1958

Never write up your diary on the day itself, for it takes longer than that to know what happened.

Christopher Morley, as quoted in *Reader's Digest*,
December 1960

Why do people always expect authors to answer questions? I am an author because I want to *ask* questions. If I had answers, I'd be a politician.

Eugène Ionesco, as quoted in *Reader's Digest*, July 1970

What is good literature, what has educational value, what is refined public information, what is good art, varies with individuals as it does from one generation to another. There doubtless would be a contrariety of views concerning Cervantes' *Don Quixote*, Shakespeare's *Venus and Adonis* or Zola's *Nana*. But a requirement that literature or art conform to some norm prescribed by an official smacks of an ideology foreign to our system . . . to withdraw the second-class rate from this publication today because its contents seemed to one official not good

42

for the public, would sanction withdrawal of the second-class rate tomorrow from another periodical whose social or economic views seemed harmful to another official.

Unanimous United States Supreme Court opinion, U.S. Post Office v. Esquire Inc. (1946)

Some places speak distinctly. Certain dank gardens cry aloud for a murder; certain old houses demand to be haunted; certain coasts are set apart for shipwrecks.

Robert Louis Stevenson, as quoted in Reader's Digest, January 1935

Fiction is not a dream. Nor is it guesswork. It is imagining based on facts, and the facts must be accurate or the work of imagining will not stand up.

Margaret Culkin Banning, as quoted in The Writer, March 1960

It is a great thing to start life with a small number of really good books which are your very own.

Sherlock Holmes, as quoted in Reader's Digest, December 1954

Great editors do not discover nor produce great authors; great authors create and produce great publishers.

John Farrar, *What Happens in Book Publishing*

Autobiography is an unrivaled vehicle for telling the truth about other people.

Philip Guedalla, as quoted in *Reader's Digest*, July 1957

I write at high speed because boredom is bad for my health. It upsets my stomach more than anything else. I also avoid green vegetables. They're grossly overrated.

Sir Noel Coward, as quoted in *Tempo*, January 15, 1956

The greatest tribute that a writer can earn is not that we keep our eyes fast on his page, forgetting all else, but that sometimes, without knowing that we have ceased to read, we allow his book to rest, and look out over and beyond it with newly opened eyes.

Charles Morgan, as quoted in *Reader's Digest*, June 1947

This will never be a civilized country until we expend more money for books than we do for chewing gum.

Elbert Hubbard, *The Philistine*

Contemporary literature can be classified under three headings: the neurotic, the erotic, and the tommy-rotic.

W. Giese, professor of French at the University of Wisconsin, as quoted in *Reader's Digest*, March 1936

Pretty women swarm around everybody but writers. Plain, intelligent women *somewhat* swarm around writers.

William Saroyan, *A Writer's Declaration*

What nonsense! No one ever seduced by books? Since the invention of writing, people have been seduced by the power of the word into all kinds of virtues, follies, conspiracies and gallantries. They have been converted to religions, urged into sin and lured into salvation.

Phyllis McGinley, as quoted in the *Ladies' Home Journal*,
July 1961

I don't really feel my poems are mine at all. I didn't create them out of nothing; I owe them to my relations with other people.

Robert Graves, as quoted in the New York *Mirror*, April 1,
1963

Who knows whether in retirement I shall be tempted to the last infirmity of mundane minds, which is to write a book.

Geoffrey Fisher, in final address as Archbishop of
Canterbury, as quoted in *Time*, May 12, 1961

A poet dares be just so clear and no clearer; he approaches lucid ground warily, like a mariner who is determined not to scrape his bottom on anything solid. A poet's pleasure is to withhold a little of his meaning to intensify by mystification. He unzips the veil from beauty, but does not remove it. A poet utterly clear is a trifle glaring.

E. B. White, *One Man's Meat*

Poetry will not save the world. But poetry can force the soul into the precincts of its last evasion.

Stanley Hopper, *The Crisis of Faith*

Poetry is the journal of a sea animal living on land, wanting to fly in the air.

Carl Sandburg, as quoted in the *Atlantic Monthly*, March
1923

To ask poetry to save us is to impose a burden upon poetry that it cannot sustain. The danger is that we shall merely get an ersatz religion and an ersatz poetry.

Cleanth Brooks, as quoted in the Sewanee Review, Winter
1953

Poetry even at its purest is not prayer, but it rises from the same depths as the need to pray.

Etienne Gilson, Choir of Muses

The intolerable wrests with words and meanings.

T. S. Eliot, on the writing of poetry, as quoted in Time,
March 6, 1950

The capacity for writing poetry is rare; the capacity for religious emotion of the first intensity is rare; and it is to be expected that the existence of both capacities in the same individual should be rarer still.

T. S. Eliot, After Strange Gods

You don't have to suffer to be a poet. Adolescence is enough suffering for anyone.

John Ciardi, as quoted in the Simmons Review, Fall 1962

It's silly to suggest the writing of poetry as something ethereal, a sort of soul-crashing emotional experience that wrings you. I have no fancy ideas about poetry. It doesn't come to you on the wings of a dove. It's something you work hard at.

Louise Bogan, as quoted in the New York World-Telegram
and Sun, January 28, 1959

Like a piece of ice on a hot stove the poem must ride on its own melting.

Robert Frost, preface to Collected Works

Poetry ennobles the heart and the eyes, and unveils the meaning of all things upon which the heart and the eyes dwell. It discovers the secret rays of the universe, and restores to us forgotten paradises.

Dame Edith Sitwell, as quoted in *Reader's Digest*, August 1955

Poetry is the opening and closing of a door, leaving those who look through to guess what is seen during a moment.

Carl Sandburg, *Ten Definitions*

When power leads man toward arrogance, poetry reminds him of his limitation. When power narrows the area of man's concern, poetry reminds him of the richness and diversity of his existence. When power corrupts, poetry cleanses.

John F. Kennedy, address at Amherst College, October 26, 1963

Poetry is no more a narcotic than a stimulant; it is a universal bittersweet mixture for all possible household emergencies and its action varies accordingly as it is taken in a wine-glass or a tablespoon, inhaled, gargled or rubbed on the chest by hard fingers covered with rings.

Robert Graves, as quoted in *The New York Times*, October 9, 1960

Readers are of two kinds—the reader who carefully goes through a book and the reader who as carefully lets the book go through him.

Douglas Jerrold, as quoted in *Reader's Digest*, November 1947

The business of a poet is not to clarify, but to suggest; to imply, to employ words with auras of association, with a reaching out toward a vision, a probing down into an emotion, beyond the compass of explicit definition.

Harold Hobson, as quoted in the New York *Journal-American*, January 31, 1958   47

An autobiography usually reveals nothing bad about its writer except his memory.

Franklin P. Jones, as quoted in *Reader's Digest*, April 1960

To note an artist's limitations is but to define his talent. A reporter can write equally well about everything that is presented to his view, but a creative writer can do his best only with what lies within the range and character of his deepest sympathies.

Willa Cather, *Not Under Forty*

The trouble with the publishing business is that too many people who have half a mind to write a book do so.

William Targ, as quoted in *Reader's Digest*, April 1947

They're fancy talkers about themselves, writers. If I had to give young writers advice, I would say don't listen to writers talking about writing or themselves.

Lillian Hellman, as quoted in *The New York Times*, February 21, 1960

An essayist is a lucky person who has found a way to discourse without being interrupted.

Charles Poore, as quoted in *The New York Times*, May 31, 1962

Poetry is the impish attempt to paint the color of the wind.

Maxwell Bodenheim, as quoted in the play *Winkleberg* by Ben Hecht

The publishers of historical novels never seem to run out of material—until they get to the girl on the cover.

Luke Neely, as quoted in *Reader's Digest*, January 1955

[Poetry is the] expression of the hunger for elsewhere.

Benjamin De Casseres, *The Muse of Lies*

It took me 15 years to discover I had no talent for writing, but I couldn't give it up because by that time I was too famous.

Robert Benchley, as quoted in *Reader's Digest*, September 1949

Rose is a rose is a rose is a rose. . . . I think that in that line the rose is red in English poetry for the first time in one hundred and fifty years.

Gertrude Stein, to a class at the University of Chicago, 1935

What is the answer? . . . in that case, what is the question?

Gertrude Stein, her last words, as quoted in *Charmed Circle*

Some novels you just can't put down. Others you don't dare to—if there are children in the house.

Carl Ellstam, as quoted in *Reader's Digest*, August 1958

I think if I had done anything else I would like to have been a doctor. This is the sort of polar opposition to being a writer . . . somebody who deals directly with human experiences, is able to cure, to mend, to 49 help. . . . I may say I'm happier writing about doctors than I would have been being one.

Sylvia Plath, as quoted in The Poet Speaks

To me the charm of an encyclopedia is that it knows—and I needn't.

Francis Yeats-Brown, as quoted in Reader's Digest,
February 1940

Theater

When you're a young man, Macbeth is a character part. When you're older, it's a straight part.

Sir Laurence Olivier, as quoted in Theatre Arts, May 1,
1958

We used to have actresses trying to become stars; now we have stars trying to become actresses.

Sir Laurence Olivier, as quoted in Reader's Digest, August
1958

Dramatizations, as a rule, prove more like sieves than containers for the virtues of a book.

John Mason Brown, as quoted in the Saturday Review of
Literature, March 6, 1948

Tyrone Power as Cassius in *Julius Caesar:* A set of vocal cords wrapped up in a toga.

John Mason Brown, as quoted in Reader's Digest,
November 1935

Tallulah Bankhead sailed down the Nile in a barge last night and sank.

John Mason Brown on Tallulah Bankhead's performance in
Shakespeare's *Anthony and Cleopatra*, as quoted in
Broadway by Brooks Atkinson

I never go to see plays. I want to be on stage, not in the audience.

Carol Lynley, as quoted in *The Player: A Profile of an Art*
by Lillian and Helen Ross

True tragedy may be defined as a dramatic work in which the outward
failure of the principal personage is compensated for by the dignity and
greatness of his character.

Joseph Wood Krutch, introduction to *Nine Plays by Eugene
O'Neill*

To flounder is the precondition of all art, and the crying shame in the
theater is only that it costs so much.

William Gibson, letter to *The New York Times*, May 31,
1964

Take some wood and canvas and nails and things. Build yourself a
theater, a stage, light it, learn about it. When you've done that you will
probably know how to write a play.

Doris Alexander, *The Tempering of Eugene O'Neill*

I love pretending, but I've never been terribly happy on the stage. I've
never found it easy to act, acting to me is agony.

Katharine Cornell, as quoted in *The Player: A Profile of an
Art* by Lillian and Helen Ross

In all ages the drama, through its portrayal of the acting and suffering
spirit of man, has been more closely allied than any other art to his
deeper thoughts concerning his nature and his destiny.

Ludwig Lewisohn, *The Modern Drama*   51

In the theatre, a hero is one who believes that all women are ladies. A villain is one who believes that all ladies are women.

> George Jean Nathan, as quoted in *The New York Times*,
> November 5, 1950

Entire review of *Tonight or Never:* Very well then, I say Never.

> George Jean Nathan, as quoted in *Reader's Digest*,
> November 1935

Mr. ____ writes his plays for the ages—the ages between five and twelve.

> George Jean Nathan, as quoted in *Reader's Digest*, January
> 1938

Has anybody ever seen a drama critic in the daytime? Of course not. They come out after dark, up to no good.

> P. G. Wodehouse, as quoted in the New York *Mirror*, May 5,
> 1952

My preoccupation with my career is minimal. Acting isn't really a creative profession. It's an interpretive one.

> Paul Newman, as quoted by the Associated Press, July 27,
> 1964

King Lear: He played the king as though someone had led the ace.

> Eugene Field, as quoted in *Reader's Digest*, November 1935

The Jukes family of journalism.

> Maxwell Anderson on drama critics, as quoted in
> *Broadway* by Brooks Atkinson

Perfectly Scandalous was one of those plays in which all of the actors, unfortunately, enunciated very clearly.

> Robert Benchley, as quoted in *Reader's Digest*, November
> 1935

She's afraid she might catch acting.

> George S. Kaufman on hearing that Katharine Hepburn
> had ordered sheets hung backstage to keep out drafts
> during her performance in *The Lake.*

It's when life creates a new play that the theatre moves its limbs and wakens from its mesmerized fixation on ordinary reality; when the danger is caught and made historic.

> Arthur Miller, as quoted in *Harper's Magazine*, August
> 1958

The most serious, tender, passionate love scenes are those that are projected over the footlights through suggestion, without actual contact. A man mauling a woman on the stage is a subject for laughter from the old roues and a matter of regret from the nice men. The greatest love scenes in the world are played free from physical contact—Shakespeare realized it, and the two greatest lovers in the world played a scene, the acme of tenderness, on the balcony and ground respectively.

> Laurette Taylor, as quoted in *Reader's Digest*, March 1936

Playing Shakespeare is so tiring. You never get a chance to sit down unless you're a king.

> Josephine Hull, as quoted in *Time*, November 16, 1953

I saw the show under unfortunate circumstances: the curtain was up.

> George S. Kaufman, as quoted in *Broadway* by Brooks
> Atkinson

Business was so bad they were shooting deer in the balcony.

> George S. Kaufman, as quoted in *Broadway* by Brooks
> Atkinson

By increasing the size of the keyhole, today's playwrights are in danger of doing away with the door.

> Peter Ustinov, as quoted in the *Christian Science Monitor*,
> November 14, 1962

I love criticism just so long as it's unqualified praise.

Noel Coward, as quoted in *Reader's Digest*, October 1959

The unencumbered stage encourages the truth operative in everyone. The less seen, the more heard. The eye is the enemy of the ear in real drama.

Thornton Wilder, as quoted by *The New York Times*,
November 6, 1961

Many plays—certainly mine—are like blank checks. The actors and directors put their own signatures on them.

Thornton Wilder, as quoted in the New York *Mirror*, July 13,
1956

Some actors think they are elevating the stage when they're merely depressing the audience.

George A. Posner, as quoted in *Reader's Digest*, July 1952

You need three things in the theatre—the play, the actors and the audience, and each must give something.

Kenneth Haigh, as quoted in *Theatre Arts*, July 1958

The person who does not get the least bit nervous at the prospect of stepping on a stage will never move an audience to wild ecstasy.

Amelita Galli-Curci, opera singer, as quoted in *Reader's*
Digest, October 1927

I got all the schooling any actress needs. That is, I learned to write enough to sign contracts.

Hermione Gingold, as quoted in *Look*, October 4, 1955

A drama critic is a man who leaves no turn unstoned.

George Bernard Shaw, as quoted in *The New York Times*,
November 5, 1950

A play should give you something to think about. When I see a play and understand it the first time, then I know it can't be much good.

T. S. Eliot, as quoted in the New York *Post*, September 22,
1963

Every playwright ought to try acting just as every public prosecutor should spend some weeks in jail to find out what he is meting out to others.

Erich Maria Remarque, as quoted in the New York *Herald
Tribune*, October 24, 1957

When Mr. Wilbur calls his play *Halfway to Hell*, he underestimates the distance.

Brooks Atkinson, as quoted in *Reader's Digest*, November
1935

Good plays drive bad playgoers crazy.

Brooks Atkinson, as quoted in *Theatre Arts*, August 1956

The mission of the playwright . . . as I see it, is to look in his heart and write, to write of whatever concerns him at the moment; to write with passion and conviction. Of course the measure of the man will be the measure of the play.

Robert Anderson, as quoted in *Theatre Arts*, March 1958

The art of acting consists in keeping people from coughing.

Sir Ralph Richardson, as quoted in *Reader's Digest*, March
1949

On the stage, you have to find truth, even if you have to lose the audience.

Anthony Quinn, as quoted in *The Player: A Profile of an Art* by Lillian and Helen Ross

An excellent play . . . but I have no feeling of reality about it. It had no more to do with me than the man on the moon.

Eleanor Roosevelt, commenting on *Sunrise at Campobello*, a play based on the life of the Roosevelt family, as quoted in *Theatre Arts*, April 1958

I don't see why people want new plays all the time. What would happen to concerts if people wanted new music all the time?

Clive Barnes, theater critic of *The New York Times*, as quoted in *Reader's Digest*, August 1972

We are a nation that has always gone in for the loud laugh, the wow, the belly laugh and the dozen other labels for the roll-'em-in-the-aisles gagerissimo. This is the kind of laugh that delights actors, directors, and producers, but dismays writers of comedy because it is the laugh that often dies in the lobby. The appreciative smile, the chuckle, the soundless mirth, so important to the success of comedy, cannot be understood unless one sits among the audience and feels the warmth created by the quality of laughter that the audience takes home with it.

James Thurber, in *The New York Times*, February 21, 1960

Nobody—but nobody—is willing to subject himself to any contemporary theatrical experience he can get out of. A rival medium has but to rear its head to draw off yet another portion of that public which had once been regarded as the theater's.

Walter Kerr, *How Not to Write a Play*

There are those who fear that *any* legal curtailment of smut on the stage will lead to censorship. I disagree. Prohibiting public display of sexual acts can hardly be construed as an attack on a playwright's

56

freedom of expression. Broadway has long dealt with sex as a part of life. If a play requires explicit sexual scenes, then the writer really hasn't much new or creative to say.

David Merrick, producer, as quoted in *Reader's Digest*, March 1970

I have the *worst* ear for criticism; even when I have created a stage set I like, I *always* hear the woman in the back of the Dress Circle who says she doesn't like blue.

Cecil Beaton, comment on BBC-TV, February 18, 1962

Tank-town performance of *Uncle Tom's Cabin:* The dogs were poorly supported by the cast.

Don Herold, as quoted in *Reader's Digest*, November 1935

Movies and TV

A wide screen just makes a bad film twice as bad.

Samuel Goldwyn, as quoted in *Quote*, September 9, 1956   57

I go to the movies every night. Why not? I've got to do something to take my mind off my business.

Samuel Goldwyn, as quoted in Reader's Digest, February
1958

Motion pictures should never embarrass a man when he brings his family to the theatre. Public morality is a very important factor on the screen. . . . I seriously object to seeing on the screen what belongs in the bedroom.

Samuel Goldwyn, as quoted in The Face on the
Cutting-Room Floor

God makes the star. God gives them the talent. It is up to the producers to recognize that talent and develop it.

Samuel Goldwyn, comment on CBS-TV, February 19, 1954

I had the great advantage of growing up in front of a camera. I know just how to turn, just what to show on my face, and when to let the other actor have it. A movie actor or actress paints with the tiniest brush.

Joan Crawford, as quoted in The Player: A Profile of an Art
by Lillian and Helen Ross

I class myself with Rin Tin Tin. At the end of the Depression, people were perhaps looking for something to cheer them up. They fell in love with a dog and with a little girl. . . . I think it won't happen again.

Shirley Temple, as quoted in the New York Post,
September 13, 1956

In Hollywood success is relative. The closer the relative, the greater the success.

Arthur Treacher, as quoted in Reader's Digest,
May 1952

58

I was the first of the Hollywood stars to have a baby. After that, it became an epidemic.

Gloria Swanson, on an interview program, ABC-TV,
October 1958

The art-house audience accepts lack of clarity as complexity; clumsiness and confusion as style.

Pauline Kael, as quoted in *Atlantic Monthly*, December
1964

Object to the Hollywood film and you're an intellectual snob, object to the avant-garde films and you're a Philistine. But, while in Hollywood, one must often be a snob; in avant-garde circles one must often be a Philistine.

Pauline Kael, as quoted in *Berkeley Book of Modern
Writing*, Vol. 3.

Hollywood isn't money. It's congealed snow.

Dorothy Parker, as quoted in the *Paris Review*, Summer
1956

Miss Neagle looked nice as Queen Victoria, she looks just as nice as Nurse Cavell: she moves rigidly onto the set, as if wheels were concealed under the stately skirt; she says her piece with flat dignity and trolleys out again—rather like a mechanical marvel from the World's Fair.

Graham Greene after the opening of the film *Nurse Cavell*
(1939)

She's all slink and mink.

Anonymous reporter in the New York *World*, May 5, 1925,
commenting on the acting of Pola Negri

She had a blind and uncritical admiration of her own genius in the blaze of which her sense of humor evaporated like a dew-drop on a million-watt arc lamp.

Rodney Ackland on Pola Negri in his memoir The Celluloid
Mistress

I think the things that are necessary in my profession are these: Taste, Talent and Tenacity. I think I have had a little of all three.

Lillian Gish, in an interview in Sight and Sound, 1957

What do I do when I'm down? I put on my lipstick, see my stockings are straight and go out there and sing "Over the Rainbow."

Judy Garland in conversation, shortly before her death in
1969

The movie camera is unbelievably hospitable, delightfully hospitable—but supremely conceited. The spectator must be a suave and wary guest, one educated in a profound, naïve-sophisticated conspiracy *to see as much as he can take away with him.*

Parker Tyler, The Hollywood Hallucination

She has a face that belongs to the sea and the wind, with large rocking-horse nostrils and teeth that you know just bite an apple every day.

Cecil Beaton, on Katharine Hepburn, as quoted in the New
York Herald Tribune, March 29, 1954

Life is like a B-picture. It is that corny. If I had my life story offered to me to film, I'd turn it down.

Kirk Douglas, as quoted in Look, October 4, 1955

I am a typed director. If I made *Cinderella*, the audience would immediately be looking for a body in the coach.

Alfred Hitchcock, as quoted in Newsweek, June 11, 1956

It is not true that I said actors are cattle. I said they should be *treated* like cattle.

Alfred Hitchcock, on an interview program, ABC-TV,
1971

Film directors say, "Stop acting!" If you stop acting, what is the point? You are then just talking and behaving.

Sir Cedric Hardwicke, as quoted in *Theatre Arts*, February
1958

I believe that God felt sorry for actors so he created Hollywood to give them a place in the sun and a swimming pool. The price they had to pay was to surrender their talent.

Sir Cedric Hardwicke, *A Victorian in Orbit*

Hollywood continued to furnish the heroes and heroines of our time. The ubiquitous cinema screen projected their images throughout the world. Sex is the ersatz, or substitute, religion of the 20th century. These were its priests and priestesses. They were the American Dream, soon to be in Technicolor—a dream in terms of material satisfactions and sensual love, whose requisite happy ending was always a long-drawn-out embrace.

Malcolm Muggeridge, comment on BBC-TV program,
January 16, 1962

I was a 14-year-old boy for 30 years.

Mickey Rooney, as quoted in the New York
Journal-American, April 15, 1958

Thereason good women like me and flock to my pictures is that there is a little bit of vampire instinct in every woman.

Theda Bara, on her many roles as a vampire, quoted in
reports of her death, April 8, 1955

The average Hollywood film star's ambition is to be admired by an American, courted by an Italian, married to an Englishman and have a French boy friend.

Katharine Hepburn, as quoted in the New York
Journal-American, February 22, 1954

I went out there for a thousand a week, and I worked Monday, and I got fired Wednesday. The guy that hired me was out of town Tuesday.

Nelson Algren, as quoted in *Writers at Work*

A mother never gets hit with a custard pie. Mothers-in-law—yes. But mothers—never.

Mack Sennett, as quoted in *The New York Times*,
November 6, 1960

Fundamentally I feel that there is as much difference between the stage and the films as between a piano and a violin. Normally you can't be a virtuoso in both.

Ethel Barrymore, as quoted in the New York *Post*, June 1,
1956

One thing I have always admired about my brother Cecil is his ability to bite off more than he can chew, and then chew it.

William C. De Mille, as quoted in *Reader's Digest*, April
1940

You can learn a lot about romance at the movies—if you don't let the picture distract you.

Franklin P. Jones, as quoted in *Reader's Digest*, August 1953

Look at us, look at these queer people who make up the picture industry. Just bums, half of us are, taken from every imaginable seat of ignorance in the world, from the fur trade to the circus troupe.

Douglas Fairbanks, as quoted in *Reader's Digest*, January 1928

When I first saw my face on the screen in a close-up six feet high I jumped up and yelled, "It's a lie!"

Joe E. Brown, as quoted in *Reader's Digest*, September 1936

Hollywood shoots too many pictures and not enough actors.

Walter Winchell, as quoted in *Reader's Digest*, March 1934

There is no legitimate actor who can resist the powerful lure of the movies. It isn't the money that fetches him. It isn't the great publicity. It is simply this: The movies enable an actor to look at himself.

George Jean Nathan, as quoted in *Reader's Digest*, June 1936

Believe it or not, it is a picture about two young people romantically in love—in love with each other—that is, not with a tractor, or the Soviet state. The Russians have finally found romance.

Bosley Crowther, reviewing the Soviet film *The Cranes Are Flying*, as quoted in *The New York Times*, March 27, 1960

There is another word for being a good trouper, a word that show business would think too grand to use. That word is dedication. And

63

that word, I think, is Mary Pickford's secret, as it is the secret of anyone who succeeds at anything.

Cecil B. De Mille, introduction to *Sunshine and Shadow*, autobiography of Mary Pickford

There never was an actress with whom it was easy to work. I have yet to see one completely unspoiled star, except for the animals—like Lassie. Each thinks she knows more than I do about her bust and hips.

Edith Head, costume designer, as quoted in the *Saturday Evening Post*, November 30, 1963

My idea of a good television mystery is one where it's hard to detect the sponsor.

Irv Leiberman, as quoted in *Reader's Digest*, August 1952

Who says television is not educational? No longer need the child wonder what those young couples are doing, reclining on the beach or cuddled in cars. Thanks to the commercials, he knows that they are discussing how many tiny filters each cigarette contains.

Bill Vaughan, as quoted in *Reader's Digest*, December 1956

With all the medical shows on television, it would seem only fair for Blue Cross to pay the repair bills on the set.

Bill Vaughan, as quoted in *Reader's Digest*, September 1962

The teacher tells the little boy down the block that the world is round, but he's been watching it on television all his life and he knows it's rectangular.

Bill Vaughan, *Half the Battle*

It's inevitable that I should seem a rather remote figure to many of you—a successor to the kings and queens of history; someone whose face may be familiar in newspapers and films but who never touches your personal lives. But now, at least for a few minutes, I welcome you to the peace of my own home.

Elizabeth II, in first telecast of her annual Christmas
address to the Commonwealth, 1957

Television may yet unify Yankees and Southerners—against Westerns.

Fletcher Knebel, as quoted in *Reader's Digest*, July 1959

Humanity is making slow but sure progress. Thus far we've been able to confine germ warfare to the TV commercials.

Fletcher Knebel, as quoted in *Reader's Digest*, May 1960

When given a choice between a gunslinger's blazing six-shooter and an information program, the majority dialed in the gunslinger.

Richard Huber, *The American Idea of Success*

Have you ever noticed how much more terrifying the old ghost stories were than the creepy stuff on TV? Today the screen shows you an electronic monster or an actor in some nasty make-up, but the old stories left something to the imagination—let you shop among your own fears. For instance: "What I saw when I opened that door burned itself into my consciousness for a frightful moment before the brain fever took my reason. Today, white-haired at 35, I live in a quiet seaside cottage to which my ruined health drove me. Even in these peaceful surroundings I sometimes wake at night screaming so loudly

65

that kindly neighbors come to comfort me. I cannot tell them what I saw. I can never tell anyone."

Heywood Hale Broun, as quoted in *Reader's Digest*, December 1972

You have debased [my] child. . . . You have made him a laughing stock of intelligence . . . a stench in the nostrils of the ionosphere.

Dr. Lee DeForest, inventor of the audion tube, speech to the National Association of Broadcasters, as quoted in *Time*, July 7, 1961

Television's first duty is to the honest search for truth. That is not a meaningless aspiration. Truth may be an elusive ideal. But there is the world of difference between a television service which is erected to *suppress* truth and one which is erected to *search* for it. To that end I want to see television not simply a gigantic image machine with one knob marked *shock* and the other marked *tranquilize*. For all its limitations it can be a mighty forum of ideas—inquiring, criticizing, exposing, illuminating. Television *can* be a weapon against prejudice, injustice and ignorance. But only if it can work in freedom, responsibility and independence.

Robin Day, as quoted in *Encounter* (London), May 1970

Television news is careful to divide things into small and easily digestible particles. There is no integrated or comprehensible world view presented. Everything is safely middle class.

Alice Embree, as quoted in *Sisterhood Is Powerful*

The primary danger of the television screen lies not so much in the behavior it produces as the behavior it prevents—the talks, the games, the family activities and the arguments through which much of the child's learning takes place and his character is formed.

Urie Bronfenbrenner, as quoted in *Reader's Digest*, April 1972

I hate television. I hate it as much as peanuts. But I can't stop eating peanuts.

Orson Welles, as quoted in the New York *Herald Tribune*, October 12, 1956

In one move, television has taken a giant step. We still have shows with comic-book plots, superman heroes and unreality. But we also have "All in the Family." America has come face to face with itself—and is laughing at what it sees.

Arnold Hano, as quoted in *Reader's Digest*, July 1972

Television: Summer stock in an iron lung.

Beatrice Lillie, as quoted in *Reader's Digest*, May 1953

Television in its present form . . . [is] the opiate of the people in the United States.

Richard M. Nixon, as quoted in *Richard Nixon: A Political and Personal Portrait*

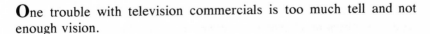

One trouble with television commercials is too much tell and not enough vision.

Marjorie Johnson, as quoted in *Reader's Digest*, August 1958

There's nothing funnier than the human animal.

Walt Disney, comment at a news conference on changing
from films about animals to shows about people, December 5,
1954

You can never hope to become a skilled conversationalist until you learn how to put your foot tactfully through the television set.

M. Dale Baughman, *The Educator's Handbook of Stories,
Quotes and Humor*

We have impressive evidence that watching television violence causes a significant increase in aggressive behavior. It is not the only or even the most significant cause of antisocial behavior, but it certainly is one of the major contributors. It also happens to be one cause we *can* change.

Dr. Robert M. Liebert, as quoted in *Reader's Digest*, April
1973

When I was nine I was the Demon King in *Cinderella* and it appears to have launched me on a long and happy life of being a monster.

Boris Karloff, as quoted in the London *Sunday Times*, July 28,
1957

Television is a kind of radio which lets people at home see what the studio audience is not laughing at.

Fred Allen, as quoted in *Reader's Digest*, April 1950

Look at television and what do you see? Thataway, giveaway, Garroway.

Corey Ford, as quoted in *Reader's Digest*, December 1958

We are drowning our youngsters in violence, cynicism and sadism piped into the living room and even the nursery. The grandchildren of the kids who used to weep because the Little Match Girl froze to death now feel cheated if she isn't slugged, raped and thrown into a Bessemer converter.

Jenkin Lloyd Jones, as quoted in *U. S. News and World Report*, May 28, 1962

A celebrity is a person who works hard all his life to become well-known, then wears dark glasses to avoid being recognized.

Fred Allen, as quoted in *Paris after Dark*

THE FAMILY AND THE GENERATIONS

Children

I am sure that if people had to choose between living where the noise of children never stopped and where it was never heard, all the good-natured and sound people would prefer the incessant noise to the incessant silence.

George Bernard Shaw, *Misalliance*

Some of our modern children are so precocious, the birds and bees should study them.

Chester L. Marks, as quoted in *Reader's Digest*, July 1966

Every child comes with the message that God is not yet discouraged of man.

Rabindranath Tagore, *Stray Birds*

I think, at a child's birth, if a mother could ask a fairy godmother to endow it with the most useful gift, that gift would be curiosity.

Eleanor Roosevelt, as quoted in *The Common Sense Wisdom of Three First Ladies*

The persons hardest to convince they're at the retirement age are children at bedtime.

Shannon Fife, as quoted in *Reader's Digest*, July 1952

You know children are growing up when they start asking questions that have answers.

John J. Plomp, as quoted in *Reader's Digest*, March 1952   73

The one thing children wear out faster than shoes is parents.

John J. Plomp, as quoted in *Reader's Digest*, November
1952

Humans are children for so long that they never get over it.

Leon J. Faul, *Emotional Maturity*

Children are a great comfort in your old age—and they help you reach it faster, too.

Lionel M. Kaufman, as quoted in *Reader's Digest*, June
1945

People who say they sleep like a baby usually don't have one.

Leo J. Burke, as quoted in *Reader's Digest*, January 1952

Babies are such a nice way to start people.

Don Herold, *There Ought to Be a Law*

Children are God's spies.

Elizabeth Bowen, as quoted in *Reader's Digest*, September
1970

All children wear the sign: "I want to be important NOW." Many of our juvenile-delinquency problems arise because nobody read the sign.

Dan Pursuit, as quoted in Reader's Digest, October 1968

Children cannot be made good by making them happy, but they can be made happy by making them good.

E. J. Kiefer, as quoted in Reader's Digest, July 1959

The first, the most fundamental right of childhood is the right to be loved. The child comes into the world alone, defenseless, without resource. Only love can stand between his infant helplessness and the savagery of a harsh world.

Paul Hanly Furfey, The Church and the Child

A baby has a way of making a man out of his father and a boy out of his grandfather.

Angie Papadakis, as quoted in Reader's Digest, January 1968

The hearts of small children are delicate organs. A cruel beginning in this world can twist them into curious shapes. The heart of a child can shrink so that forever afterward it is hard and pitted as the seed of a peach. Or again, the heart of such a child may fester and swell until it is a misery to carry within the body, easily chafed and hurt by the most ordinary things.

Carson McCullers, The Member of the Wedding

Whenever poets want to give the idea that something is particularly
    meek and mild,
They compare it to a child,
Thereby proving that though poets with poetry may be rife
They don't know the facts of life.

Ogden Nash, as quoted in Reader's Digest, July 1952   75

My own lawn—which is where my neighbors' children play—is no credit at all to this gardening community. It is a scarred and scuffed ledger that records the urgent enterprises of childhood, and childhood's four-legged companions. What grows there, grows with my blessing and my profound respect.

Scott Seegers, as quoted in Reader's Digest, May 1973

Some of my best friends are children. In fact, all of my best friends are children.

J. D. Salinger, as quoted in Time, July 16, 1951

My three children are at the perfect age—too old to cry at night and too young to borrow my car.

Walter Slezak, as quoted in Reader's Digest, October 1959

When we adults want to enjoy ourselves, we almost always seek to be entertained by others—on television, at the theater, at a baseball game. Or we fall back on things that provide us with a kind of programmed play: cards, dominoes, bowling balls, golf clubs. We let places and objects tell us what to do, how we should react.

When a child plays, he is the manipulator; he makes do with whatever is at hand. His imagination transforms the commonplace into the priceless. A wooden clothespin, rescued from under the kitchen table and wrapped in a dishcloth, becomes a baby; a penny thrust under a cushion becomes a buried treasure.

Eda J. LeShan, as quoted in PTA Magazine, June 1968

Children don't want to be told; they want to be shown. It takes years of telling to undo one unwise showing.

Eileen M. Haase, as quoted in Reader's Digest, April 1961

By the time the youngest children have learned to keep the house tidy, the oldest grandchildren are on hand to tear it to pieces.

Christopher Morley, as quoted in Reader's Digest,
November 1949

What was wonderful about childhood is that anything in it was a wonder. It was not merely a world full of miracles, it was a miraculous world.

G. K. Chesterton, *Autobiography*

I teach my child and I tell other children of all ages—preschool, in school, in college, and out:
That nothing is done finally and right.
That nothing is known positively and completely.
That the world is theirs, all of it.

Lincoln Steffens, as quoted in *Reader's Digest*, December 1942

Children grow by leaps and bounds—especially in the apartment overhead.

George Allen, as quoted in *Reader's Digest*, March 1949

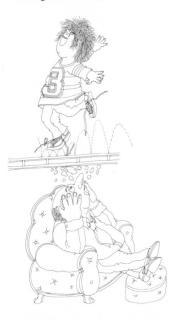

Children are our most valuable natural resource.

Herbert Hoover, cited in his obituary, October 21, 1964   77

Don't worry about the size of your Christmas tree. In the eyes of children they are all 25 feet tall.

Bill Vaughan, as quoted in *Reader's Digest*,
December 1957

A three-year-old child is a being who gets almost as much fun out of a $56 set of swings as it does out of finding a small green worm.

Bill Vaughan, as quoted in *Reader's Digest*, October 1955

Remember when your mother used to say "Go to your room—" This was a terrible penalty. Now when a mother says the same thing, a kid goes to his room. There he's got an air-conditioner, a TV set, an inter-com, a short-wave radio—he's better off than he was in the first place.

Sam Levenson, as quoted in *Reader's Digest*,
October 1956

The average child is an almost non-existent myth. To be normal one must be peculiar in some way or other.

Heywood Broun, *Sitting in the World*

You can learn many things from children. How much patience you have, for instance.

Franklin P. Jones, as quoted in *Reader's Digest*, June 1956

Children often hold a marriage together—by keeping their parents too busy to quarrel with each other.

Franklin P. Jones, as quoted in *Reader's Digest*, July 1950

Children need love, especially when they do not deserve it.

 Harold S. Hulbert, as quoted in *Reader's Digest*, May 1949

The unwarped child, with his spontaneous faith and confidence in goodness, is the best illustration of that spirit which fits the Kingdom of God.

Rufus M. Jones, *The Testimony of the Soul*

The best way to keep children home is to make the home atmosphere pleasant—and let the air out of the tires.

Dorothy Parker, as quoted in *Reader's Digest*, May 1961

Everyone is the Child of his past.

Edna G. Rostow, as quoted in *The Woman in America*

Children are small people who are not permitted to act as their parents did at that age.

Josephus Henry, as quoted in *Reader's Digest*, June 1949

Children never put off until tomorrow that which will keep them out of bed tonight.

Glen Preston Burns, as quoted in *Reader's Digest*,
December 1951

In very early youth the soul can still remember its immortal habitation, and clouds and the edges of hills are of another kind from ours, and every scent and color has a savor of Paradise.

Hilaire Belloc, *The Path to Rome*

Give me a newborn child, and in ten years I can have him so scared he'll never dare to lift his voice above a whisper, or so brave that he'll fear nothing.

Dr. George A. Dorsey, as quoted in *Reader's Digest*, March
1937   79

Doting parents would do well to remember that in doing everything for a child and expecting nothing we do the child a disservice. Children as a rule do not want to be indulged; they want to be responsible. Overindulgence is the ultimate insult, for when you "spoil" a child you are practically saying, "I know you aren't capable of being civilized and considerate and contributing and I won't expect it of you."

Hannah Lees, as quoted in Reader's Digest, July 1960

Children are the true connoisseurs. What's precious to them has no price—only value.

Bel Kaufman, television interview, 1967

The secret with dealing successfully with a child is not to be its parent.

Mell Lazarus, as quoted in Reader's Digest, March 1974

Training a baby by the book is a good idea, only you need a different book for each baby.

Dan Bennett, as quoted in Reader's Digest, July 1955

I've just learned what makes a newborn babe cry. It's hungry, naked and already owes the Government $1700.

Arthur Godfrey, as quoted in Reader's Digest, July 1952

Lessons from Life

A child that lives with ridicule learns to be timid.
A child that lives with criticism learns to condemn.
A child that lives with distrust learns to be deceitful.
A child that lives with antagonism learns to be hostile.
A child that lives with affection learns to love.
A child that lives with encouragement learns confidence.
A child that lives with truth learns justice.
A child that lives with praise learns to appreciate.
A child that lives with sharing learns to be considerate.
A child that lives with knowledge learns wisdom.

A child that lives with patience learns to be tolerant.
A child that lives with happiness will find love and beauty.

Ronald Russell, as quoted in Reader's Digest,
October 1972

Youth is a wonderful thing. What a crime to waste it on children.

George Bernard Shaw, as quoted in Reader's Digest, April
1940

To show a child what has once delighted you, to find the child's delight added to your own, so that there is now a double delight seen in the glow of trust and affection, this is happiness.

J. B. Priestley, as quoted in Reader's Digest, March 1962

Marriage and Divorce

Marriage always demands the greatest understanding of the art of insincerity possible between two human beings.

Vicki Baum, And Life Goes On

When one thinks how many people there are that one does not in the least want to marry, and how many there are that do not in the least want to marry one, and how small one's social circle really is, any marriage at all seems a miracle.

Barry Pain, as quoted in Reader's Digest,
September 1952

In marriage reverence is more important even than love. . . . A steady awareness in each that the other has a kinship with the eternal.

F. J. Shield, Society and Sanity　81

The honeymoon is over when he phones that he'll be late for supper—and she has already left a note that it's in the refrigerator.

Bill Lawrence, as quoted in Reader's Digest, January 1955

Marriage . . . is still a contract, not so much a business contract settling property right or a religious sacrament establishing eternal bonds, but a personal contract in which each undertakes to do his best to make the relationship meaningful.

Edna Rostow, as quoted in The Woman in America

However cooperative the relation between husband and wife, there is usually the tacit assumption that the household is basically the wife's responsibility. If she can cope with that and another job, fine, but the domestic burden is primarily hers.

Edna G. Rostow, as quoted in The Woman in America

The secret of happy marriage is simple: Just keep on being as polite to one another as you are to your friends.

R. Quillen, as quoted in Reader's Digest, November 1952

Marriage: the state or condition of a community consisting of a master, a mistress, and two slaves, making in all, two.

Ambrose Bierce, The Devil's Dictionary

When a girl marries, she exchanges the attention of all other men she knew for the inattention of one.

Helen Rowland, as quoted in Reader's Digest,
January 1955

Love, the quest; marriage, the conquest; divorce, the inquest.

Helen Rowland, as quoted in Reader's Digest, July 1936

[The wedding] has joined the mink coat and powerboat as a status symbol. It has been transformed from a dignified ritual into a gaudy, nerve-racking rite. To the mounting dismay of the clergy, its spiritual significance has been seriously overshadowed.

Kitty Hanson, as quoted in *Reader's Digest*, February 1971

To wed is to bring not only our worldly good but every potential capacity to create more values in living together. . . . In becoming one these two create a new world that had never existed before.

Paul E. Johnson, *Christian Love*

If family breakups contribute to juvenile crime, more family breakups will produce more crime. Are more families breaking up? Census figures show that one of every four marriages performed in 1931–33 ended in divorce. By the mid-'50s, this rate had leaped to one of every three. By 1971, it had hit 41 percent.

Lester Velie, *Reader's Digest*, August 1972

The system of law and custom which upheld the old theological conception of marriage is today a crumbling, motheaten, dangerously toppling ruin which has served its purpose and now needs to be junked.

Judge Ben B. Lindsey and Wainwright Evans, *The Companionate Marriage*

Our young are being bombarded with the notion that they may be the last generation to experience traditional marriage and family life—and also with some pretty curious notions as to what they might try instead. The tragedy is that they're subjected to this before they've even had a chance to start a family and learn about family life themselves.

Carlfred B. Broderick, as quoted in *Reader's Digest*, January 1973

A good marriage is that in which each appoints the other guardian of his solitude. Once the realization is accepted that even between the closest human beings infinite distances continue to exist, a wonderful 83 living side by side can grow up, if they succeed in loving the distance between them which makes it possible for each to see the other whole and against a wide sky.

> Rainer Maria Rilke, as quoted in *Reader's Digest*,
> May 1957

A sound marriage is not based on complete frankness; it is based on a sensible reticence.

> Morris L. Ernst, as quoted in *Reader's Digest*, August 1957

Most domestic quarrels could be checked by a timely use of arms.

> Don Marshall, as quoted in *Reader's Digest*, August 1954

What a holler would ensue, if people had to pay the minister as much to marry them as they have to pay a lawyer to get them a divorce.

> Claire Trevor, as quoted in the New York
> *Journal-American*, October 12, 1960

The proper time for divorce is during the courtship.

> Dr. Reuben Hill, as quoted in *Reader's Digest*, November
> 1948

A shotgun wedding may be defined as troth or consequences.

> Pete Simer, as quoted in *Reader's Digest*, December 1948

Love God and laugh at the devil. Assuming that a husband and wife obey these twin commandments, and thereby keep their love for each other this side of idolatry, what can Christian marriage do but bring them nearer to God?

> Chad Walsh, *Behold the Glory*

A marriage is like a long trip in a tiny rowboat: if one passenger starts to rock the boat, the other has to steady it; otherwise, they will go to the bottom together.

Dr. David R. Reuben, as quoted in *Reader's Digest*, January 1973

Marriage is the only sacrament which transforms a human action into an instrument of the divine action, using a human act which up to then had been used for a natural end.

Jacques Leclercq, *Marriage a Great Sacrament*

Society, when it rules "thumbs down" on extramarital relations, is guarding itself against destruction.

Mario A. Castallo, as quoted in *Reader's Digest*, June 1948

I doubt if there is one married person on earth who can be objective about divorce. It is always a threat, admittedly or not, and such a dire threat that it is almost a dirty word.

Nora Johnson, as quoted in the *Atlantic Monthly*, July 1962

The constant talk today about marriage, whether it's positive or negative, has only led to greater hopes for it. What's difficult to remember is that marriages of all kinds, bad and good, cannot stand the abuse of unmet expectations. If only we could realize that the better the marriage is, the worse we will sometimes feel, then we might prevent incidents that occur in any marriage from leading to separation and divorce. Such an understanding could give us the insight to make one good marriage last a lifetime.

Richard Farson, as quoted in Reader's Digest, December 1971

I have learned that only two things are necessary to keep one's wife happy. First, let her think she's having her way. And second, let her have it.

Lyndon B. Johnson, to Lord Snowden at a White House reception, November 1965

If all of one's married days are as happy as these new ones have been to me, I have deliberately fooled away 30 years of my life. If I were to do it over again I would marry in early infancy instead of wasting time cutting teeth and breaking crockery.

Mark Twain, as quoted in Reader's Digest, August 1973

"I'll cook dinner for you tonight" implies it's really your job and isn't he a nice guy to do some of it for you?

Pat Mainardi, as quoted in Sisterhood Is Powerful

There are pretenses which are very sincere, and marriage is their school.

Miguel de Unamuno, Two Mothers

Almost all married people fight, although many are ashamed to admit it. Actually, a marriage in which no quarreling at all takes place may well be one that is dead or dying from emotional undernourishment. If you care, you probably fight.

86

Flora Davis, as quoted in Glamour, March 1969

Matrimony is a process by which a grocer acquired an account the florist had.

Frances Rodman, as quoted in *Reader's Digest*, February 1956

Marriage probably has the poorest public relations of any institution in the world, but its business is only slightly short of spectacular.

Douglas Meador, as quoted in *Reader's Digest*, July 1962

It is nature's way, the gentle trickery of nature, to lead man and woman in virtue of the psychical need they have of each other to form that close relationship of marriage by which those who are already one in mind and heart become one physical principle for the propagation of the human race.

Ignatius W. Cox, *The Divine Romance of Marriage*

Success in marriage requires continence as well as potency. In other words, character is indispensable in well-ordered sexual life.

Dr. Alexis Carrel, as quoted in *Reader's Digest*, July 1939

I know what I wish Ralph Nader would investigate next. Marriage. It's not safe—it's not safe at all.

Jean Kerr, as quoted in *Family Circle*, February 1970

Marrying . . . is like buying something you've been admiring for a long time. . . . You may love it when you get home, but it doesn't always go with everything else in the house.

Jean Kerr, *The Snake Has All the Lines*

Hundreds of birds in the air
And millions of leaves on the pavement
Then the bells pealing on
Over palace and people outside,

All for the words of "I will"
To love's most holy enslavement—
What can we do but rejoice
With a triumphing bridegroom and bride?

Sir John Betjeman, Poet Laureate of England, on the marriage of Princess Anne to Mark Phillips, August 14, 1973

It is often said that couples have to work at making a success of marriage. The term seems unfortunate, particularly in relation to sex. If there is one thing a couple should not do, it is to work at the relationship as though it were some kind of task. Yet this is the message carried by a discouraging number of books on the subject.

Dr. William H. Masters and Virginia E. Johnson, as quoted in Reader's Digest, July 1973

Matrimony is not a word, it's a sentence.

Eddie Cantor, as quoted in Reader's Digest, March 1934

Never go around with a married woman unless you can go two rounds with her husband.

Eddie Cantor, as quoted in Reader's Digest, May 1934

Two dollars will buy all the happiness or all the misery in the world. At least that used to be the price of a marriage license.

Eddie Cantor, radio-show comment, October 1938

Marriage itself is not solely an institution for the propagation of children, but is also for the fruition of that richer fellowship God intended when he saw that it was not good for man to live alone.

George Hockman, Religion in Modern Life

Men have a tendency to marry women who are their intellectual inferiors. They thus preserve the male ego from excessive strain.

Paul Popenoe, as quoted in Reader's Digest, August 1935

One of the best things about marriage is that it gets young people to bed at a decent hour.

M. M. Musselman, as quoted in *Reader's Digest*, February 1955

Any married man should forget his mistakes—no use two people remembering the same thing.

Duane Dewel, as quoted in *Reader's Digest*, August 1954

The cooing stops with the honeymoon, but the billing goes on forever.

Galen Drake, as quoted in *Reader's Digest*, June 1956

In married conversation, as in surgery, the knife must be used with care.

André Maurois, as quoted in *Reader's Digest*, February 1955

Adultery in America is rare. Its place is filled by multiple divorce.

André Maurois, as quoted in *Reader's Digest*, September 1936

A happy marriage is a long conversation that always seems too short.

André Maurois, as quoted in *Reader's Digest*, April 1944

Marriage is an edifice that must be rebuilt every day.

André Maurois, as quoted in *Reader's Digest*, April 1972

Marriage is a job. Happiness or unhappiness has nothing to do with it. There was never a marriage that could not be made a success, nor a marriage that could not have ended in bitterness and failure.

Kathleen Norris, as quoted in *Reader's Digest*, April 1944

Back of every achievement is a proud wife and a surprised mother-in-law.

Brooks Hays, as quoted in the New York *Herald Tribune*,
December 2, 1961

When a woman marries again, it is because she detested her first husband; when a man marries again, it is because he adored his first wife. Women try their luck; men risk theirs.

Oscar Wilde, as quoted in *Reader's Digest*, September 1935

Marriage is a deal in which a man gives away half his groceries in order to get the other half cooked.

John Gwynne, as quoted in *The Left Handed Dictionary*

Trial marriage? Whose isn't?

Lane Olinghouse, as quoted in *Reader's Digest*, May 1967

Marriage starts out as a private affair, but it sure doesn't stay that way for long. That quiet country lane you strolled together, hand in hand, leads all too quickly into a kind of Times Square, where if any man and woman hold hands at all, it's more for mutual protection than for romance.

Jean Bradford, as quoted in *Contemporary*, April 13, 1969

The only real argument for marriage is that it remains the best method for getting acquainted.

Heywood Broun, as quoted in *Reader's Digest*, October 1944

It is not marriage that fails; it is people that fail. All that marriage does is to show them up.

Harry Emerson Fosdick, as quoted in *Reader's Digest*, July 1936

When I hear people say they have lived together 25 years and never had the least difference, I wonder whether they have not had a good deal of indifference.

Robert Collyer, as quoted in Reader's Digest, September 1937

Rarely are marriages wrecked on a big rock of adversity. It is on the smaller pebbles that they founder.

Velora Buscher, as quoted in Reader's Digest, October 1955

Nothing makes a man and wife feel closer, these days, than a joint tax return.

Gil Stern, as quoted in Reader's Digest, April 1974

What makes a marriage is the consent of the partners, their serious intention to live together in some sense, however dimly perceived, as "one flesh," a union of their two separate existences into still a third existence, the marriage itself.

William G. Cole, Sex in Christianity and Psychoanalysis

It is a fusion of two hearts—the union of two lives—the coming together of two tributaries, which after being joined in marriage, will flow in the same channel in the same direction . . . carrying the same burdens of responsibility and obligation.

Peter Marshall, as quoted in A Man Called Peter

A man should sleep sometime between lunch and dinner in order to be at his best in the evening when he joins his wife and friends at dinner. My wife and I tried two or three times in the last forty years to have breakfast together, but it was so disagreeable we had to stop.

Sir Winston Churchill, letter to an American friend, as quoted in The New York Times, December 4, 1950

My marriage was the most fortunate and joyous event which happened to me in the whole of my life.

> Sir Winston Churchill, as quoted in *My Darling Clementine,*
> a biography of Lady Churchill

Woman accepts man for the sake of matrimony and man accepts matrimony for the sake of woman.

> Gregory Mason, as quoted in *Reader's Digest,*
> April 1944

A perfect marriage is a hearth and a horizon.

> Elizabeth Asquith Bibesco, as quoted in *Reader's Digest,*
> October 1950

Often the difference between a successful marriage and a mediocre one consists of leaving about three or four things a day unsaid.

> Harlan Miller, as quoted in *Reader's Digest,*
> July 1946

Marriage is our last, best chance to grow up.

> Rev. Joseph Barth, as quoted in the *Ladies' Home Journal,*
> April 1961

A man has no business to marry a woman who can't make him miserable; it means that she can't make him happy.

> Gerald Villiers-Stuart, as quoted in *Reader's Digest,*
> December 1951

Much marriage difficulty and unhappiness are due to the failure of the partners to accept the fact of their finiteness and its meaning. Instead, they hold themselves up to ideals of performance possible only to God.

> Reuel L. Howe, *Sex and Religion Today*

Marriage is popular because it combines the maximum of temptation with the maximum of opportunity.

> George Bernard Shaw, as quoted in *Reader's Digest*,
> January 1943

Marriage is a great institution, but I'm not ready for an institution, yet.

> Mae West, as quoted in *Reader's Digest*, December 1939

He's certain to get the divorce vote and remember that's one in four these days.

> Cleveland Amory, on Governor Rockefeller's political
> future following his divorce, as quoted in the London *Daily*
> *Telegraph*, February 8, 1962

When a man declares: "I am sure of my wife," it means that he is sure of his wife. But when a woman declares: "I am sure of my husband," it means she is sure of herself.

> Francis de Croisset, as quoted in *Reader's Digest*, January
> 1943

When the wedding march sounds the resolute approach, the clock no longer ticks; it tolls the hour. . . . The figures in the aisle are no longer individuals; they symbolize the human race.

> Anne Morrow Lindbergh, *Dearly Beloved*

When a man decides to get married, it may be the last decision he is allowed to make.

> Kenneth L. Krichbaum, as quoted in *Reader's Digest*,
> December 1948

When I was a young man I vowed never to marry until I found the ideal woman. Well, I found her—but, alas, she was waiting for the perfect man.

> Robert Schuman, French Foreign Minister, as quoted in
> news summaries of December 31, 1952

93

The trouble with marriage is that, while every woman is at heart a mother, every man is at heart a bachelor.

E. V. Lucas, as quoted in *Reader's Digest*, April 1941

I sincerely regret all my divorces, because I don't like anything to be unsuccessful.

John Paul Getty, as quoted in *Time*, February 24, 1958

Wives and Mothers

Two hundred years ago, women had no identity problem. The family could not function without them. Today even those women who find complete fulfillment in bringing up their children face a forced early retirement after 20 years on the job, when most of them still have many vigorous years ahead.

Joyce Brothers, as quoted in *Reader's Digest*, March 1973

Perhaps the most vicious weapon used against women is the psychological line that tells us, "If you're not satisfied with your life, if you can't adjust to the feminine role, then something is wrong with *you.*"

Robin Morgan, as quoted in *Sisterhood Is Powerful*

Wives suffer from just as many ulcers as husbands do. The same ones.

Franklin P. Jones, as quoted in *Reader's Digest*, October 1953

American wives and American mothers, as surely as "the hand that rocks the cradle is the hand that rules the world," have, through their nurture of children and their influence over men, the destinies of our Nation in their keeping to a greater extent than any other single agency.

Grover Cleveland, as quoted in the *Ladies' Home Journal*, May 1905

As a pediatrician, I know that we do not know enough about nurturing to be able to tell mothers that if they find a person or an institution that meets such-and-such standards, this will be an adequate mother substitute. We can list people's credentials, pinpoint the standards for a day-care center, but, just as breast milk cannot be duplicated, neither can a mother. We cannot put mothering into a formula and come up with a person who has the special feeling for your child that you do.

Dr. Sally E. Shaywitz, as quoted in *Reader's Digest*, October 1973

If a woman's adult efforts are concentrated exclusively on her children, she is more likely to stifle than broaden her children's perspective and preparation for adult life.

Alice S. Rossi, as quoted in *The Woman in America*

Tired mothers find that spanking takes less time than reasoning and penetrates sooner to the seat of memory.

Will Durant, as quoted in *Reader's Digest*, December 1934

Our sabotage has ranged from . . . housemaids accidentally breaking china to mothers teaching their children to *love them* a little bit better than their fathers.

Robin Morgan, as quoted in *Sisterhood Is Powerful*

The ideal wife is one who knows when her husband wants to be forced to do something against his will.

Sydney J. Harris, as quoted in *Reader's Digest*, December 1954

Feminists are *not* against individual women being housewives. We are against the "housewife system," which says that no matter what a particular woman's talents and interests may be, it is "natural" and good for her to sacrifice such interests and ambitions to the task of making a home.

Women are individual; it makes no more sense to expect all 95 women to be happy with the same job in life than it would be to expect all men to enjoy being carpenters.

Yet we have been taught differently; we have learned that to be assertive, logical, adventurous and independent is to be masculine; that to be passive, irrational, timid and submissive—characteristics historically associated with subject peoples—is to be feminine.

Lucy Komisar, as quoted in Reader's Digest, August 1971

Instant availability without continuous presence is probably the best role a mother can play.

Lotte Bailyn, as quoted in The Woman in America

The only time a woman wishes she were a year older is when she is expecting a baby.

Mary Marsh, as quoted in Reader's Digest, July 1957

Being an old maid is like death by drowning—a really delightful sensation after you have ceased struggling.

Edna Ferber, as quoted in Sisterhood Is Powerful

The ability to listen with the eyes, to appear to be fascinated while the portals of the ear close tight and the mind goes off on pleasant journeys of its own, is a purely feminine accomplishment. God gives that gift to woman so she may stay married to the same man for years, and still smile.

Frank Case, as quoted in Reader's Digest,
January 1943

The graveyards are full of women whose houses were so spotless you could eat off the floor. Remember, the second wife always has a maid.

Heloise Cruse, as quoted in the Saturday Evening Post,
March 2, 1963

As my child struggles to sit, to search out the sounds and feel of the world, I sense that my role these six months has been beneath him, supporting. From now on my role will be from above, lifting.
Motherhood feels comfortable.

Judith Geissler, as quoted in Reader's Digest, December
1972

A mother is not a person to lean on but a person to make leaning unnecessary.

Dorothy Canfield Fisher, Her Son's Wife

No matter how happily a woman may be married, it always pleases her to discover that there is a nice man who wishes she were not.

H. L. Mencken, as quoted in Reader's Digest,
May 1957

Each suburban housewife spends her time presiding over a power plant sufficient to have staffed the palace of a Roman emperor with 100 slaves.

Margaret Mead, as quoted in Reader's Digest, February
1969

Women should receive a higher education, not in order to become doctors, lawyers, or professors, but to rear their offspring to be valuable human beings.

Dr. Alexis Carrel, *Man, the Unknown*

Just about the time a woman thinks her work is done, she becomes a grandmother.

Edward H. Dreschnack, as quoted in *Reader's Digest*, September 1955

No woman can call herself free who does not own and control her body. No woman can call herself free until she can choose consciously whether she will or will not be a mother.

Margaret Sanger, as quoted in *Parade*, December 1, 1963

There are two kinds of mothers: those who place a child's bouquet in a milk bottle on top of the refrigerator, and those who enthrone it in a vase on the piano.

Marcelene Cox, as quoted in *Reader's Digest*, November 1955

Why does a woman work ten years to change a man's habits and then complain that he's not the man she married?

> Barbra Streisand, as quoted in *Reader's Digest*, September 1967

The housewife is the most important person. She holds the world together. Mothers are the most unselfish, the most responsible people in the world.

> Bernard M. Baruch, as quoted in *U. S. News & World Report*, August 31, 1959

As long as a woman can look ten years younger than her daughter she is perfectly satisfied.

> Oscar Wilde, as quoted in *Reader's Digest*, January 1947

Sooner or later—and I think it should be sooner—women have to face the question of who they are besides their children's mother.

> Alice S. Rossi, as quoted in *The Woman in America*

If you want to know how your girl will treat you after marriage, just listen to her talking to her little brother.

> Sam Levenson, as quoted in *Reader's Digest*, March 1960

American women expect to find in their husbands a perfection that English women only hope to find in their butlers.

> W. Somerset Maugham, as quoted in *Reader's Digest*, June 1944

Most wives have already been relieved of such duties as milking cows, churning butter, stoking fires, making quilts, and preserving food. Many are now free of broom pushing, mop swinging, vegetable peeling, and bread baking. Television has become a combined babysitter and storyteller. The modern wife is expected to function at a higher level. As the rung is moved up, she becomes the family economist, child psychologist, and career woman. Many women who would have been competent wives in an earlier era reach their level of incompetence on this higher rung.

Laurence J. Peter and Raymond Hull, *The Peter Principle*

A working girl is one who quit her job to get married.

E. J. Kiefer, as quoted in *Reader's Digest*, May 1955

One of the best hearing aids a man can have is an attentive wife.

Groucho Marx, as quoted in *Reader's Digest*, May 1952

I demand for the unmarried mother, as a sacred channel of life, the same reverence and respect as for the married mother; for Maternity is a cosmic thing and once it has come to pass our conventions must not be permitted to blaspheme it.

Ben B. Lindsey and Wainwright Evans, *The Revolt of Modern Youth*

The test of a happily married—and a wise—woman is whether she can say, "I love you" far oftener than she asks, "Do you love me?"

Dorothy Dayton, as quoted in *Reader's Digest*, April 1944

Nobody objects to a woman being a good writer or sculptor or geneticist if at the same time she manages to be a good wife, good mother, good-looking, good-tempered, well-groomed—and unaggressive.

Leslie M. McIntyre, as quoted in *Reader's Digest*, May 1970

Without the full capacity to limit her own reproduction, a woman's other "freedoms" are tantalizing mockers that cannot be exercised.

100   Lucinda Cisler, as quoted in *Sisterhood Is Powerful*

An ideal wife is one who remains faithful to you but tries to be just as charming as if she weren't.

Bill Ballance, as quoted in Reader's Digest,
February 1960

A woman is not a whole woman without the experience of marriage. In the case of a bad marriage, you win if you lose. Of the two alternatives—bad marriage or none—I believe bad marriage would be better. It is a bitter experience and a high price to pay for fulfillment, but it is the better alternative.

Fannie Hurst, as quoted in Parade, September 18, 1960

Variability is one of the virtues of a woman. It avoids the crude requirement of polygamy. So long as you have one good wife you are sure to have a spiritual harem.

G. K. Chesterton, as quoted in Reader's Digest, August
1935

An American wife is wholly incapable of opening a door or even lighting a match. She will wait by a door as patiently as any poodle for her husband or some other man to come to the rescue; she will retain an unlighted cigarette in her lovely lips until some man has handed her a match.

Harold Nicolson, as quoted in Reader's Digest, September
1936

Husbands and Fathers

Seems to me there's one reason for today's generation gap which most of us would sooner not talk about—the fact that a lad's father is no longer his teacher.

H. Gordon Green, as quoted in Reader's Digest, June 1971   101

An archeologist is the best husband any woman can have; the older she gets, the more interested he is in her.

Agatha Christie, as quoted in the New York *Herald Tribune*, March 9, 1954

An ideal husband is one who treats his wife like a new car.

Dan Bennett, as quoted in *Reader's Digest*, October 1951

The husband who doesn't tell his wife everything probably reasons that what she doesn't know won't hurt him.

Leo J. Burke, as quoted in *Reader's Digest*, March 1952

Build me a son, O Lord, who will be strong enough to know when he is weak, and brave enough to face himself when he is afraid, one who will be proud and unbending in honest defeat and humble and gentle in victory.

General Douglas MacArthur, as quoted in *MacArthur: Rendezvous with History*

Many a man today is living by the seat of his frau.

102

O. O. McIntyre, as quoted in *Reader's Digest*, May 1933

The Perfect Husband
He tells you when you've got on too much lipstick,
And helps you with your girdle when your hips stick.

> Ogden Nash, as quoted in *Reader's Digest*, May 1949

There's nothing like a dish towel for wiping that contented look off a married man's face.

> Glen Preston Burns, as quoted in *Reader's Digest*, March 1953

The reason the average bachelor of 35 remains a bachelor is very simple. No ordinarily attractive and intelligent woman has ever made a serious and undivided effort to marry him.

> H. L. Mencken, *A Mencken Chrestomathy*

No man is genuinely happy, married, who has to drink worse whiskey than he used to drink when he was single.

> H. L. Mencken, *Prejudices: Fourth Series*

Bachelors know more about women than married men. If they didn't they'd be married to one.

> H. L. Mencken, *A Mencken Chrestomathy*

The way to hold a husband is to keep him a little bit jealous. The way to lose him is to keep him a little bit more jealous.

> H. L. Mencken, as quoted in *Reader's Digest*, November 1950

A New Jersey company conducted a contest among youngsters with the theme: "The Nicest Thing My Father Ever Did for Me." One answer: "He married my mother."

> Robert Sylvester, as quoted in *Reader's Digest*, August 1968

Fathers are pals nowadays mainly because they haven't got guts enough to be fathers.

Sam Levenson, as quoted in *Reader's Digest*, October 1959

The most important thing a father can do for his children is to love their mother.

Theodore Hesburgh, as quoted in *Reader's Digest*, January 1963

Perhaps host and guest is really the happiest relation for father and son.

Evelyn Waugh, as quoted in the *Atlantic Monthly*, March 1963

Nothing takes weight off a man faster than a wife who's reducing.

Franklin P. Jones, as quoted in *Reader's Digest*, October 1955

Let your wife know who's boss right from the start. There's no use kidding yourself.

Franklin P. Jones, as quoted in *Reader's Digest*, September 1952

You can't always tell what makes a man tick until you meet his wife. She may be the works.

Franklin P. Jones, as quoted in *Reader's Digest*, January 1961

There is only one thing for a man to do who is married to a woman who enjoys spending money, and that is to enjoy earning it.

Edgar Watson Howe, as quoted in *Reader's Digest*, November 1968

Whatever a woman looks askance at,
Her husband takes a second glance at.

George Walton, as quoted in *Reader's Digest*, December
1952

Being a husband is like any other job. It helps if you like the boss.

Leo J. Burke, as quoted in *Reader's Digest*, June 1957

A valiant man takes pride in being himself the founder of a race; impotence alone worships the pedigree.

Friedrich Hertz, *Race and Civilization*

A husband is the kind of man
Who drives me to a rage;
He can't recall my birthday
But he always knows my age.

Mrs. Vashti Balker, as quoted in *Reader's Digest*,
December 1947

A man likes his wife to be just clever enough to comprehend his cleverness, and just stupid enough to admire it.

Israel Zangwill, as quoted in *Reader's Digest*, November
1952

A smart husband is one who saves all the barbershop gossip until after dinner—so that his wife will help him with the dishes.

Edna May Bush, as quoted in *Reader's Digest*, February
1955

A husband is really broken in when he can understand every word his wife isn't saying.

Shannon Fife, as quoted in *Reader's Digest*, January 1956   105

Freedom, we are often told, is our most precious possession, and it was, perhaps, the fear of irreparable damage to that freedom that led me to contemplate with more anxiety than eagerness the life growing in my wife's fertile belly.

Yet now that this permanent houseguest is among the living, I am surprised to find that my pleasure in his company generally exceeds earlier estimates.

Jeff Davidson, as quoted in *McCall's*, March 1969

God help the man who won't marry until he finds a perfect woman, and God help him still more if he finds her.

Ben Tillett, as quoted in *Reader's Digest*, May 1959

My husband will never chase another woman. He's too fine, too decent, too old.

Gracie Allen, as quoted in *Reader's Digest*, January 1949

The fundamental defect of fathers is that they want their children to be a credit to them.

Bertrand Russell, as quoted in *The New York Times*, June 9, 1963

The young man who wants to marry happily should pick out a good mother and marry one of her daughters—any one will do.

J. Ogden Armour, as quoted in *Reader's Digest*, February 1974

Grandchildren don't make a man feel old; it's the knowledge that he's married to a grandmother.

G. Norman Collie, as quoted in *Reader's Digest*, July 1955

Parenthood

The best combination of parents consists of a father who is gentle beneath his firmness, and a mother who is firm beneath her gentleness.

Sydney J. Harris, as quoted in *Reader's Digest*, March 1967

Parenthood remains the greatest single preserve of the amateur.

Alvin Toffler, *Future Shock*

A parental group leader wants the two-child family made popular and fashionable again. How about the two-parent family?

Dave Keniston, as quoted in *Reader's Digest*, October 1964

The reason parents no longer lead their children in the right direction is because the parents aren't going that way themselves.

Kin Hubbard, as quoted in *Reader's Digest*, August 1962

It's great. It's wonderful *per se.*

Chief Justice Earl Warren, comment on learning of the birth of a grandson, as quoted in *Newsweek*, March 19, 1956

Was there ever a grandparent, bushed after a day of minding noisy youngsters, who hasn't felt the Lord knew what He was doing when He gave little children to young people?

Joe E. Wells, as quoted in *Reader's Digest*, January 1954

One way to curb delinquency is to take parents off the streets at night.

Morrie Gallant, as quoted in *Reader's Digest*, November 1955

Who of us is mature enough for offspring before the offspring themselves arrive? The value of marriage is not that adults produce children but that children produce adults.

Peter De Vries, *The Tunnel of Love*

One thing certain about parenthood is that the way you treat your children will turn out five years from now to have been completely wrong.

Bill Vaughan, as quoted in *Reader's Digest*, June 1961

Life was so much simpler a few months ago when all we had to worry about was whether Johnny could read, not whether he understood nuclear physics.

Bill Vaughan, as quoted in *Reader's Digest*, March 1958

Any couple with five or six kids is happier than a couple with five or six million dollars. They don't keep straining for more.

Oren Arnold, as quoted in *Reader's Digest*, May 1955

Nothing is so soothing to our self-esteem as to find our bad traits in our forbears. It seems to absolve us.

Van Wyck Brooks, *From a Writer's Notebook*

A lot of parents pack up their troubles and send them off to a summer camp.

Raymond Duncan, as quoted in *Reader's Digest*,
July 1954

Things are pretty well evened up in this world. Other people's troubles are not so bad as yours, but their children are a lot worse.

Claude Callan, as quoted in *Reader's Digest*, May 1949

Yerou don't raise heroes, you raise sons. And if you treat them like sons, they'll turn out to be heroes, even if it's just in your own eyes.

Walter Schirra, Sr., father of the six-orbit astronaut, as quoted in *This Week*, February 3, 1963

If you can give your son only one gift, let it be enthusiasm.

Bruce Barton, as quoted in *Reader's Digest*, December 1934

Heredity is an omnibus in which all our ancestors ride, and every now and then one of them puts his head out and embarrasses us.

Oliver Wendell Holmes, as quoted in *Reader's Digest*, July 1935

God knows that a mother needs fortitude and courage and tolerance and flexibility and patience and firmness and nearly every other brave aspect of the human soul. But because I happen to be a parent of almost fiercely maternal nature, I praise *casualness*. It seems to me the rarest of virtues. It is useful enough when children are small. It is important to the point of necessity when they are adolescents.

Phyllis McGinley, as quoted in *McCall's*, May 1959

When I was a boy of 14, my father was so ignorant I could hardly stand to have the old man around. But when I got to be 21, I was astonished at how much the old man had learned in seven years.

Mark Twain, as quoted in *Reader's Digest*, September 1937

It must come as a shock to most mothers when, after struggling years to civilize a son, a little five-foot girl with a sweet face tames him in a week.

Marcelene Cox, as quoted in *Reader's Digest*, April 1952

Why do so many young couples have children before their love is mature? In part because they want children, but in larger part because they want to play the role of parents. Relatives, neighbors and friends all exert subtle pressure to "join the club," to accept adult responsibilities and settle down like everyone else. In trying to win approval and acceptance, many husbands and wives become parents before they are emotionally ready.

Morton M. Hunt, as quoted in *Redbook*, October 1968

A mother spends the first 15 years teaching her son to be a man; the son spends the next 15 years teaching his mother that he is.

Fred Steiger, as quoted in *Reader's Digest*, April 1952

There are only two lasting bequests we can hope to give our children. One of these is roots; the other, wings.

Hodding Carter, as quoted in *Reader's Digest*, May 1953

There is little use to talk about your child to anyone; other people either have one or haven't.

Don Herold, *There Ought to Be a Law*

Before I got married I had six theories about bringing up children. Now I have six children—and no theories.

Lord Rochester, as quoted in *Reader's Digest*, June 1947

I love the two of them so much because they are the we of me.

Carson McCullers, *The Member of the Wedding*

If a woman talks and acts as if her husband were just the provider for little Cindy, he can be forgiven for behaving as if she were just little Cindy's mother.

Joyce Brothers, as quoted in *Reader's Digest*,
October 1972

Modern parents divide their time between worrying over how their children will turn out and when they will turn in.

Hawley R. Everhart, as quoted in *Reader's Digest*, June
1947

The thing that impresses me most about America is the way parents obey their children.

Edward, Duke of Windsor, as quoted in *Look*, March 5,
1957

Mother Nature is providential. She gives us 12 years to develop a love for our children before turning them into teen-agers.

William A. Galvin, as quoted in *Reader's Digest*, February
1960

The best time for parents to put the children to bed is while they still have the strength.

Homer Phillips, as quoted in *Reader's Digest*, February 1958

Who, I ask you, can take, dare take, on himself the rights, the duties, the responsibilities of another human soul?

Elizabeth Cady Stanton, as quoted in *Growing Up Female in America*

Oh, what a tangled web do parents weave
When they think that their children are naïve.

Ogden Nash, as quoted in *Reader's Digest*, March 1974

The best way to raise one child is to have two.

Marcelene Cox, as quoted in *Reader's Digest*, February 1954

Every parent is at some time the father of the unreturned prodigal, with nothing to do but keep his house open to hope.

John Ciardi, as quoted in *Saturday Review*, January 23, 1957

By the time parents are ready to enjoy the comforts of life, their children are using them.

Bob Brown, as quoted in *Reader's Digest*, April 1968

In no arena, perhaps, can recognition be more valuable—or less likely to be bestowed—than in the bosom of the family. In the unremitting dailiness of family life, insight can be blunted, virtues taken for granted and minor irritations magnified into frustrations so that people forget to give honor where it is due. Yet children may need recognition more than they need criticism, and their parents cannot fail to profit from making mutual positive assessments.

Margaret Cousins, as quoted in *Reader's Digest*, April 1972

That we are what we are is due to these two factors, mothers and fathers.

Charlotte Perkins Gilman, *The Home*

I believe that a baby or small child should be cared for *mainly* by one or two people, even though others may help out at times. In my opinion, the close emotional ties of an all-round good family provide the strongest stimulus to mental development.

Dr. Benjamin Spock, as quoted in *Reader's Digest*, May 1973

Most parents don't worry about a daughter until she fails to show up for breakfast. Then it is too late.

Kin Hubbard, as quoted in *Reader's Digest*, August 1962

I have found the best way to give advice to your children is to find out what they want and then advise them to do it.

Harry S. Truman, in an interview on CBS-TV, May 27, 1955

Although the hippie communards profess to be building a new society, it would be hard to find one—modern or primitive—that cares less for its children. Rebelling against parents is an old and honorable custom. But rebelling against one's children is suicide for any society.

Lester Velie, as quoted in *Reader's Digest*, March 1973

Youth and Changing Generations

The present-day adolescent, in addition to all the usual problems, is experiencing the effects of adult hopelessness. If parents believe that the world is going to hell, or feel defeated and trapped in a job, why

113

should their adolescent feel that learning self-discipline is worth the struggle?

> Dr. Martin Symonds, as quoted in *Reader's Digest*, March
> 1973

Young men have a passion for regarding their elders as senile.

> Henry Adams, *The Education of Henry Adams*

I don't go along with all this talk of a generation gap. We're all contemporaries. There's only a difference in memories, that's all.

> W. H. Auden, as quoted in *Reader's Digest*, August 1973

Possibly the factor that makes the adult-youth controversy more difficult than ever is that for the first time parents are outnumbered. Worse yet, they can't blame it on the children.

> Troy Gordon, as quoted in *Reader's Digest*, February 1968

A boy becomes an adult three years before his parents think he does, and about two years after he thinks he does.

> General Lewis B. Hershey, address, December 31, 1951

All that I know I learned after I was 30.

> Georges Clemenceau, as quoted in *Reader's Digest*,
> February 1947

All any grownup expects of an adolescent is that he act like an adult and be satisfied to be treated like a child.

> John Gran, as quoted in *Reader's Digest*, January 1957

Each youth is like a child born in the night who sees the sun rise and thinks that yesterday never existed.

> W. Somerset Maugham, *A Writer's Notebook*

The joy of the young is to disobey—but the trouble is, there are no longer any orders.

Jean Cocteau, as quoted in *Reader's Digest*, August 1960

Most teen-agers are keenly aware of the value of the dollar. It buys about three gallons of gasoline.

Pep Mealiffe, as quoted in *Reader's Digest*, October 1960

The young do not know enough to be prudent, and therefore they attempt the impossible—and achieve it, generation after generation.

Pearl S. Buck, *The Goddess Abides*

It's hard to know exactly when one generation ends and the next one begins. But it's somewhere around nine o'clock at night.

Charles Ruffing, as quoted in *Reader's Digest*, December 1960

In America, the young are always ready to give those who are older than themselves the full benefit of their inexperience.

Oscar Wilde, as quoted in *Reader's Digest*, October 1952

Each new generation must improve upon its parents; else the world stands still or retrogrades.

Charlotte Perkins Gilman, *The Woman's Movement*

It is a strange but mathematical fact that when a 17-year-old boy borrows the family car, he can in one night subtract five years from the life of the car and add them to the age of his father.

Bett Anderson, as quoted in *Reader's Digest*, August 1962

Puberty is when you and the guys light up during recess and you're the one that gets strangled. Puberty is when the boy you're crazy about calls and your mom gets to the phone first and starts asking questions. Puberty is when you write love letters to the girl you're crazy about and she starts passing it around. Puberty is when all the other girls in class have bras whether they need them or not, but *your* mom says you're going to wait until you have a reason. Puberty is when you kiss a girl for the first time and neither one of you makes the smacking noise. Puberty is when you're fixing to kiss a girl for the first time and don't know who's supposed to make the smacking noise. Puberty is when you first start thinking about the good old days. Puberty is when you have to laugh at dirty jokes you don't understand.

William Allen, as quoted in *Reader's Digest*, January 1968

Of all curable illnesses that afflict mankind, the hardest to cure, and the one most likely to leave its victim a chronic invalid, is adolescence.

Bonaro W. Overstreet, *Understanding Fear*

Father to teen-ager: "What kind of *in* crowd do you travel with—in doubt, in debt or in trouble?"

Mike Glynn, as quoted in *Reader's Digest*, January 1967

Oh, to be only half as wonderful as my child thought I was when he was small, and only half as stupid as my teen-ager now thinks I am.

Rebecca Richards, as quoted in *Reader's Digest*, November 1970

Every generation revolts against its fathers and makes friends with its grandfathers.

Lewis Mumford, *The Brown Decades*

At 20 I wanted to save the world. Now I'd be satisfied just to save part of my salary.

H. G. Hutcheson, as quoted in *Reader's Digest*, September 1955

Boys nowadays take advice and then do as they please.

John D. Rockefeller, as quoted in *Reader's Digest*, February 1922

It is the malady of our age that the young are so busy teaching us that they have no time left to learn.

Eric Hoffer, as quoted in *Reader's Digest*, August 1973

Young people everywhere share a kind of experience that none of the elders ever have had or will have. Conversely, the older generation will never see repeated in the lives of young people their own unprecedented experience of sequentially emerging change. This break between generations is wholly new; it is planetary and universal.

Margaret Mead as quoted in *The New York Times Magazine*, April 26, 1970

We spared the rod and wound up with the beat generation.

L. J. Wolf, as quoted in *Reader's Digest*, April 1961

It's hard for the modern generation to understand Thoreau, who lived beside a pond but didn't own water skis or a snorkel.

Bill Vaughan, as quoted in *Reader's Digest*, September 1962   117

Youth, as distinguished from childhood or middle age, is that brief period when the sexes talk to each other at a party.

Bill Vaughan, as quoted in Reader's Digest, June 1956

One of my aunts feels apologetic every time she reads about how unhappy young people are. She thought she enjoyed being young but realizes now it must have been because she wasn't paying attention.

Bill Vaughan, as quoted in Reader's Digest, March 1965

The universe is not altogether as God meant it to be. We are here partly to change it. One of his mercies is that as men grow older and used to things, he takes them away and puts the universe in the hands of young, fresh men.

Cleland B. McAfee, Near to the Heart of God

It is said that hope goes with youth; but I fancy that hope is the last gift given to man, and the only gift not given to youth. For youth the end of every episode is the end of the world. But the power of hoping through everything, the knowledge that the soul survives its adventures—that great inspiration comes to the middle-aged.

G. K. Chesterton, as quoted in Reader's Digest, August 1951

Everyone likes to think that he has done reasonably well in life, so that it comes as a shock to find our children believing differently. The temptation is to tune them out; it takes much more courage to listen.

John D. Rockefeller III, speech at Family of Man awards dinner, October 1968

When I was very young I was disgracefully intolerant, but when I passed the thirty mark I prided myself on having learned the beautiful lesson that all things were good, and equally good. That, however, was really laziness.

Now, thank goodness, I've sorted out what matters and what doesn't. And I'm beginning to be intolerant again.

118   G. B. Stern, as quoted in Reader's Digest, February 1940

Snow and adolescence are the only problems that disappear if you ignore them long enough.

Earl Wilson, as quoted in *Reader's Digest*, January 1963

You can say this for these ready-mixes—the next generation isn't going to have any trouble making pies exactly like mother used to make.

Earl Wilson, as quoted in *Reader's Digest*, November 1972

A fellow has come up with a sure money-maker to reach the teen-age market—he wants to put jukeboxes in phone booths.

Earl Wilson, as quoted in *Reader's Digest*, April 1965

Never grow a wishbone, daughter, where your backbone ought to be.

Clementine Paddleford, as quoted in *This Week*, May 11, 1958

My interest in young people is in rumpling their brains as you might rumple a good head of hair.

Robert Frost, as quoted in *Reader's Digest*, December 1962

Why can't life's problems hit us when we're 17 and know everything?

A. C. Jolly, as quoted in *Reader's Digest*, December 1956

The young don't know what age is, and the old forget what youth was.

Leumas MacManus, *Heavy Hangs the Golden Grain*

Adolescence isn't a period; it's a coma.

Richard Armour, as quoted in *Reader's Digest*, August 1956

The best substitute for experience is being 16.

Raymond Duncan, as quoted in *Reader's Digest*, July 1954   119

Youth is very mixed up—so what else is new? Adults are very mixed up too, which is one of the reasons the youth are as they are. Let them be. But the responsibility of the adult world is to hang on to one's sanity.

William F. Buckley, Jr., *Quotations from Chairman Bill*

An older man befurring his face is betraying his anxieties. He wants too much to be "with it," to swing, however stiff in the knees, with the Now Generation. As McLuhan would say, it's the surrender of the individual to the tribal soul.

Harriet Van Horne, as quoted in *Reader's Digest*, March 1973

Hippies are lost sheep masquerading as shepherds.

Sam Levenson, as quoted in *Reader's Digest*, July 1968

The deepest definition of youth is life as yet untouched by tragedy.

Alfred North Whitehead, *Adventures of Ideas*

The extremely important years after childhood and before adulthood are a period to which we, as a society, do not assign a clearly defined cultural role. It is time for us to evolve a national philosophy regarding this important stage of life.

S. I. Hayakawa, as quoted in *Reader's Digest*, November 1970

Don't laugh at youth for his affectations: he's only trying on one face after another till he finds his own.

Logan Pearsall Smith, *All Trivia*

What is more enchanting than the voices of young people—when you can't hear what they say.

Logan Pearsall Smith, as quoted in *Reader's Digest*, May 1942

Denunciation of the young is a necessary part of the hygiene of older people, and greatly assists the circulation of their blood.

Logan Pearsall Smith, as quoted in *Reader's Digest*, July 1935

During the Beatles' TV dress rehearsal, Ed Sullivan silenced his screaming teen-age studio audience by yelling, "Quiet—or I'll call a barber!"

Frank Judge, as quoted in *Reader's Digest*, May 1964

Trouble is, kids feel they have to shock their elders, and each generation grows up into something harder to shock.

Cal Craig, as quoted in *Reader's Digest*, December 1968

We owe the "younger generation" what all "older generations" have owed younger generations—love, protection to a point, and respect when they deserve it. We do not owe them our souls, our privacy, our whole lives—and, above all, we do not owe them immunity from our mistakes, or their own.

K. Ross Toole, as quoted in *Reader's Digest*, June 1970   **121**

My generation was lost and beat, as a matter of course; the difference was, we forgot to mention it.

R. L. Duffus, *The Waterbury Record*

We have not passed that subtle line between childhood and adulthood until we move from the passive voice to the active voice—that is, until we have stopped saying, "It got lost," and say, "I lost it."

Sydney J. Harris, as quoted in *Reader's Digest*, November 1962

It is inherently difficult for all modern youth to find tasks and causes worthy of their enthusiasm—tasks that can satisfy high standards of craftsmanship and causes which satisfy the need for an ideal.

Edna G. Rostow, as quoted in *The Woman in America*

Early youth is a baffling time. The present moment is nice but it does not last. Living in it is like waiting in a junction town for the morning limited. The junction may be interesting, but someday you will have to leave it and you do not know where the limited will take you. Sooner or later you must move down a mysterious road that leads to something beyond the range of the imagination, and the only certainty is that the trip has to be made. In this respect early youth is like old age; it is a time of waiting before a big trip to an unknown destination. The chief difference is that youth waits for the morning limited and age waits for the night train.

Bruce Catton, as quoted in *Reader's Digest*, October 1972

Ours seems to be the only nation on earth that asks its teenagers what to do about world affairs, and tells its golden-agers to go out and play.

Julian F. Grow, as quoted in *Reader's Digest*, February 1967

A few years ago, adolescence was a phase; then it became a profession; now it is a new nationality.

Donald Barr, as quoted in *Reader's Digest*, April 1972

What makes the youthful disaffiliation of our time a cultural phenomenon, rather than merely a political movement, is the fact that it strikes beyond ideology to the level of consciousness, seeking to transform our deepest sense of the self, the other, the environment.

Theodore Roszak, *The Making of a Counter Culture*

It's fashionable nowadays to blame permissiveness for everything that seems wrong with the younger generation. This is a dangerous over-simplification because it implies that the remedy is the reverse: authoritarianism, repression, law-and-order. There has to be limit-setting, to be sure. But one extreme is as bad as the other. Harshness just makes adolescents fight harder.

Dr. Roy W. Menninger, as quoted in *Reader's Digest*, March 1972

I do beseech you to direct your efforts more to preparing youth for the path and less to preparing the path for the youth.

Judge Ben Lindsey, as quoted in *Reader's Digest*, January 1968

Teenagers haven't changed much. They still grow up, leave home and get married. The big difference is that today they don't always do it in that order.

Herbert Miller, as quoted in *Reader's Digest*, December 1968

To be left alone on the tightrope of youthful unknowing is to experience full freedom and the threat of eternal indecision. Few, if any, survive their teens. Most surrender to the vague but murderous

123

pressure of adult conformity. It becomes easier to die and avoid conflicts than to maintain a constant battle with the superior forces of maturity.

Maya Angelou, I Know Why the Caged Bird Sings

Aging

At the same time doctors are extending our lives, we are seemingly intent on cutting out some of the opportunities for spending those added years. Until we come up with a better theory of what people are supposed to do when they get old, I am not prepared to encourage retirement at all.

W. Willard Wirtz, as quoted in Reader's Digest, August
1972

Middle age is when you don't have to have fun to enjoy yourself.

Franklin P. Jones, as quoted in Reader's Digest, May 1972

You've reached middle age when you know how to take care of yourself—and intend to, one of these days.

Franklin P. Jones, as quoted in Reader's Digest, August
1954

A man has reached middle age when the girl he winks at thinks he has something in his eye.

Franklin P. Jones, as quoted in Reader's Digest, October
1951

You've reached middle age when all you exercise is caution.

Franklin P. Jones, as quoted in Reader's Digest, September
1955

You've reached middle age when your wife tells you to pull in your stomach—and you already have.

Franklin P. Jones, as quoted in Reader's Digest, April 1951

Nothing is so terrible as a man who gets old and tries to tell everybody what to do.

Bernard M. Baruch, as quoted in U. S. News & World Report, August 31, 1959

To me, old age is always fifteen years older than I am.

Bernard Baruch, on his eighty-fifth birthday, as quoted in news summaries of August 20, 1955

Age is only a number, a cipher for the records. A man can't retire his experience. He must use it. Experience achieves more with less energy and time.

Bernard M. Baruch, in a speech to senior citizens in New York City, August 20, 1955

Crossing the Border
Senescence begins
And middle age ends
The day your descendants
Outnumber your friends.

Ogden Nash, as quoted in Reader's Digest, September 1971

As soon as you feel too old to do a thing, do it.

Margaret Deland, as quoted in Reader's Digest, February 1946

I am an old man and have known a great many troubles, but most of them never happened.

Mark Twain, as quoted in Reader's Digest, April 1934   125

Lyndon, I want to go home to the hill country. That's part of the world where people know when you're sick, miss you when you die, and love you while you live.

Samuel Ealy Johnson, to his son Lyndon, 1937, as quoted in *The New York Times*, April 20, 1964

Old people don't get tired—it's only the young who tire. Confusion exhausts them. I've got more energy now than when I was younger because I know exactly what I want to do.

George Balanchine, as quoted in *Reader's Digest*, December 1971

It's not how old you are but how you are old.

Marie Dressler, as quoted in *Reader's Digest*, March 1934

Some men mellow with age, like wine; but others get still more stringent, like vinegar.

Henry C. Rowland, as quoted in *Reader's Digest*, March 1936

Most people say that as you get old, you have to give up things. I think you get old because you give up things.

Senator Theodore Francis Green at age 87, as quoted in the Washington *Post*, June 28, 1954

When I die my epitaph, or whatever you call the signs on gravestones, is going to read: "I joke about every prominent man of my time, but I never met a man I didn't like." I am proud of that. I can hardly wait to die so it can be carved, and when you come around to my grave you'll probably find me sitting there proudly reading it.

Will Rogers, as quoted in *Reader's Digest*, October 1935

I hate funerals, and would not attend my own if it could be avoided, but it is well for every man to stop once in a while to think of what sort of a collection of mourners he is training for his final event.

Robert T. Morris, as quoted in Reader's Digest, October
1936

Growing old is no more than a bad habit which a busy man has no time to form.

André Maurois, as quoted in Reader's Digest, October 1946

Old age may be a distinction, but in itself it is not an honor.

Israel T. Deyo, as quoted in New York State Bar
Association Bulletin, December 1947

I wish that on some long-ago, high-summer day, a day that was hot and smothery-damp, smelling of cut grass and sun-warm hollyhocks, I had scooped at least a pint of air into a mason jar. Then I could open that jar today and inhale deeply the scent of summer past.

Oh, surely then I'd feel like a kid again. Surely then my heart would once more give a thump of innocent delight, and I could toss away my most confining middle-aged proprieties, and seize upon a zillion breezy notions. Surely then I'd have the wisdom to be cool.

Joan Mills, as quoted in Reader's Digest, July 1972

I begin to realize that I am growing old: the taxi driver calls me "Pop" instead of "Buddy."

Alexander Woollcott, as quoted in Reader's Digest, April
1934

Let me give a word of advice to you young fellows who have been looking forward to retirement: Have nothing to do with it.

Listen: it's like this. Have you ever been out for a late autumn walk in the closing part of the afternoon, and suddenly looked up to realize that the leaves have practically all gone? And the sun has set   127 and the day gone before you knew it—and with that a cold wind blows across the landscape? That's retirement.

Stephen Leacock, as quoted in *Reader's Digest*, February 1941

The golden age only comes to men when they have, if only for a moment, forgotten gold.

G. K. Chesterton, as quoted in *The New York Times*, May 3, 1931

A man is not old until regrets take the place of dreams.

John Barrymore, as quoted in *Reader's Digest*, October 1941

Eat half as much, sleep twice as much, drink three times as much, laugh four times as much, and you will live to a ripe old age.

John Harvey Kellogg, as quoted in *Reader's Digest*, November 1944

The idea that society can provide only a limited number of jobs, and that the elderly are the logical ones to be left out, is no longer tenable. There are unlimited goods and services needed and desired in American society. Among the greatest resources that could be channeled toward these ends are the experience, skill and devotion of America's elderly millions.

Mae Rudolph, as quoted in *Family Health*, March 1970

No man is really old until his mother stops worrying about him.

William Ryan, as quoted in *The Treasury for Special Days and Occasions*

We grow neither better nor worse as we get old, but more like ourselves.

May Lamberton Becker, as quoted in *Reader's Digest*, September 1945

One of the many things nobody ever tells you about middle age is that it's such a nice change from being young.

> Dorothy Canfield Fisher, as quoted in *Reader's Digest*,
> September 1940

That the end of life should be death may sound sad; yet what other end can anything have?

> George Santayana, *Some Turns of Thought in Modern*
> *Philosophy*

Beautiful young people are accidents of nature. But beautiful old people are works of art.

> Marjorie Barstow Greenbie, as quoted in *Reader's Digest*,
> November 1938

Being 70 is not a sin. It's not a joy, either.

> Golda Meir, as quoted in *Reader's Digest*, July 1971

Middle age is the time when a man is always thinking that in a week or two he will feel as good as ever.

> Don Marquis, as quoted in *Reader's Digest*, February 1955

My memory is very good: I can make the same mistakes today that I made 50 years ago.

> Simon Rothschild, as quoted in *Reader's Digest*, January
> 1928

129

Middle age: When you're grounded for several days after flying high for one night.

Marjorie Johnson, as quoted in *Reader's Digest*, June 1955

The best thing about getting old is that all those things you couldn't have when you were young you no longer want.

L. S. McCandless, as quoted in *Reader's Digest*, May 1954

Age is bothersome only when you stop to coddle it.

Maurice Chevalier, as quoted in *Reader's Digest*,
April 1957

A great thing about Middle Age is that one is usually in charge of one's own life more completely than ever before. For the first time you're neither Acting Parent nor Acted-Upon Child. . . .

It is invigorating to be simply an autonomous, free person, setting your own alarm clock, table, goals, standards, patterns.

Peg Bracken, *I Didn't Come Here to Argue*

The older I get, the less I pine for
Things that I have to stand in line for.

Richard Armour, as quoted in *Reader's Digest*,
March 1953

We are happier in many ways when we are old than when we were young. The young sow wild oats. The old grow sage.

Sir Winston Churchill, as quoted in *Reader's Digest*,
December 1961

It is well known that the older a man grows, the faster he could run as a boy.

Red Smith, as quoted in *Reader's Digest*, August 1954

Middle age had been said to be the time of a man's life when, if he has two choices for an evening, he takes the one that gets him home earlier.

Alvan L. Barach, as quoted in the *Journal of the American Medical Association*, August 4, 1962

Middle age is that period in a man's life when he'd rather not have a good time than have to get over it.

Don McNeil, as quoted in *Reader's Digest*, March 1938

When a man is pushing 60, that's exercise enough.

Shannon Fife, as quoted in *Reader's Digest*, March 1955

Those who love deeply never grow old; they may die of old age, but they die young.

Arthur Wing Pinero, as quoted in *Reader's Digest*, August 1942

Old age is like everything else. To make a success of it you've got to start young.

Felix Marten, as quoted in *Reader's Digest*, November 1961

The only way any woman may remain forever young is to grow old gracefully.

W. Béran Wolfe, as quoted in *Reader's Digest*, September 1942

About the time we get old enough to be brave enough to be as wicked as we want to be, we don't want to be so very wicked after all.

Don Herold, *There Ought to Be a Law*

Middle age is when a person starts thinking about resigning from the Jet Set and joining the Set Set.

Dan Bennett, as quoted in *Reader's Digest*, July 1968

The big shock in becoming middle-aged is that you discover you keep on growing older, even after you are old enough.

Don P. Radde, as quoted in Reader's Digest, October 1964

Middle age is when your narrow waist and broad mind begin to change places.

Ben Klitzner, as quoted in Reader's Digest, July 1960

The years between fifty and seventy are the hardest. You are always being asked to do things, and yet you are not decrepit enough to turn them down.

T. S. Eliot, as quoted in Time, October 23, 1950

Nothing ages you and tires you as much as inactivity, and the avoidance of rest is one of the things that enables you to go on in old age.

Dr. Percy Fridenberg, as quoted in Reader's Digest,
September 1960

It feels good to reach 94, except for seeing your children become depressingly middle-aged.

Mrs. Rosina Sherwood, mother of playwright Robert E.
Sherwood, as quoted in Reader's Digest, September 1949

Death is a very dull, dreary affair, and my advice to you is to have nothing whatever to do with it.

W. Somerset Maugham, A Writer's Notebook

The compensation of growing old was simply this: that the passions remain as strong as ever, but one has gained—at last!—the power which adds the supreme flavor to existence, the power of taking hold of experience, of turning it round, slowly, in the light.

Virginia Woolf, as quoted in Reader's Digest, May 1960

We've put more effort into helping folks reach old age than into helping them enjoy it.

Frank A. Clark, as quoted in Reader's Digest, September
1973

At my age . . . you are either well or dead.

George Bernard Shaw, after the writer turned ninety.

Pressure on the American male begins in boyhood, when more is expected of him than of his sister, continues throughout college and graduate school, and reaches a killing pace in early manhood and middle age. At the turn of the century, the average man died two years and ten months earlier than the average woman. Today's average male dies six years earlier than the female.

Lester Velie, as quoted in Reader's Digest, April 1973

Ironically, the middle-age blues and adolescence are remarkably similar: both are natural developmental crises, times of change and stress related to the need to make an adjustment to a new phase of life. The middle-age crisis is adolescence renewed and reviewed. Again you are asking yourself: Who am I? Where am I going? What does it all mean? The answers don't come much more easily than when you were 15, and the situation is compounded by a sense of urgency, a knowledge that you haven't got all the time in the world.

Dr. Martin Symonds, with Joan Rattner Heilman, as quoted
in Reader's Digest, November 1971

The Home and the Family

Home is a destination—the ultimate destination. "Going home" has a meaning more poignant than perhaps any other phrase in our language.

It is first spoken with true feeling by the child just turned loose from his playpen to explore the wide world of the next-door yards. His   133 first crushing experience with disappointment, or anger, or physical hurt brings a rushing torrent of emotion that ends with a tiny voice piping: "I'm going home."

Home is the sanctuary where the healing is. . . . Nothing brings as quickly to mind the horror of natural upheaval, civil strife or war as the picture of the "homeless." The deprivation of the security of home is the worst of the mass tragedies.

Walter Cronkite, as quoted in *Reader's Digest*, August 1970

Justice was born outside the home and a long way from it; and it has never been adopted there.

Charlotte Perkins Gilman, *The Home*

No remark today could sound more ludicrously quaint than "Children should be seen and not heard." Increasingly, children are permitted and encouraged to speak their minds, to ask for what they want, and to decide what they like.

This trend has not made for serene and tranquil homes—nor for notably happy children. Yet even those who most deplore the trend know in their hearts that the family will not turn back toward the old authoritarian model. Understandably parents do not want to rear submissive children who will join the dwindling ranks of the order-takers.

Max Ways, as quoted in *Reader's Digest*, June 1971

The external characteristics of home are not the same for each of us. On the coast of Maine, families labor to bring in their livelihood from the gray seas. In the vast reaches of the West many families live isolated from their neighbors. For each American, the meaning of home is unique and personal.

Dwight D. Eisenhower, address to the National Council of Catholic Women, November 9, 1954

Home is where you hang your head.

Groucho Marx, as quoted in *Reader's Digest*, February 1973

When a household is running like clockwork, you find yourself waiting for an alarm to ring.

Lane Clinghouse, as quoted in Reader's Digest, September 1967

Home is the place where, when you have to go there,
they have to take you in.

Robert Frost, "The Death of the Hired Man"

The greatest thing in family life is to take a hint when a hint is intended—and not to take a hint when a hint isn't intended.

Robert Frost, as quoted in Vogue, March 15, 1963

Domestic strife is nothing new. As Sir Edward Coke said four centuries ago, "A man's house is his hassle."

Fletcher Knebel, as quoted in Reader's Digest, January 1961

[The Family:] The only preserving and healing power counteracting any historical, intellectual or spiritual crisis no matter of what depth.

Ruth Nanda Anshen, The Family: Its Function

I realize that the subject of abortion is deeply divisive, with reaction felt more in the emotions than in the mind. For this reason, dispassionate factual discussions are more beneficial than the tossing about of violent slogans. I also realize that legalized abortion is far from the ideal solution to unwanted conception. Yet a lifetime of work in the field has convinced me that liberalized abortion is an absolutely essential tool to ease the lot of many women and families in a tough, tough world.

Dr. Alan F. Guttmacher, as quoted in Reader's Digest, November 1973

135

The men and women who, for good reasons and bad, revolt against the family are, for good reasons and bad, simply revolting against mankind.

G. K. Chesterton, *Heretics*

Of all modern notions, the worst is this: that domesticity is dull. Inside the home, they say, is dead decorum and routine; outside is adventure and variety. But the truth is that the home is the only place of liberty, the only spot on earth where a man can alter arrangements suddenly, make an experiment or indulge in a whim. The home is not the one tame place in a world of adventure; it is the one wild place in a world of rules and set tasks.

G. K. Chesterton, as quoted in *Reader's Digest*, June 1938

The professional and technical populations are among the most mobile of all Americans. (It is a house joke among executives of the International Business Machines Corp. that IBM stands for "I've Been Moved.") This moving of executives from house to house as if they were life-size chessmen on a global board has led one psychologist to propose facetiously a money-saving scheme called "The Modular Family." Under this system the executive could leave not only his house behind, but his family as well. The company would then find him a matching wife and children at the new site.

Alvin Toffler, as quoted in *Reader's Digest*, August 1971

No matter how many communes anybody invents, the family always creeps back.

Margaret Mead, as quoted in Reader's Digest, June 1972

Absence is one of the most useful ingredients of family life, and to dose it rightly is an art like any other.

Freya Stark, The Journey's Echo

The fellow who owns his own home is always just coming out of a hardware store.

Frank McKinney Hubbard, as quoted in Reader's Digest,
February 1956

For individuals the breakdown of the family means the gloomy despair of a life without happiness, of a life which not even pleasure can light up. For nations it means slow death through sterility, and it can even mean this for the human race.

Jacques Leclercq, Marriage and the Family

Science is immeasurably ahead of nature. For example, in the modern household the children are about the only things left that still have to be washed by hand.

Bill Vaughan, as quoted in Reader's Digest, September 1958

Home is not a way station: it is a profession of faith in life.

Sol Chaneles, The New Civility

The man who boasts only of his ancestors confesses that he belongs to 'a family that is better dead than alive.

J. Gilchrist Lawson, as quoted in Reader's Digest. January
1949

If the right of privacy means anything, it is the right of the individual, married or single, to be free from unwarranted governmental intrusion into matters so fundamentally affecting a person as the decision whether to bear or beget a child.

Judge Jon O. Newman, as quoted in *Reader's Digest*,
March 1973

Distrust all mothers-in-law. They are completely unscrupulous in what they say in court. The wife's mother is always more prejudiced against her husband than even the most ill-tempered wife. If I had my way, I am afraid I would abolish mothers-in-law entirely.

Sir Geoffrey Wrangham, British High Court justice, in a
court opinion, October 10, 1960

It's when you're safe at home that you wish you were having an adventure. When you're having an adventure you wish you were safe at home.

Thornton Wilder, as quoted in *Reader's Digest*, February
1959

A "good" family, it seems, is one that used to be better.

Cleveland Amory, *Who Killed Society?*

The average American home is no longer a harbor and a haven, but rather a mere place of debarkation.

George Jean Nathan, as quoted in *Reader's Digest*, October
1927

COMMUNICATIONS

The Art of Conversation

Think twice before you speak—and you'll find everyone talking about something else.

Frances Rodman, as quoted in *Reader's Digest*, January 1957

An orator is a man who says what he thinks and feels what he says.

William Jennings Bryan, as quoted in *The Peerless Leader*

We tolerate differences of opinion in people who are familiar to us. But differences of opinion in people we do not know sound like heresy or plots.

Brooks Atkinson, as quoted in *Reader's Digest*, October 1972

I never resort to a prepared script—anyone who does not have it in his head to do 30 minutes' extemporaneous talking is not entitled to be heard.

Bishop Sheen, as quoted in *Reader's Digest*, December 1954

Rumor: the news service of the weak.

C. W. Ceram, *Gods, Graves and Scholars*

Repartee: What a person thinks of after he becomes a departee.

Dan Bennett, as quoted in *Reader's Digest*, January 1957

A gossip is one who talks to you about others; a bore is one who talks to you about himself; a brilliant conversationalist is one who talks to you about yourself.

Lisa Kirk, as quoted in the New York *Journal-American*, March 9, 1954

What the world needs is a good loudspeaker for the still, small voice.

Herbert V. Prochnow, as quoted in *Reader's Digest*, August 1954

Conversation in this country has fallen upon evil days. It is drowned out in singing commercials. It is hushed and shushed in dimly lighted parlors by television audiences who used to read, argue and even play bridge, an old-fashioned card game requiring speech.

Conversation laid the foundation of the civilization we are dedicated to defend. . . . Great books, scientific discoveries, works of art, great perceptions of truth and beauty in any form, all require great conversation to complete their meaning; without it they are abracadabra—color to the blind or music to the deaf. Conversation is the handmaid of learning, true religion and free government. If Thomas Carlyle could define a university as a collection of books, Socrates might well have defined it as a conversation about wisdom.

A. Whitney Griswold, as quoted in *Reader's Digest*, June 1956

To say the right thing at the right time, keep still most of the time.

John W. Raper, as quoted in *Reader's Digest*, March 1952

The best time for you to hold your tongue is the time you feel like you must say something or bust.

Josh Billings, as quoted in *Reader's Digest*, February 1952

Silence is one of the hardest arguments to refute.

 Josh Billings, as quoted in *Reader's Digest*, July 1952

The four-letter word for psychotherapy is Talk.

Eric Hodgins, *Episode*

When somebody says, "I hope you won't mind my telling you this," it's pretty certain that you will.

Sylvia Bremer, as quoted in *Reader's Digest*, November 1955

To make a speech immortal you don't have to make it everlasting.

Lord Leslie Hore-Belisha, as quoted in *Reader's Digest*, October 1955

Before a man speaks it is always safe to assume that he is a fool. After he speaks, it is seldom necessary to assume it.

H. L. Mencken, *A Mencken Chrestomathy*

What this country needs is more free speech worth listening to.

Hansell B. Duckett, as quoted in *Reader's Digest*, February 1947

Extremists think "communication" means agreeing with them.

Leo Rosten, *A Trumpet for Reason*

Discussion is an exchange of intelligence. Argument is an exchange of ignorance.

Bill Gold, as quoted in *Reader's Digest*, February 1958

When a fellow says, "Well, to make a long story short," it's too late.

Don Herold, as quoted in *Reader's Digest*, February 1958

If we discovered that we had only five minutes left to say all we wanted to say, every telephone booth would be occupied by people calling other people to stammer that they loved them.

Christopher Morley, as quoted in *Reader's Digest*, February 1960   **143**

The older I grow, the more I listen to people who don't talk much.

Germain G. Glidden, as quoted in *Reader's Digest*, May
1974

The voice of dissent must be heard.

Henry Ford, from his will, as quoted in the *Listener*, May 14,
1953

Conversation is the art of telling people a little less than they want to know.

Franklin P. Jones, as quoted in *Reader's Digest*, March
1970

For good or ill, your conversation is your advertisement. Every time you open your mouth you let men look into your mind.

Bruce Barton, as quoted in *Reader's Digest*, January 1974

There is too much speaking in the world, and almost all of it is too
long. The Lord's Prayer, the Twenty-third Psalm, Lincoln's Gettysburg

Address are three great literary treasures that will last forever; no one of them is as long as 300 words. With such striking illustrations of the power of brevity it is amazing that speakers never learn to be brief.

Bruce Barton, as quoted in *Reader's Digest*, February 1941

A new idea is delicate. It can be killed by a sneer or a yawn; it can be stabbed to death by a quip and worried to death by a frown on the nightman's brow.

Charles Brower, as quoted in *Advertising Age*, October 10. 1959

A lecture is an occasion when you numb one end to benefit the other.

John Gould, as quoted in *Reader's Digest*, January 1952

The greatest freedom of speech is the greatest safety, because if a man is a fool the best thing to do is to encourage him to advertise the fact by speaking.

Woodrow Wilson, as quoted in *Reader's Digest*, August 1954

Good communication is as stimulating as black coffee, and just as hard to sleep after.

Anne Morrow Lindbergh, as quoted in *Reader's Digest*, September 1971

The best argument is that which seems merely an explanation.

Dale Carnegie, as quoted in *Reader's Digest*, August 1958

What this country needs is less public speaking and more private thinking.

Roscoe Drummond, as quoted in *Reader's Digest*, June 1949

She had lost the art of conversation, but not, unfortunately, the power of speech.

> George Bernard Shaw, as quoted in *Reader's Digest*, June 1949

I often quote myself. It adds spice to my conversation.

> George Bernard Shaw, as quoted in *Reader's Digest*, June 1943

The American's conversation is much like his courtship. . . . He gives an inkling and watches for a reaction; if the weather looks fair, he inkles a little more. Wishing neither to intrude nor be intruded upon, he advances by stages of acceptance, by levels of agreement, by steps of concurrence.

> Donald Lloyd, as quoted in *Harper's*, September 1963

The most lucid and elegant manner of speaking is for naught when you have nothing to say.

> Sol Chaneles, *The New Civility*

The prime purpose of eloquence is to keep other people from speaking.

> Louis Verneuil, as quoted in *Reader's Digest*, January 1953

The art of conversation isn't lost—it's hidden behind the TV set.

> Sidney Brody, as quoted in *Reader's Digest*, July 1962

Listening is a magnetic and strange thing, a creative force. The friends who listen to us are the ones we move toward, and we want to sit in their radius. When we are listened to, it creates us, makes us unfold and expand.

> Dr. Karl Menninger, *Love Against Hate*

A speech is a solemn responsibility. The man who makes a bad 30-minute speech to 200 people wastes only a half hour of his own time. But he wastes 100 hours of the audience's time—more than four days—which should be a hanging offense.

Jenkin Lloyd Jones, as quoted in Reader's Digest, January
1972

The world of conversationalists, in my experience, is divided into two classes: Those who listen to what the other person has to say, and those who use the interval to plan their next remark.

Bruce Bliven, as quoted in Reader's Digest, July 1936

In general, American social life constitutes an evasion of talking to people. Most Americans don't, in any vital sense, get together; they only do things together.

Louis Kronenberger, Company Manners

We make conversation to get away from ourselves and the people we are talking to. Talk is a world in itself, and there we are perfectly safe even from the things we are talking about.

Edwin Mue, as quoted in Reader's Digest, February 1941

Oratory: the art of making deep noises from the chest sound like important messages from the brain.

H. I. Phillips, as quoted in Reader's Digest, January 1945

The big trouble with communication today is the short supply of those willing to be communicated with.

Don Fraser, as quoted in Reader's Digest, February 1971

The real art of conversation is not only to say the right thing in the right place but to leave unsaid the wrong thing at the tempting moment.

Dorothy Nevill, Under Five Reigns   147

The most eloquent lines are neither written nor spoken—they're worn.

Elinor Tempily, as quoted in *Reader's Digest*, May 1941

To say what you think will certainly damage you in society; but a free tongue is worth more than a thousand invitations.

Logan Pearsall Smith, *Afterthoughts*

Another good thing about gossip is that it is within
    everybody's reach
And it is much more interesting than any other
    form of speech.

Ogden Nash, *I'm a Stranger Here Myself*

There are two kinds of people who blow through life like a breeze
And one kind is gossipers, and the other kind is gossipees.

Ogden Nash, *I'm a Stranger Here Myself*

Good talk has always flourished in taverns, but it dies in the hotel de luxe. It springs up naturally around campfires. It results from conditions which strip off social veneer and bring people together on a plane of elementary humanity.

Marjorie Barstow Greenbie, as quoted in *Reader's Digest*,
June 1935

Speeches are like babies—easy to conceive, hard to deliver.

Pat O'Malley, as quoted in *Reader's Digest*, July 1937

Why did they not speak out? Because they dreaded (and could not bear) the disapproval of the people around them. . . . The same reason has restrained me.

Mark Twain, *What Is Man?*

Beware of the man who goes to cocktail parties not to drink but to listen.

Pierre Daninos, as quoted in Reader's Digest, March 1960

There aren't any embarrassing questions—just embarrassing answers.

Carl T. Rowan, as quoted in The New Yorker, December 7, 1963

People love to talk but hate to listen. Listening is not merely not talking, though even that is beyond most of our powers; it means taking a vigorous, human interest in what is being told us. You can listen like a blank wall or like a splendid auditorium where every sound comes back fuller and richer.

Alice Duer Miller, as quoted in Reader's Digest, July 1951

Speech may sometimes do harm; but so may silence, and a worse harm at that. No offered insult ever caused so deep a wound as a tenderness expected and withheld; and no spoken indiscretion was ever so bitterly regretted as the words that one did not speak.

Jan Struther, as quoted in Reader's Digest, May 1947

I am well aware that an after-dinner speech which is very short to him who makes it is often very long to those who have to listen to it.

Joseph H. Choate, as quoted in Joseph H. Choate

While the right to talk may be the beginning of freedom, the necessity of listening is what makes the right important.

Walter Lippmann, as quoted in Reader's Digest, June 1971

Whenever two people meet there are really six people present. There is each man as he sees himself, each man as the other person sees him, and each man as he really is.

William James, as quoted in Reader's Digest, October 1962　149

Do you know that conversation is one of the greatest pleasures in life? But it wants leisure.

W. Somerset Maugham, *The Trembling of a Leaf*

It's just as important to listen to someone with your eyes as it is with your ears.

Martin Buxbaum, as quoted in *Reader's Digest*, January 1967

The ancient sage who concocted the maxim, "Know Thyself" might have added, "Don't tell anyone."

H. F. Henrichs, as quoted in *Reader's Digest*, March 1965

If you keep your mind sufficiently open people will throw a lot of rubbish into it.

William A. Orton, *Everyman Amid the Stereotype*

It's all right to hold a conversation, but you should be part of it now and then.

Richard Armour, as quoted in *Reader's Digest*, March 1951

My father gave me these hints on speech-making: "Be sincere . . . be brief . . . be seated."

James Roosevelt, addressing a meeting in Hollywood, as quoted in *Reader's Digest*, June 1940

The right to be heard does not automatically include the right to be taken seriously. To be taken seriously depends entirely upon what is being said.

Hubert H. Humphrey, address at the University of Wisconsin, August 23, 1965

Amen! Wisconsin state representative Stanley York, who is a minister, gave an invocation in the state assembly: "O Lord, you have given us minds, you have given us mouths. Help us keep the two connected."

Eugene C. Harrington, as quoted in *Reader's Digest*, April 1972

The argument seemed sound enough, but when a theory collides with a fact, the result is a tragedy.

Louis Nizer, *My Life in Court*

Bores can be divided into two classes; those who have their own particular subject, and those who do not need a subject.

A. A. Milne, in *Best Detective Stories of the Year*, 1951

A speech is like a love affair. Any fool can start it, but to end it requires considerable skill.

Lord Mancroft, as quoted in *Reader's Digest*, February 1967

The cruelest lies are often told in silence.

Robert Louis Stevenson, as quoted in *Reader's Digest*, March 1933

Beware of the conversationalist who adds "in other words." He is merely starting afresh.

Robert Morley, as quoted in *Reader's Digest*, February 1968

No one means all he says, and yet very few say all they mean, for words are slippery and thought is viscous.

Henry Adams, *The Education of Henry Adams*　151

There is no inspiration in evil . . . no man ever made a great speech on a mean subject.

Eugene V. Debs, *Efficient Expression*

The best way to send an idea around the world is to wrap it in a man.

Sol Linowitz, as quoted in *Reader's Digest*, January 1969

It is impossible to defeat an ignorant man in argument.

William G. McAdoo, as quoted in *Reader's Digest*, April 1972

It's among the intelligentsia, and especially among those who like to play with thoughts and concepts without really taking part in the cultural endeavors of their epoch that we often find the glib compulsion to explain everything and to understand nothing.

Dr. Joost A. M. Meerloo, *The Rape of the Mind*

If nobody ever said anything unless he knew what he was talking about, a ghastly hush would descend upon the earth.

Sir Alan Herbert, as quoted in *Reader's Digest*, August 1959

Language

The day of the printed word is far from ended. Swift as is the delivery of the radio bulletin, graphic as is television's eyewitness picture, the task of adding meaning and clarity remains urgent. People cannot and need not absorb meaning at the speed of light.

Erwin Canham, as quoted in *The New York Times*, January 5, 1958

Why shouldn't we quarrel about a word? What is the good of words if they aren't important enough to quarrel over? Why do we choose one word more than another if there isn't any difference between them?

G. K. Chesterton, *The Ball and the Cross*

The test of a good letter is a very simple one. If one seems to hear the other person talking as one reads, it is a good letter.

A. C. Benson, as quoted in *Reader's Digest*, January 1936

Independence is normally achieved when, for one thing, we rid ourselves of logophobia, the irrational fear of words.

Francis Meehan, *The Temple of the Spirit*

We never tire of the words which man in his folly and stupidity cannot smirch and debase. . . . [These] never grow drab or stale. It is, for the most part, the words which express mental concepts that we tire of, that we come to use with misgiving or distaste—the words that we have sullied or betrayed, words like *liberty* and *honor, freedom* and *democracy, faith* and *glory*. These are the words that need renewal and repair from time to time, and that need to be thought about as we use them.

J. Donald Adams, *Literary Frontiers*

Architecture, painting, sculpture, music, science—all demand a material intermediary of some sort; words alone are as disembodied as when man first drew them from his stream of thought.

J. Donald Adams, *Literary Frontiers*

You're an old-timer if you can remember when setting the world on fire was a figure of speech.

Franklin P. Jones, as quoted in *Reader's Digest*, April 1962

At the present time we have a population that is literate, in the sense that everybody is able to read and write; but, owing to the emphasis 153 placed on scientific and technical training at the expense of the humanities, very few of our people have been taught to understand and handle language as an instrument of power.

Dorothy Sayers, *Unpopular Opinions*

It is of interest to note that while some dolphins are reported to have learned English—up to 50 words used in correct context—no human has been reported to have learned dolphinese.

Carl Sager, as quoted in the *Christian Science Monitor,*
November 15, 1965

The best slang of today becomes the language of tomorrow.

George P. Brett, as quoted in *Reader's Digest*, March 1922

The end of reading is not more books but more life.

Holbrook Jackson, *The Reading of Books*

Ninety percent of the friction of daily life is caused by tone of voice.

Arnold Bennett, as quoted in *Reader's Digest*, June 1957

It took me years to understand that words are often as important as experience, because words make experiences last.

Willie Morris, *North Toward Home*

But children, you know, do really talk rather formally if you listen to them. Colloquialism comes later. It is what people pick up.

Joy Compton-Burnett, as quoted in *The House of Fiction*

An epigram is a half-truth so stated as to irritate the person who believes the other half.

Shailer Mathews, as quoted in *Reader's Digest*, July 1937

As sheer casual reading-matter, I still find the English dictionary the most interesting book in our language.

Albert Jay Nock, *Memoirs of a Superfluous Man*

The spoken and the written language must not be too near together, as they must not be too far apart.

T. S. Eliot, *Selected Essays*

If we spoke as we write we should find no one to listen; and if we wrote as we speak we should find no one to read.

T. S. Eliot, *Selected Essays*

. . . why wasn't I born, alas, in an age of adjectives; why can one no longer write of silver-shedding Tears and moontailed Peacocks, of eloquent Death, of the Negro and star-enameled Night?

Logan Pearsall Smith, *More Trivia*

Aphorisms are salted, not sugared, almonds at Reason's feast.

Logan Pearsall Smith, *Afterthoughts*

A book is the only place in which you can examine a fragile thought without breaking it, or explore an explosive idea without fear it will go off in your face. . . . It is one of the few havens remaining where a man's mind can get both provocation and privacy.

Edward P. Morgan, in *Clearing the Air*

The more cant there is in politics, the better. Cant is nothing in itself; but attached to even the smallest quantity of sincerity, it serves like a naught after a numeral, to multiply whatever genuine good-will may exist. Politicians who cant about humanitarian principles find themselves sooner or later compelled to put those principles into practice— and far more thoroughly than they had ever originally intended. Without political cant there would be no democracy.

Aldous Huxley, *Jesting Pilate*   155

It is the little writer rather than the great writer who seems never to quote, and the reason is that he is really never doing anything else.

Havelock Ellis, *The Dance of Life*

A good catchword can obscure analysis for fifty years.

Johan Huizinga, *The Waning of the Middle Ages*

When something defies description, let it.

Arnold H. Glasow, as quoted in *Reader's Digest*, May 1962

To write or to speak is almost inevitably to lie a little. It is an attempt to clothe an intangible in a tangible form; to compress an immeasurable into a mold. And in the act of compression, how Truth is mangled and torn!

Anne Morrow Lindbergh, *The Wave of the Future*

All of us communicate with one another nonverbally, as well as with words. . . .

Every culture has its own body language, and children absorb its nuances along with spoken language. A Frenchman talks and moves in French. The way an Englishman crosses his legs is nothing like the way a male American does it. . . .

The person who is truly bilingual is also bilingual in body language. New York's famous mayor, Fiorello La Guardia, politicked in English, Italian and Yiddish. When films of his speeches are run without sound, it's not too difficult to identify from his gestures the language he was speaking.

Flora Davis, as quoted in *Glamour*, September 1969

If only everyone talked the way we do in my household. I mean . . . if only everyone . . . like . . . talked . . . you know . . . the way we do . . . right?

It would be so much . . . like . . . easier to . . . you know . . . understand . . . right?

Roderick Nordell, as quoted in *Reader's Digest*, September
1972

Language specialists claim that the five sweetest phrases in English are: "I love you." "Dinner is served." "All is forgiven." "Sleep until noon." "Keep the change." There are those who choose to add: "You've lost weight."

L. M. Boyd, as quoted in *Reader's Digest*,
September 1973

Near the end of his [Aaron Burr's] life a lady said to him: "Colonel, I wonder if you were ever the gay Lothario they say you were." The old man turned his eyes, the luster still undiminished, toward the lady—and lifting his trembling finger said in his quiet, impressive whisper: "They say, they say, they say. Ah, my child, how long are you going to continue to use those dreadful words? Those two little words have done more harm than all others. Never use them, my dear, never use them."

William Carlos Williams, *In the American Grain*

I wonder what language truck drivers are using, now that everyone is using theirs?

Beryl Pfizer, as quoted in *Reader's Digest*, April 1973

Words are more interesting than letters, and sentences are more interesting than words.

Fannie Jackson Coppin, *Black Women in White America*   157

The dropping of "etc." from the language would necessitate a lot of thinking that is not being done at present.

Wellman L. France, as quoted in Reader's Digest, May
1952

One of the most beautiful phrases in our language are the words an American uses when he says to those with whom he has been in disagreement: "I'll go along."

David E. Lilienthal, This I Do Believe

English is a funny language. A fat chance and a slim chance are the same thing.

Jack Herbert, as quoted in Reader's Digest, December 1968

All the skills of speech are of no use if our words are insincerely spoken.

Wesley Wiksell, Do They Understand You?

Letters that should never have been written and ought immediately to be destroyed are the only ones worth keeping.

Sydney Tremayne, as quoted in Reader's Digest, December
1948

Despite what science, instinct and common sense tell us, many Americans seem to cut down—almost deliberately—on the amount and quality of physical contact. After infancy, words replace touches; distance replaces closeness. . . .

Norman M. Lobsenz, as quoted in Woman's Day, February
1970

Words must surely be counted among the most powerful drugs man ever invented.

Leo Rosten, as quoted in Reader's Digest, July 1973

The two words "information" and "communication" are often used interchangeably, but they signify quite different things. Information is *giving out*; communication is *getting through*.

Sydney J. Harris, as quoted in *Reader's Digest*, March, 1972

The great letter writer must be an egotist.

Lytton Strachey, *Biographical Essays*

To communicate love, parents need a language of acceptance: words that value feelings, responses that change moods, replies that radiate respect. The world talks to the mind. Parents speak more intimately—they talk to the heart.

Dr. Haim Ginott, as quoted in *Reader's Digest*, January 1973

The birth of language is the dawn of humanity. The line between man and beast—between the highest ape and the lowest savage—is the language line.

Susanne K. Langer, *Philosophy in a New Key*

With every foreign language, you develop a tiny bit of insight into the people who speak it as you study it. As one small example, the Japanese word for "husband" is the same as the word for "boss," if you see what I mean.

Florence Rome, as quoted in Reader's Digest, March 1973

He who wants to persuade should put his trust not in the right argument, but in the right word. The power of sound has always been greater than the power of sense.

Joseph Conrad, A Personal Record

Media

A newspaper is always a weapon in somebody's hands.

Claude Cockburn, In Time of Trouble

Radio announcer: A man who talks until you have a headache, then tries to sell something to relieve it.

John Carruthers, as quoted in Reader's Digest, October 1953

We tell the public which way the cat is jumping. The public will take care of the cat.

Arthur Hays Sulzberger, as quoted in Time, May 8, 1950

Along with responsible newspapers we must have responsible *readers*. No matter how conscientiously the publisher and his associates perform their work, they can do only half the job. Readers must do the rest. The fountain serves no useful purpose if the horse refuses to drink.

Arthur Hays Sulzberger, address to the Southern Newspaper Publishers Association, October 4, 1955

A good newspaper, I suppose, is a nation talking to itself.

> Arthur Miller, as quoted in the London *Observer*,
> November 26, 1961

Journalism allows its readers to witness history; fiction gives its readers an opportunity to live it.

> John Hersey, as quoted in *Time*, March 13, 1953

I find television very educating. Every time somebody turns on the set I go into the other room and read a book.

> Groucho Marx, as quoted in *Reader's Digest*, August 1950

Our republic and its press will rise or fall together.

> Joseph Pulitzer, quotation used on a three-cent
> commemorative stamp, 1947

What you *see* is news, what you *know* is background, what you *feel* is opinion.

> Lester Markel, *While You Were Gone*

The laws of libel do not permit the public assassination of private character.

> Walter Lippmann, in a syndicated column, July 21, 1964

In every field of human endeavor, he that is first must perpetually live in the white light of publicity.

> Theodore F. MacManus, as quoted in the *Saturday Evening
> Post*, January 2, 1915

Radio will never be wholly satisfactory to the listener until he can turn off unpopular programs with a click that will be heard in the studio.

> Irving Hoffman, as quoted in *Reader's Digest*, December
> 1952

If you want to get on the front page of a newspaper you should attack someone, especially when you're in politics.

Harry S. Truman, news conference in New York, January 9, 1964

Acceptance by government of a dissident press is a measure of the maturity of a nation.

Justice William O. Douglas, *An Almanac of Liberty*

It is our attitude toward free thought and free expression that will determine our fate. There must be no limit on the range of temperate discussion, no limits on thoughts. No subject must be taboo. No censor must preside at our assemblies.

Justice William O. Douglas, address to the Authors' Guild, December 3, 1952

The medium is the massage.

Marshall McLuhan, *The Medium Is the Massage*

The reader deserves an honest opinion. If he doesn't deserve it, give it to him anyhow.

John Ciardi, as quoted in the Saturday Review, February 1957

All censorships exist to prevent any one from challenging current conceptions and existing institutions. All progress is initiated by challenging current conceptions, and executed by supplanting existing institutions. Consequently the first condition of progress is the removal of censorships.

George Bernard Shaw, preface to Mrs. Warren's Profession

Assassination is the extreme form of censorship.

George Bernard Shaw, The Rejected Statement

It is very difficult to have a free, fair, and honest press anywhere in the world. In the first place, as a rule, papers are largely supported by advertising, and that immediately gives the advertisers a certain hold over the medium which they use.

Eleanor Roosevelt, If You Ask Me

It is a seldom proffered argument as to the advantages of a free press that it has a major function in keeping the government itself informed as to what the government is doing.

Walter Cronkite, as quoted in Reader's Digest, April 1974

One answer to the problem of how to treat reporters is, "Treat them frequently."

F. H. Brennan, as quoted in Reader's Digest, January 1933

Women, wampum and wrongdoing are always news.

Stanley Walker, city editor of the New York Herald Tribune, as quoted in Reader's Digest, February 1935 163

One of the disturbing things about world news is that we know we're going to have to read it in the newspapers after we hear it over the radio before we see it on television.

Harold Coffin, as quoted in *Reader's Digest*,
October 1956

You don't have a democracy. It's a photocracy.

Sir Robert Gordon Menzies, former Prime Minister of
Australia, on being followed by news photographers in
Washington, D.C., as quoted in news reports of November 6,
1954

The men with the muckrakes are often indispensable to the well-being of society; but only if they know when to stop raking the muck.

Theodore Roosevelt, at the laying of cornerstone of the
House Office Building, April 14, 1906

Freedom of the press is not an end in itself but a means to the end of a free society.

Justice Felix Frankfurter, concurring opinion in *Penchamp*
v. *Florida*

Advertising is the organized effort to extend and intensify craving—to extend and intensify . . . the working of that force which is the principal cause of suffering and wrong-doing and the greatest obstacle between the human soul and its divine Ground.

Aldous Huxley, *The Perennial Philosophy*

We keep our radio right on top of the TV set. With the radio playing there it gives us something to think about while we're watching television.

Herb Shriner, as quoted in *Reader's Digest*,
September 1958

The relationship between a reporter and a President is exactly the same as that between a pitcher and a batter . . . they both are trying to keep each other away.

Merriman Smith, interview on NBC-TV, August 2, 1961

According to American principle and practice the public is the ruler of the State, and in order to rule rightly it should be informed correctly.

William Randolph Hearst, in the New York
Journal-American, November 11, 1954

Perhaps the quickest and best phrasemaker who ever inhabited the White House, F. D. R. was a President after a newsman's heart. He talked in headline phrases. He acted, he emoted; he was angry, he was smiling; he was persuasive, he was demanding; he was philosophical, he was elemental; he was sensible, he was unreasonable; he was benevolent, he was malicious; he was satirical, he was soothing; he was funny, he was gloomy; he was exciting, he was human; he was copy.

Jack Bell, *The Splendid Misery*

The tabloids make eavesdroppers of reporters, sensual meddlers of journalists, and reduce the highest ideals of the newspaper to the process of fastening a camera lens to every boudoir keyhole.

Abden Kandel, as quoted in *Reader's Digest*, October 1927

The immense impact of commercial advertising and the mass media on our lives is—let us make no mistake about it—an impact that tends to encourage passivity, to encourage acquiescence and uniformity, to place handicaps on individual contemplation and creativeness.

George F. Kennan, address at Notre Dame University,
May 15, 1953

For forty years he has carried out, rather literally, the dictum of Mr. Dooley that the mission of a modern newspaper is to "comfort the afflicted and afflict the comfortable."

John K. Winkler, *W. R. Hearst*

I am a Protestant, Republican and a free enterpriser, which means that I am biased in favor of God, Eisenhower and the stockholders of Time Inc., and if anyone who objects doesn't know this by now, why the hell are they still spending 35 cents for the magazine?

Henry R. Luce, as quoted in *Reader's Digest*, November 1972

THE WORKING WORLD

Work, Achievement and Success

The typical successful American businessman was born in the country, where he worked like hell so he could live in the city, where he worked like hell so he could live in the country.

Don Marquis, as quoted in *Reader's Digest*, August 1940

I am only an average man, but, by George, I work harder at it than the average man.

Theodore Roosevelt, as quoted in *Reader's Digest*, March 1933

There are two kinds of success. One is the very rare kind that comes to the man who has the power to do what no one else has the power to do. That is genius. But the average man who wins what we call success is not a genius. He is a man who has merely the ordinary qualities that he shares with his fellows, but who has developed those ordinary qualities to a more than ordinary degree.

Theodore Roosevelt, as quoted in *Reader's Digest*, August 1960

In life as in a football game, the principle to follow is: Hit the line hard.

Theodore Roosevelt, *The Strenuous Life*

No man needs sympathy because he has to work. . . . Far and away the best prize that life offers is the chance to work hard at work worth doing.

Theodore Roosevelt, address in Syracuse, New York, Labor Day, 1903

Work is accomplished by those employees who have not yet reached their level of incompetence.

Laurence J. Peter and Raymond Hull, The Peter Principle

I'm a self-made man, but I think if I had it to do over again, I'd call in someone else.

Roland Young, as quoted in Reader's Digest, January 1943

Success is getting what you want; happiness is wanting what you get.

Anonymous, as quoted in Reader's Digest, April 1944

Hardships, poverty and want are the best incentives and the best foundation for the success of a man.

Bradford Merrill, as quoted in Reader's Digest, November 1937

I like work; it fascinates me. I can sit and look at it for hours.

Jerome K. Jerome, as quoted in Reader's Digest, April 1930

Happiness, I have discovered, is nearly always a rebound from hard work.

David Grayson, as quoted in Reader's Digest, March 1936

Men are failures, not because they are stupid, but because they are not sufficiently impassioned.

Struthers Burt, as quoted in Reader's Digest, April 1937

The lash may force men to physical labor; it cannot force them to spiritual creativity.

Sholem Asch, What I Believe

The sovereign source of melancholy is repletion. Need and struggle are what excite and inspire us.

William James, as quoted in Reader's Digest, June 1945

Most of us can learn to live in perfect comfort on higher levels of power. Everyone knows that on any given day there are energies slumbering in him which the incitements of that day do not call forth. Compared with what we ought to be, we are only half awake. Our fires are damped, our drafts are checked. We are making use of only a small part of our possible mental and physical resources. . . .

It is evident that our organism has stored-up reserves of energy that are ordinarily not called upon—deeper and deeper strata of explosible material, ready for use by anyone who probes so deep. The human individual usually lives far within his limits. In rough terms, we may say that a man who energizes below his normal maximum fails by just so much to profit by his chance at life.

William James, as quoted in Reader's Digest, September 1971

Not that I would not, if I could, be both handsome and fat and well-dressed and a great athlete, and make a million a year, be a wit, a bon vivant, and a lady-killer, as well as a philosopher, a philanthropist, a statesman, warrior, and African explorer, as well as a "tone-poet" and a saint. The thing is simply impossible. The millionaire's work   171 would run counter to the saint's, the bon vivant and the philanthropist would trip each other up; the philosopher and the lady-killer could not well keep house in the same tenement of clay.

William James, *Principles of Psychology*

Relief work costs twice as much as ordinary labor. That's because it takes two men for every task—one to dilly and one to dally.

Howard Brubaker, as quoted in *Reader's Digest*, August 1935

Nothing recedes like success.

Walter Winchell, as quoted in *Reader's Digest*, December 1937

For every talent that poverty has stimulated it has blighted a hundred.

John W. Gardner, *Excellence*

The best-kept secret in America today is that people would rather work hard for something they believe in than enjoy a pampered idleness.

John W. Gardner, as quoted in *Reader's Digest*, August 1968

If one defines the term "dropout" to mean a person who has given up serious effort to meet his responsibilities, then every business office, government agency, golf club and university faculty would yield its quota.

John W. Gardner, as quoted in *Reader's Digest*, September 1971

What we gave, we have;
What we spent, we had;
What we left, we lost.

Epitaph of the Earl of Devon, as quoted in *Reader's Digest*,
April 1946

Nothing is really work unless you would rather be doing something else.

Sir James Barrie, as quoted in Reader's Digest, October 1936

To live is to function. That is all there is in living.

Justice Oliver Wendell Holmes, Jr., radio address on his
ninetieth birthday, March 8, 1931

A manpower policy should lead us to a society in which every person has full opportunity to develop his—or her—earning powers, where no willing worker lacks a job, and where no useful talent lacks an opportunity.

Lyndon B. Johnson, Manpower Report of the President,
March 1966

If you want to know whether you are destined to be a success or a failure in life, you can easily find out. The test is simple and it is infallible. Are you able to save money? If not, drop out. You will lose. You may think not, but you will lose, as sure as you live. The seed of success is not in you.

James J. Hill, as quoted in Reader's Digest, June 1922

When a man blames others for his failures, it's a good idea to credit others with his successes.

Howard W. Newton, as quoted in Reader's Digest, July
1951

There's nothing wrong with being a self-made man if you don't consider the job finished too soon.

John Mooney, as quoted in Reader's Digest, June 1949

You will eat bye and bye,
In that glorious land above the sky;

173

Work and pray, live on hay,
You'll get pie in the sky when you die.

Joe Hill, as quoted in The IWW Songbook

A society that gives to one class all the opportunities for leisure, and to another all the burdens of work, dooms both classes to spiritual sterility.

Lewis Mumford, Faith for Living

Show me a man who cannot bother to do little things and I'll show you a man who cannot be trusted to do big things.

Lawrence D. Bell, as quoted in Reader's Digest, January
1957

Only a mediocre person is always at his best.

W. Somerset Maugham, as quoted in Reader's Digest, June
1957

We speak of alcohol and drugs as being addictive. So is work. Driving, ambitious people become slaves to work—and the resultant stress can cause serious problems. All work and no play doesn't make Jack a dull boy; it makes him a dead boy. This isn't to argue that hard work should be avoided, but to suggest that the hard driver allow some time for diverting recreation. It can be his best life-insurance policy.

J. D. Ratcliff, as quoted in Today's Health, July 1970

If at first you don't succeed, try, try again. Then quit. There's no use being a damn fool about it.

W. C. Fields, as quoted in Reader's Digest, September 1949

A man who works with his hands is a laborer; a man who works with his hands and his brain is a craftsman; but a man who works with his hands and his brain and his heart is an artist.

Louis Nizer, as quoted in Reader's Digest, July 1949

If I would be a young man again and had to decide how to make my living, I would not try to become a scientist or scholar or teacher. I would rather choose to be a plumber or a peddler, in the hope to find that modest degree of independence still available under present circumstances.

Albert Einstein, letter to the Reporter, November 18, 1954

We must beware of trying to build a society in which nobody counts for anything except a politician or an official, a society where enterprise gains no reward and thrift no privileges.

Sir Winston Churchill, as quoted in Reader's Digest,
October 1943

There is no dignity quite so impressive, and no independence quite so important, as living within your means.

Calvin Coolidge, as quoted in Reader's Digest, August 1953

We cannot do everything at once, but we can do something at once.

Calvin Coolidge, as quoted in Reader's Digest, October
1950

The reason why worry kills more people than work is that more people worry than work.

Robert Frost, as quoted in Vogue, March 15, 1963 175

By working faithfully eight hours a day, you may eventually get to be a boss and work 12 hours a day.

Robert Frost, as quoted in Reader's Digest, August 1956

The world is full of willing people; some willing to work, the rest willing to let them.

Robert Frost, as quoted in Reader's Digest, April 1947

If a boy is lucky and ambitious in this country, he may grow up to be President. If he is unlucky, he may grow up to be Secretary of State.

Neal O'Hara, as quoted in Reader's Digest, June 1956

If people really liked to work, we'd still be plowing the ground with sticks and transporting goods on our backs.

William Feather, as quoted in Reader's Digest, September 1949

Success is that old ABC—ability, breaks and courage.

Charles Luckman, as quoted in the New York Mirror, September 19, 1955

It is the feeling of exerting effort that exhilarates us, as a grasshopper is exhilarated by jumping. A hard job, full of impediments, is thus more satisfying than an easy job.

H. L. Mencken, as quoted in Reader's Digest, September 1962

Man is the only creature that consumes without producing.

George Orwell, Animal Farm

176 A modest man often seems conceited because he is delighted with what he has done, thinking it better than anything of which he believed

himself capable, whereas the conceited man is inclined to express dissatisfaction with his performances, thinking them unworthy of his genius.

Hesketh Pearson, as quoted in *Reader's Digest*, February
1953

A man never knows what he can do until he tries to undo what he has done.

Frances Rodman, as quoted in *Reader's Digest*, January
1956

Never give a man up until he has failed at something he likes.

Lewis E. Lawes, as quoted in *Reader's Digest*, January
1961

Keep on going and chances are you will stumble on something, perhaps when you are least expecting it. I have never heard of anyone stumbling on something sitting down.

Charles F. Kettering, as quoted in *Reader's Digest*, October
1961

There exists limitless opportunity in every industry. Where there is an open mind, there will always be a frontier.

Charles F. Kettering, as quoted in *Reader's Digest*,
September 1946

There never has been any 30-hour week for men who had anything to do.

Charles F. Kettering, as quoted in *Reader's Digest*, April
1935

If at first you don't succeed you're running about average.

M. H. Alderson, as quoted in *Reader's Digest*, February
1955

You can't hold a man down without staying down with him.

Booker T. Washington, as quoted in *The New York Times*,
February 20, 1955

Don't go around saying the world owes you a living. The world owes you nothing. It was here first.

Mark Twain, as quoted in *Reader's Digest*, March 1963

The man of character finds an especial attractiveness in difficulty, since it is only by coming to grips with difficulty that he can realize his potentialities.

Charles de Gaulle, as quoted in *Reader's Digest*, April 1961

The world stands aside to let anyone pass who knows where he is going.

David Starr Jordan, as quoted in *Reader's Digest*, June 1961

Ambition: n. An overmastering desire to be vilified by enemies while living and made ridiculous by friends when dead.

Ambrose Bierce, *The Devil's Dictionary*

I believe in the tragic element of history. I believe there is the tragedy of a man who works very hard and never gets what he wants. And then

I believe there is the even more bitter tragedy of a man who finally gets what he wants and finds out that he doesn't want it.

Henry Kissinger, as quoted in *Reader's Digest*, January 1974

People are always blaming their circumstances for what they are. I don't believe in circumstances. The people who get on in this world are the people who look for the circumstances they want, and if they can't find them, make them.

George Bernard Shaw, as quoted in *Reader's Digest*, December 1952

When I was a young man I observed that nine out of ten things I did were failures. I didn't want to be a failure, so I did ten times more work.

George Bernard Shaw, as quoted in *Reader's Digest*, March 1960

Anything one man can imagine, other men can make real.

Jules Verne, as quoted in *Reader's Digest*, June 1962

Most people like hard work. Particularly when they are paying for it.

Franklin P. Jones, as quoted in *Reader's Digest*, January 1953

Maybe they call it take-home pay because there is no other place you can afford to go with it.

Franklin P. Jones, as quoted in *Reader's Digest*, April 1953

Superior achievement, or making the most of one's capabilities, is to a very considerable degree a matter of habit. This was the reason why Joe used to say to the children, "We don't want any losers around here. In this family we want winners." They were encouraged to be winners, leaders, and victors in whatever they set their hand to, and to develop the habit.

Rose Fitzgerald Kennedy, Times to Remember

No one ever got very far by working a 40-hour week. Most of the notable people I know are trying to manage a 40-hour day.

Channing Pollock, as quoted in Reader's Digest, May 1937

The only good luck many great men ever had was being born with the ability and determination to overcome bad luck.

Channing Pollock, as quoted in Reader's Digest, April 1940

Anybody can win unless there happens to be a second entry.

George Ade, Forty Modern Fables

The trouble with some self-made men is that they insist on giving everybody their recipe.

Maurice Seitter, as quoted in Reader's Digest, June 1960

There ain't no man can avoid being born average. But there ain't no man got to be common.

Satchel Paige, as quoted in Reader's Digest, October 1958

Show me a thoroughly satisfied man—and I will show you a failure.

Thomas A. Edison, as quoted in Reader's Digest, July 1952

Never confuse motion with action.

Ernest Hemingway, as quoted in Reader's Digest, January 1974

True success is overcoming the fear of being unsuccessful.

Paul Seeney, as quoted in *Reader's Digest*, March 1974

Thinking is the hardest work there is, which is the probable reason why so few engage in it.

Henry Ford, as quoted in *Reader's Digest*, May 1929

A generation ago there were a thousand men to every opportunity, while today there are a thousand opportunities to every man.

Henry Ford, as quoted in *Reader's Digest*, October 1927

Nothing is particularly hard if you divide it into small jobs.

Henry Ford, as quoted in *Reader's Digest*, March 1934

Most people spend more time and energy in going around problems than in trying to solve them.

Henry Ford, as quoted in *Reader's Digest*, August 1955

You can't build a reputation on what you are *going* to do.

Henry Ford, as quoted in *Reader's Digest*, September 1968

Before everything else, getting ready is the secret of success.

Henry Ford, as quoted in *Reader's Digest*, January 1963

Whatever you have, you must either use or lose.

Henry Ford, as quoted in *Reader's Digest*, October 1953

The majority prove their worth by keeping busy. A busy life is the nearest thing to a purposeful life.

Eric Hoffer, *The Ordeal of Change*

The haves and the have-nots can often be traced back to the dids and the did-nots.

D. O. Flynn, as quoted in *Reader's Digest*, May 1962

For all his drudgery, the farmer enjoys certain psychic rewards. He lives and works in the open, far away from the grime, crime and tension that beset some big cities. As often as not, he still leaves his door unlocked at night. Faith and convictions remain more intact in the countryside, where they are closely linked to soil and season.

Time essay, as quoted in *Reader's Digest*, July 1973

In many businesses, today will end at five o'clock. Those bent on success, however, make today last from yesterday right through tomorrow.

Lawrence H. Martin, as quoted in the *Wall Street Journal*, March 9, 1967

Look around and you'll agree that the really happy people are those who have broken the chains of procrastination, those who find satisfaction in doing the job at hand. They're full of eagerness, zest, productivity. You can be, too.

Norman Vincent Peale, as quoted in *Reader's Digest*, January 1972

I've met a few people in my time who were enthusiastic about hard work. And it was just my luck that all of them happened to be men I was working for at the time.

Bill Gold, as quoted in *Reader's Digest*, March 1955

If a man loves the labor of his trade, apart from any question of success or fame, the gods have called him.

Robert Louis Stevenson, as quoted in *Reader's Digest*, March 1963

Don't come home a failure.

> William Herschell Cobb, to his son, Ty, as quoted in *My Life in Baseball*

After you've done a thing for two years, you should look at it carefully. After five years, look at it with suspicion. After ten years, throw it away and start all over.

> Alfred E. Perlman, as quoted in *Reader's Digest,* July 1955

The only thing that keeps a man going is energy. And what is energy but liking life?

> Louis Auchincloss, *A World of Profit*

The mightiest works have been accomplished by men who have somehow kept their ability to dream great dreams.

> Walter Russell Bowie, as quoted in *Reader's Digest*, August 1952

Nothing splendid has ever been achieved except by those who dared believe that something inside them was superior to circumstance.

> Bruce Barton, as quoted in *Reader's Digest*, December 1948

There's plenty of room at the top, but there's no room to sit down.

> Helen Downey, as quoted in *Reader's Digest*, February 1960

A job *per se* does not provide a woman, or a man either, with any magical path to self-fulfillment, not does just any community volunteer work, or half-hearted dabbling in creative art.

> Alice S. Rossi, in *The Woman in America* 183

A widely prevalent notion today seems to demand instant achievement of goals, without any of the wearying, frustrating preparation that is indispensable to any task. As the exemplar of a way of life, the professional—that man or woman who invests every new task or duty, no matter how small, with discipline of mind and spirit—is a vanishing American, particularly among those who too often believe that dreams come true because they ought to and not because they are *caused* to materialize.

Jack Valenti, as quoted in *Reader's Digest*, April 1972

Much of the good work of the world has been that of dull people who have done their best.

Senator George F. Hoar, as quoted in *Reader's Digest*, June 1958

We lay too much stress on stick-to-it-iveness. I once had a professor who wisely hung this sign over his desk: "Oh, Lord, teach me when to let go."

W. G. Carleton, as quoted in *Reader's Digest*, October 1960

One of the greatest labor-saving inventions of today is tomorrow.

Vincent T. Foss, as quoted in *Reader's Digest*, August 1947

There is no failure except in no longer trying.

Elbert Hubbard, *Note Book*

The big shots are only the little shots who keep shooting.

Christopher Morley, as quoted in *Reader's Digest*, February 1958

Luck is what happens when preparation meets opportunity.

Elmer G. Leterman, as quoted in *Reader's Digest*, February 1958

I'm a great believer in luck. The harder I work, the more of it I seem to have.

F. L. Emerson, as quoted in *Reader's Digest*,
March 1947

Times have changed. Forty years ago people worked 12 hours a day, and it was called economic slavery. Now they work 14 hours a day, and it's called moonlighting.

Robert Orben, as quoted in *Reader's Digest*,
April 1965

America's competitive spirit, the work ethic of this people, is alive and well. The dignity of work, the value of achievement, the morality of self-reliance—none of these is going out of style.

Richard M. Nixon, as quoted in *Reader's Digest*,
January 1972

Success is not a harbor but a voyage with its own perils to the spirit. The game of life is to come up a winner, to be a success, or to achieve what we set out to do. Yet there is always the danger of failing as a human being. The lesson that most of us on this voyage never learn, but can never quite forget, is that to win is sometimes to lose.

Richard M. Nixon, as quoted in *The American Idea of Success*

There is no future in any job. The future lies in the man who holds the job.

Dr. George W. Crane, as quoted in *Reader's Digest*,
September 1950

When the going gets tough, the tough get going.

Maxim adopted by Joseph P. Kennedy as a motto for his sons, as quoted in *The New York Times Magazine*, August 22, 1965

Trouble is only opportunity in work clothes.

> Henry J. Kaiser, as quoted in *Reader's Digest*, February 1947

There is no security on this earth. There is only opportunity.

> General Douglas MacArthur, as quoted in *Reader's Digest*, October 1950

The dictionary is the only place where success comes before work.

> Arthur Brisbane, as quoted in *Reader's Digest*, October 1957

If living conditions don't stop improving in this country, we're going to run out of humble beginnings for our great men.

> Russell P. Askue, as quoted in *Reader's Digest*, December 1948

There are two kinds of men who never amount to much—those who cannot do what they are told and those who can do nothing else.

> Cyrus H. K. Curtis, as quoted in *Reader's Digest*, July 1951

The formula for complete happiness is to be very busy with the unimportant.

> A. Edward Newton, *This Book-Collecting Game*

Happiness consists in activity—it is a running stream, not a stagnant pool.

> John Mason Good, as quoted in *Reader's Digest*, April 1951

America celebrates success, but occasionally it pauses to regret the men who didn't quite make it—the also-rans, the good men who arrived near the top at the wrong time, the rejected and the disappointed.

> James Reston, as quoted in *The New York Times*, July 15, 1965

I have a kind of contempt for intelligence all by itself. Coupled with energy and willingness, it'll go. Alone, it winds up riding the rails.

John Hersey, as quoted in *Reader's Digest*,
August 1972

Quite a few people are already working a four-day week. Trouble is, it takes 'em five or six days to do it.

Earl Wilson, as quoted in *Reader's Digest*, August 1958

The labor of a human being is not a commodity or article of commerce. You can't weigh the soul of a man with a bar of pig iron.

Samuel Gompers, *Seventy Years of Life and Labor*

The worst crime against working people is a company which fails to operate at a profit.

Samuel Gompers, as quoted in *Reader's Digest*, September 1952

If my sister or I took one of those school examinations where you are required to answer only 10 questions out of 12, Mother's comment on hearing this would be, "I hope you chose the hardest ones." Reject the easy path. Do it the hard way.

Margaret Bourke-White, as quoted in *Reader's Digest*,
August 1972

Happiness is essentially a state of going somewhere, wholeheartedly, one-directionally, without regret or reservation.

William H. Sheldon, *Psychology and the Promethean Will*

I loathe drudgery as much as any man; but I have learned that the only way to conquer drudgery is to get through it as neatly, as efficiently, as one can. You know perfectly well that a dull job slackly done becomes twice as dull; whereas a dull job which you try to do just as well as you 187 can becomes half as dull. Here again, effort appears to me the main art of living.

Sir Harold Nicolson, as quoted in *Reader's Digest*, April
1972

For labor a short day is better than a short dollar.

William McKinley, letter to Henry Cabot Lodge,
September 8, 1900

Work and love—these are the basics. Without them there is neurosis.

Theodor Reik, *Of Love and Lust*

Money and Property

In a society in which money determines value, women are a group who work outside the money economy.

Margaret Benston, as quoted by Robin Morgan in
Sisterhood Is Powerful

The law of work does seem utterly unfair—but there it is, and nothing can change it: the higher the pay in enjoyment the worker gets out of it, the higher shall be his pay in money also.

Mark Twain, *A Connecticut Yankee in King Arthur's Court*

Just about the time you think you can make both ends meet, somebody moves the ends.

Pansy Penner, as quoted in *Reader's Digest*, December 1944

Dollars cannot buy yesterday.

Admiral Harold R. Stark, as quoted in *Time*, December 16,
1940

188

We ought to change the legend on our money from "In God We Trust" to "In Money We Trust." Because, as a nation, we've got far more faith in money these days than we do in God.

Arthur Hoppe, as quoted in Way, June 1963

It is wrong to assume that men of immense wealth are always happy.

John D. Rockefeller, Sr., as quoted in The Age of the Moguls

Finance is the art of passing currency from hand to hand until it finally disappears.

Robert W. Sarnoff, as quoted in Reader's Digest, May 1973

Men make counterfeit money; in many more cases, money makes counterfeit men.

Sydney J. Harris, as quoted in Reader's Digest, April 1968

Men may be divided almost any way we please, but I have found the most useful distinction to be made between those who devote their lives to conjugating the verb "to be," and those who spend their lives conjugating the verb "to have."

Sydney J. Harris, as quoted in Reader's Digest, April 1972

The rich who are unhappy are worse off than the poor who are unhappy; for the poor, at least, cling to the hopeful delusion that more money would solve their problems—but the rich know better.

Sydney J. Harris, as quoted in Reader's Digest, November 1959

Remember when people worried about how much it took to buy something, instead of how long?

Earl Wilson, as quoted in Reader's Digest, May 1962

At today's prices it looks as if the nickel has gone the way of the other buffaloes.

Earl Wilson, as quoted in *Reader's Digest*,
June 1961

When you let money speak for you, it drowns out anything else you meant to say.

Mignon McLaughlin, *The Second Neurotic's Notebook*

The universal regard for money is one hopeful fact in our civilization.

George Bernard Shaw, preface to *Major Barbara*

The crying need of the nation is not for better morals, cheaper bread, temperance, liberty, culture, redemption of fallen sisters and erring brothers, nor the grace, love and fellowship of the Trinity, but simply for enough money.

George Bernard Shaw, preface to *Major Barbara*

The seven deadly sins . . . Food, clothing, firing, rent, taxes, respectability and children. Nothing can lift those seven millstones from man's neck but money: and the spirit cannot soar until the millstones are lifted.

George Bernard Shaw, *Major Barbara*

Lack of money is the root of all evil.

George Bernard Shaw, *Man and Superman*

A gentleman of our days is one who has money enough to do what every fool would do if he could afford it: that is, consume without producing.

George Bernard Shaw, *The Quintessence of Ibsenism*

Money-giving is a good criterion of a person's mental health. Generous people are rarely mentally ill people.

Dr. Karl Menninger, as quoted in *Reader's Digest*,
November 1970

There is nothing in saving money. The thing to do with it is to put it back into yourself, into your work, into the thing that is important, into whatever you are so much interested in that it is more important than money.

Henry Ford, as quoted in *Reader's Digest*, June 1922

Old men are always advising young men to save money. That is bad advice. Don't save every nickel. Invest in yourself. I never saved a dollar until I was 40 years old.

Henry Ford, as quoted in *Reader's Digest*, March 1960

It is not the employer who pays wages—he only handles the money. It is the product that pays wages.

Henry Ford, as quoted in *Reader's Digest*, February 1973

Humanly speaking, it is only when the hair is white, when . . . life is almost over, that men begin to realize how hopelessly elusive is the happiness promised by wealth and fame.

Joseph McSorley, *Be of Good Heart* 191

The great curse of our modern society is not so much the lack of money as the fact that the lack of money condemns a man to a squalid and incomplete existence.

Christopher Dawson, The Modern Dilemma

In a country where there are no rich there will be only the poor—the very poor.

Walter Rathenau, as quoted in Reader's Digest, June 1922

Love is the grandest thing on God's earth, but fortunate the lover who has plenty of money.

Russell H. Conwell, What You Can Do with Your Will
Power

Money is like manure. If you spread it around, it does a lot of good. But if you pile it up in one place, it stinks like hell.

Clint Murchison, Jr., as quoted in Time, June 16, 1961

When a feller says it ain't the money but the principle of the thing, it's the money.

Abe Martin, as quoted in Reader's Digest, March 1955

All forms of government fall when it comes up to the question of bread—bread for the family, something to eat. Bread to a man with a hungry family comes first—before his union, before his citizenship, before his church affiliation. Bread!

John L. Lewis, as quoted in the Saturday Evening Post,
October 12, 1963

The love of money is a form of infantilism. The man who loves money is the man who has never grown up. He has never passed from the world of fairy tales into the world of philosophy.

192

Robert Lynd, Searchlights and Nightingales

If a man runs after money, he's money-mad; if he keeps it he's a capitalist; if he spends it, he's a playboy; if he doesn't get it, he's a ne'er-do-well; if he doesn't try to get it, he lacks ambition. If he gets it without working for it, he's a parasite; and if he accumulates it after a lifetime of hard work, people call him a fool who never got anything out of life.

Vic Oliver, as quoted in Reader's Digest, June 1940

Money itself isn't the primary factor in what one does. A person does things for the sake of accomplishing something. Money generally follows.

Colonel Henry Crown, as quoted in The New York Times,
February 21, 1960

Undoubtedly the desire for food has been, and still is, one of the main causes of great political events.

Bertrand Russell, as quoted in the Atlantic Monthly,
January 1952

Money is like a sixth sense—and you can't make use of the other five without it.

W. Somerset Maugham, as quoted in The New York Times
Magazine, October 18, 1958

Status seekers are altering our society by their preoccupation, in the midst of plenty, with acquiring evidences of status. The people of this country have become increasingly preoccupied with status primarily because of the impact on their lives of big housing developments, big advertisers, big trade-unions, and big corporate hierarchies. As a result, democracy is still more of an ideal than a reality.

Vance Packard, The Status Seekers

Starting out to make money is the greatest mistake in life. Do what you feel you have a flair for doing, and if you are good enough at it the money will come.

Lord Rootes, as quoted in Reader's Digest, September 1960   193

Let me tell you about the very rich. They are different from you and me. They possess and enjoy early, and it does something to them, makes them soft where we are hard, and cynical where we are trustful, in a way that, unless you were born rich, it is very difficult to understand.

F. Scott Fitzgerald, "The Rich Boy"

Civilization and profits go hand in hand.

Calvin Coolidge, speech in New York, November 27, 1920

Time is really the only capital that any human being has, and the one thing that he can't afford to lose.

Thomas Edison, as quoted in *Reader's Digest*, October 1927

Money has become the grand test of virtue.

George Orwell, *Down and Out in Paris and London*

Wealth in modern societies is distributed according to opportunity; and while opportunity depends partly upon talent and energy, it depends still more upon birth, social position, access to education and inherited wealth; in a word, upon property.

R. H. Tawney, *The Acquisitive Society*

The journalist who says that "private property is the foundation of civilization" agrees with Proudhon, who said it was theft, in this respect at least that, without further definition, the words of both are meaningless. . . . Property is not theft, but a good deal of theft becomes property.

R. H. Tawney, *The Acquisitive Society*

Those who would administer wisely must, indeed, be wise, for one of the serious obstacles to the improvement of our race is indiscriminate charity.

194

Andrew Carnegie, *The Gospel of Wealth*

All is well since all grows better.

Andrew Carnegie, *Wealth*

There is inherited wealth in this country and also inherited poverty.

John F. Kennedy, address at Amherst College, October 26,
1963

A man who shows me his wealth is like the beggar who shows me his poverty; they are both looking for alms, the rich man for the alms of my envy, the poor man for the alms of my guilt.

Ben Hecht, *A Child of the Century*

We don't want a thing because we have found a reason for it; we find a reason for it because we want it.

Will Durant, as quoted in *Reader's Digest*, September 1962

Funny how a dollar can look so big when you take it to church, and so small when you take it to the store.

Frank Clark, as quoted in *Register and Tribune Syndicate*,
October 1970   195

Before borrowing money from a friend, decide which you need more.

Addison H. Hallock, as quoted in Reader's Digest,
September 1962

Americans have an abiding belief in their ability to control reality by purely material means. Hence . . . airline insurance replaces the fear of death with the comforting prospect of cash.

Cecil Beaton, It Gives Me Great Pleasure

Nobody was ever meant
To remember or invent
What he did with every cent.

Robert Frost, "The Hardship of Accounting"

America is not a mere body of traders; it is a body of free men. Our greatness built upon our freedom—is moral, not material. We have a great ardor for gain; but we have a deep passion for the rights of man.

Woodrow Wilson, speech, December 6, 1911

Money: a blessing that is of no advantage to us excepting when we part with it.

Ambrose Bierce, The Devil's Dictionary

Money, material though it be, does lie at the base of the most useful work you do. In itself nothing, it is the basis of much of the best effort which can be made for spiritual purposes.

Arthur J. Balfour, Earl of Balfour, as quoted in The Mind
of A. J. Balfour

Economic distress will teach men, if anything can, that realities are less dangerous than fancies, that fact finding is more effective than fault finding.

Carl Becker, Progress and Power

In the past, we have perhaps depended too much on the hope that creating new wealth would automatically provide us a better life. Now, we are finding that growth itself causes problems.

Charles B. Reeder, as quoted in *Reader's Digest*, April 1973

The best investment on earth *is* earth.

Louis Glickman, as quoted in the New York *Post*,
September 3, 1957

Worry, the interest paid by those who borrow trouble.

Judge George W. Lyon, as quoted in *The New York Times
Book Review*, October 23, 1932

I've never been poor, only broke. Being poor is a frame of mind. Being broke is only a temporary situation.

Mike Todd, as quoted in *Newsweek*, March 31, 1954

A status symbol is anything you can't afford, but did.

Harold Coffin, as quoted in *Reader's Digest*, March 1961

We forget what gives money its value—that someone exchanged work for it.

Neal O'Hara, as quoted in *Reader's Digest*, March 1961

A man is never so on trial as in the moment of excessive good fortune.

Lew Wallace, *Ben-Hur*

I have no complex about wealth. I have worked hard for my money, producing things people need. I believe that the able industrial leader who creates wealth and employment is more worthy of historical notice than politicians or soldiers.

J. Paul Getty, as quoted in *Time*, February 24, 1958   197

I was born into it and there was nothing I could do about it. It was there, like air or food or any other element. . . . The only question with wealth is what you do with it.

> John D. Rockefeller, Jr., as quoted in *Time*, September 24, 1956

Of course money is the Christmas gift everyone in the family would appreciate most—but the trouble is, you can't charge it.

> Bill Vaughan, as quoted in *Reader's Digest*, December 1958

Business and Labor

I don't meet competition. I crush it.

> Charles Revson, as quoted in *Time*, June 16, 1958

Bigness [in the economy] taxes the ability to manage intelligently. . . . The growth of bigness has resulted in ruthless sacrifices of human values. The disappearance of free enterprise has submerged the
198   individual in the impersonal corporation. When a nation of shopkeep-

ers is transformed into a nation of clerks, enormous spiritual sacrifices are made.

Justice William O. Douglas, to an audience of businessmen, as quoted in the New York *Post*, August 11, 1963

The conflict between the legal condemnation of monopoly and its de facto acceptance in slightly imperfect form as oligarchy is stark.

John Kenneth Galbraith, as quoted in *The Closed Enterprise*

The business of America is business.

Calvin Coolidge, speech to the Society of American Newspaper Editors, Washington, D. C., January 17, 1925

There is no right to strike against the public safety by anybody, anywhere, anytime.

Calvin Coolidge, as Governor of Massachusetts, in a letter to Samuel Gompers, September 1919, referring to the strike of the Boston police force

Private enterprise is ceasing to be free enterprise.

Franklin D. Roosevelt, message to Congress proposing the Monopoly Investigation, 1938

[Ours is] a program whose basic thesis is not that the system of free private enterprise has failed . . . but that it has not yet been tried.

Franklin D. Roosevelt, message on concentration of economic power, 1938

Concentration of economic power in all-embracing corporations . . . represents a kind of private government which is a power unto itself—a regimentation of other people's money and other people's lives.

Franklin D. Roosevelt, acceptance speech at the Democratic National Convention, 1936 199

Practices of the unscrupulous money changers stand indicted in the court of public opinion, rejected by the hearts and minds of men. . . . The money changers have fled from their high seats in the temple of our civilization. We may now restore the temple to the ancient truths.

Franklin D. Roosevelt, First Inaugural Address, March 4,
1933

In the field of modern business, so rich in opportunity for the exercise of man's finest and most varied mental faculties and moral qualities, mere money-making cannot be regarded as the legitimate end . . . since with the conduct of business human happiness or misery is inextricably interwoven.

Justice Louis D. Brandeis, address at Brown University,
1912

There must be a division not only of profits, but a division also of responsibilities. . . . We must insist upon labor sharing the responsibilities for the result of the business.

Justice Louis D. Brandeis, testimony before the U. S.
Commission on Industrial Relations, 1915

May. This is one of the peculiarly dangerous months to speculate in stocks in. The others are July, September, April, November, October, March, June, December, August, and February.

Mark Twain, as quoted in *Reader's Digest,*
May, 1933

Suppose you go to Washington and try to get at your government. You will always find that while you are politely listened to, the men really consulted are the men who have the biggest stake—the big bankers, the big manufacturers, the big masters of commerce. . . . The government of the United States at present is a foster child of special interests.

Woodrow Wilson, as quoted in *The Closed Enterprise
System*

There was a time when corporations played a minor part in our business affairs, but now they play the chief part, and most men are the servants of corporations.

Woodrow Wilson, *The New Freedom*

To me oligopoly just sounds like an immoral sex act.

Basil Mazines, as quoted in *The Closed Enterprise System*

American capitalism has been both overpraised and overindicted . . . it is neither the Plumed Knight nor the monstrous Robber Baron.

Max Lerner, *America as a Civilization*

When two men in a business always agree, one of them is unnecessary.

William Wrigley, Jr., as quoted in *Reader's Digest*, July 1940

Business men in America, as far as our experience reaches back, have seldom been enthusiastic about trade unionism.

Heywood Broun, *The Fight*

Business more than any other occupation is a continual dealing with the future; it is a continual calculation, an instinctive exercise in foresight.

Henry R. Luce, as quoted in *Fortune* promotional material, October 1960

You can be social minded without being a socialist.

Charles E. Wilson, speech at Dartmouth College, May 5, 1959

What's good for the country is good for General Motors, and vice versa.

Charles E. Wilson, as quoted in *The New York Times*,
January 23, 1953

He who builds a better mousetrap these days runs into design difficulties, material shortages, patent-infringement suits, work stoppages, collusive bidding, discount discrimination—and taxes.

H. E. Martz, as quoted in *Reader's Digest*, May 1962

The great companies did not know that the line between hunger and anger is a thin line.

John Steinbeck, *The Grapes of Wrath*

The notion that a business is clothed with a public interest and has been devoted to the public use is little more than a fiction intended to beautify what is disagreeable to the sufferers.

Justice Oliver Wendell Holmes, Jr., opinion in *Tyson* v.
Banton

There is no more demoralizing theory than that which imputes all human evils to Capitalism or any other single agency.

Samuel Gompers, *Seventy Years of Life and Labor*

Show me the country in which there are no strikes and I'll show you that country in which there is no liberty.

Samuel Gompers, as quoted in *American Labor Leaders*

What does Labor want? We want more schoolhouses and less jails; more books and less arsenals; more learning and less vice; more leisure and less greed; more justice and less revenge; in fact, more of the opportunities to cultivate our better natures, to make manhood more noble, womanhood more beautiful, and childhood more happy and bright.

Samuel Gompers, as quoted in *Labor*,
August 4, 1956

If you are ready and able to give up everything else, and will study the market and every stock listed there as carefully as a medical student studies anatomy, and will glue your nose to the ticker tape at the opening of every day of the year and never take it off till night; if you can do all that, and in addition have the cool nerve of a gambler, the sixth sense of a clairvoyant and the courage of a lion—you have a Chinaman's chance.

Bernard Baruch, as quoted in the New York *Mirror*,
January 3, 1957

WALL STREET LAYS AN EGG

Headline announcing stock-market crash, as quoted in
Variety, October 23, 1929

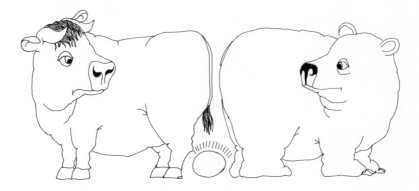

Business men must learn they cannot be in bed with elements of organized crime and then when trouble comes just say they are sorry.

Judge Arnold Bauman, in Manhattan Federal Court, March
1973   203

A bank is the thing that will always lend you money if you can prove that you don't need it.

Joe E. Lewis, as quoted in Reader's Digest, January 1949

Democratic capitalism, combined with industrial democracy, is unquestionably the best way of life for mankind.

David J. McDonald, as quoted in the New York Post,
October 30, 1957

Some people regard private enterprise as a predatory tiger to be shot. Others look on it as a cow they can milk. Not enough people see it as a healthy horse pulling a sturdy wagon.

Sir Winston Churchill, as quoted in Reader's Digest, April
1960

The capitalist process, not by coincidence but by virtue of its mechanism, progressively raises the standards of life of the masses. It does so through a sequence of vicissitudes, the severity of which is proportional to the speed of the advance.

Joseph A. Schumpeter, Capitalism, Socialism and
Democracy

"The trouble with socialism," a European observer once remarked, "is socialism. The trouble with capitalism is capitalists."

William F. Buckley, Jr., Quotations from Chairman Bill

The forces of a capitalist society, if left unchecked, tend to make the rich richer and the poor poorer.

Jawaharlal Nehru, as quoted in The New York Times
Magazine, September 7, 1958

If this country ever gets a system of governmental regulation, labor will suffer most.

William Green, president of the American Federation of
Labor, as quoted in Reader's Digest, February 1944

Too many businessmen never stop to ponder what they are doing; they reject the need for self-discipline; they are satisfied to be clever, when they need to be wise.

Louis Finkelstein, *Businessmen's Moral Failure*

To hire a man because he needs a job, rather than because the job needs him, is to assure him that he is useless. On the other side of the coin, to help a man because it is in your own interest to help him is to treat him as an equal.

Henry Ford, as quoted in *Reader's Digest*, October 1973

Labor unions are the worst thing that ever struck the earth because they take away a man's independence.

Henry Ford, from a booklet distributed to Ford workmen during the CIO organizing drive, 1936

A bank is a place where they lend you an umbrella in fair weather and ask for it back again when it begins to rain.

Robert Frost, as quoted in *Reader's Digest*, September 1949

After God had finished the rattlesnake, the toad, the vampire, He had some awful substance left with which He made a scab.

Jack London, as quoted in the *C.I.O. News*, Septmber 13, 1946

The man who gives me employment, which I must have or suffer, that man is my master, let me call him what I will.

Henry George, *Social Problems*

One of the chief arguments used in support of the policy of an open shop is that every man has an inalienable and constitutional right to work. I never found that in the Constitution. If a man has a constitutional right to work, he ought to have a constitutional right to a   205 job. . . . A man has a right to work only if he can get a job, and he has also a right not to work.

Clarence Darrow, in the Railroad Trainman, November
1909

With all their faults, trade unions have done more for humanity than any other organization of men that ever existed. They have done more for decency, for honesty, for education, for the betterment of the race, for the developing of character in man, than any other association of men.

Clarence Darrow, as quoted in the Railroad Trainman,
November 1909

No tin hat brigade of goose-stepping vigilantes or Bible-babbling mob of blackguarding and corporation-paid scoundrels will prevent the onward march of labor.

John L. Lewis, as quoted in Time, September 9, 1937

You can't dig coal with bayonets.

John L. Lewis, as quoted in the New York Post, March 1,
1956

Both business and labor have fostered the notion that any form of mandatory settlement will inhibit genuine efforts to reach agreement through bargaining. Yet it is difficult to see why the prospect of arbitration should stymie fruitful bargaining any more than the prospect of formal resolution of any other area of human disagreement would stymie voluntary settlement. Why not say that outlawing of duels inhibits private settlement of personal disputes?

O. Glenn Stahl, as quoted in *Reader's Digest*, October 1971

Nobody wins a strike against schoolchildren, or against the sick, or against bus or subway riders. We can avoid such strikes. The challenge is to improve collective bargaining—not to replace it.

Theodore W. Kheel, as quoted in *Reader's Digest*, August 1969

If capitalism is fair, then unionism must be. If men have a right to capitalize their ideas and the resources of their country, then that implies the right of men to capitalize their labor.

Frank Lloyd Wright, as quoted in *Labor*, May 2, 1959

A U. S. labor leader of an earlier generation summed up labor's philosophy in one four-letter word: "More." Nowadays the philosophy might be summed up in two four-letter words: "Much more." At times, indeed, organized labor seems to be chasing the delusion that a society can consume more than it produces, and that everybody can prosper by beggaring his neighbor. But wage increases in excess of productivity or output per man-hour are inevitably followed by unemployment or price increases or both. And it is the unorganized, the unemployed and the aged who pay.

Gilbert Burck, as quoted in *Reader's Digest*, April 1971

It is essential that there should be organizations of labor. This is an era of organization. Capital organizes and therefore labor must organize.

Theodore Roosevelt, speech in Milwaukee, October 14, 1912

Bulls and bears aren't responsible for as many stock losses as bum steers.

Olin Miller, as quoted in *Reader's Digest*, March 1936

Organizations and Organization Men

When a man retires and time is no longer a matter of urgent importance, his colleagues generally present him with a watch.

R. C. Sherriff, as quoted in Reader's Digest, July 1955

For each individual, for *you*, for *me*, the final promotion is from a level of competence to a level of incompetence. . . . In time, every post tends to be occupied by an employee who is incompetent to carry out its duties.

Laurence J. Peter and Raymond Hull, The Peter Principle

A tragic error occurs when a man who is doing a job well is promoted to a position of incompetence. It is almost impossible to unpromote him.

Laurence J. Peter and Raymond Hull, The Peter Principle

In most hierarchies, super-competence is more objectionable than incompetence. Ordinary incompetence, as we have seen, is no cause for dismissal: it is simply a bar to promotion. Super-competence often leads to dismissal, because it disrupts the hierarchy, and thereby violates the first commandment of hierarchical life: the hierarchy must be preserved.

Laurence J. Peter and Raymond Hull, The Peter Principle

It isn't the incompetent who destroy an organization. The incompetent never get in a position to destroy it. It is those who have achieved something and want to rest upon their achievements who are forever clogging things up.

Charles Sorenson, My 40 Years with Ford

It's going to be a tough decision when the purchasing agent starts negotiating to buy the machine that's to replace him.

Dave Murray, as quoted in Reader's Digest, November 1962

The mark of a true executive is usually illegible.

Leo J. Farrell, Jr., as quoted in *Reader's Digest*, December
1962

A good manager is a man who isn't worried about his own career but rather the careers of those who work for him. My advice: Don't worry about yourself. Take care of those who work for you and you'll float to greatness on their achievements.

H. S. M. Burns, as quoted in *Men at the Top*

The executive exists to make sensible exceptions to general rules.

Elting E. Morison, *Men, Machines and Modern Times*

Electronic engineers have yet to devise a better interoffice communications system than the water cooler.

Leo Ellis, as quoted in *Reader's Digest*, November
1961

Executive: A man who talks to visitors so the other employes can get their work done.

Cedric Adams, as quoted in Reader's Digest, June 1956

In the business world an executive knows something about everything, a technician knows everything about something—and the switchboard operator knows everything.

Harold Coffin, as quoted in Reader's Digest, May 1960

You can delegate authority, but you can never delegate responsibility for delegating a task to someone else. If you picked the right man, fine, but if you picked the wrong man, the responsibility is yours—not his.

Richard E. Krafve, as quoted in the Boston Globe, May 22, 1960

A former executive of a company which had been taken over in a corporate merger gave this description of what had happened to his company's executive personnel: "We got the mushroom treatment. Right after the acquisition we were kept in the dark. Then they covered us with manure. Then they cultivated us. After that they let us stew a while. Finally, they canned us."

Isadore Barmash, as quoted in Reader's Digest, March 1973

Taxes

There is just one thing I can promise you about the outer-space program: Your tax dollar will go farther.

Werner von Braun, as quoted in Reader's Digest, May 1961

The politician's promises of yesterday are the taxes of today.

W. L. Mackenzie King, as quoted in Reader's Digest,
February 1960

Collecting more taxes than is absolutely necessary is legalized robbery.

Calvin Coolidge, as quoted in The New York Times, March 6,
1955

Never sell America short. In what other country can a boy start with nothing and wind up with enough after taxes to give him a fresh start?

Fletcher Knebel, as quoted in Reader's Digest, December
1958

Our forefathers made one mistake. What they should have fought for was representation without taxation.

Fletcher Knebel, as quoted in Reader's Digest, March 1962

Trouble with being a breadwinner nowadays is that the Government is in for such a big slice.

Mary McCoy, as quoted in Reader's Digest, October 1955

Somebody has got to pay, but we would rather that somebody were somebody else. . . . We are placing the burdens on the broad shoulders. Why should I put burdens on the people?

David Lloyd George, on the "people's budget," July 30,
1909

Capital punishment: The income tax.

Jeff Hayes, as quoted in Reader's Digest, April 1957

Government bureau: Where the taxpayer's shirt is kept.

Herb Stein, as quoted in Reader's Digest, December 1951   211

There is one difference between a tax collector and a taxidermist—the taxidermist leaves the hide.

Mortimer J. Caplin, former director of the Internal
Revenue Service, as quoted in *Time*, February 1, 1963

America's tax system needs major surgery—now. Multimillion-dollar loopholes for certain industries and certain classes of individuals, combined with onerously high rates for the great mass of middle- and lower-income taxpayers, are endangering public confidence in the entire federal tax structure. The system cries out for fundamental, broad-scale reform—reform that can be accomplished.

Mortimer M. Caplin, former director of the Internal
Revenue Service, as quoted in *Reader's Digest*, September
1969

Instead of THINK, the signs on the wall of an Internal Revenue Service office say REMEMBER.

Art Paul, as quoted in *Reader's Digest*, April 1968

Blessed are the young, for they shall inherit the national debt.

Herbert Hoover, as quoted in *Reader's Digest*,
April 1965

We can trace the personal history of a man, and his successes and failures, just by looking at his tax returns from his first job to his retirement.

Charles Alden Church, as quoted in *The New York Times*,
March 10, 1964

Ah, for those good old days when Uncle Sam lived within his income—and without most of yours.

Barclay Braden, as quoted in *Reader's Digest*, February
1948

I've saved the money to pay my income tax, now all I have to do is borrow some to live on.

Lou Costello, as quoted in *Reader's Digest*, February 1942

I want to be the President who helped to feed the hungry and to prepare them to be taxpayers instead of tax eaters.

Lyndon B. Johnson, address to joint session of Congress
on voting rights for Negroes, March 15, 1965

Every person born in the U.S.A. is endowed with life, liberty and a substantial share of the national debt.

Francis Bacon, as quoted in *Reader's Digest*, March 1963

I'm proud to be paying taxes in the United States. The only thing is—I could be just as proud for half the money.

Arthur Godfrey, as quoted in *Reader's Digest*, October 1951

The Income Tax has made more Liars out of the American people than golf has.

Will Rogers, *The Illiterate Digest*

A man owes it to himself to become successful—after that he owes it to the Bureau of Internal Revenue.

Edward H. Dreschnack, as quoted in *Reader's Digest*, July 1951

Why does a slight tax increase cost you $200 and a substantial tax cut save you 30 cents?

Peg Bracken, *I Didn't Come Here to Argue*

Taxes are going up so fast that government is likely to price itself right out of the market.

Dan Bennett, as quoted in *Reader's Digest*, May 1960

In seventeen hundred and seventy-six
A group of American mavericks
Renounced a yoke of tyranny—
The tax on stamps, the tax on tea.
Our fathers felt that we were fit
To tax ourselves and you'll admit
We have been very good at it.

Howard Dietz, as quoted in Reader's Digest,
July 1961

The magnitude of our space program now taxes the imagination too.

Chester L. Marks, as quoted in Reader's Digest, December
1961

By most measures of private wealth, the United States is the world's richest country. But in terms of its ability to pay for public services, we seem almost to be going broke. . . . Americans will have to get used to

214

the idea that a greater portion of the country's wealth must be devoted to the public sector if they are to enjoy clean air, safe streets and better health and education. Paying the bill cannot be made pleasant. By reflecting on the observation of Justice Oliver Wendell Holmes that taxes are the price of civilization, it can perhaps be made at least tolerable.

Time essay, as quoted in *Reader's Digest*,
August 1972

Economy and Economics

Everyone is always in favor of general economy and particular expenditure.

Sir Anthony Eden, as quoted in *Reader's Digest*,
April 1959

If we are to establish the secure foundations of equal-opportunity society and master the sensitive arts of building a life-encouraging environment, then at this moment in history we need to realize that: Bigger is not better; slower may be faster; less may well mean more.

Stewart L. Udall, as quoted in *Urban Planning in
Transition*, edited by Ernest Erber

If the nation's economists were laid end to end, they would still point in all directions.

Arthur H. Motley, as quoted in *Reader's Digest*, February
1954

A recession is like an unfortunate love affair. It's a lot easier to talk your way in than it is to talk your way out.

Bill Vaughan, as quoted in *Reader's Digest*, July 1958   215

The truth is we are all caught in a great economic system which is heartless.

Woodrow Wilson, *The New Freedom*

America is like Gulliver in Lilliput—a giant, held down by a mass of small doubts and restrictions, needing only to exert the strength of its convictions to realize its full potential. The hard truth of the matter is that nothing—nothing—is needed to put this country on a full-employment basis except the decision to do it.

W. Willard Wirtz, *Labor and the Public Interest*

I favor the policy of economy, not because I wish to save money, but because I wish to save people.

Calvin Coolidge, as quoted in *Reader's Digest*, November
1961

Our nation's economy seems to be based on the belief that we shouldn't practice it.

> Harold Coffin, as quoted in *Reader's Digest*, March 1962

Inflation: When nobody has enough money because everybody has too much.

> Harold Coffin, as quoted in *Reader's Digest*, October 1956

A study of economics usually reveals that the best time to buy anything is last year.

> Marty Allen, as quoted in *Reader's Digest*, February 1960

We now know that anything which is economically right is also morally right; there can be no conflict between good economics and good morals.

> Henry Ford, as quoted in *Christian Morals* by T. Browne
> and Samuel Johnson, edited by S. C. Roberts

One of the most damaging misconceptions about economics is that inflation, somehow or other, promotes growth.

> Raymond J. Saulnier, as quoted in *Reader's Digest*, March
> 1970

If ignorance paid dividends, most Americans could make a fortune out of what they don't know about economics.

> Luther H. Hodges, as quoted in the *Wall Street Journal*,
> March 14, 1962

Productivity in the American economy—the output per man hour—has tended to go up at a rate of three percent a year, and with good economic management we can hold it at that rate or even increase it. In any event, that is all we have to distribute, and wage increases of ten percent a year are simply a monetary illusion.

> Arthur F. Burns, as quoted in *Reader's Digest*, January
> 1972

A completely planned economy ensures that when no bacon is delivered, no eggs are delivered at the same time.

J. L. Frain, as quoted in Time and Tide

There can't be anything too seriously wrong with the economy of a country whose most vexing problems are still: (1) how to reduce and (2) how to find a place to park.

General Melvin Maas, as quoted in Reader's Digest, August
1958

The mere absence of war is not peace. The mere absence of recession is not growth.

John F. Kennedy, speech, January 4, 1963

Planned economy: Where everything is included in the plans except economy.

Carey Williams, as quoted in Reader's Digest, June 1949

The instability of the economy is equaled only by the instability of economists.

John H. Williams, as quoted in The New York Times,
June 2, 1956

In the old days we used to say that when the United States economy sneezed the rest of the world went to bed with pneumonia. Now when the United States economy sneezes the other countries say *"Gesundheit."*

Walter W. Heller, as quoted in The New York Times, May 8,
1961

Democracy in economics, aristocracy in thought.

George V. Russell, as quoted in A Writer's Notebook by
W. Somerset Maugham

EDUCATION

Schools

You must adjust. . . . This is the legend imprinted in every school-book, the invisible message on every blackboard. Our schools have become vast factories for the manufacture of robots.

Dr. Robert Lindner, Must You Conform?

We must recover the element of quality in our traditional pursuit of equality. We must not, in opening our schools to everyone, confuse the idea that all should have equal chance with the notion that all have equal endowments.

Adlai E. Stevenson, address to the United Parents
Association, as quoted in The New York Times, April 6,
1958

Our schools are still set up as though every mother were at home all day and the whole family needed the summer to get the crops in.

Sidney Callahan, as quoted in Reader's Digest, October
1972

No greater nor more affectionate honor can be conferred on an American than to have a public school named after him.

Herbert Hoover, speech, June 5, 1956

What are our schools for if not indoctrination against Communism?

Richard M. Nixon, as quoted in Avant-Garde, January 1968

I feel that busing for the purpose of achieving racial balance in our schools is wrong, and that the great majority of Americans are right in wanting to bring it to an end.

The purpose of such busing is to help end segregation. But experience in case after case has shown that busing is a bad means to a good end. Recognition of that fact does not reduce our commitment to desegregation—it simply tells us we have to come up with a better means to that good end.

Richard M. Nixon, as quoted in Reader's Digest, June 1972

Schoolmasters and parents exist to be grown out of.

Sir John F. Wolfenden, as quoted in the London Sunday
Times, July 13, 1958

People don't learn to function very well in multiracial societies when they do all their learning in uniracial schools.

The choice is not "to bus or not to bus," but to teach children to read, and to live among the wide variety of people. We can either integrate—sometimes using buses as a tool—or we can choose to create a future generation of cripples, savages and bigots.

Roger Wilkins, as quoted in Reader's Digest, June 1972

In the Middle West, the high school is the place where the band practices.

Robert M. Hutchins, as quoted in the New York Herald
Tribune, April 22, 1963

I have never let my schooling interfere with my education.

Mark Twain, as quoted in Reader's Digest, October 1946

The bridges between the races are too few and fragile anyway, and they must be preserved at all costs. The best way to strengthen and increase them is not to try to force middle-class whites to send their children to school in the ghettos, but to open up middle-class jobs and the middle-class suburbs to Negroes.

Stewart Alsop, as quoted in Newsweek, February 23, 1970

"Whom are you?" said he, for he had been to night school.

George Ade, *Bang! Bang!*

Education is that which remains when one has forgotten everything he learned in school.

Albert Einstein, *Out of My Later Years*

Those who worry about radicalism in our schools and colleges are often either reactionaries who themselves do not bear allegiance to the traditional American principles, or defeatists who despair of the success of our own philosophy in an open competition.

James Bryant Conant, *Education in a Divided World*

The three R's of our school system must be supported by the T's—teachers who are superior, techniques of instruction that are modern, and thinking about education which places it first in all our plans and hopes.

Lyndon B. Johnson, message to Congress, January 12, 1965

The shocking presence of 11 million crippled readers contaminates virtually every aspect of education. . . . Primary responsibility for reading instruction, however, belongs to the schools. U. S. taxpayers foot a $38-billion annual bill for primary and secondary public education. What a tragic waste to spread this kind of educational banquet before 45 million children, and then fail to provide 11 million of them

223

with the reading skills—the knife and fork, if you will—essential for sharing in the feast!

James E. Allen, Jr., former U. S. Commissioner of Education, as quoted in *Reader's Digest*, April 1970

We send Johnny to school "to help him lead a better life in the future." But how many of us have taken the time to think seriously about what that future will be like? Most of us, teachers included, assume that today's way of life will be repeated in the future. Yet all the evidence points toward a radically changed tomorrow. Johnny must learn to anticipate the directions and rate of change. All of this will require broad, imaginative innovations in our educational system.

Alvin Toffler, *Future Shock*

Teachers

In one of the most famous and fateful incidents in the Bible, the Lord summoned Moses to the top of Mount Sinai. There he appeared to Moses in the form of a fiery cloud, and there—to the appropriate accompaniment of thunder and lightning—he presented Moses with the Ten Commandments. That, so far as I know, is the earliest recorded use of audio-visual techniques for mass education.

Harold Howe II, former U.S. Commissioner of Education, as quoted in *Reader's Digest*, February 1969

I wish that I could persuade every teacher in an elementary school to be proud of his occupation—not conceited or pompous, but proud. People who introduce themselves with the shameful remark that they are "just an elementary teacher" give me despair in my heart. Did you ever hear a lawyer say deprecatingly that he was only a little patent attorney? Did you ever hear a physician say "I am just a brain surgeon"? I beg of you to stop apologizing for being a member of the most important section of the most important profession in the world.

Draw yourself up to your full height, look anybody squarely in the eye, and say, *I am a teacher.*

> William G. Carr, as quoted in *Reader's Digest*, October 1946

Reformers are those who educate people to appreciate the things they need.

> Elbert Hubbard, *Note Book*

I took violin lessons from age 6 to 14, but had no luck with my teachers, for whom music did not transcend mechanical practicing. I really began to learn only after I had fallen in love with Mozart's sonatas. The attempt to reproduce their singular grace compelled me to improve my technique. I believe, on the whole, that love is a better teacher than sense of duty.

> Albert Einstein, as quoted in *Reader's Digest*, August 1972

The teaching of reading—all over the United States, in all the schools, in all the text books—is totally wrong and flies in the face of all logic and common sense. Johnny couldn't read . . . for the simple reason that nobody ever showed him how. Johnny's only problem was that he was unfortunately exposed to an ordinary American school.

> Rudolf Flesch, *Why Johnny Can't Read*

He who can, does. He who cannot, teaches.

> George Bernard Shaw, *Maxims for Revolutionists*

Educators, black and white, should speak out more boldly than they have against this corruption of the young by militants. This does not lessen the parallel responsibility of society to wipe out conditions which are the breeding ground for resentment and crime. But no social problem will be more rapidly solved through the calculated transformation of the chief sufferers into beings who wantonly rob and kill. Evil conditioning can only make evil conditions worse.

> Marie Syrkin, as quoted in *Reader's Digest*, February 1972

The close observer soon discovers that the teacher's task is not to implant facts but to place the subject to be learned in front of the learner and, through sympathy, emotion, imagination, and patience, to awaken in the learner the restless drive for answers and insights which enlarge the personal life and give it meaning.

Nathan M. Pusey, as quoted in *The New York Times*,
March 22, 1959

Teaching is not a lost art, but the regard for it is a lost tradition.

Jacques Barzun, as quoted in *Newsweek*, December 5, 1955

I never reprimand a boy in the evening—darkness and a troubled mind are a poor combination.

Frank Boyden, speech at Deerfield Academy, January 2,
1954

The greatest job of teachers is to cultivate talent until it ripens for the public to reap its bounty.

Jascha Heifetz, as quoted in *Newsweek*, February 11, 1963

You can teach a student a lesson for a day; but if you can teach him to learn by creating curiosity, he will continue the learning process as long as he lives.

Clay P. Bedford, as quoted in *Reader's Digest*, June 1969

Many a child called dull would advance rapidly under a patient, wise, and skillful teacher, and the teacher should be as conscientious in the endeavor to improve himself as he is to improve the child.

Fannie Jackson Coppin, in *Black Women in White America*

The specialist who is trained but uneducated, technically skilled but culturally incompetent, is a menace.

David B. Truman, speech in Chicago to Columbia
University alumni, April 15, 1964

I am quite sure that in the hereafter she will take me by the hand and lead me to my proper seat. I always have a great reverence for teachers. For teachers, both lay and clerical, and for nurses. They are the most underpaid people in the world for what they do.

Bernard M. Baruch, recalling one of his early teachers, as quoted in *The New York Times*, August 29, 1955

Experience is a hard teacher because she gives the test first, the lesson afterwards.

Vernon Law, Pittsburgh Pirates pitcher, as quoted in *This Week*, October 14, 1969

The best insurance against old age and disability is an interesting mind. In my life of professional teaching, I have never endeavored to make young men more efficient; I have tried to make them more interesting. I like to hang pictures on the walls of the mind; I like to make it possible for a man to live with himself, so that he will not be bored with himself.

William Lyon Phelps, as quoted in *Reader's Digest*, May 1939

The best teacher, until one comes to adult pupils, is not the one who knows most, but the one who is most capable of reducing knowledge to that simple compound of the obvious and the wonderful which slips into the infantile comprehension. A man of high intelligence, perhaps, may accomplish the thing by a conscious intellectual feat. But it is vastly easier to the man (or woman) whose habits of mind are naturally on the plane of a child's. The best teacher of children, in brief, is one who is essentially childlike.

H. L. Mencken, in the New York *Evening Mail*, January 23, 1918

If I had a child who wanted to be a teacher, I would bid him Godspeed as if he were going to a war. For indeed the war against prejudice, greed and ignorance is eternal, and those who dedicate themselves to it give their lives no less because they may live to see some fraction of the battle won.

James Hilton, as quoted in *Reader's Digest*, October 1946 227

In education, the closeness of students to a good and great man or woman is the finest we can offer our children.

Seymour St. John, as quoted in Vogue,
January 15, 1958

Students

Someone should invent a real educational toy for children—one that would teach the youngster to put it away when he's finished playing with it.

Monte Feuerstein, as quoted in Reader's Digest, August
1961

It is the malady of our age that the young are so busy teaching us that they have no time left to learn.

Eric Hoffer, Reflections on the Human Condition

I wouldn't attach too much importance to these student riots. I remember when I was a student at the Sorbonne in Paris I used to go out and riot occasionally.

John Foster Dulles, as quoted in The New York Times,
April 15, 1958

A student is not a professional athlete. . . . He is not a little politician or junior senator looking for angles . . . an amateur promoter, a gladhander, embryo Rotarian, cafe-society leader, quiz kid, or man about town. A student is a person who is learning to fulfill his powers and to find ways of using them in the service of mankind.

Harold Taylor, as quoted in the New York Herald Tribune,
September 3, 1956

A father who wants his children to get an education these days may have to pull a few wires—the television wire, the hi-fi wire and the radio wire.

Lavonne Mathison, as quoted in Reader's Digest,
November 1961

Reading should be for children an integral part of life, like eating and loving and playing. An early familiarity with books unconsciously introduces the child to a fundamental, liberating truth: that the largest part of the universe of space and time can never be apprehended by direct first-hand experience. The child who has never really understood this truth remains, in the most literal sense, mentally unbalanced.

Clifton Fadiman, as quoted in Reader's Digest, July 1962

If we turn our little children into performing intellectual seals, what will we have accomplished?

Trouble, that's what. For when we rush our children into clever performance of skills, when we organize their daily lives so that there is not a moment for inner contemplation, we decrease the possibilities for genuine thought and individual growth.

Eda LeShan, The Conspiracy Against Childhood   229

Two thirds of a person's intellectual development occurs before he even begins his formal education. For many children—particularly children of poverty—lack of intellectual stimulus then preordains almost certain disaster in school and adult life. "By the age of five or six," according to one report, "slum children trail so far behind middle-class children that they are already remedial cases."

> Evan McLeod Wylie, as quoted in the *PTA Magazine*, May 1970

To take a child's lunch from him is a great mistake. There is no use in attempting to teach a hungry child.

> Fannie Jackson Coppin, as quoted in *Black Women in White America*

Higher Education

Economists report that a college education adds many thousands of dollars to a man's lifetime income—which he then spends sending his son to college.

> Bill Vaughan, as quoted in *Reader's Digest*, December 1962

American students wait until they graduate before taking over the world. Students in other countries are demanding it in their freshman year.

> Bill Vaughan, as quoted in *Reader's Digest*, September 1960

It might be said now that I have the best of both worlds. A Harvard education and a Yale degree.

> John F. Kennedy, receiving honorary degree from Yale University, as quoted in *The New York Times*, June 12, 1962

The time may come when a course entitled "Repairman, TV" carries as much weight—and worth—as one called "English Lit., A.B."

William H. Stringer, as quoted in Reader's Digest,
December 1972

Two delusions fostered by higher education are that what is taught corresponds to what is learned, and that it will somehow pay off in money.

William Feather, as quoted in The William Feather
Magazine, July 1974

The peculiar thing about some Rhodes scholars is that they lose their Indiana accent after six months' residence in England, whereas when they return home, their Oxford accent clings to them for the rest of their lives.

William Feather, as quoted in The William Feather
Magazine, August 1974

I early learned that a Ph.D. thesis consists of transferring bones from one graveyard to another.

J. Frank Dobie, as quoted in Reader's Digest, September
1950 231

The aim of a college education is to teach you to know a good man when you see one.

William James, speaking at a women's college, as quoted in
Reader's Digest, February 1954

What the colleges . . . should at least try to give us is a general sense of what, under various disguises, *superiority* has always signified and may still signify. The feeling for a good human job anywhere, the admiration of the really admirable, the disesteem of what is cheap and trashy and impermanent—this is that we call the critical sense, the sense for ideal values. It is the better part of what men know as wisdom.

William James, *Memories and Studies*

I find the three major administrative problems on a campus are sex for the students, athletics for the alumni, and parking for the faculty.

Clark Kerr, as quoted in *Time*, November 17, 1958

The freshmen bring a little in and the seniors take none out, so it accumulates through the years.

President Lowell of Harvard explaining why universities
have so much learning, as quoted in *Reader's Digest*, May
1949

Those who go to college and never get out are called professors.

George Givot, as quoted in *Reader's Digest*, April 1936

The idea that going to college is one of the inherent rights of man seems to have obtained a baseless foothold in the minds of many of our people.

A. Lawrence Lowell, address at Haverford College, April 17,
1931

The best way to see America nowadays is to try to get your son, or daughter, into college.

Earl Wilson, as quoted in *Reader's Digest*, January 1961

How ironic it will be if history records that the most democratic educational system in the world produced an educated class that could not lead because it could not conceal its contempt for the people who might have been its followers!

John W. Gardner, *Recovery of Confidence*

Students don't come to the university to educate themselves. They throw themselves down in front of their teachers like a pile of boards to be turned into furniture.

William A. Albrecht, as quoted in *Reader's Digest*, May 1961

The scramble to get into college is going to be so terrible in the next few years that students are going to put up with almost anything, even an education.

Barnaby C. Keeney, as quoted in *Time*, August 1955

What we need for young men and women in America now are two things. First, all who want higher education and cannot now get it should be given a chance to get it. Second—and this applies especially to the upper middle class—all who don't want higher education, or are not sure they want it should have the freedom to postpone college or not go to college at all.

S. I. Hayakawa, as quoted in *Reader's Digest*, November 1970

Let the clever young blacks go to a university to study engineering, medicine, chemistry, economics, law, agriculture and comparable subjects. And let the clever whites go to college to read black novels, to learn Swahili, and to record the exploits of Negro heroes of the past: they are the ones to whom this will come as an eye-opener.

Sir Arthur Lewis, as quoted in *University: A Princeton Quarterly*, August 1969

A college education is usually the most expensive product—aside from a house—that a parent can buy. At a good private college, it costs more than two Cadillacs; at a public university in one's home state, more than a Lincoln Continental.

Loren Pope, as quoted in *Reader's Digest*, December 1972

Why is it that the boy or girl who on June 15 receives his degree, eager, enthusiastic, outspoken, idealistic, reflective, and independent, is on the following September 15, or even on June 16 . . . dull, uninspiring, shifty, pliable and attired in a double-breasted blue serge suit? The answer must lie in the relative weakness of the higher education, compared with the forces that make everybody think and act like everybody else.

Robert Hutchins, as quoted in *Time*, February 12, 1951

It is not so important to be serious as to be serious about the important things. The monkey wears an expression of seriousness which would do credit to any college student, but the monkey is serious because he itches!

Robert Hutchins, as quoted in *Quote*, August 3, 1958

The college graduate is presented with a sheepskin to cover his intellectual nakedness.

Robert Hutchins, as quoted in *Reader's Digest*, August 1940

Our American professors like their literature clear and cold and pure and very dead.

Sinclair Lewis, address in Stockholm, December 12, 1930, upon receiving the Nobel Prize for literature

The right to interfere with the rights of others is no part of academic freedom.

Grayson Kirk, as quoted in *The New York Times*, June 4,
1965

The ends are achieved by indirect means—something said in private conversation one day in the street, a remark by a teacher in the middle of a discussion, a book picked up in someone's room.

Harold Taylor, as quoted in *Saturday Review*, January 7,
1961

One way to stop a student-protest movement is to make it a required course.

Jerry Robinson, as quoted in *Reader's Digest*, April 1968

I'm still waiting for some college to come up with a march protesting student ignorance.

Paul Larmer, as quoted in *Reader's Digest*, February 1967

It takes me several days, after I get back to Boston, to realize that the reference "the president" refers to the president of Harvard and not to a minor official in Washington.

Oliver Wendell Holmes, as quoted in *Reader's Digest*,
November 1936

Four-fifths of our undergraduates feel inferior for life.

Nathan M. Pusey, *Observations on Education in a
Troubled Decade*

Will "black studies" really lead to higher black achievement? Or will black separatists find easy refuge in a reverse-racist cocoon, instead of facing their more important task—preparing to be doctors, lawyers and the like—in the larger American community?

Joseph Alsop, as quoted in *Reader's Digest*, May 1969   235

The chief value in going to college is that it's the only way to learn it really doesn't matter.

> George Edwin Howes, as quoted in *Reader's Digest*,
> January 1952

Be part of the answer, not part of the problem, as the American revolution proceeds.

> Buell G. Gallagher, address to graduating class of City
> College, New York, June 18, 1964

The American university system is built on the two false premises that all teachers must add to the existing stock of knowledge by research and that all self-respecting institutions fulfill their role only by employing productive scholars.

> Jacques Barzun, as quoted in *Reader's Digest*, June 1961

Lecture: Something that can make you feel numb on one end and dumb on the other.

> Cy N. Peace, as quoted in *Reader's Digest*, October 1956

As a general proposition, colleges are best administered by administrators, next best by faculty, and most worst by students.

> William F. Buckley, Jr., *Quotations from Chairman Bill*

A college education is a taste for knowledge, a taste for philosophy, a capacity to explore, question and perceive relationships between fields of knowledge and experience.

> A. Whitney Griswold, as quoted in *The New York Times*,
> April 20, 1963

Fathers send their sons to college either because they went to college or because they didn't.

236

> L. L. Hendren, as quoted in *Reader's Digest*, March 1936

Surely the shortest commencement address in history—and for me one of the most memorable—was that of Dr. Harold E. Hyde, president of New Hampshire's Plymouth State College. He reduced his message to the graduating class to these three ideals: "Know thyself—Socrates. Control yourself—Cicero. Give yourself—Christ."

Walter T. Tatara, as quoted in Reader's Digest, March 1973

I feel about my work as President Eliot felt about Harvard: "Things seem to be going fairly well, now that a spirit of pessimism prevails in all departments."

Van Wyck Brooks, A Chilmark Miscellany

If you feel that you have both feet planted on level ground, then the university has failed you.

Robert Goheen, as quoted in Time, June 23, 1961

Education and the Educated

Learning learns but one lesson: Doubt!

George Bernard Shaw, The Admirable Bashville

Today, educational levels are replacing class structures as the significant vertical stratification of society. Income and status distinctions are based upon education, all over the world. . . .

We have recently turned an important corner from which we can now see that greater equality does not necessarily mean greater   237 homogeneity. Blacks can have equality without forcing those blacks who cherish negritude to become just like whites. Women can become more equal *and* also more feminine. Possibly—and this may be the hardest task of the next 50 years—we may even discover how to preserve and enhance the self-respect of those who fall far behind in the education race.

Max Ways, as quoted in Reader's Digest, June 1972

At the desk where I sit, I have learned one great truth. The answer for all our national problems—the answer for all the problems of the world—comes down to a single word. That word is "education."

Lyndon B. Johnson, address to the bicentenary
convocation at Brown University, September 28, 1964

We have entered an age in which education is not just a luxury permitting some men an advantage over others. It has become a necessity without which a person is defenseless in this complex, industrialized society. . . . We have truly entered the century of the educated man.

Lyndon B. Johnson, Tufts University commencement
address, June 9, 1963

We must open the doors of opportunity. But we must also equip our people to walk through those doors.

Lyndon B. Johnson, address at National Urban League
conference, Washington, D. C., December 10, 1964

The library is not a shrine for the worship of books. It is not a temple where literary incense must be burned or where one's devotion to the bound book is expressed in ritual. A library, to modify the famous metaphor of Socrates, should be the delivery room for the birth of ideas—a place where history comes to life.

Norman Cousins, as quoted in the American Library
Association Bulletin, October 1954

The vice of the modern notion of mental progress is that it is always something concerned with the breaking of bonds, the effacing of boundaries, the casting away of dogmas.

G. K. Chesterton, Heretics

Man's fear of ideas is probably the greatest dike holding back human knowledge and happiness.

Morris L. Ernst, as quoted in Reader's Digest, August 1973

There is no common faith, no common body of principle, no common body of knowledge, no common moral and intellectual discipline. . . . We have established a system of education in which we insist that while everyone must be educated, yet there is nothing in particular that an educated man must know.

Walter Lippmann, address to the American Association for
the Advancement of Science, December 29, 1940

A little learning is *not* a dangerous thing to one who does not mistake it for a great deal.

William Allen White, as quoted in Reader's Digest, August
1958

You ought not to educate a woman as if she were a man, or to educate her as if she were not.

George N. Shuster, The Ground I Walked On

Self-education is fine when the pupil is a born educator.

John A. Shedd, Salt from My Attic

The test of a truly educated man is what he is, and what he thinks, and what his mind absorbs, or dreams, or creates, when he is alone.

Donald K. David, as quoted in Reader's Digest, June 1950   239

Education doesn't change life much. It just lifts trouble to a higher plane of regard. . . . College is a refuge from hasty judgment.

Robert Frost, as quoted in *Quote*, July 9, 1961

Education is the ability to listen to almost anything without losing your temper or your self-confidence.

Robert Frost, as quoted in *Reader's Digest*, April 1960

The more a man thinks, the better adapted he becomes to thinking, and education is nothing if it is not the methodical creation of the habit of thinking.

Ernest Dimnet, as quoted in *Reader's Digest*, March 1962

Education is a kind of continuing dialogue, and a dialogue assumes, in the nature of the case, different points of view.

240

Robert Hutchins, as quoted in *Time*, December 8, 1952

The object of education is to prepare the young to educate themselves throughout their lives.

Robert Hutchins, as quoted in *Reader's Digest*, November 1973

My idea of education is to unsettle the minds of the young and to inflame their intellects.

Robert Hutchins, as quoted in *Reader's Digest*, July 1935

Creative minds always have been known to survive any kind of bad training.

Anna Freud, annual Freud lecture to the New York Psychoanalytic Society, 1968

I am defeated, and know it, if I meet any human being from whom I find myself unable to learn anything.

George Herbert Palmer, as quoted in *Reader's Digest*, August 1937

We have created for ourselves a manner of living in America in which a little learning can no longer serve our needs.

Nathan M. Pusey, *The Age of the Scholar: Observations of Education in a Troubled Decade*

When we look at the troubled state of the present world . . . one thing becomes manifest. This is the failure of recent educational practice to prepare men in terms of heart and will to prevent the strife, misunderstanding, and willfulness that now arise.

Nathan M. Pusey, *Religion and Freedom of Thought*

The true business of liberal education is greatness.

Nathan M. Pusey, as quoted in *Time*, March 1, 1954   241

Love of learning is seldom unrequited.

Arnold H. Glasow, as quoted in *Reader's Digest*, February 1963

There is nothing so stupid as an educated man, if you get off the thing that he was educated in.

Will Rogers, as quoted in *On the Meaning of Life*

Intelligence appears to be the thing that enables a man to get along without education. Education appears to be the thing that enables a man to get along without the use of his intelligence.

Albert E. Wiggam, *The New Decalogue of Science*

There is no lack of opportunity for learning among us. What is lacking is a respect for it . . . an honest respect such as we now have for technical competence or business success. . . . We honor learning, but we do not believe in it. We reward it with lengthy obituaries and a wretched living wage. Rather than submit to it ourselves, we hire substitutes; rather than cultivate our own brains, we pick theirs. We spend as much time and energy on short-cuts to learning and imitations of learning as we do on learning itself.

A. Whitney Griswold, address to the American Academy and National Institute of Arts and Letters, May 22, 1958

In the long run of history, the censor and the inquisitor have always lost. The only sure weapon against bad ideas is better ideas. The source of better ideas is wisdom. The surest path to wisdom is a liberal education.

A. Whitney Griswold, *Essays on Education*

To be able to be caught up into the world of thought—that is educated.

Edith Hamilton, as quoted in the *Saturday Evening Post*, September 27, 1958

Education is discipline for the adventure of life.

Alfred North Whitehead, as quoted in *Reader's Digest*,
February 1967

The man who reads only for improvement is beyond the hope of much improvement before he begins.

Jonathan Daniels, *Three Presidents and Their Books*

The ability to think straight, some knowledge of the past, some vision of the future, some skill to do useful service, some urge to fit that service into the well-being of the community—these are the most vital things education must try to produce. If we can achieve them in the citizens of our land, then, given the right to knowledge and the free use thereof, we shall have brought to America the wisdom and the courage to match her destiny.

Virginia C. Gildersleeve, *Many a Good Crusade*

Discipline means power at command; mastery of the resources available for carrying through the actions undertaken. To know what one is to do and to move to do it promptly and by the use of the requisite means is to be disciplined whether we are thinking of an army or the mind. Discipline is positive.

John Dewey, *Democracy and Education*

There may be times when men and women in the turmoil of change lose touch with the civilized gains of centuries of education; but the gains of education are never really lost. Books may be burned and cities sacked, but truth, like the yearning for freedom, lives in the hearts of humble men and women. The ultimate victory of tomorrow is with democracy, and through democracy with education, for no people in all the world can be kept eternally ignorant or eternally enslaved.

Franklin D. Roosevelt, address to the National Education
Association, New York City, June 30, 1938

Being educated means to prefer the best not only to the worst but to the second best.

William Lyon Phelps, as quoted in Reader's Digest, August 1962

The trouble with present-day education is that it covers the ground without cultivating anything in it.

E. N. Ferris, as quoted in Reader's Digest, January 1941

The primary purpose of education is not to teach you to earn your bread, but to make every mouthful sweeter.

James Angell, as quoted in Reader's Digest, November 1963

The uneducated tend to overvalue their own abilities.

Admiral Hyman G. Rickover, in the Saturday Evening Post, November 28, 1959

Education would be much more effective if its purpose was to ensure that by the time they leave school every boy and girl should know how much they do *not* know, and be imbued with a lifelong desire to know it.

Sir William Haley, as quoted in Reader's Digest, December 1963

The imposition of passive self-images can seriously hinder intellectual creativity.

Dr. Mary Daly, as quoted in Sisterhood Is Powerful

I respect faith, but doubt is what gets you an education.

Wilson Mizner, as quoted in Reader's Digest, March 1943

The end product of education, yours and mine and everybody's, is the total pattern of reactions and possible reactions we have inside ourselves.

S. I. Hayakawa, in the Saturday Evening Post, December 27,
1958

There are only two ways of changing men—one is by education of spirit, mind, and body, and the other is by violence. . . . Education is the one peaceful technique for creating changes for the better.

Howard H. Brinton, as quoted in The Quaker Approach to
Contemporary Problems

Thinking is like loving and dying. Each of us must do it for himself.

Josiah Royce, as quoted in Reader's Digest,
May 1963

A democratic form of government, a democratic way of life, presupposes free public education over a long period; it presupposes also an education for personal responsibility that too often is neglected.

Eleanor Roosevelt, Let Us Have Faith in Democracy

I am always ready to learn, although I do not always like being taught.

Sir Winston Churchill, as quoted in Reader's Digest, April
1957

My definition of an educated man is the fellow who knows the right thing to do at the time it has to be done. . . . You can be sincere and still be stupid.

Charles F. Kettering, as quoted in The Professional
Amateur

245

Adults can learn most things better than children, though it may take them longer.

Cyril O. Houle, *Continuing Your Education*

The most important function of education at any level is to develop the personality of the individual and the significance of his life to himself and to others. This is the basic architecture of a life; the rest is ornamentation and decoration of the structure.

Grayson Kirk, as quoted in *Quote,* January 27, 1963

It is true that education is intended to benefit the entire personality. But it is not possible, not even desirable, to show that many of the most important subjects which are taught as part of education will make the learner rich, fit him for social life or find him a job.

Some values must be postulated. Poetry is better than pinball. The man who does not know anything about biology is in that respect inferior to the man who does, even though he may be richer. Training in philosophy makes few men wealthy, but it satisfies an instinct in them which cries for fulfillment.

Gilbert Highet, as quoted in *Reader's Digest,* February 1972

Human history becomes more and more a race between education and catastrophe.

H. G. Wells, *The Outline of History*

The test and the use of man's education is that he finds pleasure in the exercise of his mind.

Jacques Barzun, in the *Saturday Evening Post,* May 3, 1958

The principal goal of education is to create men who are capable of doing new things, not simply of repeating what other generations have done—men who are creative, inventive and discoverers.

Jean Piaget, as quoted in *Reader's Digest,* August 1969

It is one of the failures of American philosophy that we confuse education and intelligence as much as we confuse plumbing and civilization. One ounce of intelligence is worth a pound of education, for where there is intelligence education will advance on its own, but where education alone exists the results can be terrifying beyond even the realms of untutored stupidity.

> Louis Bromfield, as quoted in *Reader's Digest*, August 1951

Love of learning is a pleasant and universal bond, since it deals with what one *is* and not what one *has*.

> Freya Stark, *The Journey's Echo*

Knowledge and Ignorance

It is harder to conceal ignorance than to acquire knowledge.

> Arnold Glasow, as quoted in *Reader's Digest*, April 1961

When the ignorant are taught to doubt they do not know what they safely may believe.

> Justice Oliver Wendell Holmes, Jr., *Law and the Court*

I find that a great part of the information I have was acquired by looking up something and finding something else on the way.

> Franklin P. Adams, as quoted in *Reader's Digest*, October
> 1960

I don't know what a moron is,
    And I don't give a damn.
I'm thankful that I am not one—
    My God! Perhaps I am.

> Henry Pratt Fairchild, as quoted in *Harper's Magazine*,
> May 1932   247

Genius is the ability to put into effect what is in your mind.

F. Scott Fitzgerald, *The Crack-up*

Piling up knowledge is as bad as piling up money. You have to begin sometime to kick around what you know.

Robert Frost, as quoted in *Reader's Digest*, February 1971

Genuine ignorance is . . . profitable because it is likely to be accompanied by humility, curiosity, and openmindedness; whereas ability to repeat catch-phrases, cant terms, familiar propositions, gives the conceit of learning and coats the mind with varnish waterproof to new ideas.

John Dewey, *Democracy and Education*

Effective knowledge is that which includes knowledge of the limitations of one's knowledge.

S. I. Hayakawa, as quoted in *Reader's Digest*, January 1968

Strange how much you've got to know before you know how little you know.

Duncan Stuart, as quoted in *Reader's Digest*, March 1974

Nothing in education is so astonishing as the amount of ignorance it accumulates in the form of inert facts.

Henry Adams, *The Education of Henry Adams*

Imagination is more important than knowledge.

Albert Einstein, as quoted in *Reader's Digest*,
May 1970

More trouble is caused in this world by indiscreet answers than by indiscreet questions.

Sydney J. Harris, as quoted in the Chicago *Daily News*,
March 27, 1958

To know a little less and to understand a little more: that, it seems to me, is our greatest need.

James Ramsey Ullman, as quoted in *Reader's Digest*,
March 1948

The larger the island of knowledge, the longer the shore line of wonder.

Rev. Ralph Sockman, *Now to Live!*

Smart's one of the grandest feelings there is but hard to hang onto. It rarely persists full-strength past first grade. Higher education and the lessons of life tend to humble a person well before middle age.

Joan Mills, as quoted in *Reader's Digest*, 1970

Knowledge is the only instrument of production that is not subject to diminishing returns.

J. M. Clark, *Overhead Costs in Modern Industry*   **249**

Everybody is ignorant, only on different subjects.

Will Rogers, *The Illiterate Digest*

A retentive memory may be a good thing, but the ability to forget is the true token of greatness.

Elbert Hubbard, *Note Book*

HEALTH

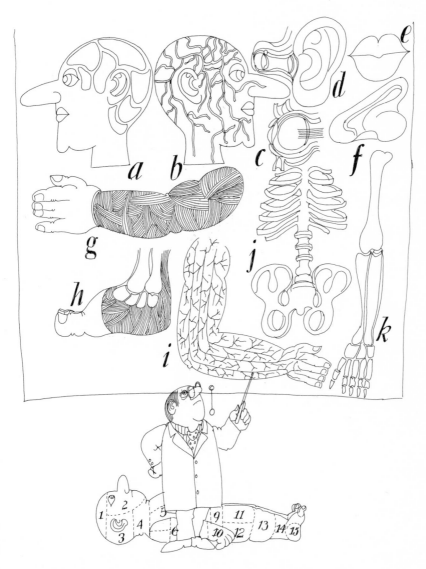

Doctors and Medicine

A man will bleed to death from a severed artery in three minutes. You can block this artery in two minutes if you are not in a hurry.

Don Herold, as quoted in *Reader's Digest*, January 1938

If a man is good in his heart, then he is an ethical member of any group in society. If he is bad in his heart, he is an unethical member. To me, the ethics of medical practice is as simple as that.

Dr. Elmer Hess, former president of the AMA, as quoted in the *American Weekly*, April 1955

The most thoughtful doctor I know holds a child's tongue down with a lollipop when he has to look down a small throat.

Elizabeth Metcalf, as quoted in *Reader's Digest*, September 1946

The longer I practice medicine, the more I am convinced every physician should cultivate lying as a fine art. There are lies which contribute enormously to the success of the physician's mission of mercy and salvation.

Dr. Joseph Collins, as quoted in *Reader's Digest*, May 1933

If you think you have caught a cold, call in a good doctor. Call in three doctors and play bridge.

Robert Benchley, *How to Avoid Colds*   253

We live on one third of what we eat and the doctors live on the rest.

Royal S. Copeland, M.D. and former Senator, as quoted in
Reader's Digest, March 1934

As with eggs, there is no such thing as a poor doctor; doctors are either
good or bad.

Dr. Fuller Albright, *Textbook of Medicine*

Our doctor would never really operate unless it was necessary. He
was just that way. If he didn't need the money, he wouldn't lay a hand
on you.

Herb Shriner, as quoted in *Reader's Digest*, June 1955

Every day you hear of something new in medicine . . . the latest is a
new wonder drug that's so powerful you have to be in perfect health to
take it.

Herb Shriner, as quoted in *Reader's Digest*, June 1955

They answered as they took their fees,
"There is no cure for this disease."

Hilaire Belloc, *Cautionary Tales*

One of the new miracle drugs is inexpensive. That's the miracle.

Harold Coffin, as quoted in *Reader's Digest*, January 1960

It's a shame we can't call a new tranquilizer "Dammitol."

Dr. Frederick Yonkman, on the problem of naming new
drugs, as quoted in *Reader's Digest*, September 1958

Doctors are given to claiming that medicine is both an art and a
science. The fact is that until a half-century ago it was virtually all art,
with scarcely a modicum of science. Recently, it has become virtually

all science, and whatever art remains has often been obscured by materialism and poor organization.

Time, February 21, 1969

A specialist is a man who knows more and more about less and less.

Dr. William J. Mayo, as quoted in *Reader's Digest*, November 1927

We now feel we can cure the patient without his fully understanding what made him sick. We are no longer so interested in peeling the onion as in changing it.

Dr. Franz Alexander, as quoted in *Time*, May 19, 1961

Some tortures are physical and some
  are mental.
But one that's both is dental.

Ogden Nash, as quoted in *Reader's Digest*, July 1952

Let no one suppose that the words doctor and patient can disguise from the parties the fact that they are employer and employee.

George Bernard Shaw, *The Doctor's Dilemma*

I learned why they're called wonder drugs—you wonder what they'll do to you.

Harlan Miller, as quoted in *Reader's Digest*, April 1953

The best doctor in the world is the Veterinarian. He can't ask his patients what is the matter—he's got to just know.

Will Rogers, *The Autobiography of Will Rogers*

A good gulp of hot whisky at bedtime—it's not very scientific, but it helps.

Sir Alexander Fleming, discoverer of penicillin, on the treatment for the common cold, as quoted in news summaries of March 22, 1954

In the final analysis, a dying person and his family can rely on an ancient pact, unwritten and usually unspoken, between a good doctor and his patient. It is simply that the doctor, backed by his training, experience and the entire history of medicine, has but the single mission of doing what is best for each individual under his care.

Leonard A. Stevens, as quoted in *Reader's Digest*, May 1969

Keep away from physicians. It is all probing and guessing and pretending with them. They leave it to Nature to cure in her own time, but they take the credit. As well as very fat fees.

Anthony Burgess, *Nothing Like the Sun*

The desire to take medicine is perhaps the greatest feature which distinguishes man from animals.

Harvey Cushing, as quoted in *Reader's Digest*, June 1938

Surgery is always second best. If you can do something else, it's better. Surgery is limited. It is operating on someone who has no place else to go.

Dr. John Kirklin, heart surgeon at the Mayo Clinic, as quoted in *Time*, May 3, 1963

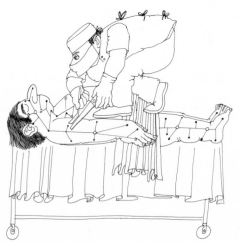

Medicine, the only profession that labors incessantly to destroy the reason for its own existence.

James Bryce, address, March 23, 1914

Mental Health

Neurotic: A person who has discovered the secret of perpetual emotion.

Dan Bennett, as quoted in *Reader's Digest*, April 1957

A neurotic is the man who builds a castle in the air. A psychotic is the man who lives in it. And a psychiatrist is the man who collects the rent.

Lord Webb-Johnson, as quoted in *Look*,
October 16, 1958

Being a good psychoanalyst . . . has the same disadvantage as being a good parent: the children desert one as they grow up.

Dr. Morton Hunt, as quoted in *The New York Times*,
November 24, 1957

A vigorous five-mile walk will do more good for an unhappy but otherwise healthy adult than all the medicine and psychology in the world.

Dr. Paul Dudley White, as quoted in *Reader's Digest*,
January 1972

The great majority of neuroses in women have their origin in the marriage bed.

Sigmund Freud, *Studies in Hysteria*   257

It might be said of psychoanalysis that if you give it your little finger it will soon have your whole hand.

Sigmund Freud, Introductory Lectures on Psychoanalysis

Psychiatry is the art of teaching people how to stand on their own feet while reclining on couches.

Shannon Fife, as quoted in Reader's Digest, August 1962

Madness comes from the refusal to develop, to adjust, to dilute one's true self in the sordid mush of the world. If we want to find the true self of each of us, we must go to the county lunatic asylum.

Gerald Brennan, A Holiday by the Sea

I'm grateful I was born before the psychiatrists got loose. They're a real danger. I was never frustrated in my life until I lied, stole, cheated and kicked my brother. Then I was frustrated and in the very spot children should be frustrated.

Lady Nancy Astor, as quoted in Reader's Digest, July 1951

If you treat a sick child like an adult and a sick adult like a child, everything usually works out pretty well.

Ruth Carlisle, as quoted in Reader's Digest, January 1969

A dream that is not understood, says the Talmud, is like an unopened letter. Every night we have important messages from the unconscious. Whether we are in a car plunging down a steep slope, or piloting a plane through heavenly skies, we will do well to ask why our unconscious puts us there.

Blake Clark, as quoted in Reader's Digest, September 1972

If you see a snake coming toward you in a jungle, you have a right to be anxious. If you see it coming down Park Avenue, you're in trouble.

Dr. Theodor Reik, psychiatrist, as quoted in *Saturday Review*, January 11, 1958

The man who once cursed his fate, now curses himself—and pays his psychoanalyst.

John W. Gardner, *No Easy Victories*

Kindliness antedates psychiatry by hundreds of years; its antiquity should not lessen your opinion of its usefulness.

Dr. J. Roswell Gallagher, as quoted in *Reader's Digest*, April 1961

This is a do-it-yourself test for paranoia: you know you've got it when you can't think of anything that's your fault.

Robert Hutchins, as quoted in *Reader's Digest*, January 1972

Love—incomparably the greatest psychotherapeutic agent—is something that professional psychiatry cannot of itself create, focus, nor release.

Gordon W. Allport, *The Individual and His Religion*

Fortunately psychoanalysis is not the only way to resolve inner conflict. Life still remains a very effective therapist.

Dr. Karen Horney, as quoted in *Reader's Digest*, November 1960

The repressed memory is like a noisy intruder being thrown out of the concert hall. You can throw him out, but he will hang on the door and continue to disturb the concert. The analyst opens the door and says, "If you promise to behave yourself, you can come back in."

Dr. Theodor Reik, as quoted in *Saturday Review*, January 11, 1958

Anybody who would go to a psychiatrist ought to have his head examined.

Samuel Goldwyn, as quoted in *Reader's Digest*, December 1948

Mental health problems do not affect three or four out of every five persons but one out of one.

Dr. William Menninger, as quoted in *The New York Times*, November 22, 1957

To "know thyself" must mean to know the malignancy of one's own instincts and to know as well one's power to deflect it.

Dr. Karl Menninger, as quoted in *Vogue*, June 1961

Man is tied to the weight of his own past, and even by a great therapeutic labor little more can be accomplished than a shifting of the burden.

Philip Rieff, preface to *Freud: The Mind of the Moralist*

To understand oneself is the classic form of consolation; to elude oneself is the romantic.

George Santayana, Winds of Doctrine

Psychology, which explains everything,
Explains nothing,
And we are still in doubt.

Marianne Moore, Collected Poems

We now feel we can cure the patient without his fully understanding what made him sick. We are no longer so interested in peeling the onion as in changing it.

Dr. Franz Alexander, address marking the 50th anniversary
of the organized practice of psychoanalysis in the U. S., as
quoted in Time, May 19, 1961

Dreaming permits each and every one of us to be quietly and safely insane every night of our lives.

Dr. William Dement, as quoted in Newsweek, November 30,
1959

The brain is viewed as an appendage of the genital glands.

Carl Jung, on Freudian psychology, as quoted in Time,
February 14, 1955

Yes, how indeed? He copes, like everybody else, as well as he can, that's all. And it's usually deplorable enough.

Carl Jung, on how a psychiatrist deals with his own
personal problems, as quoted in Portraits of Greatness by
Yousef Karsh

Man's task is to become conscious of the contents that press upward from the unconscious. . . . As far as we can discern, the sole purpose of human existence is to kindle a light in the darkness of mere being. It   261 may even be assumed that just as the unconscious affects us, increase in our consciousness likewise affects the unconscious.

Carl Jung, *Memories, Dreams, Reflections*

Health and Illness

The trouble with being a hypochondriac these days is that antibiotics have cured all the good diseases.

Caskie Stinnet, *Out of the Red*

It's funny, you can always say that your foot hurts, and it sounds all right; but if you say that your feet hurt, it sounds perfectly lousy.

Joan Crawford, as quoted in *Reader's Digest*, September 1936

When it comes to your health, I recommend frequent doses of that rare commodity among Americans—common sense. We are rapidly becoming a land of hypochondriacs, from the ulcer-and-martini executives in the big city to the patent medicine patrons in the sulphur-and-molasses belt.

Dr. Vincent Askey, speech to a medical convention, Bakersfield, California, October 1960

Very few people go to a doctor when they have a cold. They go to the theater instead.

W. Boyd Gatewood, as quoted in *Reader's Digest*, June 1949

There are no diseases of the aged, but simply diseases among the aged.

Dr. Leonard Larsen, former president of American Medical Association, to U. S. Senate Finance Committee, June 1960

Last year, the United States spent an estimated $83 billion for all health purposes, and there is much to be said for what those dollars bought. But our great challenge now is to make the system work better for everybody. Somehow, without creating a giant federal health-care bureaucracy, we must endeavor to lift the fear and worry from the sick in this country.

Paul Friggens, as quoted in Reader's Digest, October 1973

I have never yet met a healthy person who worried very much about his health, or a really good person who worried much about his own soul.

J. B. S. Haldane, Adventures of a Biologist

The major puzzle is that acupuncture as I observed it apparently does induce a certain relaxation in selected patients and helps them to endure surgical procedures that would be quite frightening to most people. Frankly, I'm as mystified by this as is anyone else who has seen it. . . .

I think that the calm behavior of the patients I saw may have a psychological rather than physiological explanation. Perhaps it is a form of self-hypnosis. I don't know. We should continue to examine it until we do have a rational explanation that either confirms or denies its usefulness. I frankly doubt that the results will significantly affect world medicine.

Dr. Michael E. DeBakey, with Don A. Schanche, as quoted
in Reader's Digest, September 1973

I have seen soul grow while bodies shrivel and the really great things of life unfold to a man when all that the world prizes most have been denied.

Dr. Edward L. Trudeau, letter to J. L. Waring, December
1907

Scientists studying the link between hunger and child development say there is little hope that a poor child—handicapped by hunger—can later pull himself out of poverty unaided. The school lunchroom may be the place to break the poverty cycle that goes on from generation to generation.

Lester Velie, as quoted in *Reader's Digest*,
March 1970

Is society ready to analyze death and the prolongation of life in terms of cost-benefit analysis, or to consider shifting the use of expensive facilities from the hopelessly ill to those whose future holds more promise? . . . A society increasingly concerned about the quality of life cannot omit the final chapter from its concern.

Dael Wolfle, as quoted in *Science*, June 19, 1970

Americans are unfit for human consumption. Animals which have seven parts for every million of DDT in their fatty tissues are judged in the United States to be unfit to eat. And it is now disclosed that the average American has 12 parts per million of the pesticide in his body.

Richard Scott, as quoted in *Reader's Digest*,
March 1970

What is the thing called health? Simply a state in which the individual happens transiently to be perfectly adapted to his environment. Obviously, such states cannot be common, for the environment is in constant flux.

H. L. Mencken, as quoted in *The American Mercury*,
March 1930

I have discovered that the flu is both affirmative and negative. Sometimes the eyes have it and sometimes the nose.

William Lyon Phelps, as quoted in *Reader's Digest*,
November 1933

I enjoy convalescence. It is the part that makes the illness worth while.

George Bernard Shaw, *Back to Methuselah*

Use your health, even to the point of wearing it out. That is what it is for. Spend all you have before you die; and do not outlive yourself.

George Bernard Shaw, *The Doctor's Dilemma*

There are people who bear their pains with a better grace when they think of greater sufferings on the part of other people, and so, in a dentist's chair, they keep their minds upon hospitals.

Booth Tarkington, as quoted in *Reader's Digest*, March 1936

I reckon being ill as one of the great pleasures of life, provided one is not too ill and is not obliged to work till one is better.

Samuel Butler, *The Way of All Flesh*

There's a device on the market that can help you not only take off weight but also *keep* it off. Last year, more than four million Americans bought and used it.

It is called a scale. If you use it faithfully, three things can happen.

First, it can tell you how much flab you need to lose to improve your health—and your looks. Second, it can motivate you to get a sensible reducing diet from your doctor, and then stick to it. Third, when you are proud or pretty again because your weight is what it ought to be, it will help you stay there.

Curtis Mitchell, as quoted in *Reader's Digest*, July 1971

All interest in disease and death is only another expression of interest in life.

Thomas Mann, The Magic Mountain

There is only one danger I find in life—you may take too many precautions.

Alfred Adler, as quoted in Reader's Digest, June 1964

One of the most difficult things to contend with in a hospital is the assumption on the part of the staff that because you have lost your gall bladder you have also lost your mind.

Jean Kerr, Please Don't Eat the Daisies

Two things are bad for the heart—running up stairs and running down people.

Bernard M. Baruch, as quoted in Reader's Digest, October 1951

I am interested in physical medicine because my father was. I am interested in medical research because I believe in it. I am interested in arthritis because I have it.

Bernard M. Baruch, as quoted in the New York Post, May 1, 1959

There are no such things as incurables, there are only things for which man has not found a cure.

Bernard M. Baruch, address to the President's Committee
on Employment of the Physically Handicapped, as quoted
in The New York Times, May 1, 1954

A fearful thing happened to us on the way to the 1970s: we became trapped in a dangerous web of noise. Whether it comes in loud, sudden blasts or as a steady high level of sound, noise is loaded with threats to the health of us all. And, ever-increasing, it must now be recognized as a plague that has reached epidemic proportions.

James Stewart-Gordon, as quoted in Reader's Digest,
February 1970

The trouble about always trying to preserve the health of the body is that it is so difficult to do without destroying the health of the mind.

G. K. Chesterton, as quoted in Come to Think of It

Health is the thing that makes you feel that now is the best time of the year.

Franklin P. Adams, as quoted in Reader's Digest, April
1938

Let the clean wind blow the cobwebs from your body. Air is medicine.

Lillian Russell, as quoted in Reader's Digest,
March 1922

There is an Arab philosophy about health. They say that health is the digit one, love is zero, glory zero, success zero. Put the one of health beside the others and you are a rich man. But without the one of health, everything is zero.

Jack Denton Scott, Passport to Adventure

A hospital should also have a recovery room adjoining the cashier's office.

Francis O'Walsh, as quoted in Reader's Digest, September
1962

Pain is no longer pain when it is past.

Margaret J. Preston, Nature's Lesson   267

What point does it make to speak of sickness if there is no health?

Viktor Frankl, as quoted in *Psychology Today*, January
1973

A hospital bed is a parked taxi with the meter running.

Groucho Marx, as quoted in *Reader's Digest*, March 1973

Health alone does not suffice. To be happy, to become creative, man must always be strengthened by faith in the meaning of his own existence.

Stefan Zweig, *Mental Healers*

Why doesn't medical science figure some way to make our ailments as interesting to others as they are to us?

Harold Coffin, as quoted in *Reader's Digest*, February 1974

Don't be afraid to enjoy the stress of a full life, nor too naïve to think you can do so without some intelligent thinking and planning. Man should not try to avoid stress any more than he would shun food, love or exercise.

Dr. Hans Selye, as quoted in *Newsweek*, March 31, 1958

Now that even cardiologists are beginning to believe that heart disease can be traced to unrelenting competitiveness and baffled fury, will a wave of concern over stress sweep over this hypochondriacal country, to match the widespread interest in jogging and polyunsaturated oils? Quite likely. There is nothing more fascinating to the layman than folklore finally validated by reputable scientists.

Walter McQuade, as quoted in *Reader's Digest*,
April 1972

The process of living is the process of reacting to stress.

Stanley Sarnoff, as quoted in *Time*, November 29, 1963

Nobody is sicker than the man who is sick on his day off.

Bill Vaughan, as quoted in *Reader's Digest*, November 1961

Psychologically, sleep can sometimes be a vehicle for retreating from reality. All of us have experienced the kinds of stresses in which the most comfortable thing to do upon awakening would be to duck under the covers and escape reality by sleeping some more. . . .

Good sleep is not the result of something you do immediately before retiring, but of a style of life and a manner of daily living. After all, we are not different persons when we turn out the light. Our sleep reflects our total selves.

Dr. Julius Segal, interviewed in *U.S. News & World Report*, December 28, 1970

Americans, as I've discovered in my medical practice, seem unable to relax. A business executive came to my office for a routine checkup. He showed visible signs of overwork. I warned him to slow down, take up a hobby—perhaps painting—to relax. He readily agreed, and left the office.

The next day he phoned and announced enthusiastically, "Doc, this painting is wonderful! I've finished a dozen already."

Dr. A. F. Johnson, as quoted in *Reader's Digest*, February
1971

HISTORY AND CIVILIZATION

What Is History?

In our concern with the present and our serious social problems, we are losing a proper perspective of history. History balances the frustration of "how far we have to go" with the satisfaction of "how far we have come." It teaches us tolerance for the human shortcomings and imperfections which are not uniquely of our generation, but of all time.

Lewis F. Powell, Jr., as quoted in *Reader's Digest*,
November 1972

History is worth reading when it tells us truly what the attitude toward life was in the .past.

Dorothy Canfield Fisher, *Vermont Tradition*

One of the lessons of history is that nothing is often a good thing to do and always a clever thing to say.

Will Durant, as quoted in *Reader's Digest*, November 1972

Civilization is a stream with banks. The stream is sometimes filled with blood from people killing, stealing, shouting and doing the things historians usually record, while on the banks, unnoticed, people build homes, make love, raise children, sing songs, write poetry and even whittle statues. The story of civilization is the story of what happened on the banks. Historians are pessimists because they ignore the banks for the river.

Will Durant, as quoted in *Life*, October 18, 1963

Neither our classroom lessons nor our sermons nor our books nor the things we live with nor the houses we live in are any longer strong ties to our past. We have become a nation of short-term doomsayers. In a word, we have lost our sense of history. . . .

To revive our sense of history is no panacea for current ills. But it may help us discover what is now curable; it may help us define the timetable of the possible—and so help us become something that we are not. If history cannot give us panaceas, it is the best possible cure of the yen for panaceas. And the only proven antidote for utopianism.

Daniel J. Boorstin, as quoted in Newsweek, July 6, 1970

The spirit of the age, as it is revealed to each of us, is too often only the spirit of the group in which the accidents of birth or education or occupation or fellowship have given us a place.

Justice Benjamin N. Cardozo, The Nature of the Judicial
Process

We have not formed the right theory of History until we see History itself as a spiritual drama, moving toward a significant denouement and at the same time a process which has meaning and value as it goes on.

Rufus Jones, The Eternal Gospel

Nostalgia isn't what it used to be.

Peter De Vries, as quoted in Reader's Digest, April 1965

History is no one's personal property.

Editorial, The New York Times, December 22, 1960

Men make history and not the other way 'round. In periods where there is no leadership, society stands still. Progress occurs when courageous, skillful leaders seize the opportunity to change things for the better.

Harry S. Truman, as quoted in This Week, February 22,
1959

History has generally shown the radical in the role of an active proponent of change and has cast the conservative for the part of the stalwart defender of things as they are.

Arthur M. Schlesinger, Sr., *New Viewpoints in American History*

For history is more than the record of man's conflict with nature and himself. It is the knowledge which gives dimension to the present direction of the future, and humility to the leaders of men. A nation, like a person, not conscious of its own past is adrift without purpose or protection against the contending forces of dissolution.

Lyndon B. Johnson, Thanksgiving Day proclamation, November 25, 1964

When great changes occur in history, when great principles are involved, as a rule the majority are wrong.

Eugene V. Debs, speech during his trial for draft obstruction, Cleveland, Ohio, September 12, 1918

I am always amazed that the people who attack me never ask the first question that a historian would ask: Is it true?

Arthur Schlesinger, Jr., as quoted in *The New York Times Magazine*, November 21, 1965

What makes a good writer of history is a guy who is suspicious. Suspicion marks the real difference between the man who wants to write honest history and the one who'd rather write a good story.

Jim Bishop, as quoted in *The New York Times*, February 5, 1955

History is the transformation of tumultuous conquerors into silent footnotes.

Paul Eldridge, *Maxims for a Modern Man*

In the realm of history, the moment we have reason to think that we are being given fiction instead of fact, be the fiction ever so brilliant, our interest collapses like a pricked balloon. To hold our interest you must tell us something we believe to be true about the men who once walked the earth. It is the fact about the past that is poetic; just because it really happened, it gathers round it all the inscrutable mystery of life and death and time. Let the science and research of the historian find the fact, and let his imagination and art make clear its significance.

G. M. Trevelyan, *History of England*

Alas! Hegel was right when he said that we learn from history that men never learn anything from history.

George Bernard Shaw, preface to *Heartbreak House*

I see History as a relay race in which each one of us, before dropping in his tracks, must carry one stage further the challenge of being a man.

Romain Gary, as quoted in *Reader's Digest*, March 1962

People are trapped in history and history is trapped in them.

James Baldwin, *Notes of a Native Son*

More history's made by secret handshakes than by battles, bills and proclamations.

John Barth, *The Sot-Weed Factor*

History: n. An account mostly false, of events mostly unimportant, which are brought about by rulers mostly knaves, and soldiers mostly fools.

Ambrose Bierce, *The Devil's Dictionary*

The history of the world is the record of the weakness, frailty and death of public opinion.

Samuel Butler, *Note-Books*

The historical sense involves a perception, not only of the pastness of the past, but of its presence.

T. S. Eliot, "Tradition and the Individual Talent"

History never looks like history when you are living through it. It always looks confusing and messy, and it always feels uncomfortable.

John W. Gardner, *No Easy Victories*

The mark of the historic is the nonchalance with which it picks up an individual and deposits him in a trend, like a house playfully moved in a tornado.

Mary McCarthy, *On the Contrary*

The history of the world is the history of a privileged few.

Henry Miller, *Sunday After the War*

History justifies whatever we want it to. It teaches absolutely nothing, for it contains everything and gives examples of everything.

Paul Valéry, *Régards sur le monde actuel*

History is all explained by geography.

Robert Penn Warren, as quoted in *Writers at Work: First Series*

Man is a history-making creature who can neither repeat his past nor leave it behind.

W. H. Auden, *The Dyer's Hand*

Truth is the only merit that gives dignity and worth to history.

Lord Acton, *The History of Freedom and Other Essays*

The history of the world is the record of a man in quest of his daily bread and butter.

Hendrik Willem van Loon, *The Story of Mankind*

When we attempt to answer the question, What is history?, our answer, consciously or unconsciously, reflects our position in time, and forms part of our answer to the broader question, what view we take of the society in which we live?

Edward Hallett Carr, *What Is History?*

Perhaps nobody has changed the course of history as much as the historians.

Franklin P. Jones, as quoted in *Reader's Digest*, September 1958

No single man makes history. History cannot be seen, just as one cannot see grass growing.

Boris Pasternak, *Doctor Zhivago*

History is like a surveyor's transit. Unless we use it frequently to look back and get our bearing, it will not be of much help to us in running a straight line ahead.

Gerald Horton Bath, as quoted in *Reader's Digest*, September 1955

If America forgets where she came from, if the people lose sight of what brought them along, if she listens to the deniers and mockers, then will begin the rot and dissolution.

Carl Sandburg, as quoted in *Reader's Digest*, January 1959

History is more or less bunk.

Henry Ford, as quoted in *Saturday Review*, January 22, 1955

There is no inevitability in history except as men make it.

Felix Frankfurter, as quoted in *Saturday Review*, October 30, 1954

History is a cruel stepmother, and when it retaliates, it stops at nothing.

V. I. Lenin, comment to Maxim Gorki, as quoted in *To the Finland Station* by Edmund Wilson

---

Change, Progress and Time

The American public has been brainwashed during recent decades into the belief that progress means introducing into our lives everything we know how to produce—an endless variety of food additives, ever more powerful automobiles, higher and higher buildings serviced by high-speed elevators, a senseless consumption of electricity to create a more artificial life. This kind of progress demands little imagination, and its likely outcome is at best a return to the Dark Ages.

René Dubos, as quoted in *Reader's Digest*, January 1973

Change means the unknown. . . . It means too many people cry insecurity. Nonsense! No one from the beginning of time has had security.

Eleanor Roosevelt, as quoted in *The New York Times Magazine*, November 3, 1963

If we wish to make a new world we have the material ready. The first one, too, was made out of chaos.

Robert Quillen, as quoted in *Reader's Digest*, August 1962

I am not a Luddite. Nor could I be one. Luddites were those frenzied traditionalists of the early 19th century who toured English districts around Nottingham, wrecking new weaving machines on the theory that if they were destroyed at the start, old jobs and old ways of life could be preserved. . . .

At certain times in his life, each man is tempted to become a Luddite, for there is always something he would like to go back to. But to be against all change—against change in the abstract—is folly.

James A. Michener, as quoted in *The New York Times Magazine*, September 6, 1971

He who believes that the past cannot be changed has not yet written his memoirs.

Torvald Gahlin, as quoted in *Reader's Digest*, July 1954

One hundred and eighty-one years ago, our forefathers started a revolution that still goes on.

Dwight D. Eisenhower, speech, April 19, 1956

Neither a wise man nor a brave man lies down on the tracks of history to wait for the train of the future to run over him.

Dwight D. Eisenhower, as quoted in *Time*, October 6, 1952

I amenthusiastic over humanity's extraordinary and sometimes very timely ingenuities. If you are in a shipwreck and all the boats are gone, a piano top buoyant enough to keep you afloat may come along and make a fortuitous life preserver. This is not to say, though, that the best way to design a life preserver is in the form of a piano top. I think that we are clinging to a great many piano tops in accepting yesterday's fortuitous contrivings as constituting the only means for solving a given problem.

R. Buckminster Fuller, as quoted in *Reader's Digest*, January 1972

Change is one thing, progress is another. "Change" is scientific, "progress" is ethical; change is indubitable, whereas progress is a matter of controversy.

Bertrand Russell, Unpopular Essays

Growth for the sake of growth is the ideology of the cancer cell.

Edward Abbey, as quoted in Reader's Digest, January 1970

Is civilization progress? The challenge, I think, is clear; and, as clearly, the final answer will be given not by our amassment of knowledge, or by the discoveries of our science, or by the speed of our aircraft, but by the effect our civilized activities as a whole have upon the quality of our planet's life—the life of plants and animals as well as that of men.

Charles A. Lindbergh, as quoted in Reader's Digest, July
1964

It is the darling delusion of mankind that the world is progressive in religion, toleration, freedom, as it is progressive in machinery.

Moncure Daniel Conway, Dogma and Science

Progress is a continuing effort to make the things we eat, drink and wear as good as they used to be.

Bill Vaughan, as quoted in Reader's Digest, August 1962

Civilization in itself is a long hard *fight* to maintain and advance.

Thornton Wilder, as quoted in The New York Times, April 15,
1962

Only in growth, reform and change, paradoxically enough, is true security to be found.

Anne Morrow Lindbergh, as quoted in Reader's Digest,
August 1973   281

The test of our progress is not whether we add more to the abundance of those who have much; it is whether we provide enough for those who have too little.

Franklin D. Roosevelt, Second Inaugural Address, January 20, 1937

We ought to spend more time "wondering" than "doubting whether." Wondering is the key to progress.

Gerald Horton Bath, *The Little Gazette*

Tradition does not mean that the living are dead but that the dead are alive.

G. K. Chesterton, as quoted in *Reader's Digest*, September 1942

All this will not be finished in the first one hundred days, nor will it be finished in the first one thousand days, nor in the life of this administration, nor even perhaps in our lifetime on this planet. But let us begin.

John F. Kennedy, Inaugural Address, January 20, 1961

I am not afraid of tomorrow, for I have seen yesterday and I love today.

William Allen White, as quoted in *Reader's Digest*, June 1938

The reasonable man adapts himself to the world: the unreasonable one persists in trying to adapt the world to himself. Therefore all progress depends on the unreasonable man.

George Bernard Shaw, *Maxims for Revolutionists*

Can a man control his future? Yes. Despite the system they live under, men everywhere have, I believe, more power over the future than ever before. The important thing is that we must choose to exercise it.

282

Boris Pasternak, as quoted in *Reader's Digest*, April 1961

We must change to master change.

Lyndon B. Johnson, State of the Union message, January 12, 1966

Yesterday is not ours to recover, but tomorrow is ours to win or lose.

Lyndon B. Johnson, address to the nation, November 28, 1963

Those who cannot remember the past are condemned to repeat it.

George Santayana, as quoted in *Reader's Digest*, June 1962

We must welcome the future, remembering that soon it will be the past; and we must respect the past, knowing that once it was all that was humanly possible.

George Santayana, as quoted in *Reader's Digest*, March 1972

Those who speak most of progress measure it by quantity and not by quality; how many people read and write, or how many people there are, or what is the annual value of their trade; whereas true progress would rather lie in reading or writing fewer and better things, and being fewer and better men, and enjoying life more.

George Santayana, *Winds of Doctrine*

I suppose I must be a "progressive," which I take to be one who insists on recognizing the facts, adjusting policies to facts and circumstances as they arise.

Woodrow Wilson, speech in New York, January 29, 1911

Problems are the price of progress. Don't bring me anything but trouble. Good news weakens me.

Charles F. Kettering, as quoted in *Reader's Digest*, April 1962

My interest is in the future because I'm going to spend the rest of my life there.

Charles Kettering, as quoted in *Reader's Digest*, January 1946

The art of progress is to preserve order amid change and to preserve change amid order.

Alfred North Whitehead, as quoted in *Forbes Magazine*, December 1, 1957

The apparent serenity of the past is an oil spread by time.

Lloyd Frankenberg, as quoted in *Reader's Digest*, August 1972

I always avoid prophesying beforehand, because it is much better policy to prophesy after the event has already taken place.

Sir Winston Churchill, as quoted in *The New York Times Magazine*, November 1, 1964

It is a mistake to look too far ahead. Only one link in the chain of destiny can be handled at a time.

Sir Winston Churchill, as quoted in *Reader's Digest*, February 1968

The farther backward you can look, the farther forward you are likely to see.

Sir Winston Churchill, as quoted in *Reader's Digest*, September 1958

It is no use saying, "We are doing our best." You have got to succeed in doing what is necessary.

Sir Winston Churchill, as quoted in *Reader's Digest*, July 1964

Every age is modern to those who are living in it.

Justice Benjamin N. Cardozo, *Selected Writings of Benjamin Nathan Cardozo*

... prophecy, however honest, is generally a poor substitute for experience.

Justice Benjamin N. Cardozo, opinion in *West Ohio Gas Co.* case, 1935

The difference between heresy and prophecy is often one of sequence. Heresy often turns out to have been prophecy—when properly aged.

Hubert H. Humphrey, as quoted in *Reader's Digest*, June 1968

I never think of the future. It comes soon enough.

Albert Einstein, interview, December 1930

Disdain for history is symptomatic of the malaise of today's youth culture and of the larger society which nurtured it. Resenting death, we murdered time. Almost too late we see that what we have slain is not time but our sense of ourselves as humans. To reject the past is to deprive today of its meaning tomorrow. To evade the significance of time is to empty life of its significance. It is that meaninglessness which pervades this age of instant gratification and instant results and permanent dissatisfaction.

William V. Shannon, as quoted in *Reader's Digest*, October 1971

Forever and a Day. High up in the North in the land called Svithjod, there stands a rock. It is 100 miles high and 100 miles wide. Once every 1000 years a little bird comes to this rock to sharpen its beak. When the rock has thus been worn away, then a single day of eternity will have gone by.

Hendrik Willem van Loon, *The Story of Mankind*   285

In times like these, it helps to recall that there have *always* been times like these.

Paul Harvey, as quoted in *Reader's Digest*, July 1968

I have seen the future, and it works.

Lincoln Steffens, returning from the Soviet Union in 1918,
as quoted in *The Autobiography of Lincoln Steffens*

When the Greco-Roman world was converted to Christianity, the divinity was drained out of nature and concentrated in a single, transcendent God. Man's greedy impulse to exploit nature used to be held in check by his awe, his pious worship of nature. Now monotheism, as enunciated in Genesis, has removed the age-old restraint. . . .

"Where your treasure is, there will your heart be also." Westerners have set their hearts on the increase of material affluence. And "verily . . . they have their reward."

Arnold J. Toynbee, as quoted in *Reader's Digest*, December
1973

To most of us the future seems unsure. But then it always has been; and we who have seen great changes must have great hopes.

John Masefield, as quoted in *Reader's Digest*, May 1973

What has been called the Revolution of Expectation has begun, and will certainly continue. The hungry believe that they could and ought to be fed, the sick that they could and ought to be healthy, the illiterate and ignorant that they could and ought to receive a decent education.

Sir Julian Huxley, as quoted in *The New York Times*,
November 20, 1959

We have to live today by what truth we can get today and be ready tomorrow to call it falsehood.

286   William James, as quoted in *Reader's Digest*, February 1973

Life is either a daring adventure or nothing. To keep our faces toward change and behave like free spirits in the presence of fate is strength undefeatable.

Helen Keller, Let Us Have Faith

The future has a way of repaying those who are patient with it.

Rev. Arthur Pringle, as quoted in Reader's Digest, January
1959

It is better that the world shall be feared than it be embraced with a good conscience.

Reinhold Niebuhr, as quoted in the Christian Century, April 22,
1926

Nothing is so dangerous as being too modern. One is apt to grow old-fashioned quite suddenly.

Oscar Wilde, as quoted in Reader's Digest, September 1958

The moral world is as little exempt as the physical world from the law of ceaseless change, of perpetual flux.

Sir James Frazer, The Golden Bough

It is change, not love, that makes the world go round—love only keeps it populated.

Charles H. Brower, as quoted in Reader's Digest, October
1960

The only limit to our realization of tomorrow will be our doubts of today.

Franklin D. Roosevelt, message for Jefferson Day, April 13,
1945

... the future is like a corridor into which we can see only by the light coming from behind.

Edward Weyer, Jr., Primitive People Today

Watching my son and daughter grow up in an age not merely of catastrophe but of wonder, a century of opportunity in the fullest and deepest sense, I perceived that to be born into an apocalyptic era may be a cause for rejoicing rather than lamentation. The problems to be resolved demand, and create, spiritual resources which the prosperous ease of a golden age will never inspire.

Vera Brittain, as quoted in Reader's Digest,
December 1960

We can pay our debt to the past by putting the future in debt to ourselves.

John Buchan, as quoted in Reader's Digest,
July 1950

The century on which we are entering can be and must be the century of the common man.

Henry A. Wallace, speech, May 8, 1942

No mariner ever enters upon a more uncharted sea than does the average human being born in the 20th century. Our ancestors knew their way from birth through eternity; we are puzzled about the day after tomorrow.

Walter Lippmann, as quoted in Reader's Digest, August
1962

We have no concern with the future. It has not come yet.

Justice Oliver Wendell Holmes, Jr., opinion in Union Trust
Co. v. Grossman (1918)

288

I have always believed that the long view of man's history will show that his destiny on earth is progress toward the good life, even though that progress is based on sacrifices and sufferings which taken by themselves seem to constitute a hideous melange of evils. This is an act of faith. We must not let ourselves be engulfed in the passing waves which obscure the current of progress. The sinfulness and weakness of man are evident to anyone who lives in the active world. But men are also great, kind and wise. Honor begets honor; trust begets trust; faith begets faith; and hope is the mainspring of life.

Henry L. Stimson, as quoted in *Reader's Digest*, September 1950

Take from me the hope that I can change the future, and you will send me mad.

Israel Zangwill, *The Melting Pot*

To quote me the authority of *precedents* leaves me quite unmoved. All human progress has been made by ignoring precedents. If mankind had continued to be the slave of precedent we should still be living in caves and subsisting on shellfish and wild berries.

Viscount Philip Snowden, as quoted in *Reader's Digest*, March 1933

It is not so much a matter of being against self-improvement as it is of being against *change*. Maturity is a *becoming*—therefore a changing, a progression toward something better.

Louis Binstock, *The Power of Maturity*

Change is an easy panacea. It takes character to stay in one place and be happy there.

Elizabeth Dunn, as quoted in *Reader's Digest*, April 1943

A fashion ten years before its time is indecent. Ten years after its time it is hideous. After a century it becomes romantic.

James Laver, as quoted in *Today's Health*

Time is a dressmaker specializing in alterations.

Faith Baldwin, *Face Toward the Spring*

A hundred years from now, I dare say, some dreamy collector will pay a cool thousand for an old milk bottle, and I wish I had the equivalent for what my hot-water bag will bring in 2034. Why we should be so beguiled by the antique is a riddle that perhaps only the interior decorator can solve.

Cornelia Otis Skinner, as quoted in *Reader's Digest*, January 1935

Why build these cities glorious
    If man unbuilded goes?
In vain we build the world, unless
    The builder also grows.

Edwin Markham, "Man-Making"

We can chart our future clearly and wisely only when we know the path which has led to the present.

Adlai E. Stevenson, speech, Richmond, Virginia, September 20, 1952

Freedom

In the end, more than they wanted freedom, they wanted security and a comfortable life. When the Athenians finally wanted not to give to the state, but for the state to give to them, when the freedom they wished for most was freedom from responsibility, then Athens ceased to be free.

Edith Hamilton, as quoted in *Reader's Digest*, January 1969

America is not a mere body of traders; it is a body of free men. Our greatness is built upon our freedom—is moral, not material. We have a great ardor for gain; but we have a deep passion for the rights of man.

Woodrow Wilson, speech in New York, January 29, 1911

Liberty does not consist in mere declarations of the rights of man. It consists in the translation of those declarations into definite actions.

Woodrow Wilson, address, July 4, 1914

America was established not to create wealth but to realize a vision, to realize an ideal—to discover and maintain liberty among men.

Woodrow Wilson, speech in Pittsburgh, January 29, 1916

The history of liberty is the history of limitations on the power of government.

> Woodrow Wilson, as quoted in *Reader's Digest*, February
> 1944

Commandment Number One of any truly civilized society is this: Let people be different.

> David Grayson, *The Countryman's Year*

The political dilemma of freedom vs. equality evolves out of the clash between the critics of the success idea and its conservative defenders.

> Richard M. Huber, *The American Idea of Success*

Every great historic change has been based upon non-conformity, has been brought either with the blood or with the reputation of non-conformists.

> Ben Shahn, as quoted in the *Atlantic Monthly*, September
> 1957

While the state exists there is no freedom; when there is freedom there will be no state.

> V. I. Lenin, *The State and Revolution*

We cannot expect that all nations will adopt like systems, for conformity is the jailer of freedom and the enemy of growth.

> John F. Kennedy, address to the UN General Assembly,
> September 26, 1961

If a nation values anything more than freedom, it will lose its freedom and the irony of it is that, if it is comfort or money that it values more, it will lose that too.

> W. Somerset Maugham, as quoted in *Reader's Digest*,
> September 1946

In one sense freedom is always in crisis, just as beauty is, and honor and truth—all those things which man has made for himself as a garment against the ever-present blasts of the barbarian spirit.

August Heckscher, address at Kenyon College, April 4,
1957

Liberty is the one thing you can't have unless you give it to others.

William Allen White, as quoted in *Reader's Digest*,
September 1940

This will remain the land of the free only so long as it is the home of the brave.

Elmer Davis, *But We Were Born Free*

Those who won our independence by revolution were not cowards. They did not fear political change. They did not exalt order at the cost of liberty.

Justice Louis D. Brandeis, concurring opinion in *Whitney* v.
California (1927)

If all that Americans want is security they can go to prison. They'll have enough to eat, a bed and a roof over their heads. But if an American wants to preserve his dignity and his equality as a human being, he must not bow his neck to any dictatorial government.

Dwight D. Eisenhower, speech in Galveston, Texas,
December 11, 1949

We must be willing to pay a price for freedom, for no price that is ever asked for it is half the cost of doing without it.

H. L. Mencken, as quoted in *Reader's Digest*, May 1941

Liberty is a different kind of pain from prison.

T. S. Eliot, *The Family Reunion*   293

The moment the slave resolves that he will no longer be a slave, his fetters fall. He frees himself and shows the way to others. Freedom and slavery are mental states.

Mohandas K. Gandhi, *Non-Violence in Peace and War*

The free way of life proposes ends, but it does not prescribe means.

Robert F. Kennedy, *The Pursuit of Justice*

You can't separate peace from freedom because no one can be at peace unless he has his freedom.

Malcolm X, *Malcolm X Speaks*

We have confused the free with the free and easy.

Adlai E. Stevenson, *Putting First Things First*

A hungry man is not a free man.

Adlai E. Stevenson, speech, September 6, 1952

Coercion, after all, merely captures man. Freedom captivates him.

Robert S. McNamara, as quoted in *Reader's Digest*, January 1967

True individual freedom cannot exist without economic security and independence. People who are hungry and out of a job are the stuff of which dictatorships are made.

Franklin D. Roosevelt, message to Congress, January 11, 1944

In the truest sense freedom cannot be bestowed, it must be achieved.

Franklin D. Roosevelt, address on the Emancipation Proclamation, September 16, 1936

Freedom is a way of life which requires authority, discipline, and government of its own kind.

Walter Lippmann, speech, August 4, 1964

Man can only be free through mastery of himself.

Samuel Eliot Morison, *Young Man Washington*

One should respect public opinion insofar as is necessary to avoid starvation and to keep out of prison, but anything that goes beyond this is voluntary submission to an unnecessary tyranny, and is likely to interfere with happiness in all kinds of ways.

Bertrand Russell, *The Conquest of Happiness*

Liberty is always dangerous, but it is the safest thing we have.

Rev. Harry Emerson Fosdick, as quoted in *Reader's Digest*, January 1968

The greatest blessing of our democracy is freedom. But in the last analysis our only freedom is the freedom to discipline ourselves.

Bernard M. Baruch, *Baruch: The Public Years*

Freedom is the freedom to say that two plus two make four. If that is granted, all else follows.

George Orwell, *1984*

Now more than ever we must keep in the forefront of our minds the fact that whenever we take away the liberties of those whom we hate, we are opening the way to loss of liberty for those we love.

Wendell L. Willkie, *One World*   295

When free people are divided, liberty is subtracted.

Walter Winchell, as quoted in *Reader's Digest*, October
1967

Liberty means responsibility. That is why most men dread it.

George Bernard Shaw, *Man and Superman*

Freedom is always, no doubt, a matter of degree; no man enjoys all the requirements of full personal development, and all men possess some of them. It is not only compatible with conditions in which all men are fellow-servants, but would find in such conditions its most perfect expression. What it excludes is a society where only some are servants, while others are masters.

R. H. Tawney, *Religion and the Rise of Capitalism*

Freedom and responsibility are like Siamese twins, they die if they are parted.

Lillian Smith, *Killers of the Dream*

There is no such thing as liberty in general, liberty so to speak, at large.

John Dewey, as quoted in the *Social Frontier*, November
1935

The essential characteristic of true liberty is that under its shelter many different types of life and character and opinion and belief can develop unmolested and unobstructed.

Charles Evans Hughes, as quoted in *Forbes*, November 1,
1957

Liberty is not a means to a higher political end. It is itself the highest political end.

296

Lord Acton, *The History of Freedom and Other Essays*

When you have robbed a man of everything, he's no longer in your power. He is free again.

Alexander Solzhenitsyn, as quoted in *Reader's Digest*,
October 1973

Restrictiveness is the outcome of unlived lives.

Erich Fromm, *Escape from Freedom*

Freedom simply means the power to carry out your own emotions.

Clarence Darrow, as quoted in *Freedom in the Modern World*

What is freedom? It consists of two things: to know each his own limitations and to accept them. That is the same thing as to know *oneself*, and to accept oneself as one is, without fear or envy or distaste; and to recognize and accept the conditions under which one lives, also without fear or envy or distaste. When you do this, you shall be free.

Ann Bridge, as quoted in *Reader's Digest*, June 1940

The phrase "give me liberty or give me death" may be trite. But liberty may indeed require a readiness to face death on its behalf.

Henry Kissinger, as quoted in *Reader's Digest*, January 1974

The story of man is the history, first, of the acceptance and imposition of restraints necessary to permit communal life; and second, of the emancipation of the individual within that system of necessary restraints.

Abe Fortas, *Civil Disobedience*

I would rather be in jail in America than to live "free" in Russia.

Emma Goldman, as quoted in *Reader's Digest*, June 1922   297

Oppression and Rebellion

Big Brother is watching you.

George Orwell, 1984

Men are not prisoners of fate, but only prisoners of their own minds.

Franklin D. Roosevelt, Pan American Day address, April 15,
1939

If black America has not written off all of white America, in spite of slavery, lynching, daily humiliation, it seems to me that white people ought to be able to hang in there. Black America has said in a thousand ways that it believes in America. It has said it in slavery; it has said it in war; it has said it in peace. It seems to me now that the time has come for America to say, "Black Americans, we believe in you."

Whitney Young, as quoted in Reader's Digest, April 1972

Modern man is master of his fate. What he suffers he suffers because he is stupid or wicked, not because it is nature's decree.

Bertrand Russell, as quoted in The New York Times
Magazine, September 3, 1950

All movements go too far.

Bertrand Russell, Unpopular Essays

Oppressed people are frequently very oppressive when first liberated. And why wouldn't they be? They know best two positions. Somebody's foot on their neck or their foot on somebody's neck.

Florence Kennedy, in Sisterhood Is Powerful

No Negro American can be free until the lowliest Negro in Mississippi is no longer disadvantaged because of his race.

Ralph Bunche, as quoted in Reader's Digest, March 1973

Sensible and responsible women do not want to vote. The relative positions to be assumed by man and woman in the working out of our civilization were assigned long ago by a higher intelligence than ours.

Grover Cleveland, in the *Ladies' Home Journal*, April 1905

A group, a nation, or a race commits murder and rape, steals and destroys, yet no individual is guilty, no one is to blame, no one can be punished. The black world squirms beneath the feet of the white in impotent fury or sullen hate.

W. E. B. DuBois, as quoted in the *Nation*, January 25, 1958

We hope that, when the insects take over the world, they will remember with gratitude how we took them along on all our picnics.

Bill Vaughan, as quoted in *Reader's Digest*, July 1968

The vast majority of human beings dislike and even actually dread all notions with which they are not familiar. . . . Hence it comes about that at their first appearance innovators have generally been persecuted, and always derided as fools and madmen.

Aldous Huxley, *Proper Studies*

There are two kinds of females in this country—colored women and white ladies. Colored women are maids, cooks, taxi drivers, crossing guards, school teachers, welfare recipients, bar maids and the only time they become ladies is when they are cleaning ladies.

Louise D. Stone, as quoted in the Washington Post,
November 13, 1966

I want to be the white man's brother, not his brother-in-law.

Rev. Martin Luther King, Jr., as quoted in the New York
Journal-American, September 10, 1962

When asked by an anthropologist what the Indians called America before the white man came, an Indian said simply, "Ours."

Vine Deloria, Jr., as quoted in Reader's Digest,
March 1973

Segregation in the South is a way of life. It is a precious and sacred custom. It is one of our dearest and most treasured possessions. It is the means whereby we live in social peace, order and security.

Judge Thomas P. Brady, speech at the Commonwealth
Club of California, San Francisco, October 4, 1957

We have come to see our planet as "spaceship earth." But we must not forget that one quarter of the passengers on that ship have luxurious first-class accommodations, and the remaining three quarters are traveling in steerage. That does not make for a happy ship, in space or anywhere else.

Robert S. McNamara, as quoted in Reader's Digest, May
1973

We have enslaved the rest of the animal creation, and have treated our distant cousins in fur and feathers so badly that beyond doubt, if they were able to formulate a religion, they would depict the devil in human form.

Rev. William Ralph Inge, *Outspoken Essays: Second Series*

The powers of the individual will are weaker than the forces of social circumstance.

James T. Farrell, as quoted in *Harper's Magazine*, October 1954

To wage a revolution, we need competent teachers, doctors, nurses, electronics experts, chemists, biologists, physicists, political scientists, and so on and so forth. Black women sitting at home reading bedtime stories to their children are just not going to make it.

Frances M. Beal, in *Sisterhood Is Powerful*

I believe that our nation, along with many others, is approaching a turning point. The growing spirit of rebellion could ruin us or save us. It could drag us down into chaos and repression. Or it could lead us to greater human fulfillment than we can now imagine. Which route we take depends on how we respond, as a people, to the nearly universal conviction that the world is not as it should be.

Henry Ford II, *The Human Environment and Business*

I am very optimistic. For one reason: this is the age of revolution. Black and White, the young people question their fathers and mothers. The world is in revolution. There are going to be some changes made.

Dara Abubakari (Virginia E. Y. Collins), as quoted in *Black Women in White America*

It doesn't take a majority to make a rebellion; it takes only a few determined leaders and a good cause.

H. L. Mencken, *Prejudices: Fifth Series*

Justice is power; and if it cannot create, it will at least destroy. So that the question for the future is not, shall there be revolution, but shall it be beneficent or disastrous?

G. Lowes Dickinson, *Justice and Liberty*   301

Every man is a revolutionist concerning the thing he understands. For example, every person who has mastered a profession is a skeptic concerning it, and consequently a revolutionist.

George Bernard Shaw, *Man and Superman*

The free souls are in revolt. And you cannot meet a Revolution with a Referendum.

Israel Zangwill, speech on woman's suffrage, London,
March 28, 1912

Revolutions, as a long and bitter experience reveals, are apt to take their color from the regime they overthrow.

R. H. Tawney, *The Acquisitive Society*

Thinkers prepare the revolution; bandits carry it out.

Mariano Azuela, *The Flies*

The successful revolutionary is a statesman, the unsuccessful one a criminal.

Erich Fromm, *Escape from Freedom*

Not actual suffering but the hope of better things incites people to revolt.

Eric Hoffer, *The Ordeal of Change*

Every social war is a battle between the very few on both sides who care and who fire their shots across a crowd of spectators.

Murray Kempton, *Part of Our Time*

If you feed the people just with revolutionary slogans they will listen today, they will listen tomorrow, they will listen the day after tomorrow, but on the fourth day they will say, "To hell with you."

Nikita Khrushchev, as quoted in *The New York Times*,
October 4, 1964

In most cases, when the lion, weary of obeying its master, has torn and devoured him, its nerves are pacified and it looks round for another master before whom to grovel.

Paul Valéry, as quoted in Reflections sur le monde actuel

If the black man is owed a debt from the past, he owes a debt, too. He owes the men who have come before him, the ones who helped him personally, and the many more who helped him by standing up when it counted and not copping out. He owes it to them not to give in to violence and anger, owes it to a lot of men as yet unborn. He owes it to himself to be a man, a human being, first and last, if not always.

You see, black *isn't* beautiful. *White* isn't beautiful. Skin-deep is never beautiful.

Jesse Owens, with Paul G. Neimark, as quoted in
Blackthink, May 1970

It is better to die on your feet than to live on your knees.

Dolores Ibarruri, Spanish Civil War fighter, called La
Pasionaria, speech in Paris, September 3, 1936

It is a terrible, an inexorable law that one cannot deny the humanity of another without diminishing one's own; in the face of one's victim, one sees oneself.

James Baldwin, Nobody Knows My Name

Reason never has failed men. Only force and oppression have made the wrecks of the world.

William Allen White, as quoted in the Emporia Gazette,
May 16, 1922

Revolution is not a dinner party, nor an essay, nor a painting, nor a piece of embroidery; it cannot be advanced softly, gradually, carefully, considerately, respectfully, politely, plainly and modestly.

Mao Tse-tung, as quoted in Time, December 18, 1950   303

The first and great commandment is, Don't let them scare you.

Elmer Davis, *But We Were Born Free*

Disobedience: the silver lining to the cloud of servitude.

Ambrose Bierce, *The Devil's Dictionary*

The path that leads from moral standards to political activity is strewn with our dead selves.

André Malraux, *L'Espoir*

Man's solidarity is founded upon rebellion, and rebellion, in its turn, can only find its justification in this solidarity. . . . In order to exist, man must rebel, but rebellion must respect the limit it discovers in itself—a limit where minds meet, and in the meeting, begin to exist.

Albert Camus, *L'Homme Révolté*

The masses go into a revolution not with a prepared plan of social reconstruction, but with a sharp feeling that they cannot endure the old regime. . . . The fundamental political process of the revolution thus consists in the gradual comprehension by a class of the problems arising from the social crisis—the active orientation of the masses by a method of successive approximations.

Leon Trotsky, preface to *The History of the Russian Revolution*

The society of excess profits for some and small returns for others, the society in which a few prey upon the many, the society in which few took great advantage and many took great disadvantage, must pass.

Wendell L. Willkie, campaign speech in Springfield, Illinois, October 18, 1940

If Karl Marx were alive today, his problem would be to find parking spaces for the American proletariat rather than break their chains of economic slavery.

304   G. K. Reddy, as quoted in *Reader's Digest*, June 1958

Power and Leadership

A friend in power is a friend lost.

> Henry Adams, *The Education of Henry Adams*

We thought, because we had power, we had wisdom.

> Stephen Vincent Benét, *Litany for Dictatorships*

To be a great autocrat you must be a great barbarian.

> Joseph Conrad, *The Mirror of the Sea*

Our sense of power is more vivid when we break a man's spirit than when we win his heart.

> Eric Hoffer, *The Passionate State of Mind*

Power corrupts the few, while weakness corrupts the many.

> Eric Hoffer, *The Ordeal of Change*

Power never takes a back step—only in the face of more power.

> Malcolm X, *Malcolm X Speaks*

The only prize much cared for by the powerful is power. The prize of the general is not a bigger tent, but command.

> Oliver Wendell Holmes, Jr., speech at Harvard Law School Association of New York, February 15, 1913

There is a homely adage which runs: "Speak softly and carry a big stick; you will go far."

> Theodore Roosevelt, speech at the Minnesota State Fair, September 2, 1901

Power undirected by high purpose spells calamity; and high purpose by itself is utterly useless if the power to put it into effect is lacking.

Theodore Roosevelt, speech in Washington, D.C.,
November 18, 1911

There is no need to fear the strong. All one needs is to know the method of overcoming them. There is a special jujitsu for every strong man.

Yevgeny Yevtushenko, *A Precocious Autobiography*

Strong men are made by opposition; like kites they go up against the wind.

Frank Harris, as quoted in *Reader's Digest*, June 1934

Either we must have power in the hands of men who use scarcity as the means of compulsion, or we must give it to men who find abundance is the instrument of freedom. . . . We must plan our civilization or we must perish.

Harold J. Laski, as quoted in the *Nation*, December 15,
1945

If I were running the world I would have it rain only between 2 and 5 A.M. Anyone who was out then ought to get wet.

> William Lyon Phelps, as quoted in *Reader's Digest*, January 1934

Is it altogether a Utopian dream, that once in history a ruling class might be willing to make the great surrender, and permit social change to come about without hatred, turmoil, and waste of human life?

> Upton Sinclair, *The Way Out*

It is a paradox that every dictator has climbed to power on the ladder of free speech. Immediately on attaining power each dictator has suppressed all free speech except his own.

> Herbert Hoover, as quoted in *Reader's Digest*, November 1938

Idealism is the noble toga that political gentlemen drape over their will to power.

> Aldous Huxley, as quoted in the New York *Herald Tribune*, November 11, 1963

Growing with every successive satisfaction, the appetite for power can manifest itself indefinitely, without interruption by bodily fatigue or sickness.

> Aldous Huxley, *The Perennial Philosophy*

What do I care about the law? Hain't I got the power?

> Cornelius Vanderbilt, as quoted in *The Worldly Philosophers*

While it is true that an inherently free and scrupulous person may be destroyed, such an individual can never be enslaved or used as a blind tool.

> Albert Einstein, *Impact* (a UNE CO publication), 1950   307

The lust for power is not rooted in strength but in weakness.

Erich Fromm, *Escape from Freedom*

Power? It's like a Dead Sea fruit. When you achieve it, there is nothing there.

Harold Macmillan, as quoted in *Parade*, July 7, 1963

In the past, those who foolishly sought power by riding the back of the tiger ended up inside.

John F. Kennedy, Inaugural Address, January 20, 1961

The main task of a free society is to civilize the struggle for power. Slavery of the acquiescent majority to the ruthless few is the hereditary state of mankind; freedom, a rarely acquired characteristic.

R. H. S. Crossman, as quoted in the *New Statesman and Nation*, April 21, 1951

We have, I fear, confused power with greatness.

Stewart L. Udall, commencement address, Dartmouth College, June 13, 1965

Insofar as national events are decided, the power elite are those who decide them.

C. Wright Mills, *The Power Elite*

Mankind is safer when men seek pleasure than when they seek the power and the glory.

Geoffrey Gorer, as quoted in *The New York Times Magazine*, November 27, 1966

Power does not corrupt men; fools, however, if they get into a position of power, corrupt power.

George Bernard Shaw, as quoted in *Days with Bernard Shaw*

Facts, when combined with ideas, constitute the greatest force in the world. They are greater than armaments, greater than finance, greater than science, business and law because they are the common denominators of all of them.

Carl W. Ackerman, speech, September 7, 1931

A leader is best
When people barely know that he exists.

Witter Bynner, The Way of Life According to Laotzu

[Robert] Taft's great attribute was that he made decisions. You never had to say "Well, what are we going to do tomorrow?" He told you. That to me is leadership.

Senator Barry Goldwater, as quoted in The New York
Times Magazine, November 24, 1963

My adversaries . . . applied the one means that wins the easiest victory over reason: terror and force.

Adolf Hitler, Mein Kampf

Adversity attracts the man of character. He seeks out the bitter joy of responsibility.

Charles de Gaulle, as quoted in Reader's Digest, December
1971

There is no necessary connection between the desire to lead and the ability to lead, and even less to the ability to lead somewhere that will be to the advantage of the led. . . . Leadership is more likely to be assumed by the aggressive than by the able, and those who scramble to the top are more often motivated by their own inner torments than by any demand for their guidance.

Bergen Evans, The Spoor of Spooks and Other Nonsense

In the last analysis all tyranny rests on fraud, on getting someone to accept false assumptions, and any man who for one moment abandons   309 or suspends the questioning spirit has for that moment betrayed humanity.

Bergen Evans, The Natural History of Nonsense

I often say of George Washington that he didn't write the Constitution—not a word of it—but he sat for it. It's his portrait. He was just a figure, but what a figure he was—one of the few in the whole history of the world who was not carried away by power. He could have been. It's something to think about.

Robert Frost, as quoted in Reader's Digest, February 1971

Can men, acting like gods, be appointed to establish heaven on earth? If we believe that they can be, then the rest follows. To fulfill their mission they must assume a godlike omnipotence. They must be jealous gods, monopolizing power, destroying all rivals, compelling exclusive loyalty.

Walter Lippmann, The Public Philosophy

Hitler has missed the bus.

Neville Chamberlain, speech in the House of Commons,
April 4, 1940

All animals are equal but some animals are more equal than others.

George Orwell, Animal Farm

The ideas of economists and political philosophers, both when they are right and when they are wrong, are more powerful than is commonly understood. Indeed, the world is ruled by little else.

John Maynard Keynes, The General Theory of
Employment, Interest and Money

Only he deserves power who every day justifies it.

Dag Hammarskjöld, as quoted in Reader's Digest, March
1965

Justice remains the greatest power on earth. To that tremendous power alone will we submit.

Harry S. Truman, address to the Conference on the United
Nations Organization, 1945

You do not lead by hitting people over the head—that's assault, not leadership.

Dwight D. Eisenhower, as quoted in *Reader's Digest*,
October 1970

No longer may the head of a state consider himself outside the law, and impose inhuman acts on the peoples of the world.

Justice Robert H. Jackson, as chief prosecutor at the
Nuremburg war crimes trials establishing personal
accountability for planning and conducting aggressive
warfare, as quoted in *The New York Times*, October 10,
1954

Civilization

The essence of taste is suitability. Divest the word of its prim and priggish implications, and see how it expresses the mysterious demand of the eye and mind for symmetry, harmony and order.

Edith Wharton, *French Ways and Their Meanings*

The ancient world, we may remind ourselves, was not destroyed because the traditions were false. They were submerged, neglected, lost. . . . May it not be that while the historical circumstances are obviously so different, something like that is happening again.

Walter Lippmann, *The Public Philosophy*   311

Where there is one Englishman there is a garden. Where there are two Englishmen there will be a club. But this does not mean any falling off in the number of gardens. There will be three. The club will have one, too.

A. W. Smith, as quoted in *Reader's Digest*,
September 1937

To have doubted one's own first principles is the mark of a civilized man.

Justice Oliver Wendell Holmes, Jr., *Collected Legal Papers*

Taste in itself is nothing. It is only what taste leads to that makes any difference in our lives.

Russell Lynes, *The Tastemakers*

. . . civilization, with its governments and establishments, is shaped by the forces of individual desire.

Charles A. Lindbergh, as quoted in *Reader's Digest*,
November 1972

Today Africa, not Asia, is favored as the most likely birthplace of the human race. However, there is great disagreement as to exactly who begat whom, for it is apparent that several species, both subhuman and human, overlapped each other in time. The descent of man is no longer regarded as a chain with some links missing, but rather as a tangled vine whose tendrils loop back and forth as species interbred to create new varieties, most of which died out.

Ronald Schiller, as quoted in Reader's Digest, August 1973

The Ganga is the river of India, beloved of her people, round which are intertwined her racial memories, her hopes and fears, her songs of triumph, her victories and her defeats. She has been a symbol of India's age-long culture and civilization, ever-changing, ever-flowing, yet ever the same Ganga.

Jawaharlal Nehru, as quoted in Reader's Digest, September 1971

The society which scorns excellence in plumbing because plumbing is a humble activity and tolerates shoddiness in philosophy because it is an exalted activity will have neither good plumbing nor good philosophy. Neither its pipes nor its theories will hold water.

John W. Gardner, Excellence

I feel sorry for the man who has never gone without his dinner to buy a book of poems, a ticket to a concert, a little statuette, or even a pretty hat for his wife.

Albert Edward Wiggam, as quoted in Reader's Digest, June 1935

Culture is on the horns of this dilemma: if profound and noble it must remain rare, if common it must become mean.

George Santayana, The Life of Reason

Society is like the air, necessary to breathe, but insufficient to live on.

George Santayana, Little Essays   313

England is the paradise of individuality, eccentricity, heresy, anomalies, hobbies, and humours.

George Santayana, Soliloquies in England

A gentleman is one who thinks more of other people's feelings than of his own rights; and more of other people's rights than of his own feelings.

Matthew Henry Buckham, as quoted in Reader's Digest,
November 1936

For others a knowledge of the history of their people is a civic duty, while for Jews it is a sacred duty.

Maurice Samuel, The Professor and the Fossil

Manners are like the cipher in arithmetic: they may not be much in themselves, but they are capable of adding a great deal to the value of everything else.

Freya Stark, as quoted in Reader's Digest, April 1946

When a man has discovered why men in Bond Street wear black hats, he will at the same moment have discovered why men in Timbucktou wear red feathers.

G. K. Chesterton, Heretics

The English are a modest people; that is why they are entirely ruled by the few of them that happen to be immodest.

G. K. Chesterton, A Miscellany of Men

The notion of primitive man possessing some inner peace which we civilized people have somehow lost, and need to regain, is a lot of nonsense. Your average New Guinea native lives not only in fear of his enemies but in terror-struck dread of the unknown.

Gordon Linsley, as quoted in Reader's Digest, February
1970

. . . the price we pay for our advance in civilization is a loss of happiness through the heightening of the sense of guilt.

Sigmund Freud, Civilization and Its Discontents

It is impossible to overlook the extent to which civilization is built up upon a renunciation of instinct, how much it presupposes precisely the non-satisfaction (by suppression, repression or some other means?) of powerful instincts.

Sigmund Freud, Civilization and Its Discontents

Civilization is just a slow process of learning to be kind.

Charles L. Lucas, as quoted in Reader's Digest, October 1962

Israel's economic and cultural progress is due to three things: the pioneering spirit that inspires the best of our immigrant and Israeli youth, who respond to the challenge of our desolate areas and the in-gathering of the exiles; the feeling of Diaspora Jewry that they are partners in the enterprise of Israel's resurgence in the ancient homeland of the Jewish people; and the power of science and technology which Israel unceasingly—and not without success—tries to enhance.

David Ben-Gurion, as quoted in the New York Herald Tribune, April 28, 1963

Tact is the knack of making a point without making an enemy.

Howard W. Newton, as quoted in Reader's Digest, October 1946

No man who is in a hurry is quite civilized.

Will Durant, as quoted in Reader's Digest, January 1941

Civilization exists by geological consent, subject to change without notice.

Will Durant, What Is Civilization? 315

Civilization is order and freedom promoting cultural activity. . . .
Civilization begins with order, grows with liberty, and dies with chaos.

Will Durant, as quoted in the *Ladies' Home Journal*,
January 1946

What increases with civilization is not so much immorality of intent as
opportunity of expression.

Will Durant, *The Story of Civilization*

Civilization is in peril? Put it correctly. Civilization *is* peril! The higher
it rises the more unstable and the more disastrous it falls. Its safety
consists in increasing the peril and going on up.

William L. Sullivan, *Epigrams and Criticisms in Miniature*

Habit is the fly-wheel of civilization.

Henry James, as quoted in *Reader's Digest*, June 1922

Social science affirms that a woman's place in society marks the level
of civilization.

Elizabeth Cady Stanton, as quoted in *Growing Up Female
in America—Ten Lives*

I hope and believe that 100 years hence there will be no British
Empire.

H. G. Wells, as quoted in *Reader's Digest*, June 1922

Comfort, opportunity, number and size are not synonymous with
civilization.

Abraham Flexner, *Universities—American, English,
German*

I believe I've found the missing link between animal and civilized man. It is us.

Dr. Konrad Lorenz, as quoted in *Reader's Digest*, August 1955

The only true hope for civilization—the conviction of the individual that his inner life can affect outward events and that, whether or not he does so, he is responsible for them.

Stephen Spender, *World Within World*

In England I would rather be a man, a horse, a dog or a woman, in that order. In America I think the order would be reversed.

Bruce Gould, as quoted in *Reader's Digest*, October 1957

What a commentary on civilization, when being alone is considered suspect; when one has to apologize for it, make excuses, hide the fact that one practices it—like a secret vice!

Anne Morrow Lindbergh, *Gift from the Sea*

In an affluent society, people are willing to devote larger and larger sums of money to programs which they hope will alleviate the misery of the poor. In the process, there is a public demand by those in poverty that builds up to the supply.

Poverty pursues society like a shadow following a running man.

Procter Thomson, as quoted in *Reader's Digest*, February 1972

A society needs more than anything else to care. An ancient Greek scholar once was asked when justice would come to Athens. He replied, "When those who are not injured are as indignant as those who are."

Whitney M. Young, Jr., *Beyond Racism: Building an Open Society*   317

Good taste is better than bad taste, but bad taste is better than no taste at all.

Arnold Bennett, as quoted in Reader's Digest, September
1957

A riot in France is one of the most remarkable things in the world. The frenzied combatants maintain perfect discipline. There is no fighting at all between 7:30 P.M. and 9, when everyone takes time out for dinner. During the riots of 1934, communists, royalists, fascists, socialists fought shoulder to shoulder under red flag and tricolor against the police and the Garde Mobile. But fighting stopped on the stroke of midnight because the Paris Métro (underground) stops running at 12:30, and no one wanted to walk home. Bloody bandaged fighters and police jostled their way into the trains together. Promptly at 7:30 the next morning, the riot started again.

John Gunther, as quoted in Reader's Digest, February 1938

Fashions exist for women with no taste, etiquette for people with no breeding.

Dowager Queen Marie of Rumania, as quoted in Reader's
Digest, April 1938

Born in iniquity and conceived in sin, the spirit of nationalism has never ceased to bend human institutions to the service of dissension and distress.

Thorstein Veblen, Absentee Ownership

We owe to the Middle Ages the two worst inventions of humanity—romantic love and gunpowder.

André Maurois, as quoted in Reader's Digest, August 1961

I am unable to find any warrant for the belief that any period has offered men the kind of peace and certainty that the modern age is clamoring for. The Middle Ages was a period of fearful maladministration. The Greeks led the most chaotic, passionate and disorderly life

318

conceivable. They preached serenity, but calm composure and discipline were with them, as they are with us, an individual achievement.

> Jacques Barzun, as quoted in *Reader's Digest*, February
> 1963

Civilizations die from philosophical calm, irony, and the sense of fair play quite as surely as they die of debauchery.

> Joseph Wood Krutch, *The Modern Temper*

Perhaps the supreme product of civilization is people who can endure it.

> Franklin P. Jones, as quoted in *Reader's Digest*, July 1959

If our civilization should perish, this will come about in part because it was not good enough to survive.

> Lewis Mumford, *Faith for Living*

A Frenchman is a man who'll risk his all on impulse. But let him stop to consider and he won't risk a thing.

> André Malraux, as quoted in *Reader's Digest*, March 1963

Deploring change is the unchangeable habit of all Englishmen. If you find any important figures who really *like* change, such as Bernard Shaw, Keir Hardie, Lloyd George, Selfridge or Disraeli, you will find that they are not really English at all but Irish, Scotch, Welsh, American or Jewish. Englishmen make changes, sometimes great changes. But, secretly or openly, they always deplore them.

> Raymond Postgate, as quoted in *Reader's Digest*, July 1963

No one can be as calculatedly rude as the British, which amazes Americans, who do not understand studied insult and can only offer abuse as a substitute.

> Paul Gallico, as quoted in *The New York Times*, January 14,
> 1962

319

Europe is finished. The American domination of the world has begun.

Georg Brandes, as quoted in Reader's Digest,
June 1922

I think the great contribution the English have made to the valuable things of world culture is this: an interest in struggling for an unpredictable goal. As you go eastward from the British Isles, you run into cultures of gradually increasing susceptibility to fatalism. The Englishman's games have made him less fatalistic, and as a result of the discipline of sport he will keep struggling even though his intellect would indicate his cause to be lost.

Wilfred Trotter, as quoted in Reader's Digest, February
1942

Those comfortably padded lunatic asylums which are known euphemistically as the stately homes of England.

Virginia Woolf, The Common Reader

A Southern lady once observed to me that gaiety is one of the surest marks of the aristocrat; and it is one of the unwritten laws of French politeness that a long face is a breach of manners.

Richard Le Gallienne, as quoted in Reader's Digest,
September 1938

Not only England, but every Englishman is an island.

M. Novalis, as quoted in Reader's Digest,
July 1940

It is not that the Englishman can't feel—it is that he is afraid to feel. He has been taught at his public school that feeling is bad form. He must not express great joy or sorrow, or even open his mouth too wide when he talks—his pipe might fall out if he did.

E. M. Forster, Abinger Harvest

In the end it may well be that Britain will be honored by the historians more for the way she disposed of an empire than for the way in which she acquired it.

David Ormsby Gore, as quoted in *The New York Times*,
October 28, 1962

This is the final test of a gentleman: His respect for those who can be of no possible service to him.

William Lyon Phelps, as quoted in *Reader's Digest*,
September 1937

The maxim of the British people is "Business as usual."

Sir Winston Churchill, speech, November 9, 1919

Our present addiction to pollsters and forecasters is a symptom of our chronic uncertainty about the future. Even when the forecasts prove wrong, we still go on asking for them. We watch our experts read the entrails of statistical tables and graphs the way the ancients watched their soothsayers read the entrails of a chicken.

Eric Hoffer, as quoted in *Reader's Digest*, February 1970

Our age will be well remembered not for its horrifying crimes nor its astonishing inventions, but because it is the first generation since the dawn of history in which mankind dared to believe it practical to make the benefits of civilization available to the whole human race.

Arnold J. Toynbee, *A Study of History*

America

The concept, the ethic and the act of concern for the welfare of one's fellow beings is, as we all know, a very deep part of the Hebraic   321 tradition. It is a foundation stone of the Judeo-Christian ethic. It is also a particularly American quality.

Elliot L. Richardson, as quoted in Reader's Digest, May
1973

I believe that we are lost here in America, but I believe we shall be found.

Thomas Wolfe, You Can't Go Home Again

The American, by nature, is optimistic. He is experimental, an inventor and a builder who builds best when called upon to build greatly.

John F. Kennedy, speech in Washington, D.C., January 1,
1960

In no other country in the world is aspiration so definite a part of life as it is in America. The most precious gift God has given to this land is not its great riches of soil and forest and mine but the divine discontent planted deeply in the hearts of the American people.

William Allen White, as quoted in Reader's Digest, October
1962

The general belief is that Americans are not destined to renounce, but to enjoy.

Herbert Croly, The Promise of American Life

Boiled down to one word, the most important difference between the early American and his modern counterpart is *awareness*. Living then was a vital experience; today we often exist in a dreamlike, mechanical world where we seem to have very little role to play in our own lives.

Eric Sloane, as quoted in Reader's Digest,
September 1973

322

Everyone knows that in the United States we have no classes. Furthermore everyone knows that he belongs to the middle class.

Sam A. Darcy, *The Idler*

The United States today is in the unhappy situation of a rich and romantic maiden. She yearns hopelessly to be loved for herself alone.

Edward Hyams, as quoted in *Reader's Digest*, February 1953

Americans think of themselves collectively as a huge rescue squad on twenty-four-hour call to any spot on the globe where dispute and conflict may erupt.

Eldridge Cleaver, *Soul on Ice*

The most serious charge which can be brought against New England is not Puritanism but February.

Joseph Wood Krutch, as quoted in *Reader's Digest*, February 1962

We [Americans] cheerfully assume that in some mystic way love conquers all, that good outweighs evil in the just balances of the universe and that at the eleventh hour something gloriously triumphant will prevent the worst before it happens.

Brooks Atkinson, *Once Around the Sun*

America has been called a melting pot, but it seems better to call it a mosaic, for in it each nation, people or race which has come to its shores has been privileged to keep its individuality, contributing at the same time its share to the unified pattern of a new nation.

King Baudouin I of Belgium, as quoted in *Reader's Digest*, October 1959

323

[Americans] expect to eat and stay thin, to be constantly on the move and ever more neighborly . . . to revere God and be God.

Daniel Boorstin, as quoted in *Newsweek*, February 26, 1962

I've discovered that what we in England call drafts you in America call cross-ventilation.

Hermione Gingold, as quoted in *Reader's Digest*, February 1959

There is nothing the matter with Americans except their ideals. The real American is all right; it is the ideal American who is all wrong.

G. K. Chesterton, as quoted in *The New York Times*, February 1, 1931

No people respond more spontaneously to fair play. If you treat Americans well, they always want to treat you better.

Sir Winston Churchill, as quoted in *Reader's Digest*, May 1965

It is natural for the ordinary American when he sees something that is wrong to feel not only that there should be a law against it, but also that an organization should be formed to combat it.

Gunnar Myrdal, *An American Dilemma*

America is a land where a citizen will cross the ocean to fight for democracy—and won't cross the street to vote in a national election.

Bill Vaughan, as quoted in *Reader's Digest*, October 1960

The three great American vices seem to be efficiency, punctuality and the desire for achievement and success. They are the things that make the Americans so unhappy and so nervous.

324   Lin Yutang, *The Importance of Living*

As for what you're calling hard luck—well, we made New England out of it. That and codfish.

Stephen Vincent Benét, as quoted in Reader's Digest,
November 1943

There is in most Americans some spark of idealism, which can be fanned into a flame. It takes sometimes a divining rod to find what it is; but when found, and . . . when disclosed to the owner, the results are often extraordinary.

Justice Louis D. Brandeis, The Words of Justice Brandeis

Americans have more timesaving devices and less time than any other group of people in the world.

Duncan Caldwell, as quoted in Reader's Digest, May 1949

The French look exactly like French, the faces of Dutchmen are Dutch. Danes look like Danes and Egyptians look very Canalish.   325

Americans have a sad countenance. They probably look like this because they developed catarrh when they landed on Plymouth Rock.

Sir Alfred Richardson, former president of the Royal
Academy of Art, address, September 17, 1956

England and America are two countries separated by the same language.

George Bernard Shaw, as quoted in *Reader's Digest*,
November 1942

I am always careful never to say a civil word to the United States. I have scoffed at their inhabitants as a nation of villagers. I have defined the 100 percent American as 90 percent idiot. And they just adore me.

George Bernard Shaw, as quoted in *Reader's Digest*,
October 1944

Intellectually, I know that America is no better than any other country; emotionally I know she is better than every other country.

Sinclair Lewis, in an interview, December 29, 1930

Our culture puts great emphasis on productivity. We feel we must always be doing something constructive with our time. We see a child swinging on a gate and we say, "Go find something to do." We fail to realize that he is already doing something—he's swinging on a gate. Inevitably, when we grow up, instead of swinging on gates when we feel like it, we go out and find something to do.

Dr. Alexander Reid Martin, as quoted in *Reader's Digest*,
July 1973

Loyalty . . . is a realization that America was born of revolt, flourished in dissent, became great through experimentation.

Henry Steele Commager, *Freedom, Loyalty, Dissent*

It would be irrational to say that all of the criticisms of America and its institutions are unfounded. Yet excessive self-flagellation is destroying the ties that bind us together.

Lewis F. Powell, Jr., as quoted in Reader's Digest,
November 1972

The great and invigorating influences in American life have been the unorthodox; the people who challenge an existing institution or way of life, or say and do things that make people think.

Justice William O. Douglas, as quoted in Report of the
Fund for the Republic, 1958

Religion and race define the next stage in the evolution of the American peoples. But the American nationality is still forming: its processes are mysterious, and the final form, if there is ever to be a final form, is as yet unknown.

Nathan Glazer and Daniel P. Moynihan, Beyond the
Melting Pot

America is the only civilized country in the world where women band together, organize myriad "movements," march in crusades, live in clubs, arrange banquets, join societies with feverish energy. You could not lure the average British woman into a woman's club even if you paid her a bonus. You could no more persuade a group of French women to lunch together than you could persuade them to jump into the Seine.

Beverley Nichols, as quoted in Reader's Digest, September
1936

In America, with all of its evils and faults, you can still reach through the forest and see the sun. But we don't know yet whether the sun is rising or setting for our country.

Dick Gregory, Nigger

Americans no longer seem mesmerized by their national problems. Somewhere in the course of our recent history, many people have shrugged off the hesitancy and doubt which characterized the country's mood and have regained their old, jaunty certainty that for every problem there is a solution. Now the country is abuzz with the issues that have been raised—on the farm no less than on the campus. . . .

America's weaknesses and contradictions are out in the open. Americans themselves have been the first to see them. Wherever I have gone, I have found Americans hard at work on their resolutions.

Charles Kuralt, as quoted in *Reader's Digest*,
March 1973

Our way of living together in America is a strong but delicate fabric. It is made up of many threads. . . . It serves as a cloak for the protection of poor and rich, of black and white, of Jew and Gentile, of foreign and native born. Let us not tear it asunder. For no man knows, once it is destroyed, where or when man will find its protective warmth again.

Wendell Willkie, *One World*

Civilization cannot go back; civilization must not stand still. We have undertaken new methods. It is our task to perfect, to improve, to alter when necessary, but in all cases to go forward. . . .

Without regard to party, the overwhelming majority of our people seek a greater opportunity for humanity to prosper and find happiness. They recognize that human welfare has not increased and does not increase through mere materialism and luxury, but that it does progress through integrity, unselfishness, responsibility and justice.

Franklin D. Roosevelt, message to Congress, January 3,
1934

Beware of thinking that, because it is without a hereditary nobility, America is without a hierarchy. I know few countries where the etiquette of contempt is so varied. The Anglo-Saxons despise the other races, and these despise one another. The Southerners scorn the Northerners; the Easterners, those of the Middle West. Those who have been in America 300 years look down on the 200-year-olds.

André Maurois, as quoted in *Reader's Digest*, September
1936

We have in America a rapidly growing society, one with impressive needs, and even more impressive wants.

James P. Mitchell, speech in Washington, D. C., January
1960

Throughout our history we believed that effort was its own reward. Partly because so much has been achieved here in America, we have tended to suppose that every problem must have a solution and that good intentions should somehow guarantee good results. Utopia was seen not as a dream, but as our logical destination if we only traveled the right road. Our generation is the first to find that the road is endless, that in traveling it we will find not Utopia but ourselves.

Henry Kissinger, as quoted in *Reader's Digest*, January
1974

America is the only nation in history which, miraculously, has gone directly from barbarism to degeneration without the usual interval of civilization.

Georges Clemenceau, as quoted in the *Saturday Review*,
December 1, 1945

From the very beginning our people have markedly combined practical capacity for affairs with power of devotion to an ideal. The lack of either quality would have rendered the other of small value.

Theodore Roosevelt, speech in Philadelphia, November 22,
1902

LAW AND JUSTICE

Lawyers, Judges and Courts

There are only two ways to be quite unprejudiced and impartial. One is to be completely ignorant. The other is to be completely indifferent. Bias and prejudice are attitudes to be kept in hand, not attitudes to be avoided.

Charles P. Curtis, A Commonplace Book

In striking down capital punishment, this Court does not malign our system of government. . . . Only in a free society could right triumph in difficult times, and could civilization record its magnificent advancement.

In recognizing the humanity of our fellow beings, we pay ourselves the highest tribute. We achieve a major milestone in the long road up from barbarism and join the approximately seventy other jurisdictions in the world which celebrate their regard for civilization and humanity by shunning capital punishment.

Justice Thurgood Marshall, majority opinion in Furman v.
Georgia (1972)

You're an attorney. It's your duty to lie, conceal and distort everything, and slander everybody.

Jean Giraudoux, The Madwoman of Chaillot

The judge who does not agonize before passing sentence is a criminal.

John Ciardi, as quoted in the Saturday Review, February 13,
1965

The Supreme Court has handed down the Eleventh Commandment: "Thou shalt not, in thy classrooms, read the first ten."

> Fletcher Knebel, as quoted in *Reader's Digest*, November 1963

The judges of England have rarely been original thinkers or great jurists. Many have been craftsmen rather than creators. They have needed the stuff of morals to be supplied to them so that out of it they could fashion the law.

> Lord Patrick Devlin, judge of the High Court, as quoted in the *Spectator*, London, September 15, 1961

The Lord Chief Justice of England recently said that the greater part of his judicial time was spent investigating collisions between propelled vehicles, each on its own side of the road, each sounding its horn and each stationary.

> Philip Guedalla, as quoted in *Reader's Digest*, July 1936

Sitting on raised platforms, all draped in black, judges (even of lower courts) sometimes have ludicrously inflated images of themselves and of the supposed Olympian qualities of their decisions.

> Marvin E. Frankel, *Bar Association Bulletin.* New York County Lawyers Association, Vol. 26, No. 2 (1968–69)

The decisions of the courts on economic and social questions depend on their economic and social philosophy.

> Theodore Roosevelt, message to Congress, December 8, 1908

I always felt from the beginning that you had to defend people you disliked and feared as well as those you admired.

> Roger Baldwin, as quoted in the *New Republic*, January 25, 1964

Litigant: n. A person about to give up his skin for the hope of retaining his bones.

> Ambrose Bierce, *The Devil's Dictionary*

We have to find ways to clear the courts of the endless stream of "victimless crimes" that get in the way of serious consideration of serious crimes. There are more important matters for highly skilled judges and prosecutors than minor traffic offenses, loitering and drunkenness.

> Richard M. Nixon, address to the National Conference on
> the Judiciary, March 11, 1971

In a society that cherishes change; in a society that enshrines diversity in its Constitution; in a system of justice that pits one adversary against another to find the truth—there will always be conflict. Taken to the street, conflict is a destructive force; taken to the courts, conflict can be a creative force.

> Richard M. Nixon, address to the National Conference on
> the Judiciary, March 11, 1971

All the signs and portents indicate that the organization lawyer will fuse into the organization man. . . . He will never sing solo, but only raise his voice in the institutional chorus. But in the grand and glorious annals of the bar, it has been through singing solo that its men of mark have gained their strength and courage.

> Bernard Botein and Murray A. Gordon, *The Trial of the
> Future*

We are not final because we are infallible, but we are infallible only because we are final.

> Justice Robert H. Jackson, opinion in *Brown* v. *Allen* (1953)

Justice, though due to the accused, is due to the accuser also. The concept of [judicial] business must not be strained till it is narrowed to a filament. We are to keep the balance true.

> Justice Benjamin N. Cardozo, opinion in *Snyder* v.
> *Commonwealth of Massachusetts* (1934)

Courts owe their prestige to the idea that they are constantly making the law more and more certain. They owe their power to the fact that 335 they never clarify total situations. They leave the cases which are just around the corner always undecided, and thus compel business men and legislators to be constantly in fear of their judicial veto. This is a characteristic of judicial government. Without it we would scarcely have what people call a government of law.

Thurman W. Arnold, *The Symbols of Government*

Th' lawyers make th' law, th' judges make th' errors, but th' editors make th' juries.

Finley Peter Dunne, in *The American Magazine*, October 1906

No matter whether th' constitution follows the flag or not, th' supreme court follows th' iliction returns.

Finley Peter Dunne, *Mr. Dooley's Opinions*

A criminal lawyer, like a trapeze performer, is seldom more than one slip from an awful fall, and because he must swing away from the clutches of the law to get top billing, he is eternally pinned in the hot arc light of controversy.

Paul O'Neal, as quoted in *Life*, June 22, 1959

I am appalled and ashamed that things should have come to such a pass that I am skeptical of the ability of black revolutionaries to achieve a fair trial anywhere in the United States. In large part the atmosphere has been created by police actions and prosecutions against the Panthers in many parts of the country. It is also one more inheritance from centuries of racial discrimination and oppression.

Kingman Brewster, Jr., president of Yale University, commenting on the trial in New Haven of the Black Panther 21 for murder and conspiracy, June 1970

Our court dockets are so crowded today it would be better to refer to it as the overdue process of law.

Bill Vaughan, as quoted in *Reader's Digest*, January 1957

No system of justice can rise above the ethics of those who administer it. Lawlessness in law enforcement is the ultimate in the cynical sophism that the end justifies the means.

Report of the National [Wickersham] Commission on Law
Observance and Law Enforcement, 1929

I deplore the need or the use of troops anywhere to get American citizens to obey the orders of constituted courts; but I want to point this one thing out: there is no person in this room whose basic rights are not involved in any successful defiance to the carrying out of court orders.

Dwight D. Eisenhower, news conference on Arkansas'
defiance of a Supreme Court desegregation order during the
Little Rock crisis, May 14, 1958

Our judges are not monks or scientists, but participants in the living stream of our natural life, steering the law between the dangers of rigidity on the one hand and of formlessness on the other. Our system faces no theoretical dilemma but a single continuous problem: how to apply to ever-changing conditions the never-changing principles of freedom.

Chief Justice Earl Warren, as quoted in *Fortune*, November
1955

We are under a Constitution, but the Constitution is what the judges say it is.

Charles Evans Hughes, later Chief Justice of the Supreme
Court, in a speech at Elmira, New York, May 3, 1907

Jury service honorably performed is as important in the defense of our country, its Constitution and laws, and the ideals and standards for which they stand, as the service that is rendered by the solider on the field of battle in time of war.

Judge George H. Boldt, concluding remarks in *U.S.* v. *Beck*
(1959)   337

We cannot safely entrust our livelihoods and our rights to the discretion of authorities, examiners, boards of control, character committees, regents, or license commissioners. We cannot permit any official or agency to pretend to sole knowledge of the public good. We cannot put the independence of any man . . . wholly in the power of other men.

Charles A. Reich, as quoted in the Yale Law Journal, April
1964

An Irish attorney was making the best of a rather shaky case when the judge interrupted him on a point of law. "Surely," he asked, "your clients are aware of the doctrine *de minimis non curat lex*?" "I assure you, my lord," came the suave reply, "that, in the remote and inhospitable hamlet where my clients have their humble abode, it forms the sole topic of conversation."

Walter Bryan, The Improbable Irish

One who belongs to the most vilified and persecuted minority in history is not likely to be insensible to the freedom guaranteed by our Constitution. . . . But as judges we are neither Jew nor Gentile, neither Catholic nor agnostic. We owe equal attachment to the Constitution and are equally bound by our judicial obligations, whether we derive our citizenship from the earliest or the latest immigrants to these shores.

Justice Felix Frankfurter, dissenting opinion in West
Virginia Board of Education v. Barnette (1943)

In a democratic society like ours, relief must come through an aroused popular conscience that sears the conscience of the people's representatives.

Justice Felix Frankfurter, opinion in *Baker* v. *Carr* (1962)
that reapportionment of electoral districts is the
responsibility of the legislative, rather than the judicial,
branch of government

The institution of trial by jury is almost 1000 years old. But it may not last another 50 unless we can show the public that it is an efficient tool for the administration of justice.

Judge Irving Kaufman, as quoted in *Reader's Digest*,
September 1973

The difficulty in modification of the Constitution makes the Supreme Court a very powerful body in shaping the course of our civilization. In dealing with the constitutional guarantees of human dignity, it often has the application of the national conscience in its keeping. It is a sort of diplomatic priesthood.

F. D. G. Ribble, as quoted in *Washington and Lee Law*
Review, Vol. 167, 1957

Judges are apt to be naif, simple-minded men, and they need something of Mephistopheles.

Justice Oliver Wendell Holmes, Jr., *Law and the Court*

Labels are generally sophomoric oversimplifications. All judges are "strict constructionists" on some portions of the Constitution, "activist" on others. I try to conserve the values of the Constitution as best I see them, and I will always seek to change and improve our system of justice to make it work better. We will fall short of all the noblest ideals and concepts of justice if we do not make the courts at every level work so that justice is prompt as well as fair for all people. I intend to continue working as hard as I can to make our court system 339 responsive to the needs of the country. If that constitutes "activism," I plead guilty.

Chief Justice Warren E. Burger, as quoted in *Reader's Digest*, February 1973

A trial is still an ordeal by battle. For the broadsword there is the weight of evidence; for the battle-axe the force of logic; for the sharp spear, the blazing gleam of truth; for the rapier, the quick and flashing knife of wit.

Lloyd Paul Stryker, noted trial lawyer, quoted in reports of his death, June 22, 1955

Our civilization has decided, and very justly decided, that determining the guilt or innocence of men is a thing too important to be trusted to trained men. When it wishes for light upon that awful matter, it asks men who know no more law than I know, but who can feel the things that I felt in the jury box. When it wants a library catalogued, or the solar system discovered, or any trifle of that kind, it uses up its specialists. But when it wishes anything done which is really serious, it collects 12 of the ordinary men standing around. The same thing was done, if I remember right, by the Founder of Christianity.

G. K. Chesterton, as quoted in *Reader's Digest*, September 1960

The President's [Supreme] Court nominations comprise the supreme political act of this nation, since they reflect the latest national plebiscite on the direction of our country.

Richard Kleindienst, as quoted in *Reader's Digest*, October 1972

Taking counsel is worthwhile; not for the sake of the counsel, which is not worth a button to you in any case, but for the sake of seeing in your counselor's eye the flame of gladness at being important to somebody.

Henry S. Haskings, *Meditations in Wall Street*

The Law and Justice

In the whole history of law and order, the longest step forward was taken by primitive man when, as if by common consent, the tribe sat down in a circle and allowed one man to speak at a time.

Curtis Bok, as quoted in *Reader's Digest*, March 1970

Law is experience developed by reason and applied continually to further experience.

Roscoe Pound, as quoted in the *Christian Science Monitor*,
April 24, 1963

There is a justice, but we do not always see it. Discreet, smiling, it is there, at one side, a little behind injustice, which makes a big noise.

Jules Renard, *Journal*

The concept of law and order is meaningless without justice. We must re-examine our assumptions—and our laws. To do so, we must open channels of communication. If we do not—if we think the only answer is to suppress dissent—then the responsibility for violence will hang as heavily on us as it does on those who protest.

John D. Rockefeller III, as quoted in *Reader's Digest*,
August 1970

Never in our full life could we hope to do such work for tolerance, for justice, for man's understanding of man, as now we do by accident.

Bartolomeo Vanzetti, letter to his son from prison shortly
before his execution, April 1927

We do not get good laws to restrain bad people. We get good people to restrain bad laws.

G. K. Chesterton, *All Things Considered*   341

If there isn't a law there will be.

Harold Farber, as quoted in *The New York Times Magazine,* March 17, 1968

The only justice is to follow the sincere intuition of the soul, angry or gentle. Anger is just, and pity is just, but judgment is never just.

D. H. Lawrence, *Studies in Classic American Literature*

There are not enough jails, not enough policemen, not enough courts to enforce a law not supported by the people.

Hubert H. Humphrey, speech in Williamsburg, Virginia, May 1, 1965

Few laws are of universal application. It is of the nature of our law that it has dealt not with man in general, but with him in relationships.

Justice Louis D. Brandeis, dissenting opinion in *Truax* v. *Corrigan* (1921)

The old idea of a good bargain was a transaction in which one man got the better of another. The new idea of a good contract is a transaction which is good for both parties to it.

Justice Louis D. Brandeis, address at Brown University, 1912

The law that will work is merely the summing up in legislative form of the moral judgment that the community has already reached.

Woodrow Wilson, address, December 20, 1915

Government can easily exist without law, but law cannot exist without government.

Bertrand Russell, *Unpopular Essays*

It is difficult to make our material condition better by the best laws, but it is easy enough to ruin it by bad laws.

Theodore Roosevelt, as quoted in *Reader's Digest*, June 1946

No man is above the law and no man is below it; nor do we ask any man's permission when we require him to obey it.

Theodore Roosevelt, message to Congress, January 1904

What seems just at one time in a man's life may come to seem unjust at other times. I grew up in a segregated society. It never occurred to me that this was unjust.

LeRoy Collins, former governor of Florida, interview on "Face the Nation" TV program

The law takes no account of the infinite varieties of temperament, intellect, and education which make the internal characters of a given act so different in different men.

Justice Oliver Wendell Holmes, Jr., *The Common Law*

Great cases like hard cases make bad law.

Justice Oliver Wendell Holmes, Jr., opinion in *Northern Securities Co.* v. *U. S.* (1904)

That naïve state of mind that accepts what has been familiar and accepted by them [jurists who believe in natural law] and their neighbors as something that must be accepted by all men everywhere.

Justice Oliver Wendell Holmes, Jr., dismissing natural-law philosophy in *Collected Legal Papers*

The fourteenth amendment does not enact Herbert Spencer's *Social Statics.*

Justice Oliver Wendell Holmes, Jr., minority opinion in *Lochner* v. *New York* (1905) supporting the passage of state laws governing maximum working hours in the baking industry   343

The prophecies of what the courts will do in fact, and nothing more pretentious, are what I mean by the law.

Justice Oliver Wendell Holmes, Jr., The Path of the Law

It is no sufficient condemnation of legislation that it favors one class at the expense of another; for much or all legislation does that; and none the less when the bona fide object is the greatest good of the greatest number. Why should the greatest number be preferred? Why not the greatest good for the most highly developed?

Justice Oliver Wendell Holmes, Jr., The Mind and Faith of
Justice Holmes

It is better for all the world, if instead of waiting to execute degenerate offspring for crime, or let them starve for their imbecility, society can prevent those who are manifestly unfit from continuing their kind. The principle that sustains compulsory vaccinations is broad enough to cover cutting the Fallopian tubes. . . . Three generations of imbeciles are enough.

Justice Oliver Wendell Holmes, Jr., opinion in Buck v. Bell
(1927)

. . . the character of every act depends upon the circumstances in which it is done.

Justice Oliver Wendell Holmes, Jr., opinion in Schenck v.
U.S. (1919)

Laws should be like clothes. They should be made to fit the people they are meant to serve.

Clarence Darrow, as quoted in Reader's Digest,
January 1963

There is no such thing as justice—in or out of court.

Clarence Darrow, as quoted in The New York Times,
April 19, 1936

The clearest way to show what the rule of law means to us in everyday life is to recall what has happened when there is no rule of law. The dreaded knock on the door in the middle of the night.

Dwight D. Eisenhower, address marking first U. S. Law
Day, May 5, 1958

Equal opportunity and mutual respect are matters not only of law, but also of the human heart and spirit, and the latter are not always amenable to law.

Dwight D. Eisenhower, as quoted in the New York Herald
Tribune, May 25, 1964

If a beachhead of cooperation may push back the jungles of suspicion, let both sides join in creating a new endeavor—not a new balance of power, but a new world of law, where the strong are just and the weak secure and the peace preserved.

John F. Kennedy, Inaugural Address, January 20, 1961

Justice has been described as a lady who has been subject to so many miscarriages as to cast serious reflections upon her virtue.

William L. Prosser, The Judicial Humorist

We have talked long enough in this country about equal rights. We have talked for 100 years or more. It is time now to write the next chapter—and to write it in the books of law.

Lyndon B. Johnson, address to Congress,
November 27, 1963

What in the name of conscience will it take to pass a truly effective gun-control law? Now in this new hour of tragedy, let us spell out our grief in constructive action.

Lyndon B. Johnson, following the death of Senator Robert
F. Kennedy by an assassin's bullet, June 6, 1968

Those who are too lazy and comfortable to think for themselves and be their own judges obey the laws. Others sense their own laws within them.

Hermann Hesse, Demian

A self-made man may prefer a self-made name.

Judge Learned Hand, on ruling that Samuel Goldfish could
change his name to Samuel Goldwyn, as quoted in The
Lion's Share by Bosley Crowther

One of the most intriguing passages in all legendary literature deals with an incident in the life of the patriarch Jacob. We are told that, having sent his household ahead on a journey, he camped alone at the edge of a river. There a strange man came up to him as he sat beside his tent. They proceeded to wrestle with each other unremittingly all through the darkness of the night, and when the sun rose in the morning Jacob still clung to the stranger until he was able to exact a blessing from him. Thereupon this mysterious adversary vanished again into the realm of unreality. Here the narrative breaks off and we are left to assign it whatever interpretation we choose. If, then, Jacob is taken to represent the concrete living individual, on the one hand, and the ghostly adversary is made to stand for abstraction, concept, or symbol, on the other, the struggle in this little incident epitomizes rather effectually the whole history of legal philosophy; but as yet no final blessing has been heard.

Edmond Cahn, The Sense of Injustice

"The work of justice," we have been told, "shall be peace; and the effect of justice, quietness and assurance forever." (Isaiah 32:17) Forever? No, surely not forever, but until the sense of injustice stirs once more and calls men again to gird themselves.

Edmond Cahn, The Sense of Injustice

American attitudes towards the law from our national beginnings down to the present day make up a history of fierce and unresolved tension. On the one side, there has been an uncritical and excessive

346

trust in what can be accomplished through legislation and policing, while on the other side, there has been an equally unwarranted mistrust of the law and of social control by means of government.

Edmond Cahn, The Moral Decision

Fragile as reason is and limited as law is as the expression of the institutionalized medium of reason, that's all we have standing between us and the tyranny of mere will and the cruelty of unbridled, unprincipled, undisciplined feeling.

Justice Felix Frankfurter, as quoted in the New York
Herald Tribune, August 30, 1962

Marriage, laws, the police, armies and navies are the mark of human incompetence.

Dora Russell, The Right to Be Happy

Law is a reflection and a source of prejudice. It both enforces and suggests forms of bias.

Diane Schulder, Does the Law Oppress Women?

The manufacturers of practically every class of articles used by human beings have been involved in legal difficulties . . . with more or less frequency during the last thirty years, including the manufacturers of the surgical instrument with which an infant may be assisted into the world, the bottle and nipple from which he may secure his food, the milk in his bottle, the blanket in which he is wrapped, the flag which his father displays in celebration of the event, and so on throughout life until he is finally laid away in a casket which was manufactured and sold under conditions which violated the law.

Edwin H. Sutherland, as quoted in Annals of the American
Academy of Political and Social Science, September 1941

Law is merely the expression of the will of the strongest for the time being, and therefore laws have no fixity, but shift from generation to generation.

Brooks Adams, The Law of Civilization and Decay   347

Revolt and terror pay a price. / Order and law have a cost.

Carl Sandburg, *The People, Yes!*

The entire jurisdiction of the Supreme Court should be carefully studied. The Supreme Court cannot perform its Constitutional and historic function if it must review more than [the present] 4000 cases a year and hear arguments in 150 or 160 highly important cases. Some limitation or some screening process must take the crushing burden off nine men and spread it over a greater number in other courts.

Chief Justice Warren E. Burger, as quoted in *Reader's Digest*, May 1971

When you cannot be just through virtue, be so through pride.

Eugenio Maria de Hostos, *Obras*

Injustice is relatively easy to bear; what stings is justice.

H. L. Mencken, *Prejudices: Third Series*

In civilized life, law floats in a sea of ethics.

Chief Justice Earl Warren, as quoted in *The New York Times*, November 12, 1962

There are no natural laws. There are only temporary habits of nature.

Alfred North Whitehead, as quoted in *Dialogues of A. N. Whitehead*

Justice is too good for some people and not good enough for the rest.

Norman Douglas, *Good-bye to Western Culture*

No Law, apart from a Lawgiver, is a proper object of reverence. It is mere brute fact.

William Temple, former Archbishop of Canterbury, *Nature, Man and God*

What we lawyers want to do is to substitute courts for carnage, dockets for rockets, briefs for bombs, warrants for warheads, mandates for missiles.

Charles Rhyne, chairman, World Conference on World Peace Through Law, as quoted in the *Wall Street Journal*, June 27, 1963

Fairness is what justice really is.

Justice Potter Stewart, as quoted in *Time*, October 20, 1958

The moral laws are deeply imbedded in the constitution of things—we do not break them, we break ourselves upon them.

E. Stanley Jones, *Victorious Living*   349

The law is not an end in itself, nor does it provide ends. It is preeminently a means to serve what we think is right.

Justice William J. Brennan, Jr., opinion in *Roth* v. *U. S.*
(1957)

There is no such thing as "natural rights"; there are only adjustments of conflicting claims.

Aldous Huxley, *Music at Night*

I tell ye Hogan's r-right whin he says "Justice is blind." Blind she is, an' deef an' dumb an' has a wooden leg!

Finley Peter Dunne, *Mr. Dooley's Opinions*

I am the law.

Frank Hague, former mayor of Jersey City as quoted in
The New York Times, November 11, 1937

Assassination on the scaffold is the worst form of assassination, because there it is invested with the approval of society.

George Bernard Shaw, *Man and Superman*

One can always legislate against specific acts of human wickedness; but one can never legislate against the irrational itself.

Morton Irving Seiden, *The Paradox of Hate: A Study in
Ritual Murder*

It ain't no sin if you crack a few laws now and then, just so long as you don't break any.

Mae West, in the film *Every Day's a Holiday* (1937)

Yet law-abiding scholars write;
Law is neither wrong nor right,

Law is only crimes
Punished by places and by times. . . .

W. H. Auden, "Law Like Love"

Crime, Prisons and Police

The problem of police corruption cannot be met by seeking out the few "rotten apples" whose supposedly atypical conduct is claimed to be sullying the reputation of an otherwise innocent department. The underlying problem is that the climate is inhospitable to attempts to uncover acts of corruption and protective of those who are corrupt. The rookie is faced with the situation where it is easier for him to become corrupt than to remain honest.

Knapp Commission report, as quoted in *Reader's Digest,*
January 1972

Remedial institutions are apt to fall under the control of the enemy and to become instruments of oppression.

Justice Louis D. Brandeis, letter to Robert W. Bruère,
1922

Crime is contagious. If the government becomes a lawbreaker, it breeds contempt for law.

Justice Louis D. Brandeis, dissenting opinion in *Olmstead*
v. *U. S.* (1928)

The price for getting a man thoroughly beaten up on the lower West Side of New York has risen to $60 per beating from a depression low of $40. This price, however, does not guarantee that the victim's legs will be broken.

Stanley Walker, as quoted in *Reader's Digest,*
November 1936   351

The reformative effect of punishment is a belief that dies hard, chiefly, I think, because it [punishment] is so satisfying to our sadistic impulses.

Bertrand Russell, *Ideas That Have Harmed Mankind*

Fraud is the homage that force pays to reason.

Charles P. Curtis, *A Commonplace Book*

I'm convinced that every boy, in his heart, would rather steal second base than an automobile.

Justice Tom Clark, as quoted in *Reader's Digest,*
January 1952

It is a rather pleasant experience to be alone in a bank at night.

Willie Sutton, *I, Willie Sutton*

A vague uneasiness: the police. It's like when you suddenly understand you have to undress in front of the doctor.

Ugo Betti, *The Inquiry*

For the middle class, the police protect property, give directions, and help old ladies. For the urban poor, the police are those who arrest you.

Michael Harrington, *The Other America*

Men and women who are released from prison must be given a fair opportunity to prove themselves as they return to society. We will not ensure our domestic tranquillity by keeping them at arm's length. If we turn our back on the ex-convict, then we should not be surprised if he again turns his back on us.

Richard M. Nixon, as quoted in *Reader's Digest,*
May 1972

Juvenile delinquency starts in the high chair and ends in the death chair.

> James D. C. Murray, as quoted in the New York
> *World-Telegram,* September 8, 1956

If you give to a thief he cannot steal from you, and he is then no longer a thief.

> William Saroyan, *The Human Comedy*

Today there's law and order in everything. You can't beat anybody for nothing. If you do beat anyone, it's got to be for the sake of order.

> Maxim Gorky, *The Lower Depths*

You stand here convicted of seeking to corrupt the administration of justice. You stand here convicted of having tampered, really, with the very soul of this nation.

> Frank W. Wilson, U. S. district judge, sentencing James R.
> Hoffa, head of the Teamsters Union, for attempting to rig a
> Federal jury, March 12, 1964

Don't steal; thou'lt never thus compete
Successfully in business. Cheat.

> Ambrose Bierce, *The Devil's Dictionary*

In the South . . . the Sheriff is the man. I don't care what people write in books, it's the Sheriff who has contact with the jury list, with the taxes and assessments, and all the legal and illegal activities going on in the country. He can make a person's life miserable by harassment—I mean white or black.

> James M. Nabrit, Jr., as quoted in the New York *Herald
> Tribune,* May 1, 1963

A man's respect for law and order exists in precise relationship to the size of his paycheck.

> Adam Clayton Powell, *Keep the Faith, Baby!* 353

Every prison is the exclamation point and every asylum is the question mark in the sentence of civilization.

Samuel A. W. Duffield, Essays

The battle against crime is greater than we realize because we're facing a new type of criminal today who kills for kicks. People who are bored with life and have no discipline from within—and it's unfashionable to discipline from without—go along for kicks, until they must try the supreme kick, to kill another human being. . . . Sometimes I think that the archcriminal was the man who invented the safety razor and eliminated the razor strap that used to hang by the sink.

Erle Stanley Gardner, address to the Bar Association of St.
Louis, October 1, 1963

Half our politicians wouldn't be where they are except for opposing crime, and the other half wouldn't be where they are except for supporting it.

Bergen Evans, The Spoor of Spooks

I am devoted to detective novels. They make such a nice change from my work. I particularly like your American ones, where the hero is invariably amorous, alcoholic and practically indestructible. But unfortunately, my dear, crime is solved not by single masterminds.

Richard Leofric Jackson of Scotland Yard and Interpol, as
quoted in the Saturday Evening Post, October 28, 1961

I hate this "crime doesn't pay" stuff. Crime in the U. S. is perhaps one of the biggest businesses in the world today.

Paul Kirk, as quoted in the Wall Street Journal,
February 26, 1960

Only the man who has enough good in him to feel the justice of the penalty can be punished; the others can only be hurt.

354   William Ernest Hocking, The Coming World Civilization

It is organized violence on top which created individual violence at the bottom. It is the accumulated indignation against organized wrong, organized crime, organized injustice, which drives the political offender to act.

Emma Goldman, address to the jury at her trial for draft
obstruction, June 15, 1917

One reason for our high crime rate is that the long arm of the law is often shorthanded.

Hal Chadwick, as quoted in *Reader's Digest,*
March 1960

The thought that I had cut off an innocent young life and the knowledge of the grief I had caused both his family and mine has been present in my consciousness every day of every year for the past quarter century. It is not, gentlemen, an easy thought to live with. At any time in the past twenty-five years, I would have welcomed joyously the chance to take Bobby Franks' place—to lay down my life if it would restore his.

Nathan Leopold, letter to the Illinois State Parole Board, as
quoted in news reports of March 18, 1955

The real significance of crime is in its being a breach of faith with the community of mankind.

Joseph Conrad, *Lord Jim*

It's not the people in prison who worry me. It's the people who aren't.

Arthur Gore, Earl of Arran, as quoted in *The New York
Times,* January 7, 1962

The extreme isolation of American prisoners from mainstream society has helped defeat the very goal of criminal justice: the reduction of crime by diverting offenders from criminal to acceptable and useful behavior. In recognition of this, our system of corrections is undergoing vast re-examination. . . . But the critical ingredient in the transition to life in the outside world is seldom available: support and understanding by those in the community with whom the ex-prisoner will work, live and search for acceptance.

Myrl E. Alexander, former director of the U. S. Bureau of
Prisons, as quoted in *Reader's Digest,* August 1970

We take on a burden when we put a man behind walls, and that burden is to give him a chance to change. If we deny him that, we deny his status as a human being, and to deny that is to diminish our own humanity and plant the seeds of future anguish for ourselves.

Chief Justice Warren E. Burger, address,
February 19, 1970

There is a widespread public complaint that the present system of criminal justice does not deter criminal conduct. . . . The simple and obvious remedy is to give the courts the manpower and the tools, including prosecutors and defense counsel, to try criminal cases within sixty days after indictment and then let us see what happens. I predict that this would sharply reduce the rate of crime.

Chief Justice Warren E. Burger, address to the American
Bar Association, August 10, 1970

Criminal justice has no easy answers. We can never achieve a system free of failures. But parole now delivers us more than our share. It is time to get rid of it and begin a fresh approach.

Herman Schwartz, as quoted in *Reader's Digest,* August
1973

When their lordships asked Bacon
How many bribes he had taken
He had at least the grace
To get very red in the face.

356

Edmund C. Bentley, *Baseless Biography*

Alphonse Capone: Our first gangster . . . A natural leader of men. A master salesman. A genius at organizing and consolidating. Would have gone far on Wall Street.

Joseph Driscoll, in an article on organized crime, as quoted in *Reader's Digest*, January 1934

We have to choose, and for my part I think it a less evil that some criminals should escape than that the government should play an ignoble part.

Justice Oliver Wendell Holmes, Jr., opinion in *Olmstead* v. *U. S.* (1928)

The fence is the key man in the operations of the shoplifter, the hijacker and the securities thief. Name any item, and you can find a fence for it. . . . Even when I was in prison, I found a fence of sorts. I used to sell baby pigs from the prison farm in Jefferson City, Mo., to a local farmer who gave me beer and cigarettes. He would purchase all the pigs I could steal.

Robert Earl Barnes, as quoted in *Reader's Digest*, September 1973

Warring on poverty, inadequate housing and employment is warring on crime. A civil rights law is a law against crime. Money for schools is money against crime. Medical, psychiatric and family counseling services are services against crime. More broadly and most important-ly, every effort to improve life in America's inner cities is an effort against crime.

Nicholas deB. Katzenbach, former Attorney General, as quoted in Report of the President's Crime Commission, 1968

An Attica massacre or an occasional exposé of reform-school horrors wakes us up, now and then, to what psychiatrist Karl A. Menninger has called "the crime of punishment." But only when we realize that community alternatives to warehousing fellow human beings are not

only more humane, but cost less and control crime more, will the tide
of change truly begin to roll.

Lester Velie, as quoted in Reader's Digest,
July 1972

The death penalty will seem to the next generation, as it seems to
many even now, an anachronism too discordant to be suffered,
mocking with grim reproach all our clamorous professions of the
sanctity of life.

Justice Benjamin N. Cardozo, Law and Literature

Murder may be done by legal means, by plausible and profitable war,
by calumny, as well as by dose or dagger.

Lord Acton, Historical Essays

We got our problems. My goodness, politicians are always saying,
"I'm for law enforcement." That's like an aviator saying, "I'm for tail
winds." Who ain't? The trick is to try and get one, see.

I got a solution for the crime problem, folks. Just legalize it and put
a heavy tax on it, that's all. Well, we tax some of our biggest businesses
right out of existence. It might work with crime, you can't tell.

Will Rogers, as quoted in Reader's Digest, June 1972

As through this world I've rambled,
I've seen lots of funny men.
Some rob you with a six-gun
And some with a fountain pen.

Woody Guthrie, from the song "Pretty Boy Floyd"

For de little stealin' dey gits you in jail soon or late. For de big stealin'
dey makes you emperor and puts you in de Hall o' Fame when you
croaks.

358

Eugene O'Neill, The Emperor Jones

With some 200 million people, the United States averages 50 times as many gun murders a year as do England, Germany and Japan combined with their total population of 218 million.

This appalling statistic calls to mind other salient features of our culture. The more than 90 million firearms privately owned by Americans give us the distinction of having the highest—by far the highest—gun-to-population ratio of any nation. About half of all American homes have a firearm: many have more than one. . . .

There can be no doubt that in a few years the right law would have a profound effect in reducing the crimes of armed robbery, aggravated assault and homicide.

Milton S. Eisenhower, as quoted in *Reader's Digest*, April 1971

Vandalism is rebellion with a cause. To prevent it, we must combat the cause itself—social indifference, apathy, the loss of community, neighborhood and family values.

Philip G. Zimbardo, as quoted in *Reader's Digest*, May 1973

If we were brought to trial for the crimes we have committed against ourselves, few would escape the gallows.

Paul Eldridge, *Maxims for a Modern Man*   359

Men are more often bribed by their loyalties and ambitions than by money.

Justice Robert H. Jackson, opinion in *U. S.* v. *Wunderlich*
(1951)

Civil Rights and Civil Liberties

The ultimate solution of the race problem lies in the willingness of men to obey the unenforceable.

Rev. Martin Luther King, Jr., *Where Do We Go from Here?*

It may be true that the law cannot make a man love me, but it can keep him from lynching me, and I think that's pretty important.

Rev. Martin Luther King, Jr., as quoted in the *Wall Street
Journal,* November 13, 1962

I have a dream that one day on the red hills of Georgia, the sons of former slaves and the sons of former slave-owners will be able to sit together at the table of brotherhood. . . . That one day even the state of Mississippi, a state sweltering with the heat of injustice, sweltering with the heat of oppression, will be transformed into an oasis of freedom and justice. . . . That my four little children will one day live in a nation where they will not be judged by the color of their skin but by the content of their character.

Rev. Martin Luther King, Jr., address at the Lincoln
Memorial to 200,000 participants in the national March on
Washington, August 28, 1963

The core of the evil in true civil disobedience is that it weakens the bonds of law and compels the state to resort to power.

Archibald Cox, *Civil Rights, the Constitution and the
Courts*

Social protest and even civil disobedience serve the law's need for growth. . . . Short of the millennium, sharp changes in the law depend partly upon the stimulus of protest.

Archibald Cox, Civil Rights, the Constitution and the Courts

We come then to the question presented: Does segregation of children in public schools solely on the basis of race, even though the physical facilities and other "tangible" factors may be equal, deprive the children of the minority group of equal education opportunities? We believe that it does. . . . We conclude that in the field of public education the doctrine of "separate but equal" has no place.

Chief Justice Earl Warren, unanimous opinion outlawing racial segregation in public schools, Brown v. Board of Education of Topeka, Kansas (1954)

Mere unorthodoxy or dissent from the prevailing mores is not to be condemned. The absence of such voices would be a sympton of grave illness in our society.

Chief Justice Earl Warren, opinion in Sweezy v. New Hampshire (1957)

If some people got their rights they would complain of being deprived of their wrongs.

Oliver Herford, as quoted in Reader's Digest, April 1962

The very purpose of a Bill of Rights was to withdraw certain subjects from the vicissitudes of political controversy, to place them beyond the reach of majorities and officials and to establish them as legal principles to be applied by the courts. One's right to life, liberty, and property, to free speech, a free press, freedom of worship and assembly, and other fundamental rights may not be submitted to vote; they depend on the outcome of no elections.

Justice Robert H. Jackson, in West Virginia Board of Education v. Barnette (1943)

If there is any fixed star in our constitutional constellation, it is that no official, high or petty, can prescribe what should be called orthodox in politics, nationalism, religion or other matters of opinion, or force citizens to confess by words or act their faith therein.

Justice Robert H. Jackson, opinion in West Virginia Board
of Education v. Barnette (1943)

The day that this country ceases to be free for irreligion, it will cease to be free for religion.

Justice Robert H. Jackson, opinion in Zerach v. Clausor
(1952)

I think under our system it is time enough for the law to lay hold of the citizen when he acts illegally, or in some rare circumstance when his thoughts are given illegal utterance. I think we must let his mind alone.

Justice Robert H. Jackson, partial dissent in the Supreme
Court's upholding of the non-Communist oath provision of
the Taft-Hartley Act, as quoted in The New York Times,
October 10, 1954

The essential corruption of racial segregation is not that it is supported by lies but that people believe the lies.

Harry Golden, Mr. Kennedy and the Negroes

Equality of opportunity is an equal opportunity to prove unequal talents.

Viscount Samuel, as quoted in Reader's Digest, September
1960

I remind you that the formulae of the rights of men, which was a criticism of things as they used to be, was at least as efficient as all the armies of the Continent put together in the revolutionary war.

Mary Antin, The Woman's Movement

The censor believes that he can hold back the mighty traffic of life with a tin whistle and a raised right hand. For after all, it is life with which he quarrels.

> Heywood Broun, as quoted in *The Fifty-Year Decline and Fall of Hollywood* by Ezra Goodman

Law enforcement is a protecting arm of civil liberties. Civil liberties cannot exist without law enforcement; law enforcement without civil liberties is a hollow mockery. They are parts of the same whole—one without the other becomes a dead letter.

> J. Edgar Hoover, as quoted in the *Iowa Law Review*, Winter 1952

Experience teaches us to be most on our guard to protect liberty when the government's purpose is beneficent.

> Justice Louis D. Brandeis, opinion in *Olmstead* v. *U. S.* (1928)

Like the course of the heavenly bodies, harmony in national life is a resultant of the struggle between contending forces. In frank expression of conflicting opinion lies the greatest promise of wisdom in governmental action; and in supression lies ordinarily the greatest peril.

> Justice Louis D. Brandeis, opinion in *Gilbert* v. *Minnesota* (1920)

The right to be alone—the most comprehensive of rights, and the right most valued by civilized man.

> Justice Louis D. Brandeis, opinion in *Olmstead* v. *U. S.* (1928)

What men value in this world is not rights but privileges.

> H. L. Mencken, *Minority Report*   363

The Fourth Amendment and the personal rights it secures have a long history. At the very core stands the right of a man to retreat into his own home and there be free from unreasonable government intrusion.

Justice Potter Stewart, in a unanimous Supreme Court decision barring police from mechanical eavesdropping, as quoted in *The New York Times*, March 6, 1961

That precious right to be let alone is violated once the police enter our conversations.

Justice William O. Douglas, address to the American Law Institute, 1953

No man was ever endowed with a right without being at the same time saddled with a responsibility.

Gerald W. Johnson, as quoted in the *Saturday Review,* July 5, 1958

God knows there is risk in refusing to act till the facts are all in; but is there not greater risk in abandoning the conditions of all rational inquiry? Risk for risk, for myself I had rather take my chance that some traitors will escape detection than spread abroad a spirit of general suspicion and distrust which accepts rumor and gossip in place of undismayed and unintimidated inquiry.

Judge Learned Hand, address to the Board of Regents, University of the State of New York, Albany, October 24, 1953

The most stringent protection of free speech would not protect a man falsely shouting fire in a theater and causing a panic.

Justice Oliver Wendell Holmes, Jr., opinion in *Schenck* v. *U. S.* (1919)

The question in every case is whether the words are used in such circumstances and are of such a nature as to create a clear and present danger.

Oliver Wendell Holmes, Jr., opinion in *Schenck* v. *U. S.* (1919) establishing judicial standards for constitutional limits of free speech

Obscenity is whatever happens to shock some elderly and ignorant magistrate.

Bertrand Russell, as quoted in *Look,* February 23, 1954

The suppression of civil liberties is to many less a matter for horror than the curtailment of the freedom to profit.

Marya Mannes, *But Will It Sell?*

The interest of the people [lies] in being able to join organizations, advocate causes, and make political "mistakes" without being subjected to government penalties.

Justice Hugo L. Black, dissenting opinion in *Barenblatt* v. *U. S.* (1957)

The liberties we talk about defending today were established by men who took their conception of man from the great religious tradition of Western civilization, and the liberties we inherit can almost certainly not survive the abandonment of that tradition.

Walter Lippmann, as quoted in the New York *Herald Tribune,* December 16, 1938

Nature gave women too much power; the law gives them too little.

Will Henry, as quoted in *Reader's Digest,* August 1971

True equality can only mean the right to be uniquely creative.

Erik Erikson, in *The Woman in America*

Government laws are needed to give us civil rights, and God is needed to make us civil.

Ralph W. Sockman, sermon, Riverside Church, New York, December 13, 1964

365

It is the right of our people to organize to oppose any law and any part of the Constitution with which they are not in sympathy.

Alfred E. Smith, address to the League of Women Voters,
December 2, 1927

There can be no doubt whatever regarding the soundness of your view of "obscenity" as residing exclusively, not in the thing contemplated, but in the mind of the contemplating person.

Havelock Ellis, as quoted in *Free Press Anthology*

Any time we deny any citizen the full exercise of his Constitutional rights, we are weakening our own claim to them.

Dwight D. Eisenhower, as quoted in *Reader's Digest*,
December 1963

Here in America we are descended in blood and in spirit from revolutionists and rebels—men and women who dare to dissent from accepted doctrine. As their heirs, we may never confuse honest dissent with disloyal subversion.

Dwight D. Eisenhower, address at Columbia University
bicentennial dinner, May 31, 1954

They [the Founding Fathers] proclaimed to all the world the revolutionary doctrine of the divine rights of the common man. That doctrine has ever since been the heart of the American faith.

Dwight D. Eisenhower, address at Columbia University
bicentennial dinner, May 31, 1954

The laws of God, the laws of man
He may keep that will and can;
Not I; let God and man decree
Laws for themselves and not for me.

366

A. E. Housman, *Last Poems*

The drums of Africa still beat in my heart. They will not let me rest while there is a single Negro boy or girl without a chance to prove his worth.

Mary McLeod Bethune, as quoted in the New York *Herald Tribune*, May 19, 1955

The dissenter is every human being at those moments of his life when he resigns momentarily from the herd and thinks for himself.

Archibald MacLeish, as quoted in *The New York Times*, December 16, 1956

The mind is the expression of the soul, which belongs to God, and must be let alone by government.

Adlai E. Stevenson, speech in Salt Lake City, October 14, 1952

Some in America today would limit our freedom of expression and of conscience. In the name of unity, they would impose a narrow conformity of ideas and opinion. . . .

Only a government which fights for civil liberties and equal rights for its own people can stand for freedom in the rest of the world.

Adlai E. Stevenson, speech, Jefferson–Jackson Day, February 14, 1953

Equality is the result of human organization. We are not born equal.

Hannah Arendt, *The Origins of Totalitarianism*

. . . we cannot suppose that some men have a right to be in this world, and others no right.

Henry George, *Progress and Poverty*

Dissent is not sacred; the right of dissent is.

Thurman Arnold, as quoted in *Reader's Digest*, September 1967

The greatest right in the world is the right to be wrong.

> Harry Weinberger, in the New York *Evening Post,* April 10,
> 1917

The majority of us are for free speech only when it deals with those subjects concerning which we have no intense convictions.

> Edmund B. Chaffee, as quoted in *Reader's Digest,* March
> 1941

Men must be free to exercise those powers which make them men.

> Robert Hutchins, *Democracy and Human Nature*

Few people are capable of expressing with equanimity opinions which differ from the prejudices of their social environment. Most people are even incapable of forming such opinion.

> Albert Einstein, *Ideas and Opinions of Albert Einstein*

The right to be wrong is as important as the right to be admired.

> Edward R. Murrow, speech at Hamilton College, June 1954

Every man has a right to his opinion, but no man has a right to be wrong in his facts.

> Bernard Baruch, as quoted in *Reader's Digest,* March 1948

No man who says, "I'm as good as you," believes it. He would not say it if he did. The Saint Bernard never says it to the toy dog, nor the scholar to the dunce, nor the employable to the bum, nor the pretty woman to the plain. The claim to equality is made only by those who feel themselves to be in some way inferior. What it expresses is the itching, smarting awareness of an inferiority which the patient refuses to accept. And therefore resents.

> C. S. Lewis, as quoted in *Reader's Digest,* April 1960

To suppress minority thinking and minority expression would tend to freeze society and prevent progress. . . . Now more than ever we must keep in the forefront of our minds the facts that whenever we take away the liberties of those whom we hate, we are opening the way to loss of liberty for those we love.

Wendell L. Willkie, *One World*

Our system is based on striking a fair balance between the needs of society and the rights of the individual. To maintain this ordered liberty requires a periodic examination of the balancing process, as an engineer checks the pressure gauges of his boilers.

Chief Justice Warren E. Burger, as quoted in *Reader's Digest,* October 1972

Diversity of opinion within the framework of loyalty to our free society is not only basic to a university but to the entire nation.

James Bryant Conant, *Education in a Divided World*

Let us not be afraid of debate or dissent—let us encourage it. For if we should ever abandon these basic American traditions in the name of fighting communism, what would it profit us to win the whole world when we have lost our soul?

John F. Kennedy, address to the National Civil Liberties
Conference, Washington, D. C., April 16, 1959

The system of liberties that exists at any time is always the system of restraints or controls that exists at that time. No one can do anything except in relation to what others can do and cannot do.

John Dewey, *Freedom and Culture*

Dissent is a serious and honorable pursuit. The responsible dissenter is of enormous help in identifying targets for action, in clarifying issues, in formulating significant goals and mobilizing support for them. He has not rejected his culture, but knows that there are always elements of injustice within it that he must combat. He comes to understand the complex machinery by which change must be accomplished. He devotes himself to the heart-breaking, back-breaking work of building social change into resistant institutions.

Another kind of critic, however, has discovered that "alienated" dissent is profitable, diverting, and a great ego-inflator. Playing at alienation, he obscures and confuses the dilemma of the truly alienated. For this kind of critic, the goal of curing social evils has lost reality. Social evils become magnificent stage props for his act. He no longer seeks redemption for society. His eye is on the audience.

John W. Gardner, *The Recovery of Confidence*

THE ROMANTIC
LIFE

Love

Romance cannot be put into quantity production—the moment love becomes casual, it becomes commonplace.

> Frederick Lewis Allen, *Only Yesterday*

Bitterness imprisons life; love releases it. Bitterness paralyzes life; love empowers it. Bitterness sickens life; love heals it. Bitterness blinds life; love anoints its eyes.

> Rev. Harry Emerson Fosdick, *Riverside Sermons*

Were there left but one rock with two loving souls upon it, that rock would have as thoroughly moral a constitution as any possible world which the eternities and immensities could harbor.

> William James, *The Will to Believe*

All you need is love / Love is all you need.

> John Lennon, "All You Need Is Love"

A man nearly always loves for other reasons than he thinks. A lover is apt to be as full of secrets from himself as is the object of his love from him.

> Ben Hecht, *A Child of the Century*

Love is a hole in the heart.

> Ben Hecht, *Winkleberg* 373

Love itself draws on a woman nearly all the bad luck in the world.

Willa Cather, My Mortal Enemy

Love is between *I* and *Thou*. The man who does not know this . . . does not know love. . . . In the eyes of him who takes his stand in love, and gazes out of it, men are cut free from their entanglement in bustling activity.

Martin Buber, I and Thou

Love must be learned, and learned again and again; there is no end to it. Hate needs no instruction, but waits only to be provoked.

Katherine Anne Porter, The Days Before

Despair is the absolute extreme of self-love. It is reached when a man deliberately turns his back on all help from anyone in order to taste the rotten luxury of knowing himself to be lost.

Thomas Merton, Seeds of Contemplation

Americans, who make more of marrying for love than any other people, also break up more of their marriages . . . but the figure reflects not so much failure of love as the determination of people not to live without it.

Morton Hunt, The Natural History of Love

The happy man is he who lives the life of love, not for the honors it may bring, but for the life itself.

R. J. Baughan, Undiscovered Country

The first man I loved was Spiros. He was extremely handsome, extremely seductive. His mouth smelled sweeter than any man's I've ever known. I adored his embraces, an embrace scented of rosewater and basil. He was strong. He was tall. He had a passion for me. It made my childhood a very happy one. Spiros was my grandfather. He was also mayor of Athens for 30 years.

Melina Mercouri, as quoted in *Reader's Digest,* April 1962

[My wife] told me one of the sweetest things one could hear—"I am not jealous. But I am truly sad for all the actresses who embrace you and kiss you while acting, for with them, you are only pretending."

Joseph Cotten, as quoted in the New York *Herald Tribune,*
January 8, 1960

On the wings of Christianity came the great truth that Love is of the soul, and with the soul coeval.

Francis Thompson, *Essays*

The love we give away is the only love we keep.

Elbert Hubbard, *Note Book*

Love is a flame to burn out human wills,
Love is a flame to set the will on fire,
Love is a flame to cheat men into mire.
One of the three, we make Love what we choose.

John Masefield, "The Widow in the Bye Street"

And if I loved you Wednesday,
    Well, what is that to you?
I do not love you Thursday—
    So much is true.

Edna St. Vincent Millay, "Thursday"

Who builds her a house with love for timber,
    Builds her a house of foam;

And I'd rather be bride to a lad gone down
   Than widow to one safe home.

Edna St. Vincent Millay, "Keen"

The heart grows weary after a little
Of what it loved for a little while.

Edna St. Vincent Millay, "The Harp-Weaver"

'Tis not love's going hurts my days,
But that it went in little ways.

Edna St. Vincent Millay, as quoted in Reader's Digest,
March 1933

If you love a person you love him or her in their stark reality, and refuse to shut your eyes to their defects and errors.

John MacMurray, Reason and Emotion

Nowhere but in this realm of love do we perceive so distinctly that man is neither angel nor beast; nowhere else do we find a clearer revelation that man's toilsome greatness resides precisely within the narrow and precarious margin that separates in him the beast from the angel.

Henri Gibert, Love in Marriage

We went to Sunday school, public school from the fifth grade through high school, graduated in the same class and marched down life's road together. For me she still has the blue eyes and golden hair of yesteryear.

Harry S. Truman, speaking of his wife in Years of Decision

Love hath no physic for a grief too deep.

Robert Nathan, A Cedar Box

Genuine romantic love is much more than mere stupefying and intoxicating sex haze. . . . True romantic love *is* real love. The characteristic mark of the experience, as in the case of all loving, is the blinding revelation that some other being can be more important to the lover than he is to himself.

J. V. L. Casserley, *The Bent World*

Love and religion are the two most volcanic emotions to which the human organism is liable, and it is not surprising that, when there is a disturbance in one of these spheres, the vibrations should readily extend to the other.

Havelock Ellis, *Studies in the Psychology of Sex*

If you haven't had at least a slight poetic crack in the heart, you have been cheated by nature. Because a broken heart is what makes life so wonderful five years later, when you see the guy in an elevator and he is fat and smoking a cigar and saying long-time-no-see. If he hadn't broken your heart, you couldn't have that glorious feeling of relief!

Phyllis Battelle, as quoted in the New York *Journal-American*, June 1, 1962

To be in love is merely to be in a state of perpetual anaesthesis—to mistake an ordinary young man for a Greek god or an ordinary young woman for a goddess.

H. L. Mencken, *Prejudices*

When love is real love, when people's souls go out to their beloved, when they lose their hearts to them, when they act in the unselfish way in which these exquisite Old English phrases denote, a miracle is produced.

Abbé Ernest Dimnet, *What We Live By*

He came into my life as the warm wind of spring had awakened flowers, as the April showers awaken the earth. My love for him was an unchanging love, high and deep, free and faithful, strong as death. Each year I learned to love him more and more.

Anna Chennault, *A Thousand Springs*   377

Sing, for faith and hope are high—
   More so true as you and I—
      Sing the Lovers' Litany;
"Love like ours can never die!"

Rudyard Kipling, "Lovers' Litany"

A compliment is a gift, not to be thrown away carelessly unless you want to hurt the giver.

Eleanor Hamilton, *Partners in Love*

Love is like the measles; we all have to go through it.

Jerome K. Jerome, *Idle Thoughts of an Idle Fellow*

How terrible when people are led to believe, or left to believe, that once they are in love they have nothing to do but live happily ever after, they have nothing further to learn.

Gerald Vann, *The Heart of Man*

A lady of 47 who has been married 27 years and has six children knows what love really is and once described it for me like this: "Love is what you've been through with somebody."

James Thurber, as quoted in *Life*, March 14, 1960

Of all the worn, smudged, dog-eared words in our vocabulary, "love" is surely the grubbiest, smelliest, slimiest. . . . And yet it has to be pronounced, for, after all, Love is the last word.

Aldous Huxley, *Tomorrow and Tomorrow and Tomorrow*

Love has ceased to be the rather fearful, mysterious thing it was, and become a perfectly normal, almost commonplace, activity—an activity, for many young people especially in America, of the same nature as dancing or tennis, a sport, a recreation, a pastime.

Aldous Huxley, *Do What You Will*

We can only love what we know, and we can never know completely what we do not love.

Aldous Huxley, *The Perennial Philosophy*

He who sows courtesy reaps friendship, and he who plants kindness reaps love.

Richard Brooks, as quoted in *Reader's Digest,* October 1964

Love is the supreme value around which all moral values can be integrated into one ethical system valid for the whole of humanity.

Pitirim A. Sorokin, *The Ways and Power of Love*

To love means to communicate to the other that you are all for him, that you will never fail him or let him down when he needs you, but that you will always be standing by with all the necessary encouragements. It is something one can communicate to another only if one has it.

Ashley Montagu, *The Cultured Man*

Scientists are today discovering that to live as if *live* and *love* were one is an indispensable condition of life—because this is the way of life which the innate nature of man demands. The idea is not new. What is new is that contemporary men should be rediscovering, by scientific means, the ancient truths of the Sermon on the Mount and the golden rule. For human beings—and for humanity—nothing could be more important.

Ashley Montagu, as quoted in *Reader's Digest,* July 1971

Love is the strongest force the world possesses, and yet it is the humblest imaginable.

Mahatma Gandhi, *Selections*

Love is a mutual self-giving which ends in self-recovery.

Bishop Fulton J. Sheen, *Three to Get Married*   379

If love has come to be less often a sin, it has come also to be less often a supreme privilege.

Joseph Wood Krutch, as quoted in the Atlantic Monthly,
August 1928

I am a lover and have not found my thing to love.

Sherwood Anderson, Winesburg, Ohio

Not many men may be willing to die for love these days. But you can't escape the fact that millions are dying daily for the very *lack* of it.

John E. Large, The Small Needle of Doctor Large

Love, to the lover, is a noble and immense inspiration; to the naturalist it is a thin veil and prelude to the self-assertion of lust.

George Santayana, Reason in Society

No one worth possessing can be quite possessed.

Sara Teasdale, as quoted in Reader's Digest, May 1960

The tragedy of love is indifference.

W. Somerset Maugham, The Trembling of a Leaf

When a woman refuses to quarrel with a man, it means that she's tired of him. True lovers fight back.

Arthur Richman, as quoted in Reader's Digest, October
1951

Love vanquishes time. To lovers, a moment can be eternity, eternity can be the tick of a clock. Across the barriers of time and the ultimate destiny, love persists, for the home of the beloved, absent or present, is always in the mind and heart. Absence does not diminish love.

Mary Parrish, All the Love in the World

People say, "I got over this, I got over that." They are a lot of fools, the people who say you get over your loves and your heroes. I never do.

Robert Frost, as quoted in Reader's Digest, December 1961

You've got to love what's lovable, and hate what's hateable. It takes brains to see the difference.

Robert Frost, as quoted in the New York Post, May 18,
1958

How it improves people for us when we begin to love them.

David Grayson, as quoted in Reader's Digest, June 1962

Love has its roots in sex, but its foliage and flowers are in the pure light of the spirit.

Salvador de Madriaga, as quoted in Reader's Digest, May
1929

There is no more disturbing experience in the rich gamut of life than when a young man discovers, in the midst of an embrace, that he is taking the episode quite calmly, and is taking the kiss for what it is worth. His doubts and fears start from this point and there is no end to them. He doesn't know, now, whether it's love or passion. In fact, in the confusion of the moment he's not quite sure it isn't something else altogether, like forgery.

E. B. White, as quoted in the New York Journal-American,
February 12, 1961

In the all-important world of family relations, three other words are almost as powerful as the famous "I love you." They are "Maybe you're right."

Oren Arnold, as quoted in Reader's Digest, April 1965

We love the things we love in spite of what they are.

Louis Untermeyer, Love   381

We too often love things and use people when we should be using things and loving people.

Reuel Howe, as quoted in *Reader's Digest,* October 1968

Love for one person implies love for man as such.

Erich Fromm, *Escape from Freedom*

The way to love anything is to realize that it might be lost.

G. K. Chesterton, as quoted in *Reader's Digest,* August 1943

How do you know love is gone? If you said that you would be there at seven and you get there by nine, and he or she has not called the police yet—it's gone.

Marlene Dietrich, *Marlene Dietrich's ABC's*

The fickleness of the women I love is only equalled by the infernal constancy of the women who love me.

George Bernard Shaw, *The Philanderer*

If I am asked to love all mankind from China to Peru, I can only confess that I do not feel equal to it.

F. L. Lucas, *The Greatest Problem*

Love is an act of endless forgiveness, a tender look which becomes a habit.

Peter Ustinov, as quoted in the *Christian Science Monitor,* December 9, 1958

The entire sum of existence is the magic of being needed by just one person.

Vi Putnam, *Hard Hearts Are for Cabbage*

Man can live his truth, his deepest truth, but cannot speak it. It is for this reason that love becomes the ultimate human answer to the ultimate human question. Love, in reason's terms, answers nothing. We say that *Amor vincit omnia,* but, in truth, love conquers nothing—certainly not death—certainly not chance. What love does is to arm. It arms the worth of life in spite of life.

Archibald MacLeish, as quoted in Time, December 22, 1958

I have found it impossible to carry the heavy burden of responsibility and to discharge my duties as King as I would wish to do without the help and support of the woman I love.

King Edward VIII, radio message following his abdication,
December 11, 1936

Love is a brilliant illustration of a principle everywhere discoverable: namely, that human reason lives by turning the friction of material forces into the light of ideal goods.

George Santayana, Reason in Society

Awake, my heart to be loved, awake, awake!
The darkness silvers away, the morn doth break!
It leaps in the sky: unrisen lustres slake
The o'ertaken moon. Awake, O heart, awake!

Robert Bridges, "Awake, my heart, to be loved"

Only the really plain people know about love—the very fashionable ones try so hard to create an impression that they soon exhaust their talents.

Katharine Hepburn, as quoted in Look, February 18, 1958

I know no one in any time who has succeeded in loving every man he met.

Martin Buber, Between Man and Men 383

Happiness comes more from loving than being loved; and often when our affection seems wounded it is only our vanity bleeding. To love, and to be hurt often, and to love again—this is the brave and happy life.

J. E. Buckrose, as quoted in *Reader's Digest*, December 1939

The man and woman who can laugh at their love, who can kiss with smiles and embrace with chuckles, will outlast in mutual affection all the throat-lumpy, cow-eyed couples of their acquaintance. Nothing lives on so fresh and evergreen as the love with a funnybone.

George Jean Nathan, as quoted in *Reader's Digest*, April 1944

Love demands infinitely less than friendship.

George Jean Nathan, *The Autobiography of an Attitude*

Love is based upon a view of woman that is impossible to any man who has had any experience with them.

H. L. Mencken, *Prejudices: Fourth Series*

Being in love heightens a woman's attractions, but a man in love dwindles in the eyes of the world, bores his friends and is often a figure of comedy to other women. For man, being infinitely single-minded, forgets himself in love, sometimes with a thoroughness verging on the fatuous; he sees only the woman his love has improvised.

Susan Ertz, as quoted in *Reader's Digest*, December 1939

In an age where the lowered eyelid is just a sign of fatigue, the delicate game of love is pining away. Freud and flirtation are poor companions.

Marya Mannes, as quoted in *Life*, June 12, 1964

It has been wisely said that we cannot really love anybody at whom we never laugh.

Agnes Repplier, as quoted in *Reader's Digest*, August 1962

I loved you, so I drew these tides of men into my hands and wrote my will across the sky in stars.

T. E. Lawrence, *The Seven Pillars of Wisdom*

It is not the desert island nor the stony wilderness that cuts you off from the people you love. It is the wildness in the mind, the desert wastes in the heart through which one wanders lost and a stranger.

Anne Morrow Lindbergh, as quoted in *Reader's Digest,*
September 1973

Ultimately we want to teach men how to be free—free to love. We hardly dare use the word in school—we are so afraid it will be taken to mean "get into bed with each other."

Rev. Hugh Dickinson, as quoted in the London *Sunday
Telegram,* February 11, 1962

Peace of mind really comes out of the harmony of life. Peace of mind is another way of saying that you've learned how to love, that you have come to appreciate the importance of giving love in order to be worthy of receiving it.

Hubert H. Humphrey, as quoted in *Reader's Digest,*
November 1971

A man is only as good as what he loves.

Saul Bellow, *Seize the Day*

Everybody has to be somebody to somebody to be anybody.

Malcolm S. Forbes, as quoted in *Reader's Digest,*
November 1972

No one can do me any good by loving me; I have more love than I need, or could do any good with; but people do me good by making *me* love *them*—which isn't easy.

John Ruskin, in a letter to Charles Eliot Norton, as quoted
in *Reader's Digest,* August 1935   385

There is a wealth of unexpressed love in the world. It is one of the chief causes of sorrow evoked by death: what might have been said or might have been done that never can be said or done.

Arthur Hopkins, as quoted in *Reader's Digest,* October 1937

To really know someone is to have loved and hated him in turn.

Marcel Jouhandeau, *Defense de l'enfer*

To love means to decide independently to live with an equal partner, and to subordinate oneself to the formation of a new subject, a "we."

Fritz Kunkel, *Let's Be Normal*

Love is a gross exaggeration of the difference between one person and everybody else.

George Bernard Shaw, as quoted in *Reader's Digest,* October 1938

Love between man and woman is really just a kind of breathing.

D. H. Lawrence, as quoted in *Adam's Rib*

At the center of non-violence stands the principle of love.

Rev. Martin Luther King, Jr., *Stride Toward Freedom*

The glances over cocktails
That seemed to be so sweet,
Don't seem quite so amorous
Over shredded wheat.

Benny Fields, as quoted in *Reader's Digest,* December 1947

So long as little children are allowed to suffer, there is no true love in this world.

Isadora Duncan, as quoted in *This Quarter,* Autumn 1929

Respect is love in plain clothes.

Frankie Byrne, as quoted in *Reader's Digest*,
April 1972

Perhaps they were right in putting love into books. . . . Perhaps it could not live anywhere else.

William Faulkner, *Light in August*

If you cannot inspire a woman with love of you, fill her above the brim with love of herself; all that runs over will be yours.

Charles Caleb Colton, as quoted in *Reader's Digest*,
January 1949

We are back in love with each other—that second stage of love which consists of nostalgia for the first stage. That second stage of love which comes when you desperately feel you are falling out of love and cannot stand the thought of another loss.

Erica Jong, *Fear of Flying*

I longed for him as he was when I first met him. The man he had become was disappointing.

Erica Jong, *Fear of Flying*

We complete ourselves. If we haven't the power to complete ourselves, the search for love becomes a search for self-annihilation; and then we try to convince ourselves that self-annihilation is love.

Erica Jong, *Fear of Flying*

Love for the same thing never makes allies. It's always hate for the same thing.

Howard Spring, as quoted in *Reader's Digest*,
April 1941

What we do not say is that love brings us face to face with the barest skeletons of our being. What we do not say is that we are all, every last one of us, scared of love's power to create and destroy.

Ingrid Bengis, *Combat in the Erogenous Zone*

There is no surprise more magical than the surprise of being loved. It is the finger of God on a man's shoulder.

Charles Morgan, as quoted in *Reader's Digest,* November 1949

My chief occupation, despite appearances, has always been love. I have a romantic soul, and have always had considerable trouble interesting it in something else.

Albert Camus, *Notebooks: 1942–51*

Love is like quicksilver in the hand. Leave the fingers open and it stays in the palm; clutch it and it darts away.

Dorothy Parker, as quoted in *Reader's Digest,* December 1939

Is it an earthquake or simply a shock?

Is it the good turtle soup or merely the mock?

Is it a cocktail—this feeling of joy,
Or is what I feel the real McCoy?
Have I the right hunch or have I the wrong?
Will it be Bach I shall hear or
　　just a Cole Porter song?

Cole Porter, "At Long Last Love"

It is love in old age, no longer blind, that is true love. For love's highest intensity doesn't necessarily mean its highest quality. Glamour and jealousy are gone; and the ardent caress, no longer needed, is valueless compared to the reassuring touch of a trembling hand. Passers-by commonly see little beauty in the embrace of young lovers on a park bench, but the understanding smile of an old wife to her husband is one of the loveliest things in the world.

Booth Tarkington, as quoted in Reader's Digest, December
1939

As soon as you cannot keep anything from a woman, you love her.

Paul Geraldy, as quoted in Reader's Digest, November 1960

Perspective, I soon realized, was a fine commodity, but utterly useless when I was in the thick of things.

Ingrid Bengis, Combat in the Erogenous Zone

Love will never be ideal until man recovers from the illusion that he can be just a little bit true, a little bit faithful or a little bit married.

Helen Rowland, as quoted in Reader's Digest, July 1958

Men are not gentle creatures who want to be loved, and who at the most can defend themselves if they are attacked; they are, on the contrary, creatures among whose instinctual endowments is to be reckoned a powerful share of aggressiveness.

Sigmund Freud, Civilization and Its Discontents　389

Someone has written that love makes people believe in immortality, because there seems not to be room enough in life for so great a tenderness, and it is inconceivable that the most masterful of our emotions should have no more than the spare moments of a few years.

Robert Louis Stevenson, as quoted in *Reader's Digest,*
April 1960

We love those we are happy with. We do. For how else can we know we love them, or how else define loving?

Nan Fairbrother, as quoted in *Reader's Digest,* April 1961

Men and Women

The ideal woman which is in every man's mind is evoked by a word or phrase or the shape of her wrist, her hand. The most beautiful description of a woman is by understatement. Remember, all Tolstoy ever said to describe Anna Karenina was that she was beautiful and could see in the dark like a cat. Every man has a different idea of what's beautiful, and it's best to take the gesture, the shadow of the branch, and let the mind create the tree.

William Faulkner, as quoted in *Reader's Digest,* March 1973

Find a man of forty who heaves and moans over a woman in the manner of a poet and you will behold either a man who ceased to develop intellectually at twenty-four or thereabout, or a fraud who has his eye on the lands, tenements and hereditaments of the lady's deceased first husband.

H. L. Mencken, *Prejudices*

The allurement that women hold out to men is precisely the allurement that Cape Hatteras holds out to sailors: they are enormously dangerous and hence enormously fascinating.

H. L. Mencken, *A Mencken Chrestomathy*

A man's womenfolk, whatever their outward show of respect for his merit and authority, are always regarding him secretly as an ass, and with something akin to pity.

H. L. Mencken, In Defense of Women

Though every normal man cherishes the soothing unction that he is the intellectual superior of all women and particularly of his wife, he constantly gives the lie to his pretension by consulting and deferring to what he calls her intuition.

Intuition? It is no more and no less than intelligence. Women decide the larger questions of life correctly and quickly, not because they are lucky guessers nor because they are divinely inspired, but simply and solely because they have sense. They see at a glance what most men could not see with searchlights and telescopes; they are the supreme realists of the race. Men, too, sometimes have brains. But it is a rare man indeed who is as steadily intelligent, as constantly sound in judgment, as little put off by appearances, as the average woman of 48.

H. L. Mencken, as quoted in Reader's Digest,
May 1948

When women kiss, it always reminds one of prize fighters shaking hands.

H. L. Mencken, as quoted in Reader's Digest, December
1947

Women prefer men who have something tender about them—especially the legal kind.

Kay Ingram, as quoted in Reader's Digest,
May 1952

A man usually falls in love with the woman who asks the kind of questions he is able to answer.

Ronald Colman, as quoted in Reader's Digest,
July 1951 391

Some women are wonderful and some of them are she-devils. Well, what are you going to do? You can't do with them, you can't do without them.

Bernarr Macfadden, on being jailed at eighty-six for failure to pay alimony, as quoted in the New York *Mirror,* June 30, 1955

A woman may race to get a man a gift but it always ends in a tie.

Earl Wilson, as quoted in *Reader's Digest,* May 1952

No man ever told a woman she talked too much when she was telling him how wonderful he is.

Earl Wilson, as quoted in *Reader's Digest,* May 1967

To sell something, tell a woman it's a bargain; tell a man it's deductible.

Earl Wilson, as quoted in *Reader's Digest,* May 1967

Some of the best boy scouts are girls.

Groucho Marx, as quoted in *Reader's Digest,* May 1952

I say, when there are spats, kiss and make up before the day is done and live to fight another day.

Rev. Randolph Ray, as quoted in the New York *World-Telegram,* June 30, 1956

Never forget to assure a woman that she is unlike any other woman in the world, which she will believe, after which you may proceed to deal with her as with any other woman in the world.

D. B. Wyndham Lewis, as quoted in *Reader's Digest,* December 1951

There's a difference between beauty and charm. A beautiful woman is one I notice. A charming woman is one who notices me.

John Erskine, as quoted in *Reader's Digest*, October 1951

Adam could not be happy even in Paradise without Eve.

Lord John Lubbock Avebury, *Peace and Happiness*

Never look for a worm in the apple of your eye.

Langston Hughes, as quoted in *Reader's Digest*, May 1973

If you're in the right, argue like a man; if you're in the wrong, like a woman.

P. J. Toulet, as quoted in *Reader's Digest*, May 1949

My advice to the Women's Clubs of America is to raise more hell and fewer dahlias.

William Allen White, as quoted in *Reader's Digest*, April 1947

A woman is as old as she looks. A man is old when he stops looking.

Rev. B. C. Preston, as quoted in *Reader's Digest*, February 1947

Woman's virtue is man's greatest invention.

Cornelia Otis Skinner, *Elegant Wits and Grand Horizontals*

A new hat has the same effect upon a woman that three cocktails have upon a man.

Jay E. House, as quoted in *Reader's Digest*, March 1953

There are three things a woman can make out of almost nothing—a salad, a hat, and a quarrel.

John Barrymore, as quoted in Reader's Digest, July 1954

The way to fight a woman is with your hat. Grab it and run.

John Barrymore, as quoted in Reader's Digest, July 1940

Men never learn anything about women, but they have a lot of fun trying.

Olin Miller, as quoted in Reader's Digest, July 1954

I often wonder what sort of woman I would have made.

Ed Howe, as quoted in Reader's Digest, February 1947

Being kissed by a man who didn't wax his moustache was like eating an egg without salt.

Rudyard Kipling, Soldiers Three

One of the difficult tasks in this world is to convince a woman that even a bargain costs money.

Ed Howe, as quoted in *Reader's Digest*, July 1951

After a woman has looked at a man three or four times she notices something that should be changed.

Ed Howe, as quoted in *Reader's Digest*, March 1922

He who believes in nothing still needs a girl to believe in him.

Eugen Rosenstock-Huessy, as quoted in *Reader's Digest*, October 1914

There is no such thing as an ugly woman—there are only the ones who do not know how to make themselves attractive.

Christian Dior, as quoted in *Reader's Digest*, March 1953

Women are most fascinating between the ages of 35 and 40, after they have won a few races and know how to pace themselves. Since few women ever pass 40, maximum fascination can continue indefinitely.

Christian Dior, as quoted in *Reader's Digest*, November 1968

Women have served all these centuries as looking glasses possessing the magic powers of reflecting the figure of man at twice its natural size.

Virginia Woolf, *A Room of One's Own*

If woman had no existence save in the fiction written by men, one would imagine her a person of the utmost importance; very various; heroic and mean; splendid and sordid; infinitely beautiful and hideous in the extreme; as great as a man, some think even greater.

Virginia Woolf, *A Room of One's Own*   395

A girl's hardest task is to prove to a man that his intentions are serious.

Helen Rowland, as quoted in *Reader's Digest*,
March 1953

To be happy with a man you must understand him a lot and love him a little. To be happy with a woman you must love her a lot and not try to understand her at all.

Helen Rowland, as quoted in *Reader's Digest*,
June 1947

From the day on which she tips the scales at 140 the chief excitement of a woman's life consists in spotting women who are fatter than she is.

Helen Rowland, as quoted in *Reader's Digest*, February
1922

A wise woman puts a grain of sugar into everything she says to a man, and takes a grain of salt with everything he says to her.

Helen Rowland, as quoted in *Reader's Digest*, October 1955

A good woman inspires a man; a brilliant woman interests him; a beautiful woman fascinates him; and a sympathetic woman gets him.

Helen Rowland, as quoted in *Reader's Digest*, March 1962

I kissed my first woman and smoked my first cigarette on the same day. I have never had time for tobacco since.

Arturo Toscanini, as quoted in *Reader's Digest*, March 1938

Leisure society is full of people who spend a great part of their lives in flirtation and conceal nothing but the humiliating secret that they have never gone any further.

George Bernard Shaw, preface to *Overruled*

Changeable women are more endurable than monotonous ones. They are sometimes murdered but seldom deserted.

George Bernard Shaw, as quoted in *Reader's Digest*, May 1960

The only way a man can get the better of a woman in an argument is to let her keep on talking after she has won it.

Richard Attridge, as quoted in *Reader's Digest*, April 1953

Women's styles may change, but their designs remain the same.

Oscar Wilde, as quoted in *Reader's Digest*, December 1948

Men always want to be a woman's first love. Women have a more subtle instinct: what they like is to be a man's last romance.

Oscar Wilde, as quoted in *Reader's Digest*, April 1940

Women are meant to be loved, not to be understood.

Oscar Wilde, as quoted in *Reader's Digest*, April 1934

It is a great mistake for men to give up paying compliments, for when they give up saying what is charming, they give up thinking what is charming.

Oscar Wilde, as quoted in *Reader's Digest*, September 1946

I believe women are designed in their deeper instincts to get more pleasure out of life—not only sexually, but socially, occupationally, maternally—when they are not aggressive.

Dr. Benjamin Spock, *Decent and Indecent*

Twenty million young women rose to their feet with the cry, "We will not be dictated to," and proceeded to become stenographers.

G. K. Chesterton, as quoted in *Reader's Digest*, January 1957   397

No matter how well a woman carries her years, she's bound to drop a few sooner or later.

Erskine Johnson, as quoted in *Reader's Digest*, October 1953

I want to make a policy statement. I am unabashedly in favor of women.

Lyndon B. Johnson, press conference, October 15, 1966

There is only one attribute that all charming women possess in common—an expressive, responsive face.

Peter Joray, as quoted in *Reader's Digest*, November 1950

A woman means by unselfishness chiefly taking trouble for others; a man means not giving trouble to others. Thus each sex regards the other as radically selfish.

C. S. Lewis, as quoted in *Reader's Digest*, June 1947

Nowadays, instead of progressing from vous to tu, from Mister to Jim, it's "darling" and "come to my place" in the first hour.

Marya Mannes, as quoted in *Life*, June 12, 1964

There is no such thing as a dangerous woman; there are only susceptible men.

Joseph Wood Krutch, as quoted in *Reader's Digest*, June 1947

There's nothing like mixing with women to bring out all the foolishness in a man of sense.

Thorton Wilder, *The Matchmaker*

No man is as anti-feminist as a really feminine woman.

Frank O'Connor, as quoted in *Reader's Digest*, April 1965

To men a man is but a mind. Who cares what face he carries or what he wears? But a woman's body is the woman.

Ambrose Bierce, In the Midst of Life

A romantic man often feels more uplifted with two women than with one: his love seems to hit the ideal mark somewhere between two different faces.

Elizabeth Bowen, The Death of the Heart

Meet success like a gentleman and disaster like a man.

Lord Birkenhead, as quoted in Reader's Digest, April 1941

The best way to hold a man is in your arms.

Mae West, as quoted in Reader's Digest, April 1942

A man in the house is worth two in the street.

Mae West, in the film Belle of the Nineties

Why is woman persistently regarded as a mystery? It is not that she has labored to conceal the organic and psychological facts of her constitution, but that men have showed no interest in exploring them.

Ruth Herschberger, Adam's Rib

One of the most persistent myths of love is that a man, once he is taken with a woman, is ensnared by her indifference toward him. The truth is that, while such indifference may keep him stepping lively for a short time, it soon causes him to get out of the race altogether.

The clever woman realizes that the best way to get her man is to throw away all traditional feminine weapons and frankly and openly tell him that she likes him. The man thus handled, all folklore to the contrary, is won.

George Jean Nathan, as quoted in Reader's Digest,
December 1939   399

What passes for woman's intuition is often nothing more than man's transparency.

George Jean Nathan, as quoted in *Reader's Digest,* May 1938

Men build bridges and throw railroads across deserts, and yet they contend successfully that the job of sewing on a button is beyond them.

Heywood Broun, as quoted in *Reader's Digest,* July 1950

When a man tells me he's going to put all his cards on the table, I always look up his sleeve.

Leslie Hore-Belisha, as quoted in *Reader's Digest,* July 1957

Many a man has fallen in love with a girl in a light so dim he would not have chosen a suit by it.

Maurice Chevalier, as reported to news summaries, July 17, 1955

Women are like citadels. Some are taken by storm and others withstand a long and vigorous siege.

David Ainsworth, as quoted in *Reader's Digest,* March 1941

One woman's poise is another woman's poison.

Katharine Brush, as quoted in *Reader's Digest,* May 1941

Whether women are better than men I cannot say—but I can say they are certainly no worse.

Golda Meir, in an interview in New York, June 17, 1973

A woman, I always say, should be like a good suspense movie: the more left to the imagination, the more excitement there is. This should be her aim—to create suspense, to let a man discover things about her without her having to tell him.

Alfred Hitchcock, as quoted in *Reader's Digest*, July 1963

A man is never so weak as when some woman is telling him how strong he is.

Steve Hannagan, as quoted in *Reader's Digest*, August 1946

I think the real difference between men and women is their way of suffering. A woman learns to accept suffering. In body and in spirit. But a man keeps struggling, and the struggle keeps weakening and finally defeats him. Suffering never weakens or defeats a woman. It becomes a part of her. It brings her closer to life. With a man it's different. It brings him closer to death.

Frederic Prokosch, as quoted in *Reader's Digest*, August 1946

Women have considerable moral sense when they don't love a man. Mighty little when they do. With man, it's the opposite. If he doesn't care for a girl, he's without scruples. If he does care, he is likely to develop a moral code only the angels can live up to.

Mark Reed, as quoted in *Reader's Digest*, August 1946

Here's to woman! Would that we could fall into her arms without falling into her hands.

Ambrose Bierce, as quoted in *Bitter Bierce* by C. H. Grattan

If a man makes a stupid mistake, the other men say: "What a fool that man is." If a woman makes a stupid mistake, the men say: "What fools women are."

H. C. L. Jackson, as quoted in *Reader's Digest*, August 1946

What is most beautiful in virile men is something feminine; what is most beautiful in feminine women is something masculine.

Susan Sontag, *Against Interpretation*

Do not expect a woman to honor your privacy. She is liquid and, unless your resolution is well calked, she will seep through.

Nicolas Samstag, as quoted in *Reader's Digest*, August 1968

It takes a man a lifetime to find out about one particular woman; but if he puts in, say, ten years, industrious and curious, he can acquire the general rudiments of the sex.

O. Henry, *Heart of the West*

Feminine intuition is a fiction and a fraud. It is nonsensical, illogical, emotional, ridiculous—and practically foolproof.

Harry Haenigsen, as quoted in *Reader's Digest*, January 1967

A woman can look both moral and exciting—if she also looks as if it was quite a struggle.

Edna Ferber, as quoted in *Reader's Digest*, December 1954

Many men spend their daytime hours away from home as vital cognitive animals and their nights and weekends in mental passivity and vegetation.

Alice S. Rossi, *The Woman in America*

Girls have an unfair advantage over men: if they can't get what they want by being smart, they can get it by being dumb.

Yul Brynner, as quoted in *Reader's Digest*, May 1964

When an Italian talks with an American, he's inclined to feel a twinge of inferiority. America is rich and strong. Italy is poor. But when he talks to me, he's more at ease. I still represent a big, strong nation, but I am a woman—and he's a man.

Clare Boothe Luce, in a newspaper interview while
Ambassador to Italy, May 5, 1959

The best thing that can happen to any girl is to have her heart broken while she is young enough to grow beautiful on it. It gives a nice limpid look to the eyes—better than eye-shadow—and increases allure fifty percent.

Norman Patterson, as quoted in *Reader's Digest*, February
1941

A married man looks comfortable and settled and finished; he looks at a woman as if he knew all about her.

A bachelor looks unsettled and funny and he always wants to be running around seeing things. He looks at a woman sharply and then looks away and then looks back again, so she knows he is thinking about her and wondering what she is thinking about him. Bachelors are always strange and that's why women like them.

James Stephens, as quoted in *Reader's Digest*, February
1941

I've been a woman for fifty years, and I've never yet been able to discover precisely what it is I am.

Jean Giraudoux, *Tiger at the Gates*

A spectacle that depresses the male and makes him shudder is that of a woman looking another woman up and down to see what she is wearing. The cold, flat look that comes into a woman's eyes when she does this, the swift coarsening of her countenance and the immediate evaporation from it of all humane quality is one reason why men fear women.

James Thurber, as quoted in *Reader's Digest*, November
1941 403

A man who won't lie to a woman has very little consideration for her feelings.

Olin Miller, as quoted in Reader's Digest, May 1942

God created man and, finding him not sufficiently alone, gave him a companion to make him feel his solitude more keenly.

Paul Valéry, Tel quel

The fundamental reason that women do not achieve so greatly as men do is that women have no wives. Until such time as science or economics corrects this blunder of nature we shall remain, I fear, the inferior sex.

Professor Marjorie Nicolson, as quoted in Reader's Digest, September 1946

Once a woman has forgiven her man, she must not reheat his sins for breakfast.

Marlene Dietrich, Marlene Dietrich's ABC's

The average man is more interested in a woman who is interested in him than he is in a woman with beautiful legs.

Marlene Dietrich, as quoted in Reader's Digest, March 1949

A man admires the woman who makes him think but he keeps away from her. He likes the woman who makes him laugh. He loves the girl who hurts him. But he marries the woman who flatters him.

Nellie B. Stull, as quoted in Reader's Digest, July 1935

Any mechanism hard to manage is usually feminine.

Miles W. Abbott, as quoted in Reader's Digest, March 1936

Does the imagination dwell the most
Upon a woman won or a woman lost?

William Butler Yeats, "The Tower"

Every man is a volume if you know how to read him.

Margaret Fuller, as quoted in Reader's Digest, December
1936

A man may be so totally lost to hope that he will refuse to believe he can ever do or be anything, but few ever get so far down that they can't imagine a woman might be in love with them.

H. L. Davis, as quoted in Reader's Digest, October 1936

What do we bring you besides our poverty and our rags? Men, women and children—the stuff that nations are built of.

Mary Antin, as quoted in The Woman's Movement

The attributes of a great lady may still be found in the rule of the four S's: Sincerity, Simplicity, Sympathy, Serenity.

Emily Post, as quoted in Reader's Digest, September 1936

If a woman has been loved, hated and envied, her life was worth living.

Akiho Yanagiwara, Japanese socialite, as quoted in
Reader's Digest, February 1937

The woman who is known only through a man is known wrong.

Henry Adams, The Education of Henry Adams

It matters more what's in a woman's face than what's on it.

Claudette Colbert, as quoted in Reader's Digest, July 1940　　405

Women like to sit down with trouble as if it were knitting.

Ellen Glasgow, *The Sheltered Life*

We women do talk too much but even then we don't tell half we know.

Lady Nancy Astor, as quoted in *Reader's Digest,*
September 1946

My vigor, vitality, and cheek repel me. I am the kind of woman I would run from.

Lady Nancy Astor, as quoted in news summaries of
March 29, 1955

Even the wisest men make fools of themselves about women, and even the most foolish women are wise about men.

Theodor Reik, *The Need to be Loved*

First time you buy a house you see how pretty the paint is and you buy it. The second time you look to see if the basement has termites. It's the same with men.

Lupe Velez, as quoted in *Reader's Digest,* April 1942

I like a man who grins when he fights.

Sir Winston Churchill, as quoted in *Reader's Digest,*
October 1944

The thing most women dread about their past is its length.

J. P. Corcoran, as quoted in *Reader's Digest,* May 1945

The trouble with lipstick is that it doesn't.

Arch Ward, as quoted in *Reader's Digest,* April 1948

Manliness is not all swagger and swearing and mountain climbing. Manliness is also tenderness, gentleness, consideration. You men think you can decide on who is a man, when only a woman can really know.

Robert Anderson, *Tea and Sympathy*

I shudder to think what the generations-to-come will think about us women when, on thumbing over museum numbers of present-day publications, they learn that we are evil-smelling, foul-mouthed, bleary-eyed, rough-skinned, constipated, anemic creatures . . . unloved, unhonored, and barely unhung.

Mary Muldoon, as quoted in *Reader's Digest*, March 1933

A woman will always cherish the memory of the man who wanted to marry her; a man, of the woman who didn't.

Viola Brothers Shore, as quoted in *Reader's Digest*,
January 1943

Woman wants monogamy; / Man delights in novelty.

Dorothy Parker, *Enough Rope*

He and I had an office so tiny that an inch smaller and it would have been adultery.

Dorothy Parker, on sharing space with Robert Benchley at
Vanity Fair, as quoted in *Writers at Work*

Men seldom make passes at girls who wear glasses.

Dorothy Parker, in an often-quoted quip

It is only women who can love and criticize in the same long look.

Maurice Hewlett, as quoted in *Reader's Digest*, December
1939

Dancing is wonderful training for girls; it's the first way you learn to guess what a man is going to do before he does it.

Christopher Morley, as quoted in *Reader's Digest,*
December 1940

I asked a Burmese why women, after centuries of following their men, now walk ahead. He said there were many unexploded land mines since the war.

Robert Mueller, as quoted in *Look,* March 5, 1957

A woman with true charm is one who can make a youth feel mature, an old man youthful, and a middle-aged man completely sure of himself.

Bob Talbert, as quoted in *Reader's Digest,* January 1968

What we owe men is some freedom from their part in a murderous game in which they kick each other to death with one foot, bracing themselves on our various comfortable places with the other.

Grace Paley, as quoted in *Sisterhood Is Powerful*

There may be something in the idea of reincarnation. Some women of 35 can remember things that happened 45 years ago.

Eleanor Wood, as quoted in *Reader's Digest,* January 1968

A man is young if a lady can make him happy or unhappy. He enters middle age when a lady can make him happy, but can no longer make him unhappy. He is old and gone if a lady can make him neither happy nor unhappy.

Moriz Rosenthal, seventy-five-year-old pianist, as quoted in
Reader's Digest, January 1937

It's the homely women who are dangerous, not the beauties. A man is armed against a beautiful woman, and is constantly alert. But with a woman who has no special claim to beauty, he *feels safe,* the poor boob. And that's his undoing. My guess is, Delilah was a homely girl with a lot of charm.

Mildred Harrington, as quoted in *Reader's Digest*, August 1940

A "woman driver" is one who drives like a man and gets blamed for it.

Patricia Ledger, as quoted in the New York *Herald Tribune*, April 15, 1958

A man in love is a stupid thing—he bores you stiff, in real life or anywhere else; but a woman in love is fascinating—she has a kind of aura.

Leslie Howard, as quoted in *Reader's Digest*, September 1938

Who says women have to give up femininity to get equal legal rights? Anyway I don't want to go through a doorway ahead of a man—it's more fun to squeeze through together.

Perle Mesta, as quoted in *Reader's Digest*, May 1962

It is the easiest thing in the world to say every broad for herself— saying it and acting that way is one thing that's kept some of us behind the eight ball where we've been living for a hundred years.

Billie Holiday, as quoted in *Sisterhood Is Powerful*

A man can be a great scholar and look like something the cat should not have dragged in—but a woman has to be pretty good to be recognized for intellectual achievement if she lets her petticoat hang.

Professor Helen White, as quoted in *Reader's Digest*, February 1940

A woman with her hair combed up always looks as if she were going some place, either to the opera or the shower bath—depending on the woman.

Orson Welles, as quoted in *Reader's Digest*, December 1938

In the beginning, said a Persian poet, Allah took a rose, a lily, a dove, a serpent, a little honey, a Dead Sea apple, and a handful of clay. When he looked at the amalgam, it was a woman.

William Sharp, as quoted in Adam's Rib

The only way women could have equal rights nowadays would be to surrender some.

Burton Hillis, as quoted in Reader's Digest, June 1960

There's something contagious about demanding freedom, especially where women, who comprise the oldest oppressed group on the face of the planet, are concerned.

Robin Morgan, as quoted in Sisterhood Is Powerful

Behind every successful man you'll find a woman who has nothing to wear.

Harold Coffin, as quoted in Reader's Digest, March 1960

I don't mind living in a man's world as long as I can be a woman in it.

Marilyn Monroe, as quoted in Reader's Digest,
April 1960

I do not think it altogether inappropriate to introduce myself to this audience. I am the man who accompanied Jacqueline Kennedy to Paris, and I have enjoyed it.

John F. Kennedy, opening a news conference shortly after
French acclaim for the First Lady, June 3, 1961

Never argue with a woman when she's tired—or rested.

H. C. Diefenbach, as quoted in Reader's Digest, November
1960

When French women talk to a man, they seem to be asking a question. American women seem already to have given the answer.

Brigitte Bardot, as quoted in *Reader's Digest*, July 1958

If a man is vain, flatter. If timid, flatter. If boastful, flatter. In all history, too much flattery never lost a gentleman.

Kathryn Cravens, *Pursuit of Gentlemen*

A woman has to be twice as good as a man to go half as far.

Fannie Hurst, as quoted in *Reader's Digest*, October 1958

The American woman's ambitions are too high. In Europe a woman decides early what type she will be—mother, cook or siren. Women here want to be all of these and also run Wall Street.

Alistair Cooke, as quoted in *Reader's Digest*, December 1958

If a woman likes another woman, she's cordial. If she doesn't like her, she's very cordial.

Irvin S. Cobb, as quoted in *Reader's Digest*, January 1953

She was handsome in spite of her efforts to be handsomer.

Ring Lardner, *The Love Nest*

I never lied save to shield a woman or myself.

Ring Lardner, *Ex Parte*

Women are unpredictable. You never know how they are going to manage to get their own way.

Franklin P. Jones, as quoted in *Reader's Digest*, September 1955

There's one thing certain about flattery—it's not done with mirrors.

Caroline Clark, as quoted in *Reader's Digest,* October 1955

A married woman who likes her husband is much more attractive to men than one who doesn't. The reason is obvious. It's much easier to like a woman who confidently expects the best of you than one who has been soured by unpleasant experiences. And the married woman who instinctively likes men because she likes her husband not only makes friends for herself but performs the interesting miracle of making all her men friends like each other. Socially she is humanity's highest achievement.

Chester T. Crowell, as quoted in *Reader's Digest,* August 1940

If women are to change, then we have to see that something in the attitude of man also changes. . . . For if things don't change, if biology cannot be harnessed to serve the needs of human beings, then we risk an anger so large as to be ultimately paralyzing, risk the solidification of a gap that closes us off completely from what every human being needs most: love.

Ingrid Bengis, *Combat in the Erogenous Zone*

Our common isolation is so profound, and our common needs so overwhelming, that the meeting of the two almost invariably produces an awareness that we cannot possibly ask so much of our relations with another human being, but cannot ask any less either.

Ingrid Bengis, *Combat in the Erogenous Zone*

A woman is as old as she looks to a man who likes to look at her.

Finley Peter Dunne, as quoted in *Reader's Digest,* December 1956

The real trouble about women is that they must always go on trying to adapt themselves to men's theories of women.

412

D. H. Lawrence, as quoted in *Fear of Flying* by Erica Jong

Women have recently been placed at a disadvantage: man can now travel faster than sound.

Edward Artin, as quoted in *Reader's Digest*, April 1949

Women must be free to determine their own life patterns and their own destinies without suffering lifelong guilt for not having lived up to society's or their family's expectations.

Boston Women's Health Collective, *Our Bodies, Ourselves*

A truthful woman is one who won't lie about anything except her age, her weight and her husband's salary.

Cal Tinney, as quoted in *Reader's Digest*, March 1949

We have but one police force, the American woman.

Herbert L. Hoover, as quoted in *Reader's Digest*, February 1922

A woman is the only being that can skin a wolf and get a mink.

Sam Cowling, as quoted in *Reader's Digest*, January 1956

In Europe, every woman is every other woman's instinctive enemy. In America, women band together in clubs, crowd happily to lectures and, so far as I can see, actually seem to like each other.

C. E. M. Joad, as quoted in *Reader's Digest*, June 1938

Taste is the mark of an educated man, imagination the sign of a productive man, and emotional balance the token of a mature man.

Philip N. Youtz as quoted in *Reader's Digest*, January 1938

The vote, I thought, means nothing to women. We should be armed.

Edna O'Brien, as quoted in *Fear of Flying* by Erica Jong   413

Bachelor: The only species of big game for which the license is taken out after the safari.

Thomas Lyness, as quoted in *Reader's Digest*, April 1957

Women have a passion for mathematics. They divide their ages by two, double the price of their dresses, treble their husbands' salaries and add five years to the ages of their best friends.

Marcel Achard, as quoted in *Reader's Digest*, May 1956

It is only in the upper-class level that each husband sits next to the other man's wife.

Louis Kronenberger, *Company Manners*

Next to the wound, what women make best is the bandage.

Barbey d'Aurevilly, as quoted in *Reader's Digest*, July 1963

The clothes that keep a man looking his best are worn by girls on beaches.

Walter Woerner, as quoted in *Reader's Digest*, August 1956

Out of the 93 persons who have sat on the Supreme Court, not one yet has been a woman. Too bad, for they always have the last word, except here, where the last word really counts.

Justice Tom Clark, as quoted in *McCall's*, September 1963

Why is it that in public a woman without a man looks forlorn but a man without a woman looks romantic?

Lawrence Jaqua, as quoted in *Reader's Digest*, April 1951

Where are the days when men used to admire the entire woman? If current trends continue, we may have to breed women the way they breed chickens—either all bosom or all leg.

Grace Downs, as quoted in *Reader's Digest*, February 1955

Rules are the only means of a girl's assessing which man she likes well enough to break them for.

Petronella Portobello, as quoted in Reader's Digest, January 1958

We have to distrust each other. It is our only defense against betrayal.

Tennessee Williams, Camino Real

Little ladies may be born, but little gentlemen are hewn, like monuments, out of solid resistance.

Marcelene Cox, as quoted in Reader's Digest, February 1953

Remember the dignity of womanhood. Do not appeal, do not beg, do not grovel. Take courage, join hands, stand beside us, fight with us.

Christabel Pankhurst, as quoted in Sisterhood Is Powerful

The way you can tell a girl from a boy in the 15-year-old set is that the girl's feet are usually bigger.

Al Capp, as quoted in Reader's Digest, May 1954

A Frenchwoman, when double-crossed, will kill her rival; the Italian woman would rather kill her deceitful lover; the Englishwoman simply breaks off relations—but they all will console themselves with another man.

Charles Boyer, as quoted in news summaries of July 20, 1954

A woman never forgets her sex. She would rather talk with a man than an angel any day.

Oliver Wendell Holmes, as quoted in Reader's Digest, August 1961

Sex

Free love is seldom free. Teens pay for it in worry—the fear that they'll get caught, or that their partner may tire of them. It's hurried and furtive and not much fun.

Helen Bottel, as quoted in *Family Circle*, November 1969

If half the engineering effort and public interest that go into the research on the American bosom had gone into our guided-missile program, we would now be running hot-dog stands on the moon.

Al Capp, as quoted in *Reader's Digest*, July 1958

Just as you can't cook without heat you can't make love without feedback (which may be the reason we say "make love" rather than "make sex"). Sex is the one place where we today can learn to treat people as people. Feedback means the right mixture of stop and go, tough and tender, exertion and affection. This comes by empathy and long mutual knowledge. Anyone who expects to get this in a first attempt with a stranger is an optimist, or a neurotic—if he does, it is what used to be called love at first sight, and isn't expendable: "skill," or variety, is no substitute. Also one can't teach tenderness.

Dr. Alex Comfort, *The Joy of Sex*

Long-term love expressed in active sex means you have to know something about the biology of people. Don't go in for mutual do-it-yourself psychoanalysis, or you'll bring down the roof on each other. We all have pregenital needs, however we were weaned, potted or reared, just as we all have fingerprints and a navel. Finding out someone else's needs and your own, and how to express them in bed, is not only interesting and educative but rewarding, and what sexual love is about.

Dr. Alex Comfort, *The Joy of Sex*

The starting point of all lovemaking is close bodily contact. Love has
been defined as the harmony of two souls and the contact of two

epiderms. It is also, from our infancy, the starting point of human relationships and needs.

Dr. Alex Comfort, The Joy of Sex

A little theory makes sex more interesting, more comprehensible, and less scary—too much is a put-down, especially as you're likely to get it out of perspective and become a spectator of your own performance.

Dr. Alex Comfort, The Joy of Sex

The whole joy of sex-with-love is that there are no rules, so long as you enjoy, and the choice is practically unlimited.

Dr. Alex Comfort, The Joy of Sex

Our idea of sex wouldn't be recognizable to some other cultures, though our range of choice is the widest ever. For a start it's over-genital: "sex" for our culture means putting the penis in the vagina.

Dr. Alex Comfort, The Joy of Sex

One of the things still missing from the "new sexual freedom" is the unashamed ability to use sex as play—in this, psychoanalytic ideas of maturity are nearly as much to blame as old-style moralisms about what is normal or perverse. . . . Play is one function of sexual elaboration—playfulness is a part of love which could well be the major contribution of the Aquarian revolution to human happiness.

Dr. Alex Comfort, The Joy of Sex

There are after all only two "rules" in good sex, apart from the obvious one of not doing things which are silly, antisocial or dangerous. One is "Don't do anything you don't really enjoy," and the other is "Find your partner's needs and don't balk them if you can help it." In other words, a good giving and taking relationship depends on a compromise. . . . This can be easier than it sounds, because unless your partner wants something you find actively off-putting, real lovers 417 get a reward not only from their own satisfactions but from seeing the other respond and become satisfied.

Dr. Alex Comfort, *The Joy of Sex*

So far as woman is concerned there are no "great" lovers. The "great" lovers of the world have all been elected to this post either on their own recognizance or on the word of other men. The qualifications have been quantitative, and women, proverbially, are not interested in mathematics. For a woman, there are no "great" lovers; there is only the man she loves. And she does not have to be a mathematician to feel that the more he is a "great" lover, the less he is hers.

Jessamyn West, as quoted in *Reader's Digest*, February
1960

One man's mate is another man's passion.

Eugene Healy, *Mr. Sandeman Loses His Life*

My child, if you finally decide to let a man kiss you, put your whole heart and soul into it. No man likes to kiss a rock.

Lady Chesterfield, as quoted in *Reader's Digest*, January
1949

In the duel of sex, woman fights from the dreadnaught and man from an open raft.

H. L. Mencken, *A Mencken Chrestomathy*

There may be some things better than sex, and some things may be worse. But there is nothing exactly like it.

W. C. Fields, as quoted in *Reader's Digest*, August 1954

I should not regard physical infidelity as a very grave cause and should teach people that it is to be expected and tolerated.

Bertrand Russell, letter to Judge Ben B. Lindsey, as quoted
in *The Companionate Marriage*

Kisses may not spread germs, but they certainly lower resistance.

Louise Erickson, as quoted in *Reader's Digest,* May 1949

Anatomy is destiny.

Sigmund Freud, *The Complete Works of Sigmund Freud*

The pace and range of modern life are reducing even domestic love to the status of a quick-lunch counter.

Rosita Forbes, as quoted in *Reader's Digest,* October 1927

Once let the public become sufficiently clean-minded to allow every adult access to all that is known about the psychology, hygiene and ethics of sex, and in two generations we will have a new humanity, with more health and joy, fewer wrecked nerves, and almost no divorces.

Theodore Schroeder, *A Challenge to the Sex Censors*

You can't kiss a girl unexpectedly—only sooner than she thought you would.

Jack Seaman, as quoted in *Reader's Digest,* January 1949   419

Make love to every woman you meet. If you get five percent on your outlay, it's a good investment.

Arnold Bennett, as quoted in Reader's Digest, June 1941

Learning to understand, accept, and be responsible for our physical selves, we can start to use our untapped energies. Once our image of ourselves is on a firmer base, we can be better friends and better lovers, better *people,* more self-confident, more autonomous, stronger and more whole.

Boston Women's Health Collective, Our Bodies, Ourselves

Preoccupation with manipulative technique turns persons into objects, and touching is turned into the science of stimulation. Instead of a sharing of private emotions, sex then comes perilously close to being an exchange of impersonal services.

For the man and woman who value each other as individuals and who want the satisfactions of a sustained relationship, it is important to avoid the fundamental error of believing that touch serves only as a means to an end. In fact it is a primary form of communication, a silent voice that avoids the pitfalls of words while expressing the feelings of the moment.

Dr. William H. Masters and Virginia E. Johnson, as quoted
in Reader's Digest, December 1972

In the vast majority of marriages where sex is a problem, it's usually assumed that it's the wife who needs help. So widespread is this assumption that it goes unquestioned by most women. More than once couples have come to our clinic for therapy on the basis of the wife's inability to experience orgasm, genuinely unaware of the real factor involved—the husband's sexual incapacity.

This traditional attitude sustains the male in a heads-I-win, tails-you-lose approach to sexual disharmony. If he is impotent, his wife worries: "What's wrong with me?" And if she is non-orgasmic, he wonders: "What's wrong with her?" He then sends her off to a doctor or psychiatrist and hopes she will come back "fixed."

Dr. William H. Masters and Virginia E. Johnson, as quoted
in Redbook, May 1971

Sex is a three-letter word which sometimes needs some old-fashioned four-letter words to convey its full meaning: words like help, give, care, love.

Sam Levenson, *Sex and the Single Child*

Sex, which is purely physical, can be demonstrated, categorized, measured, identified and promoted like popcorn or mouthwash. Love, which is a state of mind, is more elusive. . . . There is a sort of rhythm involved in sex—an ebb and flow. The urge builds up, and then, after the physical release, it is satisfied and desire fades away.

Love, however, is different. Love is a deep and constant feeling for another person. Time has no importance. The most remarkable thing is that the other person's happiness becomes at least as important as your own. A person who loves you wants you to be happy *forever*.

Allan Martin Kaufman, as quoted in *Reader's Digest*, April 1972

Homosexuality has always existed, of course, but only recently has it been openly talked about. With this new openness, many myths about homosexuality are being dispelled. One is that a homosexual cannot be a useful, happy, productive person. Many committed homosexuals are. . . . Disappearing, too, is the idea that an individual who has engaged in homosexual practices cannot lead a normal, heterosexual life. He can—if he wants to.

Dr. Lawrence J. Hatterer, as quoted in *Reader's Digest*, September 1971

A curved line is the loveliest distance between two points.

Mae West, as quoted in *Reader's Digest*, January 1934

Rape is not practiced among lower animals, but only among industrialized primates.

Ruth Herschberger, *Adam's Rib*

The sexual organs are simply the means of exchanging sexual sensations. The real business is transacted at the emotional level. Thus, the

421

foundation for sexual happiness—or misery—is laid not in the bedroom but at the breakfast table.

Dr. David R. Reuben, as quoted in *Reader's Digest,* January
1973

By the end of the first week of marriage even the most skeptical husband usually recognizes that his wife has sexual needs just as real as his own. The fellow who refuses to provide his wife with sexual satisfaction is just begging for someone else to stand in for him. Unfortunately the male version of the "sick headache" is more common than most men are willing to admit.

Dr. David R. Reuben, as quoted in *Reader's Digest,* August
1973

Sex is everywhere—in the skies, on the earth. Comets are born, trees take root and grow. Yet we go merrily on our way totally unmindful of it all, or a reasonable facsimile of same.

Loretta Young, as quoted in *Reader's Digest,* April 1942

In most marriages, at some time, a husband or wife will refuse lovemaking because of distraction, excitement or, most likely, personal hurt. This is a powerful weapon because it touches the innermost sensitivities of the partner. But it is a weapon that should never be used. To do so is a sin against the spirit.

Marion Hilliard, *Women and Fatigue: A Woman Doctor's
Answer*

If a woman hasn't got a tiny streak of a harlot in her, she's a dry stick as a rule.

D. H. Lawrence, *Pornography and Obscenity*

I am not in the least disturbed when people regard my legs intently. I know they are doing so in pursuance of their inherent artistic instinct.

Marlene Dietrich, as quoted in *Reader's Digest,* April 1942

The orgasm has replaced the Cross as the focus of longing and the image of fulfillment.

Malcolm Muggeridge, *The Most of Malcolm Muggeridge*

To be very frank for a moment, the extra-matrimonial love affair has never struck me as so much an offense against religion, or a violation of what "the new morality" calls "sex-taboos," as a breach of that loyalty and good faith that one partner expects of another under every other contract.

Channing Pollock, as quoted in *Reader's Digest*, February 1933

Nothing can vex
Like the opposite sex.

Georgie Starbuck Galbraith, as quoted in *Reader's Digest*, November 1956

Sex is the great amateur art. The professional, male or female, is frowned on; he or she misses the whole point and spoils the show.

David Cort, *Social Astonishments*

When everything is linked to sex, it becomes difficult to determine and appreciate what is truly sexual. For sexiness is remote from sexuality. Sexiness remains very much on the surface in its distorted emphasis on the external aspects of human beings. To look sexy is not necessarily to be sexual. True sexuality is a function of the total personality, and is experienced and expressed only in the lives of truly mature people.

Father Eugene C. Kennedy, as quoted in *Reader's Digest*, September 1972

So long as the emotional feelings between the couple are right, so long as there is mutual trust and love, their bodies will invariably make the appropriate responses.

Dr. David R. Mace, as quoted in *Time*, March 10, 1958   423

A woman's reaching orgasm means giving up her hold on the world around her. In a woman who subconsciously feels that people and things are undependable or transitory, this fading process can be so alarming that it can prevent sexual excitement from building up.

Seymour Fisher, as quoted in *Reader's Digest*, February
1973

The ability to make love frivolously is the chief characteristic which distinguishes human beings from the beasts.

Heywood Broun, *It Seems to Me*

From best-sellers to comic books, any child who hasn't acquired an extensive sex education by the age of 12 belongs in remedial reading.

Will Stanton, as quoted in *Reader's Digest*, March 1971

The only method of creating sex appeal is by clothes. The woman of the 19th century was a masterpiece of sex appeal from the crown of her head to the soles of her feet. Everything about her except cheeks and nose was a secret.

George Bernard Shaw, as quoted in *Reader's Digest*,
December 1934

If I became dictator of the world I'd give all the poor a cottage and birth-control pills—and I'd make damn sure they didn't get one if they didn't take the other!

Lyndon B. Johnson, as quoted in *The Atlantic Monthly*,
September 1973

For the first time a woman can plan a career with the certainty that it will not be disrupted by an unwanted pregnancy. . . .

Every day we see increasing world problems because of rapidly expanding populations. Safe and effective contraception is essential in man's battle to control his environment. Thus far, the Pill remains one of our most effective weapons. Taken properly, under careful medical

424

supervision, it is still the most reliable means of preventing unwanted pregnancy that man has yet been able to devise for wide-scale use.

Elizabeth B. Connell, as quoted in Reader's Digest, October
1970

. . . and then I asked him with my eyes to ask again yes and then he asked me would I yes to say yes my mountain flower and first I put my arms around him yes and drew him down to me so he could feel my breasts all perfume yes and his heart was going like mad and yes I said yes I will Yes.

James Joyce, Ulysses

A good girl, whose grandmother would have refused to kiss her fiance until the engagement was sealed, now has to decide "how far to go" on each date to keep her reputation poised between prudish and loose.

Connie Brown and Jane Seitz, as quoted in Sisterhood Is
Powerful

Although man has learned through evolution to walk in an upright position, his eyes still swing from limb to limb.

Margaret Schooley, as quoted in Reader's Digest, January
1956

REASON AND EMOTION

Musings of the Mind

Nothing can be unconditional; consequently nothing can be free.

George Bernard Shaw, *Maxims for Revolutionists*

The man who listens to Reason is lost: Reason enslaves all whose minds are not strong enough to master her.

George Bernard Shaw, *Man and Superman*

This is the true joy in life, the being used for a purpose recognized by yourself as a mighty one.

George Bernard Shaw, as quoted in *Reader's Digest*, August 1948

When a stupid man is doing something he is ashamed of, he always declares that it is his duty.

George Bernard Shaw, *Caesar and Cleopatra*

The great secret is not having bad manners or good manners or any other particular sort of manners, but having the same manners for all human souls.

George Bernard Shaw, *Pygmalion*

Man is the only animal of which I am thoroughly and cravenly afraid. I have never thought much of the courage of a lion-tamer. Inside the cage he is at least safe from other men. There is not much harm in a

429

lion. He has no ideals, no religion, no politics, no gentility; in short, no reason for destroying anything that he does not want to eat.

> George Bernard Shaw, as quoted in *Reader's Digest*,
> August 1938

The open mind never acts: when we have done our utmost to arrive at a reasonable conclusion, we still, when we can reason and investigate no more, must close our minds for the moment with a snap, and act dogmatically on our conclusions. The man who waits to make an entirely reasonable will dies intestate.

> George Bernard Shaw, preface to *Androcles and the Lion*

We are only cave men who have lost their cave.

> Christopher Morley, *The Man Who Made Friends with
> Himself*

Many people today don't want honest answers insofar as honest means unpleasant or disturbing. They want a soft answer that turneth away anxiety.

> Louis Kronenberger, as quoted in *Reader's Digest*,
> February 1972

An untruth is not always a lie. Romancing, as we use the term, means the telling of untruths that are not falsehoods.

> Edward A. Strecker and Vincent T. Lathbury, *Their
> Mothers' Daughters*

Wisdom is knowing when you cannot be wise.

> Paul Engle, as quoted in *Reader's Digest*, January 1973

What man knows is everywhere at war with what he wants.

> Joseph Wood Krutch, *The Modern Temper*

The average man never really thinks from end to end of his life. The mental activity of such people is only a mouthing of clichés. What they

430

mistake for thought is simply repetition of what they have heard. My guess is that well over 80% of the human race goes through life without having a single original thought. Whenever a new one appears the average man shows signs of dismay and resentment.

H. L. Mencken, *The Intimate Notebooks of George Jean Nathan*

Run your eye back over the list of martyrs, lay and clerical: nine-tenths of them, you will find, stood accused of nothing worse than honest efforts to find out and announce the truth.

H. L. Mencken, *The Vintage Mencken*

Criticism, like rain, should be gentle enough to nourish a man's growth without destroying his roots.

Frank A. Clark, as quoted in *Reader's Digest*, September 1971

An honest man can never surrender an honest doubt.

Walter Malone, *The Agnostic's Creed*

These terrible sociologists, who are the astrologers and alchemists of our twentieth century.

Miguel de Unamuno, *Fanatical Skepticism*

The intellectual world is divided into two classes—dilettantes, on the one hand, and pedants, on the other.

Miguel de Unamuno, *The Tragic Sense of Life*

Use harms and even destroys beauty. The noblest function of an object is to be contemplated.

Miguel de Unamuno, *Mist*

Men fear thought as they fear nothing else on earth—more than ruin, more than death.

Bertrand Russell, *Selected Papers of Bertrand Russell*

Real life is, to most men, a long second-best, a perpetual compromise between the ideal and the possible.

Bertrand Russell, *The Study of Mathematics*

Tidiness is one of those virtues that never will be assimilated with pleasure. It makes life easier and more agreeable, does harm to no one, actually saves time and trouble to the person who practices it—yet there must be some ominous flaw to explain why, in spite of the concerted effort of humanity to teach it to the young, millions in every generation continue to reject it.

Freya Stark, as quoted in *Reader's Digest*, March 1973

The big, strong and rich are always unpopular with the small, weak and poor. . . . When a smaller dog finds itself boxed up with a larger dog, the smaller dog is inclined to snarl and bristle. This is not only dog nature, it is human nature.

Arnold J. Toynbee, as quoted in *The New York Times Magazine*, November 3, 1963

Life is never so bad at its worst that it is impossible to live; it is never so good at its best that it is easy to live.

Gabriel Heatter, as quoted in *Reader's Digest*, August 1954

Philosophy has the task and the opportunity of helping banish the concept that human destiny here and now is of slight importance in comparison with some supernatural destiny.

John Dewey, as quoted in *Fortune*, August 1944

A thing is not truth until it is so strongly believed in that the believer is convinced that its existence does not depend on him. This cuts off the pragmatist from knowing what truth is.

John Jay Chapman, *Essays*

If most of us are ashamed of shabby clothes and shoddy furniture, let us be more ashamed of shabby ideas and shoddy philosophies.

Albert Einstein, as quoted in *Reader's Digest*, February 1974

The man who regards his own life and that of his fellow creatures as meaningless is not merely unhappy but hardly fit for life.

Albert Einstein, as quoted in *The New York Times Magazine*, April 24, 1955

I cannot prove scientifically that truth must be conceived as a truth that is valid independent of humanity; but I believe it firmly.

Albert Einstein, as quoted in *The Religion of Men*

The individual who has experienced solitude will not easily become a victim of mass suggestion.

Albert Einstein, letter to Queen Elizabeth, 1939

Everybody acts not only under external compulsion but also in accordance with inner necessity.

Albert Einstein, *The World as I See It*

Most mistakes in philosophy and logic occur because the human mind is apt to take the symbol for the reality.

Albert Einstein, *Cosmic Religion*

The great enemy of the truth is very often not the lie—deliberate, contrived and dishonest—but the myth—persistent, persuasive and unrealistic.

John F. Kennedy, commencement address, Yale University, June 11, 1962

Too often we . . . enjoy the comfort of opinion without the discomfort of thought.

> John F. Kennedy, speech at Yale University, 1962

If seed in the black earth can turn into such beautiful roses, what might not the heart of man become in its long journey toward the stars?

> G. K. Chesterton, as quoted in *Reader's Digest*, August 1952

People have fallen into the foolish habit of speaking of orthodoxy as something heavy, humdrum, and safe. There never was anything so perilous or so exciting as orthodoxy. It was sanity: and to be sane is more dramatic than to be mad.

> G. K. Chesterton, *Orthodoxy*

Truth must necessarily be stranger than fiction; for fiction is the creation of the human mind and therefore congenial to it.

> G. K. Chesterton, *The Club of Queer Trades*

There is only one thing certain and that is that nothing is certain.

> G. K. Chesterton, as quoted in *Reader's Digest*, June 1922

Do not try to bend, any more than the trees try to bend. Try to grow straight, and life will bend you.

> G. K. Chesterton, *Alarms and Discursions*

In everything worth having, even in every pleasure, there is a point of pain or tedium that must be survived, so that the pleasure may revive and endure. The joy of battle comes after the first fear of death; the glow of the sea-bather comes after the icy shock of the sea bath; and the success of the marriage comes after the failure of the honeymoon. All human vows, laws and contracts are so many ways of surviving with success this breaking point, this instant of potential surrender.

> G. K. Chesterton, as quoted in *Reader's Digest*, October 1936

Among all the strange things that men have forgotten, the most universal lapse of memory is that by which they have forgotten they are living on a star.

G. K. Chesterton, as quoted in *Reader's Digest,*
November 1939

Every man is dangerous who only cares for one thing.

G. K. Chesterton, as quoted in *Reader's Digest,* June 1968

In a world where everything is ridiculous, nothing can be ridiculed. You cannot unmask a mask.

G. K. Chesterton, *Generally Speaking*

Out of our beliefs are born deeds. Out of our deeds we form habits; out of our habits grow our character; and on our character we build our destination.

Henry Hancock, as quoted in the *Alpha Xi Delta Magazine,* 1957

Hypocrisy is the tribute vice pays to virtue.

Kenneth W. Thompson, as quoted in *Reader's Digest,*
February 1961

There can *be* no difference anywhere that doesn't *make* a difference elsewhere—no difference in concrete fact and in conduct consequent upon the fact, imposed on somebody, somehow, somewhere, and somewhen. The whole function of philosophy ought to be to find out what definite difference it will make to you and me, at definite instances in our life, if this world-formula or that world-formula be the true one.

William James, *Pragmatism*

Philosophy is only a matter of passionate vision rather than of logic—logic only finding reasons for the vision afterwards.

William James, *The Pluralistic Universe*   435

Habit is the enormous flywheel of society, its most precious conservative agent. There is no more miserable human being than one in whom nothing is habitual but indecision. Full half the time of such a man goes to the deciding, or regretting, of matters which ought to be so ingrained in him as practically not to exist for his consciousness at all.

William James, as quoted in *Reader's Digest,* July 1951

When you have to make a choice and don't make it, that is in itself a choice.

William James, *Memories and Studies*

The great use of life is to spend it for something that will outlast it.

William James, as quoted in *Reader's Digest,*
November 1943

It is not easy to find happiness in ourselves, and it is not possible to find it elsewhere.

Agnes Repplier, as quoted in *Reader's Digest,* October 1951

The clearsighted do not rule the world, but they sustain and console it.

Agnes Repplier, *Eight Decades*

A man's life, like a piece of tapestry, is made up of many strands which interwoven make a pattern; to separate a single one and look at it alone not only destroys the whole but gives the strand itself a false value.

Judge Learned Hand, as quoted in *Proceedings in Memory
of Mr. Justice Brandeis*

We must not try to manipulate life; rather we must find out what life demands of us, and train ourselves to fulfill these demands. It is a long and humble business.

Phyllis Bottome, as quoted in *Reader's Digest,*
November 1943

Philosophy has become either the errand boy of the natural sciences or the playboy of linguistic shellgames whose name at present is logical positivism.

Allen Tate, as quoted in The New York Times Book Review, March 8, 1952

One is daily annoyed by some little corner that needs clearing up, and when by accident one at last is stirred to do the needful, one wonders that one should have stood the annoyance so long when such a little effort would have done away with it. Moral: When in doubt, do it.

Justice Oliver Wendell Holmes, Jr., as quoted in Reader's Digest, July 1964

If you want to hit a bird on the wing, you must have all your will in a focus, you must not be thinking about yourself, and equally, you must not be thinking about your neighbor; you must be living in your eye on that bird. Every achievement is a bird on the wing.

Justice Oliver Wendell Holmes, Jr., Speeches

Many ideas grow better when transplanted into another mind than in the one where they sprang up.

Justice Oliver Wendell Holmes, Jr., as quoted in Reader's Digest, October 1962

Time and again I have emerged from a course of reading in philosophy with the conviction that the authors were really avoiding specific problems by converting them into tenuous sophistries that have very little real meaning.

Ernest Jones, Free Associations

What you are doing is, of course, in the first place, living. And life involves passions, faiths, doubts and courage. The critical inquiry into what these things mean and imply is philosophy.

Josiah Royce, The Spirit of Modern Philosophy   437

The world is not innocent. It does not ignore evil; it possesses and still conquers evil.

Josiah Royce, The Spirit of Modern Philosophy

Unless you can find some sort of loyalty, you cannot find unity and peace in your active living.

Josiah Royce, The Philosophy of Loyalty

Bread, beauty and brotherhood are the three great needs of man. We shall create a new social order in which everyone who renders honest service shall have these things.

Edwin Markham, as quoted in Reader's Digest, August 1936

There is no doubt that the most radical division of humanity it is possible to make is that which splits it into two classes: those who make great demands on themselves, piling up difficulties and duties; and those who demand nothing special of themselves, but for whom to live is to be every moment what they already are, without imposing on themselves any effort towards perfection; mere buoys that float on the waves.

José Ortega y Gasset, as quoted in Reader's Digest,
September 1936

From the moment of birth we are immersed in action, and can only fitfully guide it by taking thought.

Alfred North Whitehead, Science and the Modern World

Ideas won't keep; something must be done about them.

Alfred North Whitehead, as quoted in Reader's Digest,
March 1962

Reality is just itself, and it is nonsense to ask whether it be true or false.

438

Alfred North Whitehead, Adventures in Ideas

Not ignorance, but the ignorance of ignorance, is the death of knowledge.

Alfred North Whitehead, as quoted in *Reader's Digest*,
December 1968

Men heap together the mistakes of their lives, and create a monster they call Destiny.

John Oliver Hobbes, as quoted in *Reader's Digest*,
September 1937

The ultimate measure of a man is not where he stands in moments of comfort and convenience, but where he stands at times of challenge and controversy.

Rev. Martin Luther King, Jr., *Strength to Love*

What we steadily, consciously, habitually think we are, that we tend to become.

John Cowper Powys, as quoted in *Reader's Digest*,
April 1935

Great men are rarely isolated mountain-peaks; they are the summits of ranges.

Thomas Wentworth Higginson, *Atlantic Essays*

The only thing sure about luck is that it will change.

Bret Harte, as quoted in Reader's Digest, May 1933

Life is a long lesson in humility.

Sir James M. Barrie, The Little Minister

An injurious truth has no merit over an injurious lie. Neither should ever be uttered.

Mark Twain, as quoted in Reader's Digest, May 1936

Truth is stranger than fiction, but it is because fiction is obliged to stick to possibilities; truth isn't.

Mark Twain, as quoted in Reader's Digest,
May 1967

The proper function of man is to live, not to exist.

Jack London, as quoted in Reader's Digest,
August 1968

I would rather live in a world where my life is surrounded by mystery than live in a world so small that my mind could comprehend it.

Rev. Harry Emerson Fosdick, The Mystery of Life

We cannot all be great, but we can always attach ourselves to something that is great.

Rev. Harry Emerson Fosdick, as quoted in Reader's Digest,
January 1973

Repetition does not transform a lie into a truth.

440
Franklin D. Roosevelt, radio address, October 26, 1939

The art of living consists in knowing which impulses to obey and which must be made to obey.

Sydney J. Harris, as quoted in *Reader's Digest*,
November 1972

It is a tribute to the spontaneous vitality of truth that we never say somebody "blurts out" a lie.

Sydney J. Harris, as quoted in *Reader's Digest*, April 1968

The first lesson of pragmatism: damn the absolute!

Henry Steele Commager, *Freedom, Loyalty, Dissent*

Never look down to test the ground before taking your step: only he who keeps his eye fixed on the far horizon will find his right road.

Dag Hammarskjöld, as quoted in *Reader's Digest*,
March 1965

Life demands from you only the strength you possess. Only one feat is possible—not to have run away.

Dag Hammarskjöld, *Markings*

It is more important to be aware of the ground for your own behavior than to understand the motives of another.

Dag Hammarskjöld, as quoted in *Reader's Digest*,
March 1965

You cannot play with the animal in you without becoming wholly animal, play with falsehood without forfeiting your right to truth, play with cruelty without losing your sensitivity of mind. He who wants to keep his garden tidy doesn't reserve a plot for weeds.

Dag Hammarskjöld, as quoted in *Reader's Digest*,
March 1963 441

A successful lie is doubly a lie; an error which has to be corrected is a heavier burden than the truth.

Dag Hammarskjöld, as quoted in *Reader's Digest*,
March 1965

The horror no less than the charm of real life consists precisely in the recurrent actualization of the inconceivable.

Aldous Huxley, *Themes and Variations*

The end cannot justify the means for the simple and obvious reason that the means employed determine the nature of the ends produced.

Aldous Huxley, *Ends and Means*

Facts do not cease to exist because they are ignored.

Aldous Huxley, as quoted in *Reader's Digest*, March 1973

Man is an intelligence in service to his organs.

Aldous Huxley, *Themes and Variations*

The art of living lies less in eliminating our troubles than in growing with them.

Bernard Baruch, as quoted in *Reader's Digest*,
September 1966

There are two ways to slice easily through life; to believe everything or to doubt everything. Both ways save us from thinking.

Alfred Korzybski, *Manhood of Humanity*

When you have eliminated the impossible, whatever remains, however improbable, must be the truth.

Sir Arthur Conan Doyle, *The Sign of Four*

Lack of something to feel important about is almost the greatest tragedy a man may have.

Arthur E. Morgan, as quoted in *Reader's Digest,*
January 1973

The superstition that the hounds of truth will rout the vermin of error seems, like a fragment of Victorian lace, quaint, but too brittle to be lifted out of the showcase.

William F. Buckley, Jr., *Quotations from Chairman Bill*

I believe that only one person in a thousand knows the trick of really living in the present. Most of us spend 59 minutes an hour living in the past, with regret for lost joys, or shame for things badly done (both utterly useless and weakening)—or in a future which we either long for or dread. Yet the past is gone beyond prayer, and every minute you spend in the vain effort to anticipate the future is a moment lost. There is only one world, the world pressing against you at this minute. There is only one minute in which you are alive, *this minute*—here and now. The only way to live is by accepting each minute as an unrepeatable miracle. Which is exactly what it is—a miracle and unrepeatable.

Storm Jameson, as quoted in *Reader's Digest*, August 1956

Man's mind stretched to a new idea never goes back to its original dimensions.

Oliver Wendell Holmes, as quoted in *Reader's Digest,*
August 1949

The longing for certainty and repose is in every human mind. But certainty generally is illusion, and repose is not the destiny of man.

Oliver Wendell Holmes, as quoted in *Reader's Digest,*
November 1961

It is our responsibilities, not ourselves, that we should take seriously.

Peter Ustinov, as quoted in *This Week,* November 1968   443

I do believe one ought to face facts. If you don't they get behind you and may become terrors, nightmares, giants, horrors. As long as one faces them one is top dog. The trouble is not to steel oneself but to face them calmly, easily—to have the habit of facing them.

Katherine Mansfield, as quoted in *Reader's Digest,*
April 1952

Wisdom consists in the highest use of the intellect for the discernment of the largest moral interest of humanity. It is the most perfect willingness to do the right combined with the utmost attainable knowledge of what is right. . . . Wisdom consists in working for the better from the love of the best.

Felix Adler, *Life and Destiny*

A great deal of talent is lost to the world for want of a little courage. Every day sends to their graves obscure men whom timidity prevented from making a first effort.

Sydney Smith, as quoted in *Reader's Digest,* April 1952

Always fall in with what you're asked to accept. Take what is given, and make it over your way. My aim in life has always been to hold my own with whatever's going. Not against: with.

Robert Frost, as quoted in *Vogue,* March 15, 1963

Any life truly lived is a risky business, and if one puts up too many fences against the risks one ends by shutting out life itself.

Kenneth S. Davis, as quoted in *Reader's Digest,* April 1952

Human kind cannot bear very much reality.

T. S. Eliot, *Four Quartets*

Miracles are so called because they excite wonder. In unphilosophical minds any rare or unexpected thing excites wonder, while in philosophical minds the familiar excites wonder also.

Each morning the sunrise excites wonder in the poet, and the order of the solar system excites it every night in the astronomer. Astronomy explains the sunrise, but what shall explain the solar system? The universe, which would explain everything, is the greatest of wonders, and a perpetual miracle.

George Santayana, as quoted in Reader's Digest,
November 1961

Nothing can be meaner than the anxiety to live on, to live on anyhow and in any shape; a spirit without any honor is not willing to live except in its own way, and a spirit with any wisdom is not over-eager to live at all.

George Santayana, Winds of Doctrine

Reason requires the fusion of two types of life . . . one a life of impulse expressed in affairs and social passions, the other a life of reflection expressed in religion, science, and the imitative arts.

George Santayana, Reason in Common Sense

A simple life is its own reward.

George Santayana, as quoted in Reader's Digest, March
1965

Fame as a noble mind conceives and desires it . . . consists in the immortality of a man's work, his spirit, his efficacy, in the perpetual rejuvenation of his soul in the world. . . . Fame is thus the outward sign of recognition of an inward representative authority residing in genius or good fortune.

George Santayana, as quoted in Reason in Society

The human being cannot live in a condition of emptiness for very long: if he is not growing *toward* something, he does not merely stagnate; the pent-up potentialities turn into morbidity and despair, and eventually into destructive activities.

Rollo May, Man's Search for Himself 445

The best argument I know for an immortal life is the existence of a man who deserves one.

William Jones, as quoted in *Reader's Digest*, April 1947

Often a liberal antidote of experience supplies a sovereign cure for a paralyzing abstraction built upon a theory.

Benjamin N. Cardozo, *Paradoxes of Legal Science*

In the war against Reality, man has but one weapon—Imagination.

Jules de Gautier, as quoted in *Reader's Digest*, May 1943

This is what I think now: that the natural state of the sentient adult is a qualified unhappiness. I think also that in an adult the desire to be finer than you are, "a constant striving" . . . only adds to this unhappiness in the end—that end that comes to our youth and hope.

F. Scott Fitzgerald, "The Crack-Up"

The test of a first-rate intelligence is the ability to hold two opposed ideas in the mind at the same time, and still retain the ability to function.

F. Scott Fitzgerald, *The Crack-Up*

The whole secret of life is to be interested in one thing profoundly and in a thousand things well.

Hugh Walpole, as quoted in *Reader's Digest*, November 1947

If to look truth in the face and not resent it when it's unpalatable, and take human nature as you find it . . . is to be cynical, then I suppose I'm a cynic.

W. Somerset Maugham, *The Back of Beyond*

446

The inevitable is only that which we do not resist.

Justice Louis D. Brandeis, as quoted in *Reader's Digest*,
June 1951

Sometimes, if we would guide by the light of reason, we must let our minds be bold.

Justice Louis D. Brandeis, opinion in *Jay Burns Baking Co.*
v. *Bryan* (1924)

Ideals are like the stars—we never reach them, but like the mariners on the sea, we chart our course by them.

Carl Schurz, as quoted in *Reader's Digest*, April 1940

As a rule people are afraid of truth. Each truth we discover in nature or social life destroys the crutches on which we used to lean.

Ernst Toller, as quoted in the *Saturday Review of
Literature*, May 20, 1944

There is no substitute for character, and there is no rule about where you find it.

Louis Nizer, *My Life in Court*

This then is the final triumph of thought—that it disintegrates all societies, and at last destroys the thinker himself.

Will Durant, *On the Meaning of Life*

You cannot run away from a weakness; you must sometime fight it out or perish. And if that be so, why not now, and where you stand?

Robert Louis Stevenson, as quoted in *Reader's Digest*,
March 1962

Hope, they say, deserts us at no period of our existence. From first to last, and in the face of smarting disillusions, we continue to expect 447 good fortune, better health and better conduct, and that so confidently that we judge it needless to deserve them.

Robert Louis Stevenson, as quoted in *Reader's Digest,*
November 1959

The cruelest lies are often told in silence—a man may have sat for hours and not opened his teeth, and yet have been a disloyal friend or a vile calumniator.

Robert Louis Stevenson, as quoted in *Reader's Digest,*
September 1938

An aim in life is the only fortune worth finding.

Robert Louis Stevenson, as quoted in *Reader's Digest,* May
1963

If we had no desires and no purposes, then, as sheer truism, one state of affairs would be as good as any other.

John Dewey, *The Quest for Certainty*

Perhaps there is only one cardinal sin: Impatience. Because of impatience we were driven out of Paradise; because of impatience we cannot return.

Franz Kafka, as quoted in *Reader's Digest,* November 1963

Maturity consists of no longer being taken in by oneself.

Kajetan von Schlaggenberg, as quoted in *Reader's Digest,*
June 1962

"You should not be discouraged; one does not die of a cold," the priest said to the bishop.

The old man smiled. "I shall not die of a cold, my son. I shall die of having lived."

Willa Cather, *Death Comes for the Archbishop*

The stomach is the only part of man which can be fully satisfied. The yearning of man's brain for new knowledge and experience and for more pleasant and comfortable surroundings never can be completely met. It is an appetite which cannot be appeased.

> Thomas A. Edison, as quoted in *Reader's Digest*,
> November 1961

We don't know one millionth of one percent about anything.

> Thomas A. Edison, as quoted in *The Golden Book*, April
> 1931

I am long on ideas, but short on time. I expect to live only about a hundred years.

> Thomas A. Edison, as quoted in *The Golden Book*, April
> 1931

Immortality is the genius to move others long after you yourself have stopped moving.

> Frank Rooney, as quoted in *Reader's Digest*, June 1958

In the hour of danger a man is proven: the boaster hides, the egotist trembles, only he whose care is for honor and for others forgets to be afraid.

> Donald Hankey, *A Student in Arms*

The other day when I was speaking at the Arts Club someone asked me what life I would recommend to young Irishmen, the thought my whole speech if it were logical should have led up to. I was glad to be able to reply, "I do not know, though I have thought much about it." Who does not distrust complete ideas?

> William Butler Yeats, *Dramatis Personae*

The idea of Utopia is mischievous as well as unrealistic. And dull to boot. Man is born pushing and shoving as the sparks fly upward.

> David E. Lilienthal, as quoted in *Reader's Digest*,
> December 1973

... there is in man a reason which demands selection, preference, negation, in conduct and in art. To say "Yes" to everything and everybody is manifestly to have no character at all.

Arthur O. Lovejoy, *The Great Chain of Being*

Life hardens what is soft within us and softens what is hard.

Dr. Joseph Fort Newton, as quoted in *Reader's Digest*,
March 1956

Man is a rebel. He is committed by his biology not to conform.

Robert M. Lindner, *Must You Conform?*

The man who cannot wonder is but a pair of spectacles behind which there is no eye.

Thomas Carlyle, as quoted in *Reader's Digest*, August 1952

Chaos is the score upon which reality is written.

Henry Miller, *Tropic of Cancer*

Man cannot discover new oceans unless he has courage to lose sight of the shore.

André Gide, as quoted in *Reader's Digest*, October 1972

The truths which are not translated into lives are dead truths, and not living truths.

Woodrow Wilson, speech, October 1904

Every man has a mob self and an individual self, in varying proportions.

450

D. H. Lawrence, as quoted in *This Quarter*, Paris, 1929

How often are we offended by not being offered something we do not really want.

Eric Hoffer, as quoted in *Reader's Digest*, April 1973

Every new adjustment is a crisis in self esteem.

Eric Hoffer, *The Ordeal of Change*

Good people are good because they've come to wisdom through failure.

William Saroyan, as quoted in the New York
Journal-American, August 23, 1961

Be the inferior of no man, nor of any be the superior. Remember that every man is a variation of yourself. No man's guilt is not yours, nor is any man's innocence a thing apart.

William Saroyan, *The Time of Your Life*

It may be that men are not equal in all respects, but they are all equally men.

Hugh Gaitskell, as quoted in *Reader's Digest*, December 1972

Man is still a super-age savage, predatory, acquisitive, primarily interested in himself.

Earnest A. Hooton, address, April 11, 1953

If we were to wake up some morning and find that everyone was the same race, creed and color, we would find some other causes for prejudice by noon.

Senator George Aiken, as quoted in *Reader's Digest*, September 1968

Ideas should be received like guests—in a friendly way, but with the reservation that they are not to tyrannize their host.

Alberto Moravia, as quoted in *Reader's Digest*, April 1965

Beauty makes idiots sad and wise men merry.

George Jean Nathan, *The House of Satan*

One man's ostentatious strut is another's self-effacing shuffle. Things have no power to speak for themselves until they have been shaped by purpose.

Sol Chaneles, *The New Civility*

The only life worth living is the adventurous life. Of such a life the dominant characteristic is that it is unafraid. In the first place, it is unafraid of what other people think. Like Columbus, it dares not only to assert a belief but to live it in the face of contrary opinion. It does not adapt either its pace or its objectives to the pace and objectives of its neighbors. It is not afraid of dreaming dreams that have no practical meaning. It thinks its own thoughts, it reads its own books, it develops its own hobbies, it is governed by its own conscience.

The herd may graze where it pleases or stampede when it pleases, but he who lives the adventurous life will remain unafraid when he finds himself alone.

Raymond B. Fosdick, as quoted in *Reader's Digest*, April 1952

The four great motives which move men to social activity are hunger, love, vanity, and fear of superior powers.

William Graham Sumner, *War*

Far better is it to dare mighty things, to win glorious triumphs, even though checkered by failure, than take rank with those poor spirits who neither enjoy much nor suffer much, because they live in the gray twilight that knows not victory nor defeat.

Theodore Roosevelt, as quoted in *Reader's Digest*, April 1952

I decline to accept the end of man. It is easy enough to say that man is immortal simply because he will endure: that when the last ding-dong of doom has clanged and faded from the last worthless rock hanging tideless in the last red and dying evening, that even then there will still be one more sound: that of his puny inexhaustible voice, still talking. I refuse to accept this. I believe that man will not merely endure: he will prevail. He is immortal, not because he alone among creatures has an inexhaustible voice, but because he has a soul, a spirit capable of compassion and sacrifice and endurance.

William Faulkner, Nobel Prize acceptance speech, recalled
in reports of his death, July 6, 1962

Courage is the first of human qualities because it is the quality which guarantees all the others.

Winston Churchill, as quoted in *Reader's Digest*, April 1952

A well-ordered life is like climbing a tower; the view halfway up is better than the view from the base, and it steadily becomes finer as the horizon expands.

William Lyon Phelps, *Autobiography*

The truth may be one, final, determined, but my apprehension of it can never be anything of the kind; it is changing continuously.

Bede Jarrett, *Meditations for Layfolk*

We do not err because truth is difficult to see. It is visible at a glance. We err because this is more comfortable.

Alexander Solzhenitsyn, as quoted in *Reader's Digest*, April
1974

Let those of us who are well-fed, well-clothed, and well-housed never forget and never overlook those who live on the outskirts of hope.

Lyndon B. Johnson, speech, August 31, 1964   453

. . . for all evolution would seem to be just the dying of something, as fast as it can, in order that something better may live in its place.

C. E. Montague, *Disenchantment*

There is no goal that is as near as it appears to the hopeful or as remote as it seems to the timid.

Lloyd George, as quoted in *Reader's Digest*, September 1922

A concept is stronger than a fact.

Charlotte Perkins Gilman, *Human Work*

It is not enough to be physically beautiful today. It is the vitality of people's relation to life that matters.

Elsie Ferguson, as quoted in *Reader's Digest*, November 1927

Most of our so-called reasoning consists in finding arguments for going on believing as we already do.

James Harvey Robinson, *The Mind in the Making*

All the tools with which mankind works upon its fate are dull, but the sharpest among them is reason.

Carl Van Doren, *Many Minds*

Man consists of body, mind and imagination. His body is faulty, his mind is untrustworthy, but his imagination can make his life on this planet an intense practice of all the lovelier energies.

John Masefield, as quoted in *Reader's Digest*, August 1952

Once in a century a man may be ruined or made insufferable by praise. But surely once in a minute something generous dies for want of it.

John Masefield, as quoted in *Reader's Digest*, October 1972

The surest cure for vanity is loneliness.

Thomas Wolfe, as quoted in the American Mercury,
October 1941

Welcome, O life! I go to encounter for the millionth time the reality of experience and to forge in the smithy of my soul the uncreated conscience of my race.

James Joyce, Portrait of the Artist as a Young Man

Many of our painful frustrations are caused by our driving desire to make an end of something or other. We work ourselves to death trying to make an end of unfinished business. We harass our dogs and our children today, training them for tomorrow. We are in a kind of cold rage to bring about a desired end in our own time and by our own means. Eternity must laugh at our pretenses. To be driven by a passion to hurry the end is to famish our lives of a living present.

Robert Raynolds, as quoted in Reader's Digest, July 1960

The worst provincialism of which America can be guilty is the provincialism of prejudice, racial prejudice, prejudice against new and challenging ideas.

Justice William O. Douglas, speech to the Amalgamated
Clothing Workers, New York, as quoted in the Nation,
May 14, 1952

Experience is awareness of encompassing the totality of things.

Sidney Hook, as quoted in The New York Times, February 16,
1958

Responsibility, the high price of self-ownership.

Eli J. Schleifer, as quoted in Reader's Digest, April 1970

The significance of man is that he is that part of the universe that asks the question, What is the significance of Man? He alone can stand apart 455 imaginatively and, regarding himself and the universe in their eternal aspects, pronounce a judgment: The significance of man is that he is insignificant and is aware of it.

Carl Becker, Progress and Power

I often think how tenuous is the thread that holds our thoughts together. Hunger, thirst, heat, cold, a bit of any of them and all the esthetic and philosophic thoughts on which we pride ourselves vanish as by a wand. For most people a mere flea inside the shirt can ruin Beethoven.

Robert Gibbings, as quoted in Reader's Digest, September 1960

There is no stigma attached to recognizing a bad decision in time to install a better one.

Laurence J. Peter and Raymond Hull, The Peter Principle

How many of our daydreams would darken into nightmares, were there any danger of their coming true.

Logan Pearsall Smith, Afterthoughts

My clothes keep my various selves buttoned up together, and enable all these otherwise irreconcilable aggregates of psychological phenomena to pass themselves off as one person.

Logan Pearsall Smith, More Trivia

What humbugs we are, who pretend to live for Beauty, and never see the Dawn!

Logan Pearsall Smith, as quoted in Reader's Digest, April 1946

Things that happen, however painful they are at the time, do not matter very much for long. Only how we behave to them matters.

456
Phyllis Bottome, as quoted in Reader's Digest, April 1936

People ask you for criticism, but they only want praise.

W. Somerset Maugham, *Of Human Bondage*

The greatest service we can do the Common Man is to abolish him.

Sir Norman Angell, *The Steep Places*

All enchantments die; only cowards die with them.

Charles Morgan, as quoted in *Reader's Digest,* April 1936

In the last resort nothing is ridiculous except the fear of being so.

Henri Faucommier, as quoted in *Reader's Digest,* January 1936

Man is the only animal that contemplates death, and also the only animal that shows any sign of doubt of its finality.

William Ernest Hocking, *The Meaning of Immortality in Human Experience*

Man is the only animal that laughs and weeps; for he is the only animal that is struck with the difference between what things are and what they ought to be.

William Hazlitt, as quoted in *Reader's Digest,* August 1940

Self-respect cannot be hunted. It cannot be purchased. It is never for sale. It cannot be fabricated out of public relations. It comes to us when we are alone, in quiet moments, in quiet places, when we suddenly realize that, knowing the good, we have done it; knowing the beautiful, we have served it; knowing the truth, we have spoken it.

Whitney Griswold, as quoted in news summaries of June 24, 1957

There are no hopeless situations; there are only men who have grown hopeless about them.

Clare Boothe, as quoted in *Reader's Digest,* December 1940   457

Curiosity is free-wheeling intelligence. . . . It endows the people who have it with a generosity in argument and a serenity in their own mode of life which spring from the cheerful willingness to let life take the forms it will.

Alistair Cooke, as quoted in Vogue, January 1953

My importance to the world is relatively small. On the other hand, my importance to myself is tremendous. I am all I have to work with, to play with, to suffer and to enjoy. It is not the eyes of others that I am wary of, but my own. I do not intend to let myself down more than I can possibly help, and I find that the fewer illusions I have about myself or the world around me, the better company I am for myself.

Noel Coward, as quoted in Cosmopolitan, March 1958

A man's country is where the things he loves are most respected.

Albert Jay Nock, Memoirs of a Superfluous Man

Personality is to man what perfume is to a flower.

Charles M. Schwab, Ten Commandments of Success

Follow impulse, and you may well be sorry. But ignore it, and you deny yourself one of the too rare moments when individuality is possible.

Sheldon Cain, as quoted in Reader's Digest, October 1964

The ear tends to be lazy, craves the familiar and is shocked by the unexpected; the eye, on the other hand, tends to be impatient, craves the novel and is bored by repetition.

W. H. Auden, The Dyer's Hand

Perhaps it is that the more we are able to control life, the less able we are to live it.

Milton S. Eisenhower, as quoted in the Educational Record, October 1963

There is something that is much more scarce, something finer by far than ability. It is the ability to recognize ability.

Elbert Hubbard, as quoted in Reader's Digest, October 1967

Always I have hoped not to mislead myself or others. The hope I have seems to me to be legitimate. The dangers I feel seem to me to be real. To me, this is life as it is.

Arthur E. Morgan, as quoted in The Manas Reader

If men were basically evil, who would bother to improve the world instead of giving it up as a bad job at the outset?

Van Wyck Brooks, From a Writer's Notebook

We are all snobs of the Infinite, parvenus of the Eternal.

James Gibbons Huneker, Iconoclasts

A complete life may be one ending in so full an identification with the not-self that there is no self left to die.

Bernard Berenson, as recalled in Time, October 19, 1959

I wonder sometimes whether memory is not the core of one's own feeling of identity.

Bernard Berenson, Sketch for a Self-Portrait

Life is infinitely stranger than anything which the mind of man could invent.

Sherlock Holmes, as quoted in Reader's Digest, December 1945

The world may end next week, or next year, and the last flash will light up the darkness in which we stumble now. . . . But then, in the last

459

flash, instead of saying, "What little can I do?" we shall say, "What little could I have done?"

Milton Mayer, as quoted in *The Manas Reader*

When you understand what you see, you will no longer be children. You will know that life is pain, that each of us hangs always upon the Cross of himself. And when you know that this is true of every man, woman and child on earth, you will be wise.

Whittaker Chambers, in his autobiography, *Witness*

There are many isms today to perplex us—nazism, communism, fascism and so forth—but most of them will cancel each other out. There is only one ism which kills the soul, and that is pessimism.

Lord John Buchan Tweedsmuir, as quoted in *Reader's Digest*, April 1939

In the midst of winter, I finally learned that there was in me an invincible summer.

Albert Camus, as quoted in the *Christian Science Monitor*, January 6, 1960

We can appreciate the miracle of life even more when we realize that human embryos a week old are so small that it would take about seven of them to cover the period which closes this sentence.

Bernard Lewis, as quoted in *Reader's Digest*, March 1945

The strongest are those who renounce their own times and become a living part of those yet to come. The strongest, and the rarest.

Milovan Djilas, former Vice President of Yugoslavia and political prisoner, *Land Without Justice*

Zest is the secret of all beauty. There is no beauty that is attractive without zest.

Christian Dior, as quoted in the *Ladies' Home Journal*, April 1956

The larger the island of knowledge, the longer the shoreline of wonder.

Ralph Sockman, as quoted in Reader's Digest,
November 1946

To be nobody-but-myself—in a world which is doing its best, night and day, to make you everybody else—means to fight the hardest battle which any human being can fight, and never stop fighting.

E. E. Cummings, as quoted in The Magic-Maker by Charles
Norman

The power of choice must involve the possibility of error—that is the essence of choosing.

Herbert L. Samuel, Belief and Action

A man who has bought a theory will fight a vigorous rear guard action against the facts.

Joseph Alsop, as quoted in Reader's Digest, October 1968

One of the functions of intelligence is to take account of the dangers that come from trusting solely to the intelligence.

Lewis Mumford, The Transformations of Man

Thought is action in rehearsal.

Sigmund Freud, as quoted in Reader's Digest, April 1973

To sensible men, every day is a day of reckoning.

John W. Gardner, No Easy Victories

Where there is an open mind, there will always be a frontier.

Charles F. Kettering, as quoted in Profile in America   461

It is man's destiny to ponder on the riddle of existence and, as a by-product of his wonderment, to create a new life on this earth.

Charles F. Kettering, as quoted in *Time*, December 8, 1958

That some good can be derived from every event is a better proposition than that everything happens for the best, which it assuredly does not.

James K. Feibleman, as quoted in *Reader's Digest*, May 1971

The older I get, the more wisdom I find in the ancient rule of taking first things first—a process which often reduces the most complex human problems to manageable proportions.

Dwight D. Eisenhower, as quoted in *Reader's Digest*, December 1963

The search for a scapegoat is the easiest of all hunting expeditions.

Dwight D. Eisenhower, *At Ease: Stories I Tell Friends*

Nothing is done. Everything in the world remains to be done or done over.

The Autobiography of Lincoln Steffens

The years slip by like grace notes in a song—only the days and nights are ever long.

Eleanor Graham Vance, as quoted in *Reader's Digest*, October 1964

What is all wisdom save a collection of platitudes? Take fifty of our current proverbial sayings—they are so trite, so threadbare, that we can hardly bring our lips to utter them. None the less, they embody the concentrated experience of the race, and the man who orders his life according to their teaching cannot go far wrong. How easy that seems!

462

Has anyone ever done so? Never. Has any man ever attained to inner harmony by pondering the experience of others? Not since the world began! He must pass through the fire.

Norman Douglas, *South Wind*

As soon as you begin to take yourself seriously and imagine that your virtues are important because they are yours, you become the prisoner of your own vanity and even your best works will blind and deceive you.

Thomas Merton, *Seeds of Contemplation*

The decisive desire of men is not for peace, however deep their longing, but for life in dignity, the sense of which burns, however feebly, in every man, however humble his status or obscure his place upon the earth.

Eric Sevareid, *Not So Wild a Dream*

Perhaps it would be a good idea, fantastic as it sounds, to muffle every telephone, stop every motor, and halt all activity for an hour some day, to give people a chance to ponder for a few minutes on what it is all about, why they are living and what they really want.

James Truslow Adams, as quoted in *Reader's Digest*, June 1945

Success is a fickle jade. The clothes on her back may be put there by hard work, but her jewels are the gifts of chance.

Sir Charles Wheeler, as quoted in the London Sunday *Times*, April 27, 1958

The perversion of the mind is only possible when those who should be heard in its defense are silent.

Archibald MacLeish, *The Irresponsibles*   463

There are two statements about human beings that are true: that all human beings are alike, and that all are different. On those two facts all human wisdom is founded.

Mark Van Doren, as quoted in *Reader's Digest,* August 1968

A man can stand a lot as long as he can stand himself. He can live without hope, without friends, without books, even without music, as long as he can listen to his own thoughts.

Axel Munthe, as quoted in *Reader's Digest,* July 1939

I forget how many thousand eggs go wrong for one codfish that gets hatched. But as Berkeley said long ago, it is idle to censure the creation as wasteful if you believe in a creator who has unlimited stuff to play with. And anyway, why be sorry for the things we don't miss?

Sir Frederick Pollock, in a letter to Justice Oliver Wendell Holmes, Jr., September 8, 1919

The excellence of a circle lies in its roundness, not in its bigness.

Samuel Coley, as quoted in *Reader's Digest,* May 1966

Prejudice is a raft onto which the shipwrecked mind clambers and paddles to safety.

Ben Hecht, *A Guide for the Bedevilled*

Man cannot accept certainties; he must discover them.

John Middleton Murry, *The Necessity of Art*

There are two ways of spreading light: to be the candle, or the mirror that reflects it.

Edith Wharton, as quoted in *Robins' Reader*

The service we render to others is really the rent we pay for our room on this earth.

Sir Wilfred Grenfell, as quoted in *Reader's Digest*, July 1972

It is a mistake to take oneself too seriously. That only ends in self-consciousness, which is just as deleterious a habit of mind as self-pity. No doubt it is an excellent thing to know oneself, but self-consciousness is a heavy price to pay for that knowledge. Indeed, perhaps the main reward of knowing oneself is the power to forget about oneself.

E. F. Benson, as quoted in *Reader's Digest*, February 1941

Don't be afraid of opposition. Remember, a kite rises against, not with, the wind.

Hamilton Mabie, as quoted in *Reader's Digest*, February 1942

The most exhausting thing in life, I have discovered, is being insincere. That is why so much social life is exhausting; one is wearing a mask.

Anne Morrow Lindbergh, *Gift from the Sea*

Wit, at its best, consists of the terse intrusion into an atmosphere of serene mental habit of some uncompromising truth.

Philander Johnson, as quoted in *Everybody's Magazine*, May 1920

I am bound to praise the simple life, because I have lived it and found it good.

John Burroughs, *Leaf and Tendril*   465

Some people mistake weakness for tact. If they are silent when they ought to speak and so feign an agreement they do not feel, they call it being tactful. Cowardice would be a much better name. Tact is an active quality that is not exercised by merely making a dash for cover. Be sure, when you think you are being extremely tactful, that you are not in reality running away from something you ought to face.

Sir Frank Medlicott, as quoted in *Reader's Digest*, July 1958

Man is not made for defeat.

Ernest Hemingway, *The Old Man and the Sea*

We have come out of the time when obedience, the acceptance of discipline, intelligent courage and resolution were most important, into that more difficult time when it is a man's duty to understand his world rather than simply fight for it.

Ernest Hemingway, introduction to *Treasury of the Free World*

One has two duties—to be worried and not to be worried.

E. M. Forster, as quoted in the London *Observer*, December 20, 1959

As long as men live upon this planet, whatever the tyrannies and cruelties they devise, they will, they *must* continue to think. It is this urgent march of the mind—imperfect but marvelous, unique in every individual—which has brought us out of savagery toward civilization and wisdom, and will take us further still.

Gilbert Highet, as quoted in *Reader's Digest*, February 1972

Nothing in life is to be feared. It is only to be understood.

Marie Curie, as quoted in *Reader's Digest*, October 1944

What strikes us at once in superior lives is their magnetism: moral beauty has only to show itself immediately to gather a following.

Abbé Ernest Dimnet, What We Live By

With the stones we cast at them, geniuses build new roads for us.

Paul Eldridge, Maxims for a Modern Man

In the battle of existence, talent is the punch; tact is the clever footwork.

Wilson Mizner, as quoted in Reader's Digest, February 1967

Nothing is easier than fault-finding; no talent, no self-denial, no brains are required to set up in the grumbling business.

Robert West, as quoted in Elbert Hubbard's Scrapbook

Life is a one-way street. No matter how many detours you take, none of them leads back. And once you know and accept that, life becomes much simpler. Because then you know you must do the best you can with what you have and what you are and what you have become.

Isabel Moore, as quoted in Reader's Digest, October 1942

Going off the track of consecutive thinking is a peculiar trick of the mystical mind. If it didn't go off the track, it would quietly stay on the same road forever, saying A leads to B and B to C which is true but very unexciting. . . . Logic and sequence are often poor guides to the seeker among shoreless seas and unpathed mountains in which many an important truth has lain hidden.

Anais Nin, "D. H. Lawrence: Mystic of Sex"

Everybody needs his memories. They keep the wolf of insignificance from the door.

Saul Bellow, Mr. Sammler's Planet   467

Every society honors its live conformists and its dead troublemakers.

Mignon McLaughlin, *The Neurotic's Notebook*

The longer one lives, the less importance one attaches to things, and also the less importance to importance.

Jean Rostand, as quoted in *Reader's Digest*, October 1963

A man, after he has brushed off the dust and chips of his life, will have left only the hard, clean question: Was it good or was it evil? Have I done well—or ill?

John Steinbeck, *East of Eden*

What really matters is what happens in us, not to us.

Rev. James W. Kennedy, *Minister's Shop-Talk*

The only tolerance in the world, the only tolerance that earns the name, is that toward intolerance.

Louis Paul, as quoted in *Reader's Digest*, December 1936

In any sense in which we can choose what action we shall do, we choose what motive we shall act from.

Charles Peirce, *Collected Papers*

Emotions and Feelings

We crucify ourselves between two thieves: regret for yesterday and fear of tomorrow.

Fulton Oursler, as quoted in *Reader's Digest*, January 1970

It is the nature of the mind to forget—and the nature of man to worry about his forgetfulness.

Gordon H. Bower, as quoted in Reader's Digest, December
1972

The fear I heard in my father's voice . . . when he realized that I really *believed* I could do anything a white boy could do, and had every intention of proving it, was not at all like the fear I heard when one of us was ill or had fallen down the stairs or strayed too far from the house. It was another fear, a fear that the child, in challenging the white world's assumptions, was putting himself in the path of destruction.

James Baldwin, The Fire Next Time

Often the finding of an exquisite thing can't be contained. Tingling with joy, we *have* to tell or show somebody. One evening the father of poet Emily Dickinson hurried to the church in Amherst, Mass., and pulled the bell rope. The villagers rushed from their homes. What was the alarm? Fire? Accident? It was neither. Mr. Dickinson, overcome by beauty, was merely summoning everyone to admire a sunset too magnificent to keep to himself.

George P. Morrill, as quoted in Reader's Digest, September
1972

Why is there such a difference between an event we can never forget and an event we shall always remember?

Marcelene Cox, as quoted in Reader's Digest, June 1971

There is no cosmetic for beauty like happiness.

Lady Marguerite Blessington, as quoted in Reader's Digest,
September 1950

And Christ himself, who preached the life of love, was yet as lonely as any man that ever lived.

Thomas Wolfe, as quoted in The American Mercury,
October 1941   469

We would much rather blame someone or something for making us feel unhappy than take the steps to make us feel better. We even talk about our own feelings as if they were visitors from outer space. We say, "This feeling came over me," as if we were helpless creatures overwhelmed by mysterious forces.

> Mildred Newman and Bernard Berkowitz with Jean Owen,
> as quoted in *Reader's Digest,* August 1973

Most of us haven't begun to tap our own potential for happiness. It's as if we're waiting for permission to start living fully, but the only person who can give us that permission is ourselves. We must realize that we are responsible for our own good time.

> Mildred Newman and Bernard Berkowitz with Jean Owen,
> as quoted in *Reader's Digest,* August 1973

Boredom is an emptiness filled with insistence.

> Leo Stein, *Journey into the Self*

Shut your eyes and you will know what I mean by thought entombed in darkness. Light comes through the senses, and not only through the sense of sight. When you see without feeling, you are still partly blind; you lack the inner light that brings awareness. Awareness requires the interplay of every faculty, the use of your entire being as an eye.

> Charles A. Lindbergh, as quoted in *Reader's Digest,* July
> 1972

The best cure for worry, depression, melancholy, brooding, is to go deliberately forth and try to lift with one's sympathy the gloom of somebody else.

> Arnold Bennett, as quoted in *Reader's Digest,* April 1951

Every scene, even the commonest, is wonderful, if only one can detach oneself, casting off all memory of use and custom and beholding it as if for the first time—simply, artlessly, ignorantly, like a baby, who lives each moment by itself and tarnishes the present by no remembrance of the past.

470

> Arnold Bennett, as quoted in *Reader's Digest,* May 1940

Man is the only creature whose emotions are entangled with his memory. And the anguish of memory is what we probably must pay for its pleasures, or whatever progress we gain from it. Bitter or sweet, we don't want any part of life to be really over; it should always be available, if only through people who have shared it. When they go, they take a part of you with them. . . . But the roots remain. The roots that will forever keep calling you back, begging, "Come home."

Marjorie Holmes, as quoted in *Reader's Digest,* September 1973

There are days when I sag, and when I am disposed to go wherever gravity leads me, which is down. But I am restored by the life of laughter, or somebody's shoulder to lean on.

Joan Mills, as quoted in *Reader's Digest,* November 1970

The emotions may be endless. The more we express them, the more we may have to express.

E. M. Forster, *Abinger Harvest*

She ran the gamut of emotions from A to B.

Dorothy Parker commenting on Katharine Hepburn's performance in the 1934 Broadway play *The Lake*

After a fire not long ago, I sat in the vestibule of a tenement. A mother and a child had been rescued by firefighters, but an 18-month-old girl was lost. A fireman came down the stairs, and sat next to me, the dead child on his lap. His face was covered with grime and burned paint chips. As we waited for the ambulance, he said over and over, "Poor little thing. She never had a chance." I looked up at his eyes; they were wet. The corneas were red from smoke, and light reflected from the watered surfaces, making them sparkle.

I wish now that each man . . . could have seen the humanity, the sympathy and the sadness of those eyes, for they explained why we fight fires. I was a part of that man sitting in a tenement hall, and together we were a part of all firefighters everywhere.

Dennis Smith, as quoted in *Reader's Digest*,
September 1971

A certain amount of monotony is essential to life, and those who always try to flee monotony cut themselves off from a life-giving force; it is the monotony of the sun rising every morning that makes variety possible.

Sydney J. Harris, as quoted in *Reader's Digest*, April 1959

Perhaps no phenomenon contains so much destructive feeling as "moral indignation," which permits envy or hate to be acted out under the guise of virtue.

Erich Fromm, as quoted in *Reader's Digest*, October 1972

To spare oneself from grief at all cost can be achieved only at the price of total detachment, which excludes the ability to experience happiness.

Erich Fromm, *Man for Himself*

To show a child what has once delighted you, to find the child's delight added to your own, so that there is now a double delight seen in the glow of trust and affection, this is happiness.

J. B. Priestley, as quoted in *Reader's Digest*, March 1962

You can't take a crash course in serenity.

Shirley MacLaine, as quoted in *Reader's Digest*, January 1973

Melancholy is not a mood which I have ever allowed to weigh for long upon my spirits. I live—as I have always worked—by the faith that with each passing day we are always approaching a new springtime. It is in that perspective that I see our country now.

Lyndon B. Johnson, as quoted in *Reader's Digest*, January 1973

Quiet minds cannot be perplexed or frightened, but go on in fortune or misfortune at their own private pace, like a clock during a thunderstorm.

Robert Louis Stevenson, as quoted in *Reader's Digest*, November 1941

Keep your fears to yourself, but share your courage with others.

Robert Louis Stevenson, as quoted in *Reader's Digest*, May 1960

Happiness? It is an illusion to think that more comfort means more happiness. Happiness comes of the capacity to feel deeply, to enjoy simply, to think freely, to risk life, to be needed.

Storm Jameson, as quoted in *Reader's Digest*, January 1948

It is only with the heart that one can see rightly; what is essential is invisible to the eye.

Antoine de Saint-Exupéry, *The Little Prince*

It is better to break one's heart than to do nothing with it.

Margaret Kennedy, as quoted in *Reader's Digest*, April 1943

The heart makes a record of every shining thing and plays it back like music through the years.

Felix Noland, as quoted in *Reader's Digest*, June 1942

I have no cure for boredom, because I have never suffered from it—life is much too interesting if one attacks it with vigor.

Frank Knox, as quoted in *Reader's Digest*, January 1942

I knew that there was something in the nature of homesickness called nostalgia, but I found that there is also a homesickness for the earth. I don't know what it should be called but it does exist. There is nothing more splendid . . . than Mother Earth on which one can stand, work and breathe the wind of the steppes.

Major Gherman Titov, Soviet cosmonaut, commenting on his 400,000-mile space flight, as quoted in the New York *Herald Tribune*, August 13, 1961

Plenty of people miss their share of happiness, not because they never found it, but because they didn't stop to enjoy it.

William Feather, as quoted in *Reader's Digest*, October 1967

Melancholy and remorse form a deep leaden keel which enables us to sail into the wind of reality; we run aground sooner than the flat-bottomed pleasure-lovers, but we venture out in weather that would sink them.

Cyril Connolly, *The Unquiet Grave*

I have read some obituaries with savage pleasure.

Clarence Darrow, as quoted in *Reader's Digest*, April 1934

Freedom simply means the power to carry out your own emotions.

Clarence Darrow, as quoted in *Freedom in the Modern World*

If qualities have odors, the odor of courage to me is the smell of smoked leather or the smell of the sea when the wind rips the top from a wave.

Ernest Hemingway, as quoted in *Reader's Digest*, January
1935

I don't want to be told that I must love a woman or a man because of their color, any more than I want to be told that I must hate them because of their color. I love and hate only a few, and their color may have as little or as much to do with it as their height or the color of their hair or the way they walk. It is for themselves in their totality that I am drawn to them or recoil from them—for their totality and their humanity.

Max Lerner, as quoted in the *Wall Street Journal*, March 29,
1963

Make it a rule of life never to regret and never to look back. Regret is an appalling waste of energy; you can't build on it; it's only good for wallowing in.

Katherine Mansfield, as quoted in *Reader's Digest*, April
1941

Life is no brief candle to me. It is a sort of splendid torch which I have got hold of for the moment, and I want to make it burn as brightly as possible before handing it on to future generations.

George Bernard Shaw, as quoted in *Reader's Digest*, July
1938

We have no more right to consume happiness without producing it than to consume wealth without producing it.

George Bernard Shaw, *Candida*

One truth we gain
From living through the years,
Fear brings more pain
Than does the pain it fears.

John Golden, as quoted in *Reader's Digest*, September 1945   475

The real reason we caved was that we were after one of the old, dependable highs in life: the risk high. It is produced by willfully choosing to do something that there is absolutely no need to do—rope up a cliff, jump out of a plane, drive 180 m.p.h. or, in our case, crawl under the roots of mountains. You keep at it until reason and instinct scream stop. The next step, the one beyond reason and instinct, is where the high begins. . . .

We are all, in some respects, caves. Our interiors are dark, confused, ancient mazes, difficult and sometimes dangerous to penetrate, but often containing unexpected, spectacular scenery. In either kind of labyrinth, those who obediently stop where reason and instinct command them to never make it to the best and highest places.

Bil Gilbert, as quoted in Sports Illustrated, November 10, 1969

Anger improves nothing except the arch of a cat's back.

Coleman Cox, as quoted in Reader's Digest, September 1953

It is never any good dwelling on good-byes. It is not the being together that it prolongs, it is the parting.

Elizabeth Asquith Bibesco, as quoted in Reader's Digest, July 1938

When happiness or sorrow becomes chronic, then it becomes dangerous. Permanent sorrow is produced by the exaggerated pictures of our imagination; the longer we allow ourselves to dwell in that state the further we drift from reality. Permanent happiness tends to make most people selfish, oblivious of reality, uninterested in anything outside their own happiness.

Rom Landau, as quoted in Reader's Digest, March 1937

The fairest thing we can experience is the mysterious. It is the fundamental emotion which stands at the cradle of true science. He who knows it not, and can no longer wonder, no longer feel amazement, is as good as dead. We all had this priceless talent when we were

476

young. But as time goes by, many of us lose it. The true scientist never loses the faculty of amazement. It is the essence of his being.

> Hans Selye, as quoted in *Newsweek*, March 31, 1958

I have my own particular sorrows, loves, delights; and you have yours. But sorrow, gladness, yearning, hope, love, belong to all of us, in all times and in all places. Music is the only means whereby we feel these emotions in their universality.

> Harry Overstreet, as quoted in *Reader's Digest*, May 1939

There may be Peace without Joy, and Joy without Peace, but the two combined make Happiness.

> Lord John Buchan Tweedsmuir, *Pilgrim's Way*

We are never more discontented with others than when we are discontented with ourselves.

> Henri Frederic Amiel, as quoted in *Reader's Digest*, September 1946

The lowest possible state to which I could sink would be one in which, before I died, I could say—I do not care whether the world is better for my having lived. The sin against the Holy Ghost is the sin against posterity. Any man who has planted a tree and knows that it will grow up and be pleasant to others years hence is experiencing in a small way what is one of the strongest emotions in humanity. This is a noble emotion. It is noble when a man lays out gardens, levels terraces and plants woods for no other benefit than for his successors.

> George Buchanan, as quoted in *Reader's Digest*, July 1935

To retreat into oneself is a common response in the face of misfortune. But the more a man is preoccupied with himself, the more he diminishes himself. If he becomes totally self-immersed, he becomes totally reduced and is nothing. He is roadblocking his own way to any form of happiness, to any plane of sanity. . . .

477

However formidable your situation, you are not alone in it. You are not the first to go through it. Many others are in it with you, right this minute. Misfortune is the only true international currency the world has ever had. . . .

To those people fortunate enough to be surrounded by those they love most, I would like to put this question: Right now, in your every speech and action, *what kind of memories are you building?* It is the quiet, day-by-day interchange that makes the richest part of all living. Right now, day by day, it is you who fill the well you must draw on when alone.

Max Wylie, as quoted in Family Health, March 1970

Misfortunes one can endure—they come from outside, they are accidents. But to suffer for one's own faults—ah—there is the sting of life.

Oscar Wilde, as quoted in Reader's Digest, July 1955

Grief can take care of itself; but to get the full value of joy you must have somebody to divide it with.

Mark Twain, as quoted in Reader's Digest, June 1939

Happiness is a delicate balance between what one is and what one has.

J. H. Denison, as quoted in Reader's Digest, April 1939

Happiness is a resultant of the relative strengths of positive and negative feelings rather than an absolute amount of one or the other.

Dr. Norman Bradburn, In Pursuit of Happiness

Regrets are as personal as fingerprints. . . . Discarding what is vain or false, facing the facts that should truly disturb your conscience, is worth whatever time it takes or pain it may cause. It can pay to the future what you owe to the past.

Margaret Culkin Banning, as quoted in Reader's Digest,
October 1958

Anger is a wind which blows out the lamp of the mind.

Robert Ingersoll, as quoted in *Reader's Digest*, October
1943

A happy life must be to a great extent a quiet life, for it is only in an atmosphere of quiet that true joy can live.

Bertrand Russell, *The Conquest of Happiness*

The whole subject of happiness has, in my opinion, been treated too solemnly. It has been thought that men cannot be happy without a "theory of life." Actually, it is the simple things that really matter. If a man delights in his wife and children, has success in work, and finds pleasure in the alternation of day and night, spring and autumn, he will be happy whatever his philosophy may be.

Bertrand Russell, as quoted in *Reader's Digest,* August 1960

People are lonely because they build walls instead of bridges.

J. F. Newton, as quoted in *Reader's Digest*, September 1952

479

Happiness is a way station between too much and too little.

Channing Pollock, as quoted in *Reader's Digest*, January 1973

Ennui, felt on proper occasions, is a sign of intelligence.

Clifton Fadiman, *Reading I've Liked*

The only time to lose your temper is when it's deliberate.

Richard M. Nixon, as quoted in *Reader's Digest*, June 1956

Normal day, let me be aware of the treasure you are. Let me learn from you, love you, savor you, bless you before you depart. Let me not pass you by in quest of some rare and perfect tomorrow. Let me hold you while I may, for it will not always be so. One day I shall dig my nails into the earth, or bury my face in the pillow, or stretch myself taut, or raise my hands to the sky, and want more than all the world your return.

Mary Jean Irion, *Yes, World: A Mosaic of Meditation*

If bravery is a quality which knows not fear, I have never seen a brave man. All men are frightened. The more intelligent they are, the more they are frightened. The courageous man is the man who forces himself, in spite of his fear, to carry on.

General George S. Patton, as quoted in *Reader's Digest*, October 1951

Happiness is a form of courage.

Holbrook Jackson, as quoted in *Reader's Digest*, November 1948

Happiness is to "become portion of that around me." . . .We are happy only when the self achieves union with the notself. Now both self and notself are states of our consciousness.

 Aldous Huxley, *Texts and Pretexts*

Speed provides the one genuinely modern pleasure.

Aldous Huxley, Music at Night

I am a confirmed believer in blessings in disguise. I prefer them undisguised when I happen to be the person blessed. But the theory that blessings in disguise are constantly happening to other people I find consoling. It enables me to bear their troubles without feeling too miserable.

Robert Lynd, as quoted in Reader's Digest, December 1951

Some sense of security is necessary to happy or healthful living, but you cannot get it by refusing to take chances, any more than a country can get it by living behind walls. Living is too dangerous a business for there to be any sense in courting danger for its own sake, but the readier we are to accept it when we have to, the less it will usually hurt us.

Lawrence Gould, as quoted in Reader's Digest, August 1951

Once people were driven—someday they will be inspired.

Walter Dill Scott, as quoted in Reader's Digest, February 1947

What I discovered in the midst of my drive toward emancipation was that sex, love, hurt, and hate were the real stuff I was made of; that fairness, rationality, and the willingness to share or give away what one had never been sure of possessing in the first place, were all secondary characteristics, carefully cultivated to be sure, but capable of collapsing the moment stronger passions reared their heads.

Ingrid Bengis, Combat in the Erogenous Zone

Anger is righteous if it has in it grief on account of what is happening to others, and not a grudge on account of what is happening to oneself.

E. Stanley Jones, as quoted in Reader's Digest, March 1952　481

The older you get the more you realize that kindness is synonymous with happiness.

Lionel Barrymore, as quoted in Reader's Digest, April 1953

An irritable man is like a hedgehog rolled up the wrong way, tormenting himself with his own prickles.

Thomas Hood, as quoted in Reader's Digest, April 1959

My idea of happiness is four feet on a fireplace fender.

Oliver Wendell Holmes, as quoted in Reader's Digest,
March 1961

You are genuinely happy if you don't know why.

Joseph Mayer, as quoted in Reader's Digest, March 1956

The happy people of this world are never free. It is only youth which really wants freedom, or those who have set up a defensive mechanism against life, since to live is also to suffer. The older and wiser know that nothing is of value unless it can be shared, and that the eternal cry of the human heart is to belong to someone else. It is its escape from loneliness, its support in weakness, a solace to its pride. Even youth should think twice before it asks for freedom. Surely to be happy is better than to be free; and to be kind to all, to like many and love a few, to be needed and wanted by those we love, is certainly the nearest we can come to happiness.

Mary Roberts Rinehart, as quoted in Reader's Digest, June
1938

Time cools, time clarifies; no mood can be maintained quite unaltered through the course of hours.

Thomas Mann, The Magic Mountain

The trouble with most people is that they think with their hopes or fears or wishes rather than with their minds.

Walter Duranty, as quoted in Reader's Digest, February
1938

When a man has quietly made up his mind that there is nothing he cannot endure, his fears leave him.

Grove Patterson, as quoted in *Reader's Digest*, March 1958

As for happiness, it isn't something you experience, it's something you remember.

Oscar Levant, as quoted in *Reader's Digest*, March 1958

Man cannot remake himself without suffering. For he is both the marble and the sculptor.

Dr. Alex Carrel, *Man, the Unknown*

Many times in my life I have repeated Rodin's saying that "slowness is beauty." To read slowly, to feel slowly and deeply; what enrichment!

In the past I have been so often greedy. I have gobbled down books—I have gobbled down work—I have even gobbled down my friends!—and indeed had a kind of enjoyment of all of them. But rarely have I tasted the last flavor of anything, the final exquisite sense of personality of spirit that secretes itself in every work that merits serious attention, in every human being at all worth knowing.

David Grayson, as quoted in *Reader's Digest*, June 1940

There are few faces that can afford to smile. A smile is sometimes bewitching, in general vapid, often a contortion. But the bewitching smile usually beams from the grave face. It is then irresistible.

Lord Beaconsfield, as quoted in *Reader's Digest*, March 1938

Being "contented" ought to mean in English, as it does in French, being pleased. Being content with an attic ought not to mean being unable to move from it and resigned to living in it; it ought to mean appreciating all there is in such a position. For true contentment is a real, even an active virtue—not only affirmative but creative. It is the power of getting out of any situation all there is in it.

G. K. Chesterton, as quoted in *Reader's Digest*, January 1940

483

There is only one thing about which I shall have no regrets when my life ends. I have savored to the full all the small, daily joys. The bright sunshine on the breakfast table, the smell of the air at dusk; the sound of the clock ticking, the light rains that start gently after midnight; the hour when the family come home; Sunday-evening tea before the fire. I have never missed one moment of beauty, not ever taken it for granted. Spring, summer, autumn or winter. I wish I had failed as little in other ways.

> Agnes Sligh Turnbull, as quoted in *Reader's Digest*, May 1951

We live by encouragement and die without it—slowly, sadly and angrily.

> Celeste Holm as quoted in *Reader's Digest*, February 1974

To feel the right emotions is fully as important as to hold the right ideas, and the great service of religion is the development of the right emotions.

> Geoffrey Parsons, as quoted in *Reader's Digest*, October 1927

I am bored with it all.

> Sir Winston Churchill, near the end of his life, as quoted in *The New York Times*, February 1, 1965

If you observe a really happy man, you will find him building a boat, writing a symphony, educating his son, growing double dahlias in his garden, or looking for dinosaur eggs in the Gobi desert. He will not be searching for happiness as if it were a collar button that has rolled under the radiator. He will not be striving for it as a goal in itself. He will have become aware that he is happy in the course of living life 24 crowded hours of the day.

> W. Beran Wolfe, as quoted in *Reader's Digest*, April 1951

Unhappiness is not knowing what we want and killing ourselves to get it.

> Don Herold, as quoted in *Reader's Digest*, October 1961

Warmth, warmth, more warmth for we are dying of cold and not of darkness. It is not the night that kills, but the frost.

Miguel de Unamuno, *The Tragic Sense of Life*

It's never safe to be nostalgic about something until you're absolutely certain there's no chance of its coming back.

Bill Vaughan, as quoted in *Reader's Digest*, October 1958

He who dies, dies once: but he who fears death dies a thousand times.

Captain Charles Nungesser, French aviator, before he was lost on a transatlantic flight, as quoted in *Reader's Digest*, November 1927

As one grows older, I think one more and more feels life in terms of things. This sounds rather material, but it isn't. Things become so saturated with their associations that they symbolize the loveliest experiences and intimacies of life.

Anne Douglas Sedgwick, as quoted in *Reader's Digest*, February 1938

I have walked with people whose eyes are full of light but who see nothing in sea or sky, nothing in city streets, nothing in books. It were far better to sail forever in the night of blindness with sense, and feeling, and mind, than to be content with the mere act of seeing. The only lightless dark is the night of darkness in ignorance and insensibility.

Helen Keller, as quoted in *Reader's Digest*, August 1952

The greatest happiness you can have is knowing that you do not necessarily require happiness.

William Saroyan, as quoted in *The New York Times*, December 16, 1957

In small, familiar things, memory weaves her strongest enchantments, holding us at her mercy with some trifle, some echo, a tone of voice, a scent of tar and seaweed on the quay; we have all been explorers in our time, even if it was only when we learned to walk upon unsteady feet on the new carpet of our world; and it is those forgotten explorations that come back. It is rare in later life to drink such draughts as we do in childhood of the world's wonder, whose first depth remains through all our days.

Freya Stark, as quoted in Reader's Digest, December 1960

Be virtuous and you'll be happy? Nonsense! Be happy and you'll begin to be virtuous.

James Gould Cozzens, as quoted in Reader's Digest,
November 1958

Humdrum is not where you live; it's what you are.

Harold MacGrath, as quoted in Reader's Digest, March
1922

Nothing is happiness which is not shared by at least one other, and nothing is truly sorrow unless it is borne absolutely alone.

Myrtle Rand, as quoted in Reader's Digest, September 1947

THE LIGHTER
SIDE OF WISDOM

Irreverent Observations

The opportunities of man are limited only by his imagination. But so few have imagination that there are ten thousand fiddlers to one composer.

Charles F. Kettering, as quoted in Reader's Digest,
February 1974

You can send a message around the world in one seventh of a second, yet it may take years to force a simple idea through a quarter inch of human skull.

Charles F. Kettering, as quoted in Reader's Digest, July
1947

To do what others cannot do is talent. To do what talent cannot do is genius.

Will Henry, as quoted in Reader's Digest, March 1974

Men are not against you; they are merely for themselves.

Gene Fowler, Skyline

What on earth would a man do with himself if something did not stand in his way?

H. G. Wells, as quoted in Reader's Digest, June 1940

The crisis of yesterday is the joke of tomorrow.

H. G. Wells, You Can't Be Too Careful   489

If everyone believes a thing, it is probably untrue.

Sir W. Arbuthnot Lane, as quoted in Genesis

An opportunist: any man who goes ahead and does what you always intended to do.

Kenneth L. Krichbaum, as quoted in Reader's Digest, June
1948

Nagging: the constant reiteration of the unhappy truth.

General Mark Clark, as quoted in Reader's Digest, June 1948

If happiness truly consisted in physical ease and freedom from care, then the happiest individual would not be either a man or a woman; it would be, I think, an American cow.

William Lyon Phelps, Happiness

Stubbornness does have its helpful features. You always know what you are going to be thinking tomorrow.

Glen Beaman, as quoted in Reader's Digest, December 1968

One man's remorse is another man's reminiscence.

Gerald Horton Bath, as quoted in Reader's Digest, August
1962

The best way I know of to win an argument is to start by being in the right.

Quintin Hogg, as quoted in The New York Times, October 16,
1960

A farm is a hunk of land on which, if you get up early enough mornings and work late enough nights, you'll make a fortune—if you strike oil on it.

"Fibber" McGee, as quoted in Reader's Digest, November
1949

The chances are about ten to one that the person who slaps you on the back is trying to make you cough up something.

Olin Miller, as quoted in *Reader's Digest*, July 1943

The handwriting on the wall is often Greek to most of us.

Olin Miller, as quoted in *Reader's Digest*, August 1972

Of all liars, the smoothest and most convincing is memory.

Olin Miller, as quoted in *Reader's Digest*, January 1952

Cynic: n. a blackguard whose faulty vision sees things as they are, not as they ought to be.

Ambrose Bierce, *The Devil's Dictionary*

Positive: mistaken at the top of one's voice.

Ambrose Bierce, *The Devil's Dictionary*

Philosophy: Route of many roads leading from nowhere to nothing.

Ambrose Bierce, *The Devil's Dictionary*

In the last analysis ability is commonly found to consist mainly in a high degree of solemnity.

Ambrose Bierce, *The Devil's Dictionary*

Contentment is the smother of invention.

Ambrose Bierce, as quoted in *Reader's Digest*, February 1961

In each human heart are a tiger, a pig, an ass, and a nightingale. Diversity of character is due to their unequal activity.

Ambrose Bierce, *The Devil's Dictionary* 491

Rules are for when brains run out.

George Papashvily, as quoted in *Reader's Digest*, June 1958

Experience is a marvelous thing. It enables you to recognize a mistake whenever you make it again.

Franklin P. Jones, as quoted in *Reader's Digest*, November 1949

The trouble with being punctual is that nobody's there to appreciate it.

Franklin P. Jones, as quoted in *Reader's Digest*, November 1949

Nothing's more responsible for the good old days than a bad memory.

Franklin P. Jones, as quoted in *Reader's Digest*, January 1953

Nobody who can read is ever successful at cleaning out the attic.

Franklin P. Jones, as quoted in *Reader's Digest*, July 1955

A fanatic is one who can't change his mind and won't change the subject.

Sir Winston Churchill, as quoted in *The New York Times*, July 5, 1954

Short skirts have a tendency to make men polite. Have you ever seen a man get on a bus ahead of one?

Mel Ferrer, as quoted in *Reader's Digest*, October 1957

Prayer of the modern American: "Dear God, I pray for patience. And I want it right now."

492

Oren Arnold, as quoted in *Reader's Digest*, June 1968

The world is round. Only one-third of the human beings are asleep at one time, and the other two-thirds are awake and up to some mischief somewhere.

Dean Rusk, in a speech to the Washington press corps,
January 26, 1966

Habits are about the only servants that will work for you for nothing. Just get them established, and they will operate even though you are going around in a trance.

Frederic Whitaker, as quoted in *Reader's Digest*, January
1968

The middle of the road is where the white line is—and that's the worst place to drive.

Robert Frost, as quoted in *Collier's*, April 27, 1956

The only difference between a rut and a grave is in their dimensions.

Ellen Glasgow, as quoted in *Reader's Digest*, January 1936

Prejudice is being down on what we are not up on.

Rachel Davis DuBois, as quoted in *Reader's Digest*,
November 1945

Not only does beauty fade, but it leaves a record upon the face as to what became of it.

Elbert Hubbard, as quoted in *Reader's Digest*, May 1942

The greatest mistake you can make is to be continually fearing that you'll make one.

Elbert Hubbard, as quoted in *Reader's Digest*, January 1953　　493

Had there been a computer in 1872, it would probably have predicted that by now there would be so many horse-drawn vehicles it would be almost impossible to clear up all the manure.

Professor K. William Kapp, as quoted in *Reader's Digest*,
September 1972

The supple, well-adjusted man is the one who has learned to hop into the meat-grinder while humming a hit-parade tune.

Marshall McLuhan, *The Mechanical Bride*

There is no such thing as bad weather; there are only good clothes.

Elizabeth Woodbridge, as quoted in *Reader's Digest*,
September 1940

Conceit is God's gift to little men.

Bruce Barton, as quoted in *Reader's Digest*, August 1935

It is a great advantage for a system of philosophy to be substantially true.

George Santayana, *The Unknowable*

Fanaticism consists in redoubling your efforts when you have forgotten your aim.

George Santayana, *The Life of Reason*

Almost every wise saying has an opposite one, no less wise, to balance it.

George Santayana, *Life of Reason*

Man is a gregarious animal, and much more so in his mind than in his body. He may like to go alone for a walk, but he hates to stand alone in his opinions.

George Santayana, as quoted in *Reader's Digest*, April 1965

What is intended as a little white lie often ends up as a double feature in Technicolor.

Madena R. Wallingford, as quoted in *Reader's Digest*, December 1944

It's not a question of who's going to throw the first stone; it's a question of who's going to start building with it.

Sloan Wilson, as quoted in *Reader's Digest*, December 1971

There are people who want to be everywhere at once and they seem to get nowhere.

Carl Sandburg, *Complete Poems*

There are two insults which no human will endure: the assertion that he hasn't a sense of humor, and the doubly impertinent assertion that he has never known trouble.

Sinclair Lewis, as quoted in *Reader's Digest*, January 1937

There are two ways to get to the top of an oak tree—you can climb it or you can sit on an acorn.

R. Frank Brown, as quoted in *Reader's Digest*, March 1965

The easiest way to get a reputation is go outside the fold, shout around for a few years as a violent atheist or a dangerous radical, and then crawl back to the shelter.

F. Scott Fitzgerald, *Notebooks*

Optimism is the content of small men in high places.

F. Scott Fitzgerald, *The Crack-up*

Being an optimist after you've got everything you want doesn't count.

Kin Hubbard, as quoted in *Reader's Digest*, August 1962   495

To give up pretensions is as blessed a relief as to get them ratified.

> William James, as quoted in *Reader's Digest*, December
> 1961

A bore is a fellow who opens his mouth and puts his feats in it.

> Henry Ford, jottings made public on the fiftieth
> anniversary of the Ford Motor Company, printed privately
> by the company, 1953

Whether you believe you can do a thing or not, you are right.

> Henry Ford, as quoted in *Reader's Digest*, December 1965

Too many people don't care what happens so long as it doesn't happen to them.

> William Howard Taft, as quoted in *Reader's Digest*, June
> 1934

Man is the only animal that blushes. Or needs to.

> Mark Twain, *Following the Equator*

Habit is either the best of servants, or the worst of masters.

> Nathaniel Emmons, as quoted in *Reader's Digest*,
> September 1966

A bigot is a person who slams his mind in your face.

> Paul H. Gilbert, as quoted in *Reader's Digest*, May 1970

Life is not a static thing. The only people who do not change their minds are incompetents in asylums, who can't, and those in cemeteries.

> Senator Everett M. Dirksen, press conference, Washington,
> D.C., January 1, 1965

Perhaps the principal objection to a quarrel is that it interrupts an argument.

> G. K. Chesterton, as quoted in *Reader's Digest*, November 1941

I am not absentminded. It is the presence of mind that makes me unaware of everything else.

> G. K. Chesterton, as quoted in *Reader's Digest*, July 1962

There nearly always is method in madness. It's what drives men mad, being methodical.

> G. K. Chesterton, *The End of the Fisherman*

The biggest liar in the world is They Say.

> Douglas Mallock, as quoted in *Reader's Digest*, February 1947

The most difficult secret for a man to keep is the opinion he has of himself.

> Marcel Pagnol, as quoted in *Reader's Digest*, July 1957

People who fly into a rage always make a bad landing.

> Will Rogers, as quoted in *Reader's Digest*, August 1951

If in the last few years you haven't discarded a major opinion or acquired a new one, investigate and see if you're not growing senile.

> Gelett Burgess, as quoted in *Reader's Digest*, October 1947

The best place to find a helping hand is at the end of your arm.

> Elmer Leterman, as quoted in *Reader's Digest*, December 1959

When a resolute young fellow steps up to that great bully, the world, and takes him boldly by the beard, he is often surprised to find that the beard comes off in his hand, that it was only tied on to scare away timid adventurers.

Oliver Wendell Holmes, as quoted in *Reader's Digest*, February 1956

No man knows his true character until he has run out of gas, purchased something on the installment plan and raised an adolescent.

Marcelene Cox, as quoted in *Reader's Digest*, April 1956

Genius is more often found in a cracked pot than in a whole one.

E. B. White, *One Man's Meat*

There are two kinds of fools. One says, "This is old, therefore it is good." The other says, "This is new, therefore it is better."

Dean Inge, as quoted in *Reader's Digest*, December 1945

Unfortunately I have an open mind. I let down a window in my brain about six or seven inches from the top even in the bitterest weather.

Heywood Broun, as quoted in *Reader's Digest* September 1936

When we are offered a penny for our thoughts, we always find that we have recently had so many things in mind that we can easily make a selection which will not compromise us too nakedly.

James Harvey Robinson, *The Mind in the Making*

The people sensible enough to give good advice are usually sensible enough to give none.

Eden Phillpotts, as quoted in *Reader's Digest*, December 1951

You can always spot a well-informed man—his views are the same as yours.

Ilka Chase, as quoted in Reader's Digest, October 1951

The thing to do is to supply light and not heat.

Woodrow Wilson, speech in Pittsburgh, January 29, 1916

What many of us need is a good vigorous kick in the seat of the can'ts!

Ame Babcock, as quoted in Reader's Digest, November 1944

There is nothing final about a mistake, except its being taken as final.

Phyllis Bottome, as quoted in Reader's Digest, February 1945

. . . almost any idea which jogs you out of your current abstractions may be better than nothing.

Alfred North Whitehead, Adventures of Ideas

As scarce as truth is, the supply is always greater than the demand.

Josh Billings, as quoted in Reader's Digest, July 1959

The centre that I cannot find
Is known to my Unconscious Mind;
I have no reason to despair
Because I am already there.

W. H. Auden, "The Labyrinth"

It's all right to have a train of thoughts, if you have a terminal.

Richard R. Bowker, as quoted in Reader's Digest, September 1936

An expert is a man who avoids the small errors as he sweeps on to the grand fallacy.

Benjamin Stolberg, as quoted in *Reader's Digest*,
September 1936

If I were reincarnated, I'd want to come back a buzzard: nothing hates him or envies him or wants him or needs him; he is never bothered or in danger, and he can eat anything.

William Faulkner, as quoted in *Writers at Work*

To his dog, every man is Napoleon; hence the popularity of dogs.

Aldous Huxley, as quoted in *Reader's Digest*, December 1934

Facts are ventriloquists' dummies. Sitting on a wise man's knee they may be made to utter words of wisdom; elsewhere they say nothing or talk nonsense.

Aldous Huxley, *Time Must Have a Stop*

Some people, instead of trying to drown their troubles, take them out and give them swimming lessons.

W. A. "Billy" Sunday, as quoted in *Reader's Digest*, March 1934

A hair's breadth is sometimes a great distance.

Robert Hugh Benson, *Confessions of a Convert*

It is easier to believe a lie that one has heard a thousand times than to believe a fact that one has never heard before.

Robert Lynd, as quoted in *Reader's Digest*, March 1959

Most men, when they think they are thinking, are merely rearranging their prejudices.

Knute Rockne, as quoted in *Reader's Digest*, October 1927

Chance is the fool's name for fate.

Fred Astaire, in the film Gay Divorcee

With man's great ability to think and reason and compute, we can now pinpoint most of our current problems. The trouble is we can't solve them.

Don Fraser, as quoted in Reader's Digest, February 1968

If you're going to be the prisoner of your own mind, the least you can do is make sure it's well furnished.

Peter Ustinov, as quoted in Reader's Digest, March 1972

I regard myself as an optimist. An optimist is a person who knows how sad a place the world can be. The pessimist is one who is forever finding out.

Peter Ustinov, as quoted in Reader's Digest, October 1958

When they come downstairs from their Ivory Towers, idealists are apt to walk straight into the gutter.

Logan Pearsall Smith, Afterthoughts

The trouble with most of us is that we would rather be ruined by praise than saved by criticism.

Rev. Norman Vincent Peale, as quoted in Reader's Digest,
June 1960

He who does not enjoy his own company is usually right.

Coco Chanel, as quoted in Reader's Digest, November 1970

Idealist: one who, on noticing that a rose smells better than a cabbage, concludes that it is also more nourishing.

H. L. Mencken, A Little Book in C Major   501

There is always an easy solution to every human problem—neat, plausible, and wrong.

H. L. Mencken, A Mencken Chrestomathy

It is most important in this world to be pushing, but it is fatal to seem so.

Benjamin Fowett, as quoted in Reader's Digest, May 1939

Faced with the choice between changing one's mind and proving that there is no need to do so, almost everyone gets busy on the proof.

John Kenneth Galbraith, as quoted in Reader's Digest,
November 1971

One of the wisest things my daddy ever told me was that "so-and-so is a damned smart man, but the fool's got no sense."

Lyndon B. Johnson, as recalled in Time, October 19, 1959

Most of us would rather risk catastrophe than read the directions.

Mignon McLaughlin, as quoted in Reader's Digest, October
1964

When one burns one's bridges, what a very nice fire it makes!

Dylan Thomas, as quoted in Reader's Digest, July 1962

Earnest people are often people who habitually look on the serious side of things that have no serious side.

Van Wyck Brooks, From a Writer's Notebook

Probably the meek really will inherit the earth; they won't have the nerve to refuse.

John M. Henry, as quoted in Reader's Digest, May 1962

The airplane, the atomic bomb and the zipper have cured me of any tendency to state that a thing can't be done.

R. L. Duffus, as quoted in *Reader's Digest*, September 1952

If you don't get what you want, it is a sign either that you did not seriously want it, or that you tried to bargain over the price.

Rudyard Kipling, *Land and Sea Tales*

Where all think alike, no one thinks very much.

Walter Lippmann, as quoted in *The Speaker's Encyclopedia*

The wheel was man's greatest invention until he got behind it.

Bill Ireland, as quoted in *Reader's Digest*, April 1962

Self-portraits usually are colored.

Harold Coffin, as quoted in *Reader's Digest*, July 1962

Status symbols are medals you buy yourself.

> Bernhard Wicki, as quoted in *Reader's Digest*, February
> 1971

I think this is the most extraordinary collection of talent, of human knowledge, that has ever been gathered together at the White House—with the possible exception of when Thomas Jefferson dined alone.

> John F. Kennedy, at a dinner in the White House for the
> American Nobel Prize winners, April 29, 1962

A fashion is nothing but an induced epidemic.

> George Bernard Shaw, as quoted in *Reader's Digest*,
> September 1967

I suppose that you seldom think. Few people think more than two or three times a year. I have made an international reputation for myself by thinking once or twice a week.

> George Bernard Shaw, as quoted in *Reader's Digest*, April
> 1959

A minority group has "arrived" only when it has the right to produce some fools and scoundrels without the entire group paying for it.

> Carl T. Rowan, as quoted in *Reader's Digest*, August 1972

Even the costliest clock owns no more than sixty minutes an hour.

> Sam Lipton, *A Vort for a Vort*

A good memory is one that is so poor you can't remember what you worried about yesterday.

> Samuel Smiles, as quoted in *Reader's Digest*, December
> 1958

Nothing has more lives than an error you refuse to correct.

> O. A. Battista, as quoted in *Reader's Digest*, January 1967

Cheer up, the worst is yet to come.

Philander C. Johnson, *Shooting Stars*

It's hard for the modern generation to understand Thoreau, who lived beside a pond but didn't own water skis or a snorkel.

Bill Vaughan, as quoted in *Reader's Digest*, September 1962

"Live dangerously!" is advice we don't hear much any more since it turned out there isn't any other way.

Bill Vaughan, as quoted in *Reader's Digest*, February 1960

Every silver lining has a cloud. I carried into the land of milk and money a heavy bundle of attitudes left over from the old days—what kids today call hang-ups.

Sam Levenson, as quoted in *Reader's Digest*, October 1973

Man is the only animal that can be skinned more than once.

Jimmy Durante, as quoted in *Reader's Digest*, March 1950

When people are free to do as they please, they usually imitate each other.

Eric Hoffer, *The Passionate State of Mind*

Many people's tombstones should read: "Died at 30. Buried at 60."

Nicholas Murray Butler, as quoted in *Reader's Digest*,
February 1935

People who have what they want are fond of telling people who haven't what they want that they really don't want it.

Ogden Nash, as quoted in *Reader's Digest*, January 1973   **505**

I regret that before people can be reformed they have to be sinners,
And that before you have pianists in the family you have to have
    beginners.

Ogden Nash, as quoted in Reader's Digest, July 1952

Early to rise and early to bed makes a male healthy and wealthy and
dead.

James Thurber, as quoted in Reader's Digest, April 1950

This is the posture of fortune's slave
One foot in the gravy, one foot in the grave.

James Thurber, Further Fables for Our Times

Let the meek inherit the earth—they have it coming to them.

James Thurber, as quoted in Life, March 14, 1960

A man who has his initials on his pajamas must be uncertain of
himself. Surely you should know who you are at bedtime.

Christopher Morley, The Man Who Made Friends with
Himself

Men can live without air for a few minutes, without water for about
two weeks, without food for about two months—and without a new
thought for years on end.

Kent Ruth, as quoted in Reader's Digest, August 1953

The pursuit of truth shall set you free—even if you never catch up
with it.

Clarence Darrow, as quoted in Reader's Digest, January
1952

Folks used to be willing to wait patiently for a slow-moving stage
coach, but now they kick like the dickens if they miss one revolution of
a revolving door.

506
Ed Wynn, as quoted in Reader's Digest, May 1933

More than one pessimist got that way by financing an optimist.

Fred W. Bender, as quoted in Reader's Digest, February 1963

A fanatic is a man who does what he thinks the Lord would do if only He knew the facts of the case.

Finley Peter Dunne, as quoted in Reader's Digest, July 1963

Horse sense is that inestimable quality in a horse that keeps it from betting on a man.

Rev. Earle P. Cochran, as quoted in Reader's Digest, May 1955

Everything comes to him who hustles while he waits.

Thomas A. Edison, as quoted in The Golden Book Magazine, April 1931

When a man has a "pet peeve" it's remarkable how often he pets it.

Sydney J. Harris, as quoted in Reader's Digest, November 1960

Self-restraint is feeling your oats without sowing them.

Shannon Fife, as quoted in Reader's Digest, July 1950

Now that fabrics are wrinkleproof, there remains the baffling problem of humans.

Shannon Fife, as quoted in Reader's Digest, October 1955

Fame is a food that dead men eat.

Austin Dobson, Poems

Maybe what this country needs is a little less touch football and a little more tackling.

Fletcher Knebel, as quoted in Reader's Digest, December 1961

There are a powerful lot of strings in a man's life: apron, heart, purse and harp.

> Terence Rattigan, as quoted in *Reader's Digest*, February
> 1960

No matter what happens, there's always somebody who knew it would.

> Lonny Starr, as quoted in *Reader's Digest*, October 1955

None are so brave as the anonymous.

> K. K. Steincke, as quoted in *Reader's Digest*, June 1957

Great minds discuss ideas, average minds discuss events, small minds discuss people.

> Admiral Hyman G. Rickover, as quoted in the *Saturday
> Evening Post*, November 28, 1959

A commentary on the times is that the word "honesty" is now preceded by "old-fashioned."

> Larry Wolters, as quoted in *Reader's Digest*, March 1961

A closed mind is an enigma indeed. Nothing ever goes in—but odd things are forever coming out.

> Laurence Dunphy, as quoted in *Reader's Digest*, October
> 1961

There's always room for improvement, you know—it's the biggest room in the house.

> Louise Heath Leber, as quoted in the New York *Post*, May 14,
> 1961

If you can't stand solitude, maybe you bore others too.

> Bob Gordon, as quoted in *Reader's Digest*, September 1947

There are more self-marred people in the world than there are self-made.

Arnold H. Glasow, as quoted in *Reader's Digest*, January 1974

He who hesitates gets bumped from the rear.

Homer Phillips, as quoted in *Reader's Digest*, July 1952

A nuisance may be merely a right thing in the wrong place—like a pig in the parlor instead of the barnyard.

Justice George Sutherland, opinion in *Euclid* v. *Ambler Co.* (1926)

Each 24 hours, the world turns over on someone who was sitting on top of it.

Hugh Allen, as quoted in *Reader's Digest*, February 1974

About the only thing that'll give you more for your money now than ten years ago is the penny scale at the drugstore.

Earl Wilson, as quoted in *Reader's Digest*, August 1958

Morale is when your hands and feet keep on working when your head says it can't be done.

Admiral Ben Moreell, as quoted in *Reader's Digest*, January 1961

If all the fools were drowned in Noah's flood, the seed was saved.

I. Stein, *Journey into the Self*

A man always has two reasons for doing anything—a good reason and the real reason.

J. Pierpont Morgan, as quoted in *Reader's Digest*, June 1940

There are trivial truths and the great truths. The opposite of a trivial truth is plainly false. The opposite of a great truth is also true.

Niels Bohr, as quoted in *The New York Times Book Review*, October 20, 1957

An optimist may see a light where there is none, but why must the pessimist always run to blow it out?

Michel de Saint-Pierre, as quoted in *Reader's Digest*, December 1958

The narrower the mind the broader the statement.

Ted Cook, as quoted in *Reader's Digest*, February 1940

If you see ten troubles coming down the road, you can be sure that nine will run into the ditch before they reach you.

Calvin Coolidge, as quoted in *Calvin Coolidge*

Blessed are those who can give without remembering and take without forgetting.

Elizabeth Asquith Bibesco, as quoted in *Reader's Digest*, November 1952

No man really becomes a fool until he stops asking questions.

Charles P. Steinmetz, as quoted in *Reader's Digest*, June 1955

Good taste and humor are a contradiction in terms, like a chaste whore.

Malcolm Muggeridge, as quoted in *Time*, September 14, 1953

A dog teaches a boy fidelity, perseverance, and to turn around three times before lying down.

510

Robert Benchley, as quoted in *Reader's Digest*, April 1963

There's an element of truth in every idea that lasts long enough to be called corny.

Irving Berlin, as quoted in *Reader's Digest*, March 1963

For most men life is a search for the proper manila envelope in which to get themselves filed.

Clifton Fadiman, as quoted in *International Celebrity Register*, 1960

Humility is like underwear—essential, but indecent if it shows.

Helen Nielsen, as quoted in *Reader's Digest*, March 1959

Sin and dandelions are very much alike. To get rid of them is a lifetime fight, and you never quite win it.

William Allen White, as quoted in *Reader's Digest*, May 1959

Experience is the name everyone gives to his mistakes.

Oscar Wilde, as quoted in *Reader's Digest*, May 1949

It is so easy to be good-natured I wonder anybody takes the trouble to be anything else.

Douglas Jerrold, as quoted in *Reader's Digest*, July 1951

Person to Person

We're not primarily put on this earth to see through one another, but to see one another through.

Peter De Vries, *Let Me Count the Ways*   511

If there is anything the nonconformist hates worse than a conformist it's another nonconformist who doesn't conform to the prevailing standards of nonconformity.

Bill Vaughan, as quoted in Reader's Digest, January 1959

Man was made to lead with his chin; he is worth knowing only with his guard down, his head up, and his heart rampant on his sleeve.

Robert Farrar Capon, The Supper of the Lamb

The most difficult thing in the world is to know how to do a thing and to watch somebody else doing it wrong, without comment.

T. H. White, as quoted in Reader's Digest, October 1955

It's better to give than to lend, and it costs about the same.

Philip Gibbs, as quoted in Reader's Digest, May 1936

For my part I would much sooner spend a month on a desert island with a veterinary surgeon than with a prime minister.

W. Somerset Maugham, The Summing Up

People are never so ready to believe you as when you say things in dispraise of yourself: and you are never so much annoyed as when they take you at your word.

W. Somerset Maugham, A Writer's Notebook

I like long walks, especially when they are taken by people who annoy me.

Fred Allen, as quoted in Reader's Digest, September 1949

The worst-tempered people I've ever met were people who knew they were wrong.

Wilson Mizner, as quoted in Reader's Digest, October 1968

When a man points a finger at someone else, he should remember that four of his fingers are pointing at himself.

Louis Nizer, *My Life in Court*

Flattery is all right—if you don't inhale.

Adlai E. Stevenson, speech, February 1, 1961

We all live under the same sky, but we don't all have the same horizon.

Konrad Adenauer, as quoted in *Reader's Digest*, July 1972

A crowd is a device for indulging ourselves in a kind of temporary insanity by all going crazy together.

Everett Dean Martin, *The Behavior of Crowds*

Compliments are like perfume, to be inhaled, not swallowed.

Charles Clark Munn, as quoted in *Reader's Digest*, June 1936

How awful to reflect that what people say of us is true.

Logan Pearsall Smith, *Afterthoughts*   513

Most of us hate to see a poor loser—or a rich winner.

Harold Coffin, as quoted in *Reader's Digest,* May 1962

The best way of answering a bad argument is to let it go on.

Sydney Smith, as quoted in *Reader's Digest,* March 1939

A real test of maturity is the ability to remain equally unruffled when the elevator boy calls you "Pop" and the senior partner calls you "Son."

Ivern Boyett, as quoted in *Reader's Digest,* December 1956

The best thing to do behind a person's back is pat it.

Franklin P. Jones, as quoted in *Reader's Digest,* January 1956

A saving grace of the adult condition is the capacity to be as amused by one's own follies as by those of others.

Robert F. Goheen, as quoted in *Reader's Digest,* September 1972

We find it hard to believe that other people's thoughts are as silly as our own, but they probably are.

James Harvey Robinson, *The Mind in the Making*

A man can give thanks if, in his lifetime, he has found one wife, one friend, and one cigarette lighter he can depend on.

Lee Farr, as quoted in *Reader's Digest,* April 1960

My father used to say: "Never suspect people. It's better to be deceived or mistaken, which is only human, after all, than to be suspicious, which is common."

Stark Young, *Feliciana*

The fellow who says he'll meet you halfway usually thinks he's standing on the dividing line.

O. A. Battista, as quoted in *Reader's Digest*, September 1968

The one thing all charming people have in common, no matter how they may differ in other respects, is an amused detachment from their common place troubles.

Sydney J. Harris, as quoted in *Reader's Digest*, January 1961

The taste of another's luck is always tart.

Samuel Hoffenstein, *Pencil in the Air*

There is nobody so irritating as somebody with less intelligence and more sense than we have.

Don Herold, as quoted in *Reader's Digest*, October 1972

An overdose of praise is like ten lumps of sugar in coffee; only a very few people can swallow it.

Emily Post, as quoted in *Reader's Digest*, February 1957

There's one way to find out if a man is honest—ask him. If he says "yes," you know he is crooked.

Groucho Marx, as quoted in news summaries of July 28, 1954

Everyone is a moon, and has a dark side which he never shows to anybody.

Mark Twain, as quoted in *Reader's Digest*, August 1960

Apologizing is a very desperate habit—one that is rarely cured. Apology is only egotism wrong side out. Nine times out of ten, the first 515 thing a man's companion knows of his shortcoming is from his apology. It is mighty presumptuous on your part to suppose your small failures of so much consequence that you must talk about them.

Oliver Wendell Holmes, as quoted in *Reader's Digest,*
August 1938

I love Virginians because Virginians are all snobs and I like snobs. A snob has to spend so much time being a snob that he has little time left to meddle with you.

William Faulkner, as quoted in the Memphis *Commercial*
Appeal, July 7, 1962

How desperately difficult it is to be honest with oneself. It is much easier to be honest with other people.

E. F. Benson, as quoted in *Reader's Digest*, May 1949

Homespun Philosophy

If you're going to do something tonight that you'll be sorry for tomorrow morning, sleep late.

Henny Youngman, as quoted in *Reader's Digest*, January
1969

There is only one way to achieve happiness on this
    terrestrial ball,
And that is to have either a clear conscience, or none at all.

Odgen Nash, *I'm a Stranger Here Myself*

Vanity, vanity, all is vanity.
That's any fun at all for humanity.

516

Ogden Nash, "Ha! Original Sin"

Angels fly, because they take themselves lightly.

G. K. Chesterton, as quoted in Reader's Digest, November 1964

I believe in getting into hot water; it keeps you clean.

G. K. Chesterton, Afterthoughts

Merely having an open mind is nothing. The object of opening the mind, as of opening the mouth, is to shut it again on something solid.

G. K. Chesterton, as quoted in Reader's Digest, March 1939

Gullibility is the key to all adventures. The greenhorn is the ultimate victor in everything; it is he that gets the most out of life.

G. K. Chesterton, as quoted in Reader's Digest, November 1962

Woe unto them that are tired of everything, for everything will certainly be tired of them.

G. K. Chesterton, Afterthoughts

There are two things to aim at in life; first, to get what you want; and, after that, to enjoy it. Only the wisest of mankind achieve the second.

Logan Pearsall Smith, Afterthoughts

If you want to be thought a liar, always tell the truth.

Logan Pearsall Smith, Afterthoughts

Never measure the height of a mountain until you have reached the top. Then you will see how low it was.

Dag Hammarskjöld, as quoted in Reader's Digest, March 1965

If you look *at* a window, you see flyspecks, dust, the crack where Junior's Frisbee hit it. If you look *through* a window, you see the world beyond.

Frederick Buechner, as quoted in *Reader's Digest,*
September 1972

There is no cure for birth and death save to enjoy the interval.

George Santayana, *Soliloquies in England*

The Difficult is that which can be done immediately; the Impossible that which takes a little longer.

George Santayana, as quoted in *Reader's Digest,* November
1939

Wisdom lies in taking everything good-humoredly, and with a grain of salt.

George Santayana, *The Life of Reason*

The world is divided into people who do things and people who get the credit. Try, if you can, to belong to the first class. There's far less competition.

Dwight Morrow, as quoted in *Reader's Digest,* April 1939

You must learn day by day, year by year, to broaden your horizon. The more things you love, the more you are interested in, the more you enjoy, the more you are indignant about—the more you have left when anything happens.

Ethel Barrymore, as quoted in the New York *Mirror,* May 6,
1955

For a long life be moderate in all things, but don't miss anything.

Adolf Lorenz, as quoted in *Reader's Digest,* June 1934

There is no right way to do the wrong thing.

Oren Arnold, as quoted in *Reader's Digest*, October 1970

No one can make you feel inferior without your consent.

Eleanor Roosevelt, as quoted in *Reader's Digest*, November 1971

Never get up with the lark. Get up only for a lark.

Lord John Boyd-Orr, as quoted in the Boston *Herald*, July 1, 1955

If we don't stand for something, we will fall for anything.

Irene Dunne, as quoted in *Reader's Digest*, July 1945

Never invest your money in anything that eats or needs repainting.

Billy Rose, as quoted in the New York *Post*, October 26, 1957

Life is the art of drawing without an eraser.

John Christian, as quoted in *Reader's Digest*, October 1963

Life is like an onion; you peel it off one layer at a time, and sometimes you weep.

Carl Sandburg, as quoted in *Reader's Digest*, July 1963

Always do one thing less than you think you can do.

Bernard Baruch, as quoted in *Newsweek*, May 28, 1956

We can't cross a bridge until we come to it; but I always like to lay down a pontoon ahead of time.

Bernard Baruch, as quoted in *Reader's Digest*, December 1960   519

One's eyes are what one is, one's mouth is what one becomes.

John Galsworthy, as quoted in *Reader's Digest*, October
1935

Snobbery sometimes is thought to be a prerogative of the rich. But no man is so poverty-stricken he can't afford to be a snob.

Hal Boyle, in an Associated Press column, January 28, 1966

So often we rob tomorrow's memories by today's economies.

John Mason Brown, as quoted in *Reader's Digest*,
September 1950

Experience is not what happens to you; it is what you do with what happens to you.

Aldous Huxley, as quoted in *Reader's Digest*, March 1956

Life is something like this trumpet. If you don't put anything in it you don't get anything out. And that's the truth.

W. C. Handy, trumpet player, as quoted in the New York
Herald Tribune, February 15, 1954

Style largely depends on the way the chin is worn.

Oscar Wilde, as quoted in *Reader's Digest*, August 1953

If you are small, death may quite likely overlook you.

> W. Somerset Maugham, at age eighty-four, as quoted in
> *Time,* February 3, 1958

It wasn't until quite late in life that I discovered how easy it is to say, "I don't know."

> W. Somerset Maugham, as quoted in *Reader's Digest,*
> January 1951

It is a funny thing about life—if you refuse to accept anything but the best you very often get it.

> W. Somerset Maugham, as quoted in *Reader's Digest,*
> February 1942

I am a believer in punctuality though it makes me very lonely.

> E. V. Lucas, as quoted in *Reader's Digest,* August 1953

I have always thought respectable people scoundrels and I look anxiously at my face every morning for signs of my becoming a scoundrel.

> Bertrand Russell, as quoted in *Bertrand Russell: The*
> *Passionate Skeptic*

In all affairs—love, religion, politics, or business—it's a healthy idea, now and then, to hang a question mark on the things you have long taken for granted.

> Bertrand Russell, as quoted in *Reader's Digest,* August 1940

It is much easier to do and die than it is to reason why.

> G. A. Studdert-Kennedy, as quoted in *Reader's Digest,*
> September 1937

It's fine to believe in ourselves, but we mustn't be too easily convinced.

> Burton Hillis, as quoted in *Reader's Digest,* August 1960   **521**

Life is ten percent what you make it and 90 percent how you take it.

Irving Berlin, as quoted in *Reader's Digest*, May 1949

Happiness makes up in height for what it lacks in length.

Robert Frost, as quoted in *Reader's Digest*, March 1959

I am an optimist. It does not seem too much use being anything else.

Sir Winston Churchill, as quoted in news summaries of
November 10, 1954

Use what talents you possess: the woods would be very silent if no birds sang there except those that sang best.

Henry Van Dyke, as quoted in *Reader's Digest*, December
1960

When a man is on the point of drowning, all he cares for is his life. But as soon as he gets ashore, he asks, "Where is my umbrella?" Wisdom, in life, consists in not asking for the umbrella.

John Wu, *Beyond East and West*

It is a good idea to take things as they come—if you can handle them that fast.

Sig Arno, as quoted in *Reader's Digest*, August 1962

Wisdom consists not so much in knowing what to do in the ultimate as in knowing what to do next.

Herbert Hoover, as quoted in *Reader's Digest*, July 1957

I don't think being well-rounded is particularly important. I would rather see people with a cutting edge on them.

Barnaby Keeney, as quoted in *Reader's Digest*, June 1967

Excuse my dust.

Dorothy Parker, her own epitaph

It is my rule never to lose me temper till it would be detrimental to keep it.

Sean O'Casey, *The Plough and the Stars*

The only gracious way to accept an insult is to ignore it; if you can't ignore it, top it; if you can't top it, laugh at it; if you can't laugh at it, it's probably deserved.

Russell Lynes, as quoted in *Reader's Digest*, October 1961

Life is what happens to us while we are making other plans.

Allen Saunders, as quoted in *Reader's Digest*, January 1957

What is elegance? Soap and water!

Cecil Beaton, as quoted in *The New York Times*, January 30, 1959

I try to be as philosophical as the old lady from Vermont who said that the best thing about the future is that it only comes one day at a time.

Dean Acheson, as quoted in *Reader's Digest*, September 1950

Nervousness causes some people to become helplessly garrulous. If this happens to you, try to steady yourself by taking deep, slow breaths. Deep breaths are very helpful at shallow parties.

Barbara Walters, as quoted in *Reader's Digest*, February 1973

Never play cards with a man called Doc. Never eat at a place called Mom's. Never sleep with a woman whose troubles are worse than your own.

Nelson Algren, quoting a convict's advice, as quoted in *Newsweek*, July 2, 1956

It is difficult to see the picture when you are inside the frame.

R. S. Trapp, as quoted in *Reader's Digest,* November 1968

We should be careful to get out of an experience only the wisdom that is in it—and stop there; lest we be like the cat that sits down on the hot stove-lid. She will never sit down on a hot stove-lid again—and that is well; but also she will never sit down on a cold one any more.

Mark Twain, as quoted in *Reader's Digest,* August 1939

To be good is noble, but to teach others how to be good is nobler—and less trouble.

Mark Twain, as quoted in *Reader's Digest,* May 1949

The essence of courage is not that your heart should not quake but that nobody else should know that it does.

E. F. Benson, as quoted in *Reader's Digest,* August 1953

Some things have to be believed
    to be seen.

Ralph Hodgson, *The Skylark and Other Poems*

Sometimes it's better to compromise—like giving a gunman your wallet without approving what he's doing.

Frank A. Clark, as quoted in *Reader's Digest,* May 1967

Aim at heaven and you will get earth thrown in. Aim at earth and you get neither.

C. S. Lewis, *Mere Christianity*

A genius is a man who takes the lemons that Fate hands him and starts a lemonade stand with them.

Elbert Hubbard, as quoted in *Reader's Digest,* October 1927

I have learned always to advise a man positively instead of negatively, for as much as he *might* regret doing a thing, he *would* regret not doing it.

Franklin P. Adams, as quoted in *Reader's Digest*, August 1939

People who want by the yard but try by the inch should be kicked by the foot.

W. Willard Wirtz, as quoted in *Reader's Digest*, January 1967

The day will happen whether or not you get up.

John Ciardi, as quoted in the *Saturday Review*, September 24, 1966

People criticize me for harping on the obvious. Perhaps some day I'll write an article on The Importance of the Obvious. If all the folks in the United States would do the few simple things they know they ought to do, most of our big problems would take care of themselves.

Calvin Coolidge, as quoted in *Reader's Digest*, July 1940

If accidents happen and you are to blame, take steps to avoid repetition of same.

Dorothy Sayers, *In the Teeth of the Evidence*

When you give honest advice, have one foot out the door.

Arnold H. Gleason, as quoted in *Reader's Digest*, May 1964

Don't be afraid to take a big step if one is indicated. You can't cross a chasm in two small jumps.

David Lloyd George, as quoted in *Reader's Digest*, June 1960

A pinch of probably is worth a pound of perhaps.

James Thurber, *Lanterns and Lances*   525

There are three ingredients in the good life: learning, earning and yearning.

> Christopher Morley, as quoted in *Reader's Digest*,
> November 1950

We can always live on less when we have more to live for.

> S. Stephen McKenney, as quoted in *Reader's Digest*,
> February 1943

All except the shallowest living involves tearing up one rough draft after another.

> Msgr. John J. Sullivan, *The Leaflet Missal*

Truth is tough. It will not break, like a bubble, at a touch; you may kick it about all day like a football, and it will be round and full at evening.

> Oliver Wendell Holmes, as quoted in *Reader's Digest*, June
> 1962

Truth is polygonal. I never feel sure that I have got it until I have contradicted myself five or six times.

> John Ruskin, as quoted in *Reader's Digest*, April 1962

I set up my pitch in life on a busy and interesting street. I did a good business and I have no regrets.

> H. L. Mencken, his own epitaph

The mind is like the stomach. It is not how much you put into it that counts, but how much it digests.

> Albert Jay Nock, as quoted in *Reader's Digest*, March 1937

Decide promptly, but never give any reasons. Your decisions may be right, but your reasons are sure to be wrong.

> Lord Mansfield, as quoted in *Reader's Digest*, July 1940

The man who is swimming against the stream knows the strength of it.

Woodrow Wilson, speech on "The New Freedom," 1913

Wisdom is knowing what to do next, skill is knowing how to do it, and virtue is doing it.

David Starr Jordan, as quoted in *Reader's Digest*, August 1960

See everything, overlook a great deal, correct a little.

Pope John XXIII, as quoted in *Reader's Digest*, December 1962

It's a wise man who profits by his experience, but it's a good deal wiser one who lets the rattlesnake bite the other fellow.

Josh Billings, as quoted in *Reader's Digest*, November 1957

Two men look out through the same bars.
One sees the mud, and one sees the stars.

Frederick Langbridge, *A Cluster of Quiet Thoughts*

Life is hard,
By the yard;
But by the inch,
Life's a cinch!

Jean L. Gordon, as quoted in *Reader's Digest*, June 1947

When down in the mouth remember Jonah—he came out all right!

Thomas A. Edison, as quoted in *Reader's Digest*, July 1947

Fools live to regret their words, wise men to regret their silence.

Will Henry, as quoted in *Reader's Digest*, February 1974   527

In life as in a football game, the principle to follow is: Hit the line hard.

Theodore Roosevelt, *The Strenuous Life*

There are three things not worth running for—a bus, a woman or a new economic panacea; if you wait a bit another one will come along.

Derick Heathcoat Amory, as quoted in *Reader's Digest,*
October 1959

One learns in life to keep silent and draw one's own confusions.

Cornelia Otis Skinner, as quoted in *Reader's Digest*, May
1941

If only one could have two lives: the first in which to make one's mistakes, which seem as if they have to be made; and the second in which to profit by them.

D. H. Lawrence, *The Collected Letters of D. H. Lawrence*

The only way on earth to multiply happiness is to divide it.

Paul Scherer, as quoted in *Reader's Digest*, October 1949

A problem well stated is a problem half solved.

Charles F. Kettering, as quoted in *Reader's Digest*, April
1953

Yesterday is a canceled check; tomorrow is a promissory note; today is ready cash—use it.

Kay Lyons, as quoted in *Reader's Digest*, March 1974

My grandfather always said that living is like licking honey off a thorn.

Louis Adamic, as quoted in *Reader's Digest*, September
1955

A word of advice; don't give it.

A. J. Volicos, as quoted in *Reader's Digest*, April 1947

Humor

Laughter is the shortest distance between two people.

Victor Borge, as quoted in *Reader's Digest*, March 1973

Humor is emotional chaos remembered in tranquility.

James Thurber, as quoted in *The Enjoyment of Laughter*

Life is a joke that's just begun.

W. S. Gilbert, *The Mikado*

I think the next best thing to solving a problem is finding some humor in it.

Frank A. Clark, as quoted in *Reader's Digest*, March 1972

The American public highly overrates its sense of humor. We're great belly laughers and prat fallers, but we never really did have a real sense of humor. Not satire anyway. We're a fat-headed, cotton-picking society. When we realize finally that we aren't God's given children, we'll understand satire. Humor is really laughing off a hurt, grinning at misery.

Bill Mauldin, as quoted in *Time*, July 21, 1961

My way of joking is telling the truth. That is the funniest joke in the world.

George Bernard Shaw, as quoted in *Reader's Digest*, January 1939

He who laughs, lasts.

Mary P. Poole, *A Glass Eye at the Keyhole*

In the language of screen comedians four of the main grades of laugh are the titter, the yowl, the belly laugh and the boffo. The titter is just a titter. The yowl is a runaway titter. Anyone who has ever had the pleasure knows all about a belly laugh. The boffo is the laugh that kills.

James Agee, as quoted in *Life*, September 5, 1949

On Telling Jokes
If you can't remember them,
Don't dismember them.

Anthony J. Pettito, as quoted in *Reader's Digest*, May 1953

Laugh at yourself first, before anyone else can.

Elsa Maxwell, NBC-TV interview, September 28, 1958

Dogs laugh, but they laugh with their tails. . . . What puts man in a higher state of evolution is that he has got his laugh on the right end.

Max Eastman, *Enjoyment of Laughter*

Wit has truth in it; wisecracking is simply calisthenics with words.

Dorothy Parker, as quoted in *The Paris Review*, Summer 1956

Fred Allen said it was bad to suppress laughter. It goes back down and spreads to your hips.

Carl Reiner, as quoted in *Reader's Digest*, August 1968

Comedy is the last refuge of the non-conformist mind.

Gilbert Seldes, as quoted in *The New Republic*, December 20, 1954

It dawned on me then that as long as I could laugh, I was safe from the world; and I have learned since that laughter keeps me safe from myself, too. All of us have schnozzles—are ridiculous in one way or another, if not in our faces, then in our characters, minds or habits. When we admit our schnozzles, instead of defending them, we begin to laugh, and the world laughs with us.

Jimmy Durante, as quoted in *Reader's Digest*, July 1937

The tendency of recent culture has been to tolerate the smile but discourage the laugh.

G. K. Chesterton, *The Common Man*

THE LIFE
OF LEISURE

Leisure and Vices

Don't put off for tomorrow what you can do today, because if you enjoy it today you can do it again tomorrow.

James A. Michener, as quoted in *Reader's Digest*, May 1973

Too many people who try to use the weekend to unwind simply unravel.

Bill Copeland, as quoted in *Reader's Digest*, July 1968

Italians come to ruin most generally in three ways—women, gambling, and farming. My family chose the slowest one.

Pope John XXIII, as quoted in *Newsweek*, December 17, 1962

Organized crime's speedy takeover of the pornography industry underlines as never before that smut constitutes a serious national problem. Any lingering thought that the stream of obscene books, magazines and films flooding the country is harmless should now be ended.

George Denison, as quoted in *Reader's Digest*, December 1971

What makes resisting temptation difficult, for many people, is that they don't want to discourage it completely.

Franklin P. Jones, as quoted in *Reader's Digest*, September 1970

535

If it weren't for having more leisure time these days, many men would never finish the work they take home from the office.

Franklin P. Jones, as quoted in *Reader's Digest*, January 1963

Husbands have always had a leisure problem. It's called waiting.

Franklin P. Jones, as quoted in *Reader's Digest*, December 1961

Now that cigarettes are so improved you get the notion that anybody who doesn't smoke can't be much interested in his health.

Franklin P. Jones, as quoted in *Reader's Digest*, August 1960

Walking isn't a lost art—one must, by some means, get to the garage.

Evan Esar, as quoted in *Reader's Digest*, June 1949

Warning: The Surgeon General Has Determined That Cigarette Smoking Is Dangerous to Your Health

Statement required by law since 1965 to appear on all cigarette packages and advertisements

Sometimes it is extremely good for you to forget that there is anything in the world that needs to be done, and to do some particular thing that you want to do. Every human being needs a certain amount of time in which he can be peaceful. Peace may take the form of exercise or reading or any congenial occupation; but the one thing which must not be connected with it is a sense of obligation to do some particular thing at some particular time. I had 200 letters waiting a few days ago and any amount of work which had to be done, and I deliberately spent two hours reading poetry.

Eleanor Roosevelt, as quoted in *Reader's Digest*, May 1957

The best way to get real enjoyment out of a garden is to put on a wide straw hat, dress in thin, loose-fitting clothes, hold a trowel in one hand and a cold drink in the other, and tell the man where to dig.

Charles Barr, as quoted in *Reader's Digest*, May 1949

When I feel like exercising, I just lie down until the feeling goes away.

Paul Terry, as quoted in *Reader's Digest*, January 1938

Hallelujah! I'm a Bum.

Song of the International Workers of the World (IWW),
c. 1905

Nothing solidifies the country more than taking a pleasure ride on Sunday afternoon.

Dan Bennett, as quoted in *Reader's Digest*, August 1961

Today my heart beat 103,389 times, my blood traveled 168,000,000 miles, I breathed 23,040 times, I inhaled 438 cubic feet of air, I spoke 4,800 words, noved 750 major muscles, and I exercised 7,000,000 brain cells. I'm tired.

Bob Hope, as quoted in *Reader's Digest*, January 1949

Few things are as hard to use in moderation as a comfortable chair.

D. O. Flynn, as quoted in *Reader's Digest*, December 1963

Men tire themselves in pursuit of rest.

Laurence Sterne, as quoted in *Reader's Digest*, November 1961

What is this life if, full of care,
We have no time to stand and stare?

W. H. Davies, "Leisure," *Songs of Joy*

Millions long for immortality who do not know what to do with themselves on a rainy Sunday afternoon.

Susan Ertz, as quoted in *Reader's Digest*, September 1944

Many of us spend half our time wishing for things we could have if we didn't spend half our time wishing.

Alexander Woollcott, as quoted in *Reader's Digest*, January 1943

All the things I really like to do are either immoral, illegal or fattening.

Alexander Woollcott, as quoted in *Reader's Digest*, December 1933

More free time means more time to waste. The worker who used to have only a little time in which to get drunk and beat his wife now has time to get drunk, beat his wife—and watch TV.

Robert Hutchins, as quoted in news summaries of January 2, 1954

To cease smoking is the easiest thing I ever did. I ought to know because I've done it a thousand times.

Mark Twain, as quoted in *Reader's Digest*, December 1945

I made it a rule never to smoke while asleep, never to stop smoking while awake and never to smoke more than one cigar at a time.

Mark Twain, as quoted in *Reader's Digest*, September 1952

There are several good protections against temptation, but the surest is cowardice.

Mark Twain, as quoted in *Reader's Digest*, March 1961

A habit cannot be tossed out the window; it must be coaxed down the stairs a step at a time.

Mark Twain, as quoted in *Reader's Digest*, June 1958

The soul is dyed with the color of its leisure thoughts.

Dean Inge, as quoted in *Reader's Digest*, April 1936

Sometimes I think it is worth while to get tired—it feels so good to rest.

Grace Coolidge, as quoted in *Reader's Digest*, March 1934

Conspicuous consumption of valuable goods is a means of reputability to the gentleman of leisure.

Thorstein Veblen, *The Theory of the Leisure Class*

The secret of being miserable is to have leisure to bother about whether you are happy or not.

George Bernard Shaw, as quoted in *Reader's Digest*, April 1935

My idea of a vacation is to rest quietly in the shade of a blonde.

Richard Powell, as quoted in *Reader's Digest*, December 1945

The only perfect climate is bed.

Frank Crowninshield, as quoted in *Reader's Digest*, June 1948

It is better to have loafed and lost than never to have loafed at all.

James Thurber, *Fables for Our Time*

Contemplation is a casualty of the American way of life. We simply do not have the time for it. We read poetry as we would a detective story. We listen to opera, chamber music and symphonies on our FM's while we do the morning dishes or prepare income tax statements. We visit art museums as we would tour the Grand Canyon. Our nation has so much leisure time that it has a "leisure problem," and yet it lacks the essential leisure of contemplation.

Andrew M. Greeley, as quoted in *Reader's Digest*, January 1961

539

Living in the lap of luxury isn't so bad except that you never know when luxury is going to stand up.

Ken Murray, as quoted in *Reader's Digest,* June 1951

Generally speaking anybody is more interesting doing nothing than doing anything.

Gertrude Stein, *Four Saints in Three Acts*

Today we use 300 horsepower to move a 150-pound man one block to purchase a one-ounce package of cigarettes—complete with filter tips so he won't know what he's smoking.

John B. MacDonald, as quoted in *Reader's Digest,* April 1961

Do you know that conversation is one of the greatest pleasures in life? But it wants leisure.

W. Somerset Maugham, *The Trembling of a Leaf*

The unfortunate thing about this world is that good habits are so much easier to get out of than bad ones.

W. Somerset Maugham, as quoted in *Reader's Digest,* July 1951

I have not been afraid of excess: excess on occasion is exhilarating. It prevents moderation from acquiring the deadening effect of a habit.

W. Somerset Maugham, as quoted in *Reader's Digest,* June 1960

The day that goes by without your having had some fun—the day you don't enjoy life—is not only unnecessary but unchristian!

Dwight D. Eisenhower, as quoted in *Reader's Digest,* January 1972

If, after I depart this vale, you ever remember me and have thought to please my ghost, forgive some sinner and wink your eye at some homely girl.

H. L. Mencken, as quoted in *Reader's Digest*, November 1955

There's a great deal to be said for a man who quits smoking, and he generally says it without letup.

G. Norman Collie, as quoted in *Reader's Digest*, June 1955

It takes application, a fine sense of value, and a powerful community-spirit for a people to have serious leisure, and this has not been the genius of the Americans.

Paul Goodman, *Growing Up Absurd*

The original mistake was inventing the calendar. This led, in due course, to having Mondays.

H. V. Wade, as quoted in *Reader's Digest*, April 1952

As kids, we started smoking because it was smart. Why don't we stop for the same reason?

Harold Emery, as quoted in *Reader's Digest*, March 1970

All the epidemics of typhoid throughout Western Europe since the beginning of the 16th century have caused fewer estimated deaths than the total known to be caused by cigarettes in one year in the United States alone.

Cigarettes have accounted for more fatalities than were caused by TB epidemics in Europe throughout the 19th century. The current annual cigarette mortality in this country surpassed the estimated total for all of the known epidemics of yellow fever in history.

S. S. Field, as quoted in *Reader's Digest*, September 1973   541

There is less leisure now than in the Middle Ages, when one-third of the year consisted of holidays and festivals.

Ralph Borsodi, *This Ugly Civilization*

The only way to stop smoking is to just stop—no ifs, ands or butts.

Edith Zittler, as quoted in *Reader's Digest,* May 1974

I have often been struck by the fact that the symptoms of laziness and fatigue are practically identical.

Frederick Lewis Allen, as quoted in *Reader's Digest,* December 1951

The way of the transgressor may be hard—but it sure isn't lonely.

Lou Erickson, as quoted in *Reader's Digest,* April 1974

A little secret sinning now and then,
Should not disturb the saintliness of men;
For when your life is spent, and sun has set,
'Tis easier to repent than to regret.

E. Y. Harburg, *Rhymes for the Irreverent*

The trouble with more leisure time is that pretty soon you're working overtime to pay for all the expensive hobbies you took up.

Fletcher Knebel, as quoted in *Reader's Digest*, March 1958

It is now proved beyond doubt that smoking is one of the leading causes of statistics.

Fletcher Knebel, as quoted in *Reader's Digest*, October 1961

Sleep, riches and health, to be truly enjoyed, must be interrupted.

Jean Paul Friedrich Richter, as quoted in *Reader's Digest*,
December 1963

More and more these days I find myself pondering on how to reconcile my net income with my gross habits.

John Kirk Nelson, as quoted in *Reader's Digest*, March
1952

Give me the luxuries of life and I will willingly do without the necessities.

Frank Lloyd Wright, as quoted in *The New York Times*,
April 9, 1959

People would be surprised to know how much I learned about prayer from playing poker.

Mary Austin, as quoted in *Reader's Digest*, December 1951

Be limp if you want your sleep to be placid; emulate the dishrag.

Joseph Collomb, as quoted in *Reader's Digest*, February
1947

Idleness is as necessary to good work as is activity. The man who can take hold hard and to some purpose is the man who knows how to let go.

Dr. Frank Crane, as quoted in *Reader's Digest*, May 1951

Travel

Restore human legs as a means of travel. Pedestrians rely on food for fuel and need no special parking facilities.

Lewis Mumford, as quoted in Reader's Digest, January 1973

The whole object of travel is not to set foot on foreign land. It is at last to set foot on one's own country as a foreign land.

G. K. Chesterton, The Man Who Was Chesterton

The only way of catching a train I have ever discovered is to miss the train before.

G. K. Chesteron, as quoted in Reader's Digest, March 1933

A good holiday is one spent among people whose notions of time are vaguer than yours.

J. B. Priestley, as quoted in Reader's Digest, May 1967

Opinions and principles are no doubt noble things, essential factors in the forward moves of humanity—and in the reactionary ones as well—but they are poor things to take along when you are going to places with the intention of seeing and knowing what is there.

Thomas Hart Benton, An American in Art

Experience has convinced me that the prime necessity for those who would go places and not bring back simply what they took with them is to be rid of all opinions before starting. If you can't be rid of opinions, then the next necessity is to learn to keep your mouth shut about them, for you will otherwise find yourself in the hot water of dispute and get in those messes of words which, among men in any stratum of life, operate to confuse understanding.

Thomas Hart Benton, An American in Art

As a nation we have become space-eaters, mile-consumers; unless we can gulp distances down, we fell laggard as lizards.

Dr. Peter J. Steincrohn, as quoted in *Reader's Digest*, August 1973

He who would travel happily must travel light.

Antoine de Saint-Exupéry, *Wind, Sand, and Stars*

I do not understand love of just one place; I believe one mustn't confuse love of life with the love of certain things in it. One cannot pick the moment and place as one pleases and say, "Enough. This is all I want. This is how it is henceforth to be." That sort of present betrays past and future. Life is its own journey; presupposes its own change and movement, and one tries to arrest them at one's eternal peril.

Laurens van der Post, travel writer, as quoted in *Reader's Digest*, February 1960

The very name London has tonnage in it.

V. S. Pritchett, *London Perceived*

Although Londoners are, more than any other city people, wary of foreigners, although London landladies are Britannias armed with helmet, shield, trident, and have faces with the word "No" stamped like a coat of arms on them, the place is sentimental and tolerant. The attitude to foreigners is like the attitude to dogs; dogs are neither human nor British, but so long as you keep them under control, give them their exercise, feed them, pat them, you will find their wild emotions are amusing, and their characters interesting.

V. S. Pritchett, *London Perceived*

Thanks to the miles of super highways under construction, America will soon be a wonderful place to drive—if you don't want to stop.

Fletcher Knebel, as quoted in *Reader's Digest*, June 1962

If you are lucky enough to have lived in Paris as a young man, then wherever you go for the rest of your life, it stays with you, for Paris is a moveable feast.

Ernest Hemingway, *A Moveable Feast*

Building model railroads has become popular as a hobby; now commuters wish somebody would take it up as a business.

Harold Coffin, as quoted in *Reader's Digest*, April 1961

The eye remembers Lora-like images: widows with beaten skin, an oyster eye and a black shawl over their heads; beggars having a good time exaggerating their poverty.

Cecil Beaton, on Spain, as quoted in *The Face of the World*

Man has pursued a lot of dreams—the golden fleece, the alchemist's stone and the idea that the car can be packed for a family vacation so that only one suitcase need be brought into the motel at night.

Bill Vaughan, as quoted in *Reader's Digest*, January 1955

A lot of friction is caused by half the drivers trying to go fast enough to thrill their girl friends and the other half trying to go slow enough to placate their wives.

Bill Vaughan, as quoted in *Reader's Digest*, October 1957

Safety experts urge that we drive five car-lengths behind the car ahead on the highway. But if you try it, you will find there are five cars in there too.

Bill Vaughan, as quoted in *Reader's Digest*, September 1956

It's a strange trend in transportation—every year there are more station wagons and fewer stations.

546

Bill Vaughan, as quoted in *Reader's Digest*, May 1960

The time to enjoy a European trip is about three weeks after unpacking.

George Ade, *Forty Modern Fables*

Too often travel, instead of broadening the mind, merely lengthens the conversation.

Elizabeth Drew, as quoted in *Reader's Digest*, March 1961

The way blood flows in them these days, it's easy to see why they're called traffic arteries.

Luke Neely, as quoted in *Reader's Digest*, May 1955

Venice is like eating an entire box of chocolate liqueurs in one go.

Truman Capote, as quoted in *The New York Times*,
November 26, 1961

Why are hotel-room walls so thin when you sleep and so thick when you listen?

Arthur Godfrey, as quoted in *Reader's Digest*, May 1955

Moscow is the city where, if Marilyn Monroe should walk down the street with nothing on but shoes, people would stare at her feet first.

John Gunther, *Inside Russia Today*

In this country there are three persons to every car—and they are always in front of it at a street crossing.

Henry Morgan, as quoted in *Reader's Digest*, December
1954

Some people would not hestitate to drive up to the gate of heaven and honk.

John Andrew Holmes, *Wisdom in Small Doses*   547

The worst thing about taking your vacation in winter is July.

John T. McCutcheon, Jr., as quoted in Reader's Digest, July
1957

The American arrives in Paris with a few French phrases he has culled from a conversational guide or picked up from a friend who owns a beret. He speaks the sort of French that is really understood by another American who also has just arrived in Paris.

Fred Allen, introduction to Paris After Dark

If we would only give, just once, the same amount of reflection to what we want to get out of life that we give to the question of what to do with a two weeks' vacation, we would be startled at our false standards and the aimless procession of our busy days.

Dorothy Canfield Fisher, The Squirrel-Cage

England is my wife—America, my mistress. It is very good sometimes to get away from one's wife.

Sir Cedric Hardwicke, as quoted in The New York Times,
August 6, 1964

Natives who beat drums to drive off evil spirits are objects of scorn to smart American motorists who blow horns to break up traffic jams.

Mary Ellen Kelly, as quoted in Reader's Digest, March 1956

When I was very young and the urge to be someplace else was on me, I was assured by mature people that maturity would cure this itch. When years described me as mature, the remedy prescribed was middle age. In middle age I was assured that greater age would calm my fever, and now that I am 58 perhaps senility will do the job.

John Steinbeck, Travels with Charley

In the space age, man will be able to go around the world in two hours—one hour for flying and the other to get to the airport.

Neil McElroy, former U.S. Secretary of Defense, as quoted
in Look, February 18, 1958

548

We may well go to the moon, but that's not very far. The greatest distance we have to cover still lies within us.

Charles de Gaulle, as quoted in *Reader's Digest*, April 1959

I'm leaving because the weather is too good. I hate London when it's not raining.

Groucho Marx, as quoted from news summaries of June 28, 1954

I have nothing to declare but my genius.

Oscar Wilde, to customs officials upon arriving in the United States, as quoted in *Reader's Digest*, March 1934

The traveler was active; he went strenuously in search of people, of adventure, of experience. The tourist is passive; he expects interesting things to happen to him. He goes "sight-seeing."

Daniel J. Boorstin, *The Image*

In the United States, "First" and "Second" class can't be painted on railroad cars, for all passengers, being Americans, are equal and it would be "un-American." But paint "Pullman" on a car, and everybody is satisfied.

Owen Wister, as quoted in *Reader's Digest*, July 1936

Man has always been an explorer. There's a fascination in thrusting out and going to new places. It's like going through a door because you find the door in front of you. I think that man loses something if he has the option to go to the moon and does not take it.

Neil Armstrong, Michael Collins and Edwin Aldrin, *First on the Moon*

One small step for man, one giant step for mankind.

Neil Armstrong, U.S. astronaut, descending onto the moon after the Apollo 11 lunar landing, July 20, 1969

Though it may be unessential to the imagination, travel is necessary to an understanding of men.

Freya Stark, *Perseus in the Wind*

Such delicate goods as justice, love and honor, courtesy, and indeed all the things we care for, are valid everywhere; but they are variously moulded and often differently handled, and some times nearly unrecognized if you meet them in a foreign land; the art of learning fundamental common values is perhaps the greatest gain of travel to those who wish to live at ease among their fellows.

Freya Stark, *Perseus in the Wind*

If there is one thing in the world that will make a man peculiarly and insufferably self-conceited, it is to have his stomach behave itself, the first day at sea, when nearly all his comrades are seasick.

Mark Twain, as quoted in *Reader's Digest*, January 1934

To forget pain is to be painless; to forget care is to be rid of it; to go abroad is to accomplish both.

550

Mark Twain, *Autobiography*

It strikes me that we're all in the same boat with Christopher Columbus. He didn't know where he was going when he started. When he got there he didn't know where he was, and when he got back he didn't know where he had been.

Owen Young, as quoted in Reader's Digest, March 1933

[My hotels] are rather like the old Spanish mission stations, strung across the countryside just one day's journey apart.

Conrad Hilton, as quoted in Life, August 30, 1963

Every year it takes less time to fly across the ocean and longer to drive to the office.

Raymond Duncan, as quoted in Reader's Digest, May 1956

If it weren't for the fun of anticipating the pleasures of travel and the fun of telling about your trip when you get back, nobody would ever go very far from home.

William Feather, as quoted in Reader's Digest, July 1971

Travel is broadening, particularly where the food and drink are good. But the journey home is an exultant occasion.

Brooks Atkinson, in The New York Times, March 1965

An example of modern progress is that every year it takes less time and more money to get where you're going.

Earl Wilson, as quoted in Reader's Digest, October 1962

In his long pursuit for those elusive objectives he has labeled peace and security, man has found them often on board a ship, away from the ghastly reminders of land. . . . After a few days at sea he achieves a sense of rhythm and balance to an extent which never seemed possible on land; his mind becomes lulled by the space and physical order and time compresses itself into the single tense: the present.

Jerre Mangione, The Ship and the Flame   551

One of the most common disrupters of marital bliss is the choice of where to spend a vacation. What this country needs is an ocean in the mountains.

Paul Sweeney, as quoted in *Reader's Digest,* May 1970

Traveling may be one of two things—an experience we shall always remember, or an experience which, alas, we shall never forget.

Rabbi Julius Gordon, *Your Sense of Humor*

The one book that really tells you where you can go on your vacation is your checkbook.

Imogene Fey, as quoted in *Reader's Digest,* May 1956

It's hardly surprising that today's Philippines are a tantalizing mélange of East and West and most places in between. Besides Brazil, it's probably the only genuine multi-racial society on earth. Imagine Chinese delicacy, Malay fire, Spanish modesty and Yankee verve, and you have Filipino girls, the world's warmest, loveliest and most devastating. Miscegenation works wonders.

Christopher Lucas, as quoted in *Reader's Digest,* January 1972

The helicopter has become the most universal vehicle ever created and used by man. It approaches closer than any other to fulfillment of mankind's ancient dreams of the flying horse and the magic carpet.

Igor Sikorsky, on the twentieth anniversary of his first practical helicopter, September 13, 1959, as quoted in *The New York Times*

I should like to spend the whole of my life traveling, if I could anywhere borrow another life to spend at home.

William Hazlitt, as quoted in *Reader's Digest,* October 1948

It is when the holiday is over that we begin to enjoy it.

A. G. Gardiner, as quoted in *Reader's Digest,* October 1948

A man may desire to go to Mecca. His conscience tells him that he ought to go to Mecca. He fares forth, either by the aid of Cook's or unassisted; he may probably never reach Mecca; he may drown before he gets to Port Said; he may perish ingloriously on the coast of the Red Sea; his desire may remain eternally frustrated. Unfulfilled aspirations may always trouble him. But he will not be tormented in the same way as the man who, desiring to reach Mecca, and harried by the desire to reach Mecca, never leaves Brixton. It is something to have left Brixton. Most of us have not left Brixton. We have not even taken a cab to Ludgate Circus.

Arnold Bennett, Howto Live on Twenty-four Hours a Day

When you travel, remember that a foreign country is not designed to make you comfortable. It is designed to make its own people comfortable.

Clifton Fadiman, as quoted in Reader's Digest, August 1960

To be really cosmopolitan, a man must be at home even in his own country.

Thomas Wentworth Higginson, Short Studies of American Authors

The sage who said "Go West" never had to figure out how to do it on a cloverleaf intersection.

Gladys Boblitt, as quoted in Reader's Digest, March 1960

Road: n. A strip of land along which one may pass from where it is too tiresome to be to where it is futile to go.

Ambrose Bierce, The Devil's Dictionary

They haven't yet decided officially what to call men who volunteer to be shot to the moon, but one lively possibility seems to be lunatics.

Franklin P. Jones, as quoted in Reader's Digest, June 1960

Sports

[On athletic scholarships:] . . . one of the greatest educational swindles ever perpetrated on American youth.

A. Whitney Griswold, former president of Yale University,
as quoted in The New York Times, April 20, 1963

Golf is an awkward set of bodily contortions designed to produce a graceful result.

Tommy Armour, as quoted in Reader's Digest, October
1973

As I understand it, sport is hard work for which you do not get paid.

Irvin S. Cobb, Sports and Pastimes

If you watch a game, it's fun. If you play it, it's recreation. If you work at it, it's golf.

Bob Hope, as quoted in Reader's Digest, October 1958

Here is no sentiment, no contest, no grandeur, no economics. From the sanctity of this occupation, a man may emerge refreshed and in control of his own soul. He is not idle. He is fishing, alone with himself in dignity and peace. It seems a very precious thing to me.

John Steinbeck, as quoted in Sports Illustrated, October 4,
1954

Our football was primitive compared to the skills and deception of today. We knew only one defense, a 7-4 diamond. We never passed on first down, seldom on second. We used a minimum of ball-handling, no laterals or pitchouts. The so-called iron men of my era would have melted down in a hurry trying to play a full game at the pace demanded today.

Harold "Red" Grange, as quoted in Reader's Digest,
September 1973

554

You gotta be a man to play baseball for a living but you gotta have a lot of little boy in you too.

Roy Campanella, as quoted in the New York
Journal-American, April 12, 1957

Fishing is the chance to wash one's soul with pure air. It brings meekness and inspiration, reduces our egotism, soothes our troubles and shames our wickedness.

Herbert Hoover, as quoted in the New York *Herald*
Tribune, May 19, 1947

The art of fishing brings meekness and inspiration from the decency of nature, charity toward tackle makers, patience toward fish, a quieting of hate, and a mockery of profits and egos. Fishing is great discipline in the equality of men—because all men are equal before fish!

Herbert Hoover, as quoted in *Reader's Digest,* May 1970

Real sport is an antidote to fatalism; the deep objective of games is really to train one's reflex of purpose, to develop a habit of keeping steadily at something you want to do until it is done. The rules of the game and the opposition of other players are devices to put obstacles in your way. The winner must keep everlastingly after his objective with intensity and continuity of purpose.

John R. Tunis, as quoted in *Reader's Digest,* February 1942

A ball player's got to be kept hungry to become a big-leaguer. That's why no boy from a rich family ever made the big leagues.

Joe Di Maggio, as quoted in *The New York Times,* April 30,
1961

The devotion of millions of Americans to professional sports is rooted in their deep faith that the games are honestly played and that the athletes give their best performance at all times. Anything less than the absolute isolation of the gambling syndicate from the world of professional sports constitutes a betrayal of that faith.

George Denison, as quoted in *Reader's Digest,* August 1973　555

It's a lot tougher to be a football coach than a President. You've got four years as President, and they guard you. A coach doesn't have anyone to protect him when things go wrong.

> Harry S. Truman, as quoted in *Sports Illustrated*, March 17, 1958

Thanks to the alertness of the sportscasters and the miracles of modern communication, it is often possible to know the score of every major football game in the country—except the one to which you are listening.

> Bill Vaughan, as quoted in *Reader's Digest*, October 1957

Texas has a rather confusing image. It's the country of rugged outdoors people, where they play baseball and football under a roof.

> Bill Vaughan, *Half the Battle*

I'd like to get a steamroller and lay [Ken] Norton down and crush him flat. Other than that, I like him.

> George Foreman, on his heavyweight title challenger, as quoted in *The New York Times*, January 27, 1974

Some people get so all they want out of life is food, sex, clothes and a well-strung racket.

> Allie Ritzenberg, Washington tennis pro, as quoted in *Reader's Digest*, August 1973

Golf is like a love affair: if you don't take it seriously, it's no fun; if you do take it seriously, it breaks your heart.

> Arnold Daly, as quoted in *Reader's Digest*, November 1933

I had pro offers from the Detroit Lions and Green Bay Packers, who were pretty hard up for linemen in those days. If I had gone into professional football the name Jerry Ford might have been a household word today.

> Gerald Ford, as quoted in *The New York Times*, February 3, 1974

When I was 40, my doctor advised me that a man in his forties shouldn't play tennis. I heeded his advice carefully and could hardly wait until I reached 50 to start again.

Justice Hugo Black, as quoted in Think, February 1963

I'll be so fast that he'll think he's surrounded. I'm going to hit him before God gets the news.

Muhammad Ali, on his title fight with George Foreman, as quoted in The New York Times, May 5, 1974

If you see a tennis player who looks as if he is working very hard, then that means he isn't very good.

Helen Wills Moody, as quoted in Reader's Digest, May 1933

If you are not afraid to just go out and compete, then you will run your best race. But if you go out with a fear of something, even against yourself or against the clock, they you have lost the race before you start.

Jim Ryun, long-distance runner, as quoted in The New York Times, April 28, 1974

Even if I'd known why he couldn't shoot foul shots, I'd never have told him.

Bill Russell, recalling Wilt Chamberlain's poor free-throw shooting and their years of basketball rivalry, as quoted in *The New York Times*, April 21, 1974

Football today is far too much a sport for the few who can play it well; the rest of us, and too many of our children, get exercise from climbing up the seats in stadiums, or from walking across the room to turn on our television sets. And this is true for one sport after another, all across the board.

John F. Kennedy, address at National Football Foundation dinner, December 5, 1961

I have no interest whatever in the women's movement, except in the sense that I believe everybody should have the right to do what he wants to do. I'm not out to prove anything. I just want to ride horses.

Robyn Smith, as quoted in *Reader's Digest*, December 1972

I don't know whether you have them here but football pools, and all that, constitutes the sustaining background of the life of a man upon whose faithful daily toil and exertion all the progress of society depends.

Sir Winston Churchill, commenting on a game of chance highly popular in Britain, as quoted in news summaries of June 29, 1954

You can map out a fight plan or a life plan, but when the action starts, it may not go the way you planned, and you're down to your reflexes—which means your training. That's where your roadwork shows. If you cheated on that in the dark of the mornin', well, you're gettin' found out now under the bright lights.

Joe Frazier, as quoted in *Reader's Digest*, January 1972

The way to succeed at quarterback is to call the unexpected consistently.

John Hadl, Los Angeles Ram quarterback, as quoted in *The New York Times*, January 6, 1974

The only reason I ever played golf in the first place was so I could afford to hunt and fish.

> Sam Snead, hinting about retiring from golf, as quoted in
> *Sports Illustrated*, January 22, 1968

No horse can go as fast as the money you bet on him.

> Nate Collier, as quoted in *Reader's Digest*, January 1938

Skiing is wonderful exercise for women, and you know why? Because it makes them look so much younger. After a day outdoors on skis, a woman of 40 looks just like a man of 30.

> Herb Shriner, as quoted in *Reader's Digest*, January 1953

The way some people talk about modern football [soccer], anyone would think the results of just one game was a matter of life and death. They don't understand. It's much more serious than that.

> Bill Shankly, manager of Liverpool soccer team, as quoted
> in *The New York Times*, January 13, 1974

Golf is a good walk spoiled.

> Mark Twain, as quoted in *Reader's Digest*, December 1948

I never made the [football] team. . . . I was not heavy enough to play the line, not fast enough to play halfback, and not smart enough to be a quarterback.

> Richard M. Nixon, as quoted in *This Is Nixon*

I was a lousy football player, but I remember Chief Newman, our coach, saying that "there's one thing about Nixon, he plays every scrimmage as though the championship were at stake."

> Richard M. Nixon, as quoted in the *Saturday Evening Post*,
> July 12, 1958

The average person can't realize what a nightmare this has been. The last 10 days of the season, all winter, spring training, right up till today. Now I'm just tired. Not let down—just tired. I'm beat.

> Henry Aaron, after hitting his 715th career home run to break Babe Ruth's record, as quoted in *The New York Times*, April 14, 1974

I get a sense of accomplishment when I think back on the season. But when you're at the bottom looking up it looks a lot nicer at the top than it is when you get there.

> Tony Waldrop, National Collegiate mile champion, as quoted in *The New York Times*, April 7, 1974

I believe that racial extractions and color hues and forms of worship become secondary to what men can do. The American public is not as concerned with a first baseman's pigmentation as it is with the power of his swing, the dexterity of his slide, and the gracefulness of his fielding or the speed of his legs.

> Branch Rickey, as quoted in *Reader's Digest,* February 1949

I felt like my bubble-gum card collection had come to life.

> James Garner, actor, describing what it was like to attend a sports-celebrity awards dinner, as quoted in *Sports Illustrated,* March 11, 1968

There's one nice thing about winning a Kentucky Derby with a horse. You don't have to feed him any more the day after the race than you fed him the day before the race, and you don't have to sign him up for next year.

> John Galbreath, president of the Pittsburgh Pirates and owner of two Kentucky Derby winners, as quoted in *Sports Illustrated,* February 5, 1968

Fishing: a delusion entirely surrounded by liars in old clothes.

> Don Marquis, as quoted in *Reader's Digest,* January 1945

Winning is not the most important thing; it's everything.

Vince Lombardi, as quoted in *Quote*, October 1968

Food and Drink

The little voice that says, "You're full; stop eating," never speaks up until it's too late. If you want to stay thin, you have to stay hungry.

Dr. William A. Nolen, as quoted in *Reader's Digest*, November 1973

To a Baked Fish
Preserve a respectful demeanor
When you are brought into the room;
Don't stare at the guests while they're eating,
No matter how much they consume.

Carolyn Wells, as quoted in . . . *And Be Merry*

Our back-yard fireplace still relieves
Our summer mealtime tedium;
I charcoal-broil our thick steaks rare—
My face and fingers medium.

Frank R. Canning, as quoted in *Reader's Digest*, August 1952

A toastmaster is a man who eats a meal he doesn't want so he can get up and tell a lot of stories he doesn't remember to people who've already heard them.

George Jessel, as quoted in *Reader's Digest*, January 1949

Ticker tape ain't spaghetti.

Fiorello H. La Guardia, address to the United Nations Relief and Rehabilitation Commission, March 29, 1946 561

Cooking is like love. It should be entered into with abandon or not at all.

Harriet Van Horne, as quoted in *Vogue*, October 15, 1956

Fat has become a dirty word. It used to mean abounding in riches, well-furnished, well-filled-out—like a fat purse—but now it only means not slim. It has been proven that fat men make better husbands and have a far lower divorce rate than thin men.

Peter Ustinov, as quoted in *Reader's Digest*, February 1969

Giving a party is very much like having a baby; its conception is more fun than its completion, and once you have begun it is almost impossible to stop.

Jan Struther, *Try Anything Twice*

Nature does her best to teach us. The more we overeat, the harder she makes it for us to get close to the table.

Earl Wilson, as quoted in *Reader's Digest*, August 1956

The second day of a diet isn't too hard—because by that time you're off of it.

Mrs. Earl Wilson, as quoted in *Reader's Digest*, January 1953

My advice if you insist on slimming: eat as much as you like—just don't swallow it.

Harry Secombe, as quoted in . . . *And Be Merry*

Man may not be able to live by bread alone, but some folks seem to get by pretty well on crust.

Bill Gold, as quoted in *Reader's Digest*, December 1952

The only time that liquor makes a man go straight is when the road curves.

Everett M. Remsburg, as quoted in *Reader's Digest*, November 1952

Don't be intimidated by foreign cookery. Tomatoes and oregano make it Italian. Wine and tarragon make it French. Sour cream makes it Russian. Lemon and cinnamon make it Greek. Soy sauce makes it Chinese. Garlic makes it good. Now you are an International Cook.

Alice May Brock, *Alice's Restaurant Cookbook*

The flavor of frying bacon beats orange blossoms.

Ed Howe, as quoted in *Reader's Digest*, February 1947

What is a croquette but hash that has come to a head?

Irvin S. Cobb, as quoted in . . . *And Be Merry*

Breakfast foods grow odder and odder;
It's a wise child that know its fodder.

Ogden Nash, as quoted in *Reader's Digest*, July 1952

Celery, raw,
Develops the jaw,
But celery, stewed,
Is more quietly chewed.

Ogden Nash, as quoted in Reader's Digest, July 1952

Candy is dandy
But liquor is quicker.

Ogden Nash, "Reflection on Ice-Breaking"

At a dinner party we should eat wisely but not too well, and talk well but not too wisely.

W. Somerset Maugham, A Writer's Notebook

Good food is the only sensual treat that can be enjoyed three times a day for a lifetime.

William F. Buckley, Jr., as quoted in Reader's Digest,
September 1971

There is more simplicity in the man who eats caviar on impulse than in the man who eats grapenuts on principle.

G. K. Chesterton, as quoted in . . . And Be Merry

The only occasion when the traditions of courtesy permit a hostess to help herself before a woman guest is when she has reason to believe the food is poisoned.

Emily Post, as quoted in Reader's Digest, November 1931

I drink to make other people interesting.

George Jean Nathan, as quoted in Reader's Digest, January
1954

Part of the secret of success in life is to eat what you like and let the food fight it out inside.

Mark Twain, as quoted in . . . And Be Merry

Eating words has never given me indigestion.

Sir Winston Churchill, as quoted in *Reader's Digest*,
Feburary 1959

What is sauce for the goose may be sauce for the gander but is not necessarily sauce for the chicken, the duck, the turkey or the guinea hen.

Alice B. Toklas, *The Alice B. Toklas Cook Book*

Years ago, I dined in a fine old restaurant in Paris where, I noticed, the paint on the ceiling was peeling. Later, I asked the proprietor why he didn't have the ceiling repainted. He was genuinely surprised. "What for? Did you ever meet a Frenchman who looks at the ceiling while he's eating?"

Joseph Wechsberg, as quoted in *Reader's Digest*, May 1973

Seeing is deceiving. It's eating that's believing.

James Thurber, *Further Fables for Our Time*

Melted ice cream is a fluid which is eternally sticky. One drop of it on a car-door handle spreads to the seat covers, to trousers, and thence to hands, and then to the steering wheel, the rear-view mirror, all the 565 knobs of the dashboard—spreads everywhere and lasts forever, in secret ways that even scientists don't understand.

L. Rust Hills, as quoted in *Reader's Digest*, May 1973

The food of the city's most celebrated dining salons, with one or perhaps two exceptions, is neither predictably elegant nor superb. More often than not it is predictably commonplace.

Craig Claiborne, on New York dining, as quoted in *The New York Times*, September 1, 1963

More wives would learn to cook if they weren't so busy trying to get meals.

Franklin P. Jones, as quoted in *Reader's Digest*, March 1953

Some people have a veneer that comes off easily with a little alcohol.

Paul Harrison, as quoted in *Reader's Digest*, March 1938

I don't drink. I don't like it. It makes me feel good.

Oscar Levant, as quoted in *Time*, May 5, 1958

The best audience is one that is intelligent, well-educated—and a little drunk.

Alben W. Barkley, as quoted in *The New York Times*, February 15, 1965

An Australian squatter said to a friend of mine who visited him on his estate far away in the wilds of the interior: "I dress for dinner to avoid losing my self-respect. If I did not dress for dinner I should end by coming in to dinner in my shirt sleeves. I should end by not troubling to wash. I should sink to the level of cattle. I dress for dinner, not to make myself pretty, but as spiritual renovation."

566

A. G. Gardiner, as quoted in *Reader's Digest*, July 1935

Of all tastes, I think none compares to these three—the light tang of cinnamon, the brown crust of cold fried chicken, and the zip of very young onions.

O. O. McIntyre, as quoted in *Reader's Digest*, April 1934

My morning-after headache was built for a hippopotamus.

O. O. McIntyre, as quoted in *Reader's Digest*, August 1935

A man is a fool if he drinks before he reaches the age of 50, and a fool if he doesn't afterward.

Frank Lloyd Wright, as quoted in *The New York Times*,
June 22, 1958

No man is lonely while eating spaghetti—it requires so much attention.

Christopher Morley, as quoted in *Reader's Digest*, May 1942

We lived for days on nothing but food and water.

W. C. Fields, describing a town which ran out of whisky,
as quoted in *Reader's Digest*, November 1941

It is WRONG to do what everyone else does—namely, to hold the wine list just out of sight, look for the second cheapest claret on the list, and say, "Number 22, please."

Stephen Potter, *One-Upmanship*

First you put in whisky to make it strong; then you add water to make it weak; you put in lemon to make it sour, then you put in sugar to make it sweet; you say "Here's to you!"—and then you drink it yourself.

Nikita Balieff, on American drinking conventions, as
quoted in *Reader's Digest*, February 1935

A gourmet can tell from the flavor whether a woodcock's leg is the one on which the bird is accustomed to roost.

Lucius Beebe, as quoted in Reader's Digest, November 1936

Said Aristotle unto Plato,
"Have another sweet potato?"
Said Plato unto Aristotle,
"Thank you, I prefer the bottle."

Owen Wister, as quoted in . . . And Be Merry

Men who call salads "rabbit food" should remember what such food does for rabbits. The male rabbit is light on his feet, has no paunch and maintains lively romantic interests.

Dr. W. W. Bauer, as quoted in Reader's Digest, March 1965

Probably nothing in the world arouses more false hopes than the first four hours of a diet.

Dan Bennett, as quoted in Reader's Digest, June 1970

Objectively alcoholics are responsible for their condition. . . . But subjectively it seems to me that not many are morally guilty. . . . Very few believe they will ever become drunks.

John Ford, Depth Psychology, Morality and Alcoholism

If you classify foods from the most useful to the least useful, you'll place meat, vegetables, fruits, milk and eggs in the first category, bread, pastas and cereals in the second category, snacks in the third, and candy, soft drinks and beer in the fourth. But if you think about it, you'll realize that the *bulk* of the food advertising is for things in categories 3 and 4—the least useful foods.

Dr. Jean Mayer, as quoted in Reader's Digest, September 1971

There is much more understanding and concern for alcoholics among abstaining Christians than among the respectable denizens of cocktail bars. . . . The alcohol problem confronts us today with one of the worst evils of our sensate culture. No form of human suffering is more tragic and none involves more people.

Albion R. King, Christian Century

Shall we never learn the worthlessness of other people's views of food? There is no authoritative body of comment on food. Like all the deeper personal problems of life, you must face it alone.

Frank Moore Colby, as quoted in Reader's Digest, October
1973

Drunkenness is temporary suicide; the happiness that it brings is merely negative, a momentary cessation of unhappiness.

Bertrand Russell, The Conquest of Happiness

THE POLITICAL ARENA

Government and Diplomacy

Usually the first thing you face is a quotation from Thomas Jefferson about how that government governs best which governs least. I think you ought to keep in mind that any politician who wrote as much as Jefferson did was bound to say something that he would like to have forgotten.

Eugene J. McCarthy, address in Indiana, Pennsylvania,
March 17, 1967

I would say the rule in Government is about the same as it is in business or any other kind of activity. For every hour that you attend a meeting, you spend at least two hours preparing for it or executing the decisions made at a meeting.

Richard M. Nixon, as quoted in *U.S. News & World Report*, May 16, 1960

The people are fed up with the government. They think it doesn't work. *And they are right.*

Richard M. Nixon, as quoted in *Reader's Digest*, April 1972

The people's right to change what does not work is one of the greatest principles of our system of government.

Richard M. Nixon, *Manpower Report of the President*, March 1972

It is not the function of the United States to guard over the political hygiene of any government, anywhere in the world; but it is most   573 definitely our function to interfere with the establishment of communist governments, because communist governments conspire against other countries' freedoms. It is a matter of pure academic concern whether a communist government is brought in by an individual, by a clique, or by a majority of voters.

> William F. Buckley, Jr., *Quotations from Chairman Bill*

I go so far as to say that theirs [the liberals'] is today the dominant voice in determining the destiny of the country.

> William F. Buckley, Jr., *Quotations from Chairman Bill*

He is forever poised between a cliché and an indiscretion.

> Harold Macmillan, former British Prime Minister, on the office of Foreign Secretary, as quoted in *Newsweek*, April 30, 1956

The prospects never looked brighter, and the problems never looked tougher. Anyone who isn't stirred by both those statements is too tired to be of much use to us in the days ahead.

> John W. Gardner, *No Easy Victories*

Democracy is good. I say this because other systems are worse.

> Jawaharlal Nehru, as quoted in *The New York Times*, January 25, 1961

No other President ever enjoyed the Presidency as I did.

> Theodore Roosevelt, as quoted in *Reader's Digest*, November 1964

The first requisite of a good citizen in this republic of ours is that he shall be able and willing to pull his weight.

> Theodore Roosevelt, speech in New York City, November 11, 1902

The United Nations was not set up to be a reformatory. It was assumed that you would be good before you got in and not that being in would make you good.

John Foster Dulles, as quoted in news reports of July 9,
1954

We're eyeball to eyeball and the other fellow just blinked.

Dean Rusk, on the Cuban missile crisis, as quoted in the
Saturday Evening Post, December 8, 1962

About all I can say for the United States Senate is that it opens with prayer and closes with an investigation.

Will Rogers, as quoted in *The New York Times Magazine*,
January 1, 1956

America never lost a war or won a conference.

Will Rogers, as quoted in *Reader's Digest*, March 1939

Democracy is the art of disciplining oneself so that one need not be disciplined by others.

Georges Clemenceau, as quoted in *Reader's Digest*, March
1971

The great society is a place where men are more concerned with the quality of their goals than the quantity of their goods.

Lyndon B. Johnson, address at the University of Michigan,
May 22, 1964

Our house is large, and it is open. It is open to all, those who agree and those who dissent.

Lyndon B. Johnson, speech in Washington, D.C., June 24,
1965

I have said that I believe in the tight fist and the open mind—a tight fist with money and an open mind to the needs of America.

Lyndon B. Johnson, speech, December 4, 1964

An assassin's bullet has thrust upon me the awesome burden of the Presidency. I am here to say that I need your help. I cannot bear this burden alone. I need the help of all Americans, in all America.

Lyndon B. Johnson, beginning his first address to Congress two days after President Kennedy's burial, November 27, 1963

Unfortunately many Americans live on the outskirts of hope—some because of their poverty, some because of their color, and all too many because of both. Our task is to help replace their despair with opportunity.

Lyndon B. Johnson, State of the Union message, opening the "war on poverty," January 8, 1964

A President's hardest task is not to do what is right, but to know what is right.

Lyndon B. Johnson, State of the Union message, January 4, 1965

My most fervent prayer is to be a President who can make it possible for every boy in this land to grow to manhood by loving his country—instead of dying for it.

Lyndon B. Johnson, speech in Washington, D.C., March 24, 1964

The vote is the most powerful instrument ever devised by man for breaking down injustice and destroying the terrible walls which imprison men because they are different from other men.

Lyndon B. Johnson, speech, August 6, 1965

The greatest leader of our time has been struck down by the foulest deed of our time. . . . No words are sad enough to express our sense of loss. No words are strong enough to express our determination to continue the forward thrust of America that he began.

Lyndon B. Johnson, beginning his first address to Congress
two days after President Kennedy's burial, November 27,
1963

All I have I would have given gladly not to be standing here today.

Lyndon B. Johnson, beginning his first address to Congress
two days after President Kennedy's burial, November 27,
1963

The office of President requires the constitution of an athlete, the patience of a mother, the endurance of an early Christian.

Woodrow Wilson, as quoted in *Reader's Digest*, November
1964

There must be, not a balance of power, but a community of power; not organized rivalries, but an organized common peace.

Woodrow Wilson, address to the U.S. Senate, January 22,
1917

The firm basis of government is justice, not pity.

Woodrow Wilson, Inaugural Address, March 4, 1912

Our whole duty, for the present at any rate, is summed up in the motto: America first.

Woodrow Wilson, speech in New York, April 20, 1915

The history of liberty is the history of the limitation of governmental power, not the increase of it.

Woodrow Wilson, speech in New York, September 9, 1912 577

The world must be made safe for democracy. Its peace must be planted on the tested foundations of political liberty.

Woodrow Wilson, address to Congress, April 2, 1917

The main task of a free society is to civilize the struggle for power. Slavery of the acquiescent majority to the ruthless few is the hereditary state of mankind; freedom, a (rarely) acquired characteristic.

R. H. S. Crossman, as quoted in the New Statesman and
Nation, April 21, 1951

You can't set a hen in one morning and have chicken salad for lunch.

George Humphrey, Secretary of the Treasury, commenting
on the impossibility of rapid economic change, as quoted in
Time, January 26, 1953

The country needs and, unless I mistake its temper, the country demands bold, persistent experimentation. It is common sense to take a method and try it; if it fails, admit it frankly and try another. But above all, try something. The millions who are in want will not stand by silently forever while the things to satisfy their needs are within each reach.

Franklin D. Roosevelt, address at Oglethorpe University,
Atlanta, May 22, 1932

A government can be no better than the public opinion that sustains it.

Franklin D. Roosevelt, speech in Washington, D.C.,
January 8, 1936

These unhappy times call for the building of plans that rest upon the forgotten, the unorganized but indispensable units of economic power, for plans like those of 1917 that build from the bottom up and not from the top down, that put their faith once more in the forgotten man at the bottom of the economic pyramid.

Franklin D. Roosevelt, radio address, April 7, 1932

We must be wary of those who with sounding brass and a tinkling cymbal preach the "ism" of appeasement. We must especially beware of that small group of selfish men who would clip the wings of the American eagle in order to feather their own nests.

> Franklin D. Roosevelt, Four Freedoms message to
> Congress, January 6, 1941

There is no indispensable man.

> Franklin D. Roosevelt, campaign speech in New York,
> November 3, 1932

The core of our defense is the faith we have in the institutions we defend.

> Franklin D. Roosevelt, speech in Dayton, Ohio, October 12,
> 1940

I have no expectation of making a hit every time I come to bat.

> Franklin D. Roosevelt, as quoted in *Reader's Digest,*
> January 1934

Democracy alone, of all forms of government, enlists the full force of men's enlightened will. . . . It is the most humane, the most advanced and in the end the most unconquerable of all forms of human society. The democratic aspiration is no mere recent phase of human history. It is human history.

> Franklin D. Roosevelt, Third Inaugural Address, January 20,
> 1941

Democracy is not a static thing. It is an everlasting march.

> Franklin D. Roosevelt, speech in Los Angeles, October 1,
> 1935

I'm tired of hearing it said that democracy doesn't work. Of course it doesn't work. It isn't supposed to work. We are supposed to work it.

> Alexander Woollcott, as quoted in *Reader's Digest*,
> November 1971

Finally, it should be clear by now that a nation can be no stronger abroad than she is at home. Only an America which practices what it preaches about equal rights and social justice will be respected by those whose choice affects our future.

> John F. Kennedy, address for delivery in Dallas, November 22,
> 1963

All free men, wherever they may live, are citizens of Berlin. And therefore, as a free man, I take pride in the words *"Ich bin ein Berliner"* [I am a Berliner].

> John F. Kennedy, address at City Hall, West Berlin, June 26,
> 1963

You have offered to trade us an apple for an orchard. We do not do that in this country.

> John F. Kennedy, on Berlin, to Soviet Foreign Minister
> Andrei Gromyko, October 6, 1961

Tell him, if he doesn't mind, we'll shake hands.

John F. Kennedy, to interpreter, on meeting Premier
Khrushchev for the first time, Vienna, June 4, 1961

Any system of government will work when everything is going well.
It's the system that functions in the pinches that survives.

John F. Kennedy, *Why England Slept*

We seek not the worldwide victory of one nation or system but a
worldwide victory of men.

John F. Kennedy, State of the Union message, January 14,
1963

I can report that the State of this old but youthful Union, in the 175th
year of its life, is good.

John F. Kennedy, State of the Union message, January 14,
1963

The basis of effective government is public confidence.

John F. Kennedy, message to Congress on ethical conduct
in government, April 27, 1961

No government is better than the men who compose it.

John F. Kennedy, campaign speech at Wittenberg College,
Ohio, October 17, 1960

If we are strong, our strength will speak for itself. If we are weak,
words will be no help.

John F. Kennedy, speech prepared for delivery in Dallas
on November 22, 1963

. . . And so, my fellow Americans: Ask not what your country can do
for you; ask what you can do for your country.

John F. Kennedy, Inaugural Address, January 20, 1961   581

The path we have chosen for the present is full of hazards, as all paths are. But it is the one most consistent with our character and courage as a nation and our commitments around the world. The cost of freedom is always high, but Americans have always paid it. And one path we shall never choose, and that is the path of surrender, or submission.

John F. Kennedy, address to the nation announcing the
blockade of Cuba to stop delivery of Soviet missiles,
October 22, 1962

Let every nation know, whether it wishes us well or ill, that we shall pay any price, bear any burden, meet any hardship, support any friend, oppose any foe to assure the survival and the success of liberty.

John F. Kennedy, Inaugural Address, January 20, 1961

We stand today on the edge of a new frontier—the frontier of the 1960s—a frontier of unknown opportunities and perils—a frontier of unfulfilled hopes and threats.

John F. Kennedy, speech accepting presidential
nomination, as quoted in *The New York Times,* July 16,
1960

It is a function of government to invent philosophies to explain the demands of its own convenience.

Murray Kempton, *America Comes of Middle Age*

As one lone citizen, I can't do much about international war, but I can refuse to war with my neighbor. I can accept the painful necessity of changing my attitudes when they are shown to be unjust. I can let my representative know my views instead of sitting back cynically; I can vote instead of letting my decisions go by default; I can seek to correct the law by lawful means, rather than by rioting or yammering. I can pick up after myself in public places. I can refuse to despair or to cry after a perfect society which no one living has ever had.

Michael Drury, as quoted in *Reader's Digest,* November
1973

I have in my hand 57 cases of individuals who would appear to be either card-carrying members or certainly loyal to the Communist Party, but who, nevertheless, are helping to shape our foreign policy.

Senator Joseph McCarthy, speech which began his
far-flung investigations of alleged Communists in
government, as quoted in *The New York Times*, Feburary 9,
1950

Within the first few months I discovered that being President is like riding a tiger. A man has to keep on riding or be swallowed.

Harry S. Truman, as quoted in *Reader's Digest*, November
1964

The attack upon Korea makes it plain beyond all doubt that Communism has passed beyond the use of subversion to conquer independent nations and will now use armed invasion and war.

Harry S. Truman, broadcast address announcing American
intervention in Korea after North Korean violation of the
38th parallel, as quoted in *Time*, July 3, 1950

When I was a little boy I read about a fairy princess. And there she is.

Harry S. Truman, welcoming Princess Elizabeth to
Washington, *Time*, November 12, 1951

Whenever you have an efficient government you have a dictatorship.

Harry S. Truman, speech at Columbia University, April 28,
1959

The greatest part of the President's job is to make decisions . . . he can't pass the buck to anybody.

Harry S. Truman, speech, January 15, 1953

My reading of history convinces me that most bad government has grown out of too much government.

John Sharp Williams, *Thomas Jefferson*   583

I probably long ago used up my time; but you know, there is one thing about being the President; it is hard to tell him to sit down.

Dwight D. Eisenhower, making a speech, as quoted in
Reader's Digest, November 1964

I firmly believe that the army of persons who urge greater and greater centralization of authority and greater dependence upon the federal treasury are really more dangerous to our form of government than any external threat that can possibly be arrayed against us.

Dwight D. Eisenhower, as quoted in *Reader's Digest,* July
1957

Primary responsibility for keeping out the disloyal and dangerous rests squarely upon the executive branch. When this branch so conducts itself as to require policing by another branch of the Government, it invites its own disorder and confusion.

Dwight D. Eisenhower, State of the Union message,
January 1953

The necessary and wise subordination of the military to civil power will be best sustained when lifelong professional soldiers abstain from seeking high political office.

Dwight D. Eisenhower, letter to a friend, as quoted in
Years of Trial and Hope by Harry S. Truman

We live . . . in a sea of semantic disorder in which old labels no longer faithfully describe. Police states are called "people's democracies." Armed conquest of free people is called "liberation." Such slippery slogans make more difficult the problems of communicating true faith, facts and beliefs. . . . We must use language to enlighten the mind, not as the instrument of the studied innuendo and distorter of truth. And we must live by what we say.

Dwight D. Eisenhower, State of the Union message,
January 7, 1960

Self-indulgence includes failure to fulfill the recognized responsibilities of citizenship. It is the worst form of laziness and leads, inevitably, to centralization of power.

> Dwight D. Eisenhower, speech to the National Governors'
> Conference, Cleveland, June 8, 1964

Firmness in support of fundamentals, with flexibility in tactics and method, is the key to any hope of progress in negotiation.

> Dwight D. Eisenhower, as quoted in *The New York Times*,
> September 11, 1959

In most communities it is illegal to cry "fire" in a crowded assembly. Should it not be considered serious international misconduct to manufacture a general war scare in an effort to achieve local political aims?

> Dwight D. Eisenhower, speech in Washington, D.C.,
> August 13, 1958

Whatever America hopes to bring to pass in this world must first come to pass in the heart of America.

> Dwight D. Eisenhower, Inaugural Address, January 20, 1953

The most important office is that of private citizen.

> Justice Louis D. Brandeis, as quoted in the Boston *Record*,
> April 4, 1903

In America any boy may become President and I suppose it's just one of the risks he takes.

> Adlai E. Stevenson, speech in Indianapolis, September 26,
> 1952

Bad administration, to be sure, can destroy good policy; but good administration can never save bad policy.

> Adlai E. Stevenson, speech in Los Angeles, September 11,
> 1952

My definition of a free society is a society where it is safe to be unpopular.

> Adlai E. Stevenson, as quoted in *Reader's Digest*, October
> 1972

Our goal is not just to win a cold *war* but to persuade a cold *world.*

> Adlai E. Stevenson, as quoted in *Reader's Digest*, February
> 1962

Self-criticism is the secret weapon of democracy, and candor and confession are good for the political soul.

> Adlai E. Stevenson, speech at the Democratic National
> Convention, July 21, 1952

The time to stop a revolution is at the beginning, not the end.

> Adlai E. Stevenson, campaign speech in San Francisco,
> September 9, 1952

The essence of a republican government is not command. It is consent.

> Adlai E. Stevenson, speech in Springfield, Illinois, August 14,
> 1952

The District of Columbia is a territory hounded on all sides by the United States of America.

> Irving D. Tressler, as quoted in *Reader's Digest*, December
> 1940

Perhaps one of the only positive pieces of advice that I was given was that supplied by an old courtier who observed: Only two rules really count. Never miss an opportunity to relieve yourself; never miss a chance to sit down and rest your feet.

> Edward, Duke of Windsor, *A King's Story*

At a time when American blood is again being shed to preserve our dream of freedom, we are constrained fearlessly and frankly to call the charges . . . what they truly are: a fraud and a hoax perpetrated on the Senate of the United States and the American people. They represent perhaps the most nefarious campaign of half-truths and untruths in the history of this republic.

U.S. Senate Sub-Committe Democratic majority report on
Senator Joseph McCarthy's charges of Communist
infiltration in government, as quoted in *Time*, July 24, 1950

We are the standard bearers in the only really authentic revolution, the democratic revolution against tyrannies. Our strength is not to be measured by our military capacity alone, by our industry, or by our technology. We will be remembered, not for the power of our weapons, but for the power of our compassion, our dedication to human welfare.

Hubert H. Humphrey, speech in Washington, D.C.,
September 15, 1966

The impersonal hand of government can never replace the helping hand of a neighbor.

Hubert H. Humphrey, speech in Washington, D.C.,
February 10, 1965

Governments last as long as the undertaxed can defend themselves against the overtaxed.

Bernard Berenson, *Rumor and Reflection*

Diplomacy—the art of jumping into trouble without making a splash.

Art Linkletter, as quoted in *Reader's Digest*, May 1962

If one man offers you democracy and another offers you a bag of grain, at what stage of starvation will you prefer the grain to the vote?

Bertrand Russell, *Silhouettes in Satire*   587

There is no nonsense so arrant that it cannot be made the creed of the vast majority by adequate governmental action.

Bertrand Russell, *Unpopular Essays*

Socialism is nothing but the capitalism of the lower classes.

Oswald Spengler, *The Hour of Decision*

Congress is so strange. A man gets up to speak and says nothing. Nobody listens—and then everybody disagrees.

Boris Marshalov, Russian actor and dramatic coach, after a visit to the House of Representatives, as quoted in *Reader's Digest*, March 1941

A good government remains the greatest of human blessings, and no nation has ever enjoyed it.

William Ralph Inge, *Outspoken Essays: Second Series*

I've never known a country to be starved into democracy

Senator George D. Aiken, commenting to reporters, March 27, 1964

The great fault of modern democracy—a fault that is common to the capitalist and the socialist—is that it accepts economic wealth as the end of society and the standard of personal happiness.

Christopher Dawson, *The Modern Dilemma*

What the Government gives you the Government can take away and once it starts taking away it can take more than it gave.

Samuel Gompers, as quoted in *Reader's Digest*, September 1952

Government is the art of making men live together in peace and with reasonable happiness.

Justice Felix Frankfurter, *The Public and Its Government*

Nature herself vindicates democracy. For nature plants gifts and graces where least expected, and under circumstances that defy all the little artifices of man.

Justice Felix Frankfurter, speech in Aaronsburg,
Pennsylvania, October 23, 1949

Nothing is easier than spending the public money. It does not appear to belong to anybody. The temptation is overwhelming to bestow it on somebody.

Calvin Coolidge, as quoted in *Reader's Digest*, June 1960

The government of the United States is a device for maintaining in perpetuity the rights of the people, with the ultimate extinction of all privileged classes.

Calvin Coolidge, speech in Philadelphia, September 25,
1924

If the age of a nation is measured by the continuity of its political institutions, the United States is the second-oldest country in the world. Only Britain is older.

Louis Heren, *The New American Commonwealth*

A little corruption in government is too much corruption.

D. L. Cohn, as quoted in *The New York Times Magazine*,
October 18, 1951

The only permanent safeguard of democratic government is that the unchanging and ultimate sanction of intellectual decision should be the conscience. We have here a realm within which the state can have no rights and where it is well that it should have none.

Harold J. Laski, *Authority in the Modern State*

This job has done wonders for my paranoia. Now I *really* have enemies.

Henry Kissinger, as quoted in *Reader's Digest*, January
1974

There cannot be a crisis next week. My schedule is already full.

Henry Kissinger, as quoted in *Reader's Digest*, January
1974

A guest of the state must have starved to death 3,000 years ago, and the Chinese are determined that will not happen again.

Henry Kissinger, on Chinese State banquets, as quoted in
Reader's Digest, January 1974

I don't stand on protocol. If you just call me "Excellency," that will be sufficient.

Henry Kissinger, on being asked by reporters how he
should be addressed after being named Secretary of State,
as quoted in *Reader's Digest*, January 1974

A system which requires a great man in each generation sets itself an almost insurmountable challenge if only because a great man tends to stunt the emergence of strong personalities. When the novelty of Bismarck's tactics had worn off and the originality of his conception came to be taken for granted, lesser men strove to operate his system while lacking his sure touch and almost artistic sensitivity.

Henry Kissinger, as quoted in *Reader's Digest*, April
1973

The dilemma of any statesman is that he can never be certain about the probable course of events. In reaching a decision, he must inevitably act on the basis of an intuition that is inherently unprovable. If he insists on certainty, he runs the danger of becoming a prisoner of events. His resolution must reside not in "facts" as commonly conceived but in his vision of the future.

Henry Kissinger, as quoted in *Reader's Digest*, January
1974

A dictatorship is a country where they have taken the politics out of politics.

Sam Himmell, *Baldwin Sells*

Nobody believes a rumor here until it's officially denied.

Edward Cheyfitz on Washington gossip, as quoted in
Reader's Digest, August 1958

Th' modhren idee iv governmint is "Snub th' people, buy th' people,
jaw th' people."

Finley Peter Dunne, *Mr. Dooley's Philosophy*

Occasionally we sigh for an earlier day when we could just look at the
stars without worrying whether they were theirs or ours.

Bill Vaughan, as quoted in *Reader's Digest*, October 1962

Everything is much simpler today—instead of solving a problem, you
just subsidize it.

Bill Vaughan, as quoted in *Reader's Digest*, October 1961

A statesman is any politician it's considered safe to name a school
after.

Bill Vaughan, as quoted in *Reader's Digest*, December 1965

It would be nice if the poor were to get even half of the money that is
spent in studying them.

Bill Vaughan, as quoted in *Reader's Digest*, February 1974

When a fellow you knew in school attains some lofty public office,
you're glad for his sake—but somewhat apprehensive for the future of
the country.

Bill Vaughan, as quoted in *Reader's Digest*, December 1954

A crisis is an international incident that lasts long enough for us to
locate it on the map.

Bill Vaughan, as quoted in *Reader's Digest*, November 1960   591

Diplomat: A person who can be disarming even though his country isn't.

Sidney Brody, as quoted in *Reader's Digest*, June 1956

That government is not best which best secures more life and property—there is a more valuable thing—manhood.

Mark Twain, *Autobiography*

The people at regulatory agencies are utterly confounded when we come to investigate them. They have forgotten what citizens look like.

Ralph Nader, as quoted in *Time,* December 12, 1969

The government is concerned about the population explosion, and the population is concerned about the government explosion.

Ruth Rankin, as quoted in *Reader's Digest*, October 1967

In the White House, the future rapidly becomes the past; and delay is itself a decision.

Theodore Sorensen, as special counsel to President Kennedy, as quoted in *Nation's Business*, June 1963

Government is actually the worst failure of civilized man. There has never been a really good one; and even those that are most tolerable are arbitrary, cruel, grasping and unintelligent. Indeed, it would not be far wrong to describe the best as the common enemy of all decent citizens.

H. L. Mencken, *Notebooks*

I am not in favor of turning out the lights at City Hall. We operate enough in the dark as it is.

Theodore R. Kupperman, as quoted in *The New York Times,* May 31, 1964

I am grateful that I live in a country where the leaders sit down on Thanksgiving Day and carve up a turkey instead of a map.

Eddie Cantor, as quoted in Reader's Digest, February 1939

We hope the scientists discover that Mars is not inhabited. This country can't afford to stretch foreign aid any farther.

Clyde Moore, as quoted in Reader's Digest, December 1956

In this modern world there is only one faith that can sustain the unity of a people, the greater unity that gives free play to the richness of difference that makes the creative life of a community—and that is the faith of democracy.

Robert M. MacIver, The Ramparts We Guard

Democracy, as has been said of Christianity, has never really been tried.

Stuart Chase, Men at Work

When a government takes over a people's economic life it becomes absolute, and when it has become absolute it destroys the arts, the minds, the liberties and the meaning of the people it governs.

Maxwell Anderson, The Guaranteed Life

Dictators ride to and fro upon tigers which they dare not dismount.

Sir Winston Churchill, While England Slept

The U. N. was set up not to get us to Heaven, but only to save us from hell.

Sir Winston Churchill, as quoted in Reader's Digest,
February 1955

An appeaser is one who feeds a crocodile—hoping it will eat him last.

Sir Winston Churchill, as quoted in Reader's Digest,
December 1959

593

I have nothing to offer but blood, toil, tears and sweat.

> Sir Winston Churchill, first statement as Prime Minister
> before the House of Commons, May 13, 1940

One of the reasons for the rarity of statesmanship is that, in a world increasingly rushed to death, the long range waits on the immediate. What is urgent takes priority over what is merely important, so that what is important will be attended to only when it becomes urgent, which may be too late.

> Louis J. Halle, as quoted in *Reader's Digest*, May 1960

Anarchy stands for the liberation of the human mind from the dominion of religion; the liberation of the human body from the dominion of property; liberty from the shackles and restraints of government.

> Emma Goldman, *Anarchism*

Socialism is workable only in heaven, where it isn't needed, and in hell, where they've got it.

> Cecil Palmer, as quoted in *Reader's Digest*, September 1949

The thing they forget is that liberty and freedom and democracy are so very precious that you do not fight to win them once and stop.

> Sergeant Alvin C. York, as quoted by Franklin D.
> Roosevelt in an Armistice Day speech, 1941

A man wrote Senator Vandenberg suggesting that the Rocky Mountains be leveled off. The project has merit, but the Administration does not feel that it is costly enough to be practical.

> Howard Brubaker, as quoted in *Reader's Digest*, July 1935

Too often our Washington reflex is to discover a problem and then throw money at it, hoping it will somehow go away.

> Kenneth Keating, as quoted in *The New York Times*,
> December 12, 1961

Sometimes when I get in a nervous dither over such current problems as inflation, war, taxes, crime, pollution, political intrigue, urban sprawl, population, and whatever, I find myself yearning for 1933, when all we had to fear was fear itself.

> Oren Arnold, as quoted in *Reader's Digest*, March 1973

A statesman is a politician who is held upright by equal pressure from all directions.

> Eric A. Johnston, as quoted in *Reader's Digest*, January 1944

A nation without controversy is politically dead.

> Herbert L. Samuel, *Grooves of Change*

Coexistence—what the farmer does with the turkey until Thanksgiving.

> Mike Connolly, as quoted in *Reader's Digest*, November 1960

A welfare state is one run for the benefit of everyone but the taxpayer.

> Imogene Fey, as quoted in *Reader's Digest*, November 1958

The first of all democratic doctrines is that all men are interesting.

> G. K. Chesterton, as quoted in *Reader's Digest*, October 1964

Democracy means government by the uneducated, while aristocracy means government by the badly educated.

> G. K. Chesterton, as quoted in *The New York Times*, February 1, 1931

Many people consider the things government does for them to be social progress, but they regard the things government does for others as socialism.

> Earl Warren, as quoted in *Reader's Digest*, November 1952

There are only two occasions when Americans respect privacy, especially in Presidents. Those are prayer and fishing.

> Herbert Hoover, as quoted in the New York *Herald Tribune*, May 19, 1947

The remedies in America are not revolution. They are, except for peace and war, mostly jobs of marginal repairs around a sound philosophy and a stout heart.

> Herbert Hoover, as quoted in *The New York Times Magazine*, August 9, 1964

When there is a lack of honor in government, the morals of the whole people are poisoned.

> Herbert Hoover, as quoted in *The New York Times Magazine*, August 9, 1964

There are only four letters of the alphabet not now in use by the Administration. When we establish the Quick Loans Corporations for Xylophones, Yachts and Zithers, the alphabet will be exhausted.

> Herbert Hoover, as quoted in *Reader's Digest*, February 1936

The average man that I encounter all over the country regards government as a sort of great milk cow, with its head in the clouds eating air, and growing a full teat for everybody on earth.

> Clarence C. Manion, as quoted in *Reader's Digest*, November 1952

Let's put the record straight. Our concern is not for some abstract concept of "states' rights." States have no rights—only people have rights. States have responsibilities.

> George Romney, testimony before the Republican platform committee, July 8, 1964

This country is composed of two kinds of people. One group believes that the government can support all the citizens. The other wonders whether all the citizens can support the government.

James A. Farley, as quoted in Reader's Digest, July 1959

An international crisis is like sex—as long as you keep talking about it, nothing happens.

Harold Coffin, as quoted in Reader's Digest, September 1961

Even though counting heads is not an ideal way to govern, it's better than breaking them.

Judge Learned Hand, as quoted in Reader's Digest, November 1972

Bad officials are elected by good citizens who do not vote.

George Jean Nathan, as quoted in Reader's Digest, October 1956

Man's capacity for justice makes democracy possible . . . his inclination to injustice makes democracy necessary.

Reinhold Niebuhr, The Children of Light and the Children of Darkness

In the United States we spend half our time worrying whether the Presidency will kill a man with overwork and the other half worrying whether he is playing too much golf.

Charles Poore, as quoted in Reader's Digest, March 1959

Popular government has not yet been proved to guarantee, always and everywhere, good government.

Walter Lippmann, The Public Philosophy   597

Democracy is not simply a political system; it is a moral movement and it springs from adventurous faith in human possibilities.

Rev. Harry Emerson Fosdick, Adventurous Religion

There are only two places where socialism works—one is a beehive and the other is an anthill.

Sir Ian Stewart-Richardson, as quoted in Reader's Digest,
February 1952

There is no such thing as discretion when it concerns public matters; public things and public people permit neither mystery nor silence unless tyranny rules.

Sol Chaneles, The New Civility

To make certain that crime does not pay, the Government should take it over and try to run it.

G. Norman Collie, as quoted in Reader's Digest, January
1952

It is not the function of our government to keep the citizens from falling into error; it is the function of the citizen to keep the government from falling into error.

Justice Robert H. Jackson, as quoted in Reader's Digest,
August 1958

Self-government is our right, a thing born in at birth; a thing no more to be doled out to us or withheld from us by another people than the right to life itself.

Sir Roger Casement, speech refuting charge of treason,
June 29, 1916, as quoted in The Trial of Roger Casement

The nearest thing to immortality in this world is a government bureau.

General Hugh S. Johnson, as quoted in Reader's Digest,
August 1942

Democracy is a small hard core of common agreement, surrounded by a rich variety of individual differences.

> Dr. James Conant, as quoted in *Reader's Digest*, December 1957

Conferences at the top level are always courteous. Name-calling is left to the foreign ministers.

> Averell Harriman, as quoted in the New York *Herald Tribune*, August 1, 1955

Democracy is good politics, but a poor religion.

> Nels F. S. Ferré, *Learning and World Peace*

One of the hardest things for a Government official to understand about money matters is that it does.

> Richard Attridge, as quoted in *Reader's Digest*, December 1951

I would remind you that extremism in the defense of liberty is no vice. And let me remind you also that moderation in the pursuit of justice is no virtue.

> Barry Goldwater, acceptance speech at the Republican National Convention, July 16, 1964

Next thing, we suppose, fishermen will be asking the government for a guaranteed annual catch.

> Dick Conway, as quoted in *Reader's Digest*, March 1955

Democracy which began by liberating man politically has developed a dangerous tendency to enslave him through the tyranny of majorities and the deadly power of their opinion.

> Ludwig Lewisohn, *The Modern Drama*

A committee of one gets things done.

> Joe Ryan, as quoted in *Reader's Digest*, October 1961

Instead of demanding only that the common man be given an opportunity to become as uncommon as possible, we make his commonness a virtue and, even in the case of candidates for high office, we sometimes praise them for being nearly indistinguishable from the average man in the street.

Joseph Wood Krutch, in *Is the Common Man Too Common?*

A society of sheep must in time beget a government of wolves.

Bertrand de Jouvenel, as quoted in *Reader's Digest,* May 1949

No one can rule guiltlessly, and least of all those whom history compels to hurry.

Edgar Snow, *Journey to the Beginning*

We will get just as bad government as we are willing to stand for, and just as good government as we are willing to fight for.

Luther W. Youngdahl, Federal District Court judge, as quoted in *Reader's Digest,* May 1967

. . . the important thing is the struggle everybody is engaged in to get better living conditions, and they are not interested too much in the form of government.

Bernard M. Baruch, press conference in New York, August 18, 1964

The perfect diplomat is adept at playing the heads-I-win, tails-I-win-something-else game.

Charles A. Cerami, as quoted in *Reader's Digest,* December 1968

Nowadays God helps those who help themselves, and the government helps those who don't.

Dan Bennett, as quoted in *Reader's Digest,* July 1958

There is a small articulate minority in this country which advocates changing our national symbol which is the eagle to that of the ostrich and withdrawing from the UN.

Eleanor Roosevelt, speech at the Democratic National
Convention in Chicago, July 23, 1952

One of the great attractions of patriotism—it fulfills our worst wishes. In the person of our nation we are able, vicariously, to bully and cheat. Bully and cheat, what's more, with a feeling that we are profoundly virtuous.

Aldous Huxley, *Eyeless in Gaza*

When people ask me whether I think the U.N. will work, I am tempted to ask them in reply whether they think that a spade will work. A spade works only if somebody works it.

William G. Carr, as quoted in *Reader's Digest*, April 1947

The freedom to persuade and suggest is the essence of the democratic process.

Edward L. Bernays, public-relations counselor, as quoted
in *Freedom and Union*, October 1947

Ours is the only country deliberately founded on a good idea.

John Gunther, *Inside U.S.A.*

My handkerchief is terribly important to me. It's the only thing in the country I can stick my nose into.

Chaim Weizmann, after retiring as the first President of
Israel, as quoted in *Time*, November 17, 1952

I think the British have the distinction above all other nations of being able to put new wine into old bottles without bursting them.

Clement Attlee, Earl Attlee, former British Prime Minister,
on rebuilding the House of Commons, as quoted in *Time*,
November 6, 1950   **601**

Freedom to many means immediate betterment, as if by magic. . . . Unless I can meet at least some of these aspirations, my support will wane and my head will roll just as surely as the tickbird follows the rhino.

Julius K. Nyerere, Prime Minister of Tanzania, as quoted in *Time*, December 15, 1961

If the Russians were really so proud of their communist experiment, they would take down the Iron Curtain and put in a picture window.

Alex Dreier, as quoted in *Reader's Digest*, October 1962

Democracy, the last refuge of cheap misgovernment.

George Bernard Shaw, *Man and Superman*

Democracy substitutes selection by the incompetent many for appointment by the corrupt few.

George Bernard Shaw, *Man and Superman*

Having served on various committees, I have drawn up a list of rules: Never arrive on time; this stamps you as a beginner. Don't say anything until the meeting is half over; this stamps you as being wise. Be as vague as possible; this avoids irritating the others. When in doubt, suggest that a subcommittee be appointed. Be the first to move for adjournment; this will make you popular; it's what everyone is waiting for.

Dr. Harry Chapman, *Greater Kansas City Medical Bulletin*

The only discovery left for the Russians to make is that nobody believes them.

Carl Forsstrom, as quoted in *Reader's Digest*, August 1954

If we in the Senate would stop calling each other "distinguished," we might have ten working days a year.

Senator Edward W. Brooke, as quoted in *Reader's Digest*, April 1972

The President doesn't make a choice or decision: he "exercises his options." He doesn't send a message to the Russians: he "initiates a dialogue"—and "hopefully" it's a "meaningful dialogue." He doesn't simply try something new: he "introduces innovative techniques."

Wallace Carroll, speaking of Richard Nixon, speech at
Marquette University, May 4, 1969

The government runs a school to teach wives how to act overseas. Now if the wives would just start a school to teach the government how to act overseas, we'd be in business.

Fletcher Knebel, as quoted in *Reader's Digest*, October
1964

Like a city in dreams, the great white capital stretches along the placid river from Georgetown on the west to Anacostia on the east. It is a city of temporaries, a city of just-arriveds and only-visitings, built on the shifting sands of politics, filled with people passing through.

Allen Drury, on Washington, D.C., *Advise and Consent*

In his conduct of the office of President of the United States, Richard M. Nixon . . . has prevented, obstructed, and impeded the administration of justice, in that:

On June 17, 1972, and prior thereto, agents of the Committee for the Re-election of the President:

Committed unlawful entry to the headquarters of the Democratic National Committee in Washington, District of Columbia, for the purpose of securing political intelligence. Subsequent thereto, Richard M. Nixon, using the powers of his high office, engaged personally and through his subordinates and agents in a course of conduct or plan designed to delay, impede, and obstruct the investigation of such unlawful entry; to cover up, conceal and protect those responsible; and to conceal the existence and scope of other unlawful covert activities.

The means used to implement this course of conduct or plan have included one or more of the following:

1. Making or causing to be made false or misleading statements to lawfully authorized investigative officers and employes of the U.S.

2. Withholding relevant and material evidence or information from lawfully authorized investigative officers and employes of the U.S.

3. Approving, condoning, acquiescing in, and counseling witnesses with respect to the giving of false or misleading statements to lawfully

authorized investigative officers and employes of the U.S. and false or misleading testimony in duly instituted judicial and Congressional proceedings.

4. Interfering or endeavoring to interfere with the conduct of investigations by the Department of Justice of the United States, the Federal Bureau of Investigation, the office of Watergate Special Prosecution Force, and Congressional committees.

5. Approving, condoning and acquiescing in the surreptitious payment of substantial sums of money for the purpose of obtaining the silence or influencing the testimony of witnesses, potential witnesses or individuals who participated in such illegal entry and other illegal activities. . . .

> Article I of impeachment proceedings adopted by the House Judiciary Committee against President Richard M. Nixon, as quoted in *The New York Times*, August 4, 1974

Using the powers of the office of President of the United States, Richard M. Nixon, in violation of his constitutional oath faithfully to execute the office of President of the United States, and to the best of his ability preserve, protect and defend the Constitution of the United States, and in disregard of his constitutional duty to take care that the laws be faithfully executed, has repeatedly engaged in conduct violating the constitutional rights of citizens, impairing the due and proper administration of justice in the conduct of lawful inquiries, or contravening the law of governing agencies or the executive branch and the purposes of these agencies. . . .

In all of this Richard M. Nixon has acted in a manner contrary to his trust as President and subversive of constitutional government to the great prejudice of the cause of law and justice and to the manifest injury of the people of the United States.

Wherefore, Richard M. Nixon by such conduct warrants impeachment and trial and removal from office.

> Article II of the three articles of impeachment adopted by the House Judiciary Committee against President Richard M. Nixon, as quoted in *The New York Times*, August 4, 1974

Oftentimes . . . I don't seem to grasp that I am President.

> Warren G. Harding, as quoted in *Reader's Digest*, November 1964

I'll be damned if I am not getting tired of this. It seems to be the profession of a President simply to hear other people talk.

William Howard Taft, as quoted in Reader's Digest, November 1964

How can you govern a nation which has 246 kinds of cheese?

Charles de Gaulle, as quoted in Reader's Digest, May 1963

Why employ intelligent and highly paid ambassadors and then go and do their work for them? You don't buy a canary and sing yourself. I therefore give notice that from about midsummer I shall go on strike and sit more in the control tower—just in time to avoid visiting a foreign secretary on the moon.

Sir Alexander Frederick Douglas-Home, former British Prime Minister, as quoted in The New York Times, April 21, 1961

People who want to understand democracy should spend less time in the library and more time on the buses and in the subways.

Simeon Strunsky, No Mean City

Politics

What is politics but persuading the public to vote for this and support that and endure these for the promise of those?

Gilbert Highet, as quoted in Vogue, January 1951

Do you ever get the feeling that the only reason we have elections is to find out if the polls were right?

Robert Orben, as quoted in Reader's Digest, November 1968

Smog: A combination of smoke, fog, and legislative inaction.

> Robert Orben, as quoted in *Reader's Digest*, November
> 1970

Any party which takes credit for the rain must not be surprised if its opponents blame it for the drought.

> Dwight W. Morrow, speech, October 10, 1930

Let's talk sense to the American people.

> Adlai E. Stevenson, campaign speech, July 26, 1952

Come in and have some fried post-mortems on toast.

> Adlai E. Stevenson, opening his door to reporters the
> morning after he was defeated for the Presidency, as
> quoted in *Time*, November 17, 1952

You know how it is in an election year. They pick a President and then for four years they pick on him.

> Adlai E. Stevenson, campaign speech, August 28, 1952

When an American says he loves his country, he means not only that he loves the New England hills, the prairies glistening in the sun or the wide rising plains, the mountains and the seas. He means that he loves an inner air, an inner light in which freedom lives and in which a man can draw the breath of self-respect.

> Adlai E. Stevenson, campaign address, as quoted in *Time*,
> September 8, 1952

The elephant has a thick skin, a head full of ivory, and as everyone who has seen a circus parade knows, proceeds best by grasping the tail of his predecessor.

> Adlai E. Stevenson, *The Stevenson Wit*

We have to serve the truth as candidates for public office and not mislead, misguide, misdirect the people merely to provoke emotional responses and win votes that way.

> Adlai E. Stevenson, television interview with Mike
> Wallace, 1958

It is easier to fight for principles than to live up to them.

> Adlai E. Stevenson, speech in New York, August 27, 1952

Someone asked me, as I came in, down on the street, how I felt, and I was reminded of a story that a fellow-townsman of ours used to tell—Abraham Lincoln. They asked him how he felt once after an unsuccessful election. He said he felt like a little boy who has stubbed his toe in the dark. He said that he was too old to cry, but it hurt too much to laugh.

> Adlai E. Stevenson, election-night speech as he faced
> defeat, November 5, 1952

The level of politics can be little higher than the level of the morality and sense of responsibility of the people.

> Adlai E. Stevenson, as quoted in *Ladies' Home Journal,*
> December 1961

If you're in politics and you can't tell when you walk into a room who's for you and who's against you, then you're in the wrong line of work.

> Lyndon B. Johnson, as quoted in *The Lyndon Johnson
> Story*

Nothing annoys a politician so much as the discovery that other politicians are playing politics.

> Wes Izzard, as quoted in *Reader's Digest,* June 1968

A voter without a ballot is like a soldier without a bullet.

> Dwight D. Eisenhower, as quoted in *The New York Times
> Book Review,* October 27, 1957 **607**

The middle of the road is all of the usable surface. The extremes, right and left, are in the gutters.

Dwight D. Eisenhower, as quoted in *The New York Times*,
November 10, 1963

I pledge you, I pledge myself, to a new deal for the American people. Let us all here assembled constitute ourselves prophets of a new order of competence and courage. This is more than a political campaign; it is a call to arms.

Franklin D. Roosevelt, speech accepting the Democratic
party nomination, 1932

A radical is a man with both feet firmly planted in the air.

Franklin D. Roosevelt, radio address, October 26, 1939

A conservative is a man with two perfectly good legs who, however, has never learned to walk forward.

Franklin D. Roosevelt, radio address, October 26, 1939

A Reactionary is a somnambulist walking backward.

Franklin D. Roosevelt, radio address, October 26, 1939

It is harder to remain radical when richer because you have to face up, at least in theory, to giving up what you've got.

Mary McCarthy, as quoted in *Life*, September 20, 1963

A compromise is the art of dividing a cake in such a way that everyone believes that he has got the biggest piece.

Ludwig Erhard, as quoted in *Reader's Digest*, March 1959

There's an honest graft, and I'm an example of how it works. I might sum up the whole thing by sayin': "I seen my opportunities and I took 'em."

Just let me explain by examples. My party's in power in the city, and it's goin' to undertake a lot of public improvements. Well, I'm tipped off, say, that they're goin' to lay out a new park at a certain place.

I see my opportunity and I take it. I go out to the place and I buy up all the land I can in the neighborhood. Then the board of this or that makes its plan public, and there is a rush to get my land, which nobody cared particularly for before.

Ain't it perfectly honest to charge a good price and make a profit on my investment and foresight? Of course it is. Well, that's honest graft.

> George Washington Plunkitt, as quoted in *Plunkitt of Tammany Hall*

We [Senators] have the power to do any damn fool thing we want to do, and we seem to do it about every ten minutes.

> J. William Fulbright, as quoted in *Time*, February 4, 1952

Politicians and wives agree on one thing—if you postpone payment until some time in the future, it's not really spending.

> Bill Vaughan, as quoted in *Reader's Digest*, February 1963

There is an increased demand for codes of ethics in politics, although most office holders are sworn in with their hand resting on one.

> Bill Vaughan, as quoted in *Reader's Digest*, June 1968

Between now and November, the straw polls will proliferate. Then the grass roots will take over.

> Bill Vaughan, as quoted in *Reader's Digest*, July 1968

The Vice Presidency is sort of like the last cooky on the plate. Everybody insists he won't take it, but somebody always does.

> Bill Vaughan, as quoted in *Reader's Digest*, July 1960

I have the experience to be Governor. I know how to play craps. I know how to play poker. I know how to get in and out of the Baptist Church and ride horses. I know the oil and gas business. I know both sides of the street.

> Earl Long, former Governor of Louisiana, speech, May 31,
> 1959

Many of the men running for offices are not politicians. They're commuters.

> Llewellyn Mitstifer, as quoted in *Reader's Digest*, October
> 1962

Any man who has the brains to think and the nerve to act for the benefit of the people of the country is considered a radical by those who are content with stagnation and willing to endure disaster.

> William Randolph Hearst, as quoted in the Cleveland *Plain*
> *Dealer*, October 24, 1932

Now that all the members of the press are so delighted I lost, I'd like to make a statement. . . . As I leave you, I want you to know—just think how much you'll be missing. You won't have Nixon to kick around anymore because, gentlemen, this is my last press conference.

> Richard M. Nixon, following his defeat in the 1962
> California gubernatorial race, as quoted in the Washington
> *Post*, Novebmer 8, 1962

Voters quickly forget what a man says.

> Richard M. Nixon, *Six Crises*

In politics . . . the time comes when you've got to pee or get off the pot.

> Richard M. Nixon, as quoted in *Nixon and Rockefeller: A*
> *Double Portrait*

Of course, we can't all be Winston Churchills. We all can't be President. I found that out.

Richard M. Nixon, as quoted in The New York Times, June 15, 1965

Some people . . . will say that Watergate demonstrates the bankruptcy of the American political system. I believe precisely the opposite is true. Watergate represented a series of illegal acts and bad judgments by a number of individuals. It was the system that has brought the facts to light and that will bring those guilty to justice. . . . It is essential now that we place our faith in that system.

Richard M. Nixon, as quoted in Reader's Digest, July 1973

We did get something—a gift. . . . It was a little cocker spaniel dog in a crate . . . sent all the way from Texas. Black and white spotted. And our little girl, Tricia, the six-year old, named it Checkers. And you know the kids love that dog and I just want to say this right now, that regardless of what they say about it, we're going to keep it.

Richard M. Nixon, in his "Checkers" speech, September 23, 1952

Pat doesn't have a mink coat. But she does have a respectable Republican cloth coat. And I always tell her she'd look good in anything.

Richard M. Nixon, denying use of a "slush fund" from California backers during his "Checkers" speech, September 23, 1952

A dictatorship is a country where they have taken the politics out of politics.

Sam Himmell, as quoted in Reader's Digest, July 1962

I can remember way back when a liberal was one who was generous with his own money.

Will Rogers, as quoted in Reader's Digest, November 1964　611

More men have been elected between Sundown and Sunup than ever were elected between Sunup and Sundown.

Will Rogers, The Illiterate Digest

I tell you folks, all politics is apple sauce.

Will Rogers, The Illiterate Digest

There is no more independence in politics than there is in jail.

Will Rogers, as quoted in The New York Times Magazine,
September 8, 1946

In my opinion, we are in danger of developing a cult of the Common Man, which means a cult of mediocrity.

Herbert Hoover, as quoted in This Week, August 5, 1956

It is a curious fact that when we get sick we want an uncommon doctor. If we have a construction job, we want an uncommon engineer. When we get into a war, we dreadfully want an uncommon admiral and an uncommon general. Only when we get into politics are we content with the common man.

Herbert Hoover, as quoted in The New York Times,
October 21, 1964

The toughest part of politics is to satisfy the voter without giving him what he wants.

Dan Bennett, as quoted in Reader's Digest, November 1962

The free society encourages the honorable expression of many beliefs. It is also a society in which the rules of the game are themselves a shared value. The "shared value" in question here might be put this way: Persuasion is the proper mode of action for American groups that would transform society; coercion, direct or indirect, or the suppression of ideas is properly held anathema.

Robert Lekachman, The Churches and the Public

Every Republican candidate for President since 1936 has been nominated by the Chase National Bank.

Robert A. Taft, after his defeat at the 1952 Republican
National Convention

Compromise: A deal in which two people get what neither of them wanted.

Mary Winchester, as quoted in *Reader's Digest*, July 1954

Such power as I possess for working in the political field derived from my experiments in the spiritual field.

Mahatma Gandhi, *Autobiography*

Men say I am a saint losing myself in politics. The fact is that I am a politican trying my hardest to be a saint.

Mahatma Gandhi, as quoted in *The Life of Mahatma
Gandhi*

I think the American public wants a solemn ass as a President. And I think I'll go along with them.

Calvin Coolidge, as quoted in *Time*, May 16, 1955

The political mind is the product of men in public life who have been twice spoiled. They have been spoiled with praise and they have been spoiled with abuse. With them nothing is natural, everything is artificial. A few rare souls escape these influences and maintain a vision and a judgment that are unimpaired. They are a great comfort to every President and a great service to their country. But they are not sufficient in number so that the public business can be transacted like a private business.

Calvin Coolidge, *Autobiography*

It is difficult for men in high office to avoid the malady of self-delusion. They are always surrounded by worshippers. They are constantly, and for the most part sincerely, assured of their greatness.

They live in an artificial atmosphere of adulation and exaltation which sooner or later impairs their judgment. They are in grave danger of becoming careless and arrogant.

Calvin Coolidge, *Autobiography*

Nothing is ever accomplished by a committee unless it consists of three members, one of whom happens to be sick and the other absent.

Hendrik van Loon, as quoted in *Reader's Digest*, June 1934

Each Congressman has got two ends,
A sitting and a thinking end.
And since his whole success depends
Upon his seat—why bother, friend?

E. Y. Harburg, *Rhymes for the Irreverent*

Although I myself do not drink, I always make a point of shaking hands with bartenders whenever I come across them, because their recommendations, voiced at that moment when men's minds are highly receptive to ideas, carry much weight in a community.

Joseph W. Martin, Jr., *My Fifty Years in Politics*

All politics is a struggle for power: the ultimate kind of power is violence.

614

C. Wright Mills, *The Power Elite*

Probably the reason many a politician stands on his record is to keep voters from examining it.

Cy N. Peace, as quoted in Reader's Digest, August 1956

There is no Republican way or Democratic way to clean the streets.

Fiorello H. La Guardia, mayor of New York City, speech
April 6, 1940

It makes no difference if I burn my bridges behind me—I never retreat.

Fiorello H. La Guardia, as quoted in Reader's Digest, April
1965

The Christian in politics should be judged by the standard of whether through his decisions and actions he has advanced the cause of justice and helped, at least, to achieve the highest degree of perfection possible in the temporal order.

Eugene McCarthy, Frontiers in American Democracy

The Senate is the last primitive society in the world. We still worship the elders of the tribe and honor the territorial imperative.

Eugene J. McCarthy, speech in Columbus, Ohio, October 10,
1968

Thomas Jefferson founded the Democratic Party; Franklin Roosevelt dumbfounded it.

Representative Dewey Short, as quoted in Reader's Digest,
December 1935

If more politicians in this country were thinking about the next generation instead of the next election, it might be better for the United States and the world.

Claude Pepper, as quoted in the Orlando Sentinel-Star,
December 29, 1946

The mistake a lot of politicians make is in forgetting they've been appointed and thinking they've been anointed.

Mrs. Claude Pepper, as quoted in *Reader's Digest,*
February 1955

Fundamentally, liberalism is an attitude. The chief characteristics of that attitude are human sympathy, a receptivity to change, and a scientific willingness to follow reason rather than faith or any fixed ideas.

Chester Bowles, speech, July 22, 1946

In present-day politics too many people are for either the extreme left or the extreme right. What this country needs is more articulate citizens who are for the extreme middle.

Harry Ruby, as quoted in *Reader's Digest,* November 1949

Politics: the conduct of public affairs for private advantage.

Ambrose Bierce, *The Devil's Dictionary*

Conservative: a statesman who is enamored of the existing evils, as distinguished from the Liberal, who wishes to replace them with others.

Ambrose Bierce, *The Devil's Dictionary*

Politicians are people who, before election, promise a car in every garage. And after election? They get busy putting up parking meters.

John Cameron Swayze, as quoted in *Reader's Digest,*
October 1968

History has amply proved the virtue of political activity by minority, dissident groups, who innumerable times have been in the vanguard of democratic thought and whose programs were ultimately accepted.

Chief Justice Earl Warren, opinion in *Sweczey* v. *New Hampshire* (1957)

Nor is it possible to devote oneself to Culture and declare that one is "not interested" in politics.

Thomas Mann, as quoted in Freedom

The friend of humanity cannot recognize a distinction between what is political and what is not. There is nothing that is not political.

Thomas Mann, The Magic Mountain

Idealism is the noble toga that political gentlemen drape over their will to power.

Aldous Huxley, as quoted in the New York Herald Tribune, November 11, 1963

It's extremely difficult to build a political platform that supports candidates without holding up taxpayers.

Harold Coffin, as quoted in Reader's Digest, October 1972

I never found, in a long experience of politics, that criticism is ever inhibited by ignorance.

Harold Macmillan, former British Prime Minister, as quoted in the Wall Street Journal, August 13, 1963

The difference between North American politics and Latin American politics is that our politicians start running for office *before* the election.

Former Senator Stephen M. Young, as quoted in Reader's Digest, May 1964

I asked a man in prison once how he happened to be there and he said he had stolen a pair of shoes. I told him if he had stolen a railroad he would be a United States Senator.

"Mother" Mary Jones, as quoted in Growing Up Female in America

In politics, it is remarkable what you can do with a hundred dollars if you spend it yourself. It is also sad to think of how little you can do in politics with a hundred dollars if you let someone else spend it.

William Allen White, *Autobiography*

A politician should have three hats. One for throwing in the ring, one for talking through, and one for pulling rabbits out of if he's elected.

Walter Trohan, as quoted in *Reader's Digest*, March 1968

I never give them hell. I just tell the truth, and they think it is hell.

Harry S. Truman, as quoted in *Look*, April 3, 1956

A statesman is a politician who's been dead 10 or 15 years.

Harry S. Truman, as quoted in the New York *World Telegram and Sun*, April 12, 1958

Reform must come from within, not without. You cannot legislate for virtue.

James Cardinal Gibbons, address in Baltimore, September 13, 1909

When a political columnist says "every thinking man," he means himself. When a candidate appeals to "every intelligent voter," he means everybody who's going to vote for him.

Franklin P. Adams, as quoted in *Reader's Digest*, November 1971

The trouble with this country is that there are too many politicians who believe, with a conviction based on experience, that you can fool all of the people all of the time.

Franklin P. Adams, *Nods and Becks*

"Straight-from-the-shoulder" politicians should talk from a little higher up.

John F. Parker, *If Elected, I Promise*

Public office is the last refuge of a scoundrel.

Senator Boies Penrose, as quoted in Collier's Weekly,
February 14, 1931

In our age there is no such thing as "keeping out of politics." All issues are political issues, and politics itself is a mass of lies, evasions, folly, hatred, and schizophrenia.

George Orwell, Orwell Reader

Political language—and with variations this is true of all political parties, from Conservatives to Anarchists—is designed to make lies sound truthful and murder respectable, and to give an appearance of solidity to pure wind.

George Orwell, Shooting an Elephant

Richard Nixon was not a very trusting person. Life had made him that way. There hung over him the wary loneliness of a man always excluded from the company of those he admired. He had been excluded all the way—from the football team at Whittier High School as a boy, from the private upper floor of the White House, even after he had become Vice President. . . . Life was always for him a bare-knuckle fight upward, at every level—and he made friends with difficulty. Most were flatterers in later life; he was a name and a property to be used—yet he hungered for loyalties.

Theodore H. White, The Making of the President 1972

Politics is the science of how who gets what, when and why.

Sidney Hillman, Political Primer for All Americans

Vote for the man who promises least; he'll be the least disappointing.

Bernard M. Baruch, as quoted in Meyer Berger's New York

A skillful politician is one who can stand up and rock the boat and make you believe he is the only one who can save you from the storm.

Roger Allen, as quoted in Reader's Digest, January 1968

A reformer is a guy who rides through a sewer in a glass-bottomed boat.

James J. Walker, speech in New York, 1928

The special form of warfare waged by OSS against Adolf Hitler was morally justified by the moral necessity to destroy Nazism. The more limited and circumspect form of warfare waged by the CIA against the KGB, and vice versa, is also justified by hard necessity. But to transfer such secret-service techniques, on an obviously planned and organized basis, to the internal American political process is a genuinely terrifying innovation. Any person proven to have used these techniques should not only be punished by the law; he should be banned forever from participation in American politics.

Stewart Alsop, as quoted in *Reader's Digest*, August 1973

Every man who takes office in Washington either grows or swells, and when I give a man an office, I watch him carefully to see whether he is swelling or growing.

Woodrow Wilson, address in Washington, D.C., May 15, 1916

It is easy to condemn wrong and to fulminate against wrongdoers in effective rhetorical phrases; but that does not bring either reform or ease of mind. Reform will come only when we have done some careful thinking as to exactly what the things are that are being done in contravention of the public interest and as to the most simple, direct, and effective way of getting at the men who do them.

Woodrow Wilson, speech upon accepting the Democratic nomination for Governor of New Jersey, September 15, 1910

By a progressive I do not mean a man who is ready to move, but a man who knows where he is going when he moves.

Woodrow Wilson, speech in St. Paul, September 9, 1919

I'd rather lose in a cause that will one day win than in a cause that will someday lose.

Woodrow Wilson, as quoted in The Splendid Misery

You cannot adopt politics as a profession and remain honest.

Louis McHenry Howe, speech, January 17, 1933

There's a rumor going around that political officials are preparing cards to hand to convention delegates saying: "Smoke-filled rooms may be hazardous to your candidate."

Troy Gordon, as quoted in Reader's Digest, July 1968

What we need is more women in politics . . . and not just to stuff envelopes, but to run for office. It is women who can bring empathy, tolerance, insight, patience, and persistence to government—the qualities we naturally have or have had to develop because of our suppression by men. . . . At present, our country needs women's idealism and determination, perhaps more in politics than anywhere else.

Representative Shirley Chisholm, speech in the 91st
Congress, as quoted in Black Women in White America

God knows that politics are intricate and that the brain and heart of man are small organs often pulsating as wildly as the wings of a linnet in a snare. But if we do not become more enraged by great wrongs, we shall never have the spirit to achieve great rights.

Harold Nicolson, as quoted in Off the Record with F.D.R.,
1942–45

People often say that, in a democracy, decisions are made by a majority of the people. Of course, that is not true. Decisions are made by a majority of those who make themselves heard and who vote—a very different thing.

Walter H. Judd, as quoted in Reader's Digest, August 1972

[Political skill] is the ability to foretell what is going to happen tomorrow, next week, next month, and next year. And to have the ability afterwards to explain why it didn't happen.

Sir Winston Churchill, *The Churchill Wit*

Politics are almost as exciting as war, and quite as dangerous. In war, you can only be killed once, but in politics many times.

Sir Winston Churchill, *The Churchill Wit*

I expect to fight that proposition until hell freezes over. Then I propose to start fighting on the ice.

Senator Russell Long of Louisiana, on President Kennedy's request for a cutoff of funds to areas practicing segregation, as quoted in *The New York Times*, July 14, 1963

He knows nothing and thinks he knows everything. That points clearly to a political career.

George Bernard Shaw, *Major Barbara*

Republicans sleep in twin beds—some even in separate rooms. That is why there are more Democrats.

Will Stanton, as quoted in *Ladies' Home Journal*, November 1962

Experience suggests that the first rule of politics is never to say never. The ingenious human capacity for maneuver and compromise may make acceptable tomorrow what seems outrageous or impossible today.

William V. Shannon, as quoted in *The New York Times*, March 3, 1968

The Democrats are too clever to solve all our problems this year. They are arranging to have a stream we mustn't change horses in the middle of.

Howard Brubaker, as quoted in *Reader's Digest*, October 1935

Political power grows out of the barrel of a gun.

> Mao Tse-tung, *Quotations from Chairman Mao*

Politics is war without bloodshed while war is politics with bloodshed.

> Mao Tse-tung, *Quotations from Chairman Mao*

Politics is like roller skating. You go partly where you want to go, and partly where the damned things take you.

> Henry Fountain Ashurst, as quoted in *Reader's Digest*,
> February 1958

The political is replacing the metaphysical as the characteristic mode of grasping reality.

> Harvey Cox, *The Secular City*

Since a politician never believes what he says, he is surprised when others believe him.

> Charles de Gaulle, as quoted in *Newsweek*, October 1, 1962

Politics, as hopeful men practice it in the world, consists mainly of the delusion that a change in form is a change in substance.

> H. L. Mencken, *Prejudices: Fourth Series*

[Adlai Stevenson] was the man of thought in an age of action.

> James Reston, in *The New York Times*, February 15, 1965

Politics is not the art of the possible. It consists in choosing between the disastrous and the unpalatable.

> John Kenneth Galbraith, *Ambassador's Journal*

There comes a time when even the reformer is compelled to face the fairly widespread suspicion of the average man that politics is an exhibition in which there is much ado about nothing.

Walter Lippmann, introduction to A Preface to Politics

Politicians are the same all over. They promise to build a bridge even where there is no river.

Nikita Khrushchev, as quoted in the New York Herald
Tribune, August 22, 1963

An empty stomach is not a good political adviser.

Albert Einstein, Cosmic Religion

The public is like a piano. You just have to know what keys to poke.

John Dewey, A Common Faith

SCIENCE AND TECHNOLOGY

Science

I sometimes ask myself why I was the one to develop the theory of relativity. The reason, I think, is that a normal adult never stops to think about problems of space and time. These are things which he has thought of as a child. But I began to wonder about space and time only when I had grown up. Naturally, I could go deeper into the problem than a child.

Albert Einstein, as quoted in *Reader's Digest*, August 1972

Science can only ascertain what *is*, but not what *should be*, and outside of its domain value judgments of all kinds remain necessary.

Albert Einstein, *Out of My Later Years*

The grand aim of all science is to cover the greatest number of empirical facts by logical deduction from the smallest number of hypotheses or axioms.

Albert Einstein, as quoted in *Life*, January 9, 1950

Science without religion is lame, religion without science is blind.

Albert Einstein, *Out of My Later Years*

Science in the making, science as an end to be pursued, is as subjective and psychologically conditioned as any other branch of human endeavor.

Albert Einstein, *The World as I See It*   627

Since I do not foresee that atomic energy is to be a great boon for a long time, I have to say that for the present it is a menace. Perhaps it is well that it should be. It may intimidate the human race into bringing order into its international affairs, which, without the pressure of fear, it would not do.

Albert Einstein, as quoted in the *Atlantic Monthly*,
November 1945

I assert that the cosmic religious experience is the strongest and the noblest driving force behind scientific research.

Albert Einstein, recalled in reports of his death, April 19,
1955

Science is the attempt to make the chaotic diversity of our sense-experience correspond to a logically uniform system of thought.

Albert Einstein, *Out of My Later Years*

We realize the absurdity of applying science to artistic or moral subjects if we try to speak of half a pound of beauty or two inches of courage.

Arthur F. Smethurst, *Modern Science and Christian Beliefs*

Our western science is a child of moral virtues; and it must now become the father of further moral virtues if its extraordinary material triumphs in our time are not to bring human history to an abrupt, unpleasant and discreditable end.

Arnold J. Toynbee, as quoted in *The New York Times
Magazine*, December 26, 1954

Before the close of the seventeenth century our forefathers consciously took their treasure out of religion and reinvested it in natural science.

Arnold J. Toynbee, as quoted in *The New York Times
Magazine*, December 26, 1954

Created by life, in definite circumstances, to act on definite things, how can it [science] embrace life, of which it is merely an emanation or aspect?

Ruth N. Anshen, *Our Emergent Civilization*

I believe in the discipline of silence, and could talk for hours about it.

George Bernard Shaw, as quoted in *Reader's Digest,* March 1961

Science is always simple and always profound. It is only the half-truths that are dangerous.

George Bernard Shaw, *The Doctor's Dilemma*

Man can be scientifically manipulated.

Bertrand Russell, *Unpopular Essays*

Mathematics possess not only truth, but supreme beauty—a beauty cold and austere, like that of sculpture.

Bertrand Russell, *The Study of Mathematics*

Whatever knowledge is attainable must be attainable by scientific methods; and what science cannot discover, mankind cannot know.

Bertrand Russell, *Religion and Science*

Mathematics takes us into the region of absolute necessity, to which not only the actual world, but every possible world, must conform.

Bertrand Russell, *The Study of Mathematics*

To pursue science is not to disparage the things of the spirit. In fact, to pursue science rightly is to furnish a framework on which the spirit may rise.

Vannevar Bush, speech at the Massachusetts Institute of Technology, October 5, 1953

Science does not exclude faith . . . science does not teach a harsh materialism. It does not teach anything beyond its boundaries, and those boundaries have been severely limited by science itself.

Vannevar Bush, *Modern Arms and Free Men*

We have grasped the mystery of the atom and rejected the Sermon on the Mount.

General Omar N. Bradley, speech in Washington, D.C., Armistice Day, 1948

There are but few saints among scientists, as among other men, but truth itself is a goal comparable to sanctity.

George Sarton, *History of Science*

It is facts that are needed; Facts, Facts, Facts. When facts have been supplied, each of us can try to reason from them.

James Bryce, *Modern Democracies*

Science is becoming the hallmark of our age and epoch. The conquest of nature is first of all a conquest of ignorance. Men can control only what they can understand. Science, in itself, is neither blessing nor terror; men make that decision—you and I.

Eric Sevareid, as quoted in Reader's Digest, March 1961

The discovery and use of knowledge has always been relevant to a humane future.

Lee DuBridge, as quoted in Science, July 24, 1970

The modern man, finding that Humanism and Sex both fail to satisfy, seeks his happiness in Science. . . . But Science fails too, for it is something more than a knowledge of matter the soul craves.

Bishop Fulton J. Sheen, The Eternal Galilean

It is rather pedantic to say that science never *explains* anything, but it is true to say that its explanations are never in terms of purpose, or deep-down meaning.

Arthur Thompson, Science and Religion

Science is supposed by many to have banished every realm of the sacred; and behold, science becomes the sacred cow!

Nels F. S. Ferré, Faith and Reason

Science can be and is being made into an escapist philosophy—into a dodge of moral disciplines and spiritual responsibilities.

Nels F. S. Ferré, Faith and Reason

Science burrows its insulted head in the filth of slaughterous inventions.

Sir Winston Churchill, in the London Evening Standard, September 14, 1936

Science has given to this generation the means of unlimited disaster or of unlimited progress. There will remain the greater task of directing knowledge lastingly towards the purpose of peace and human good.

Sir Winston Churchill, speech, January 3, 1944

We have not the reverent feeling for the rainbow that the savage has, because we know how it is made. We have lost as much as we gained by prying into that matter.

Mark Twain, as quoted in *Reader's Digest*, May 1967

The life of reason is no fair reproduction of the universe, but the expression of man alone.

George Santayana, *The Life of Reason*

Science is nothing but developed perception, interpreted intent, common sense rounded out and minutely articulated.

Geroge Santayana, *The Life of Reason*

The man of science, like the artist, may easily have more facts than he can use. Both seek the one fact out of a million that will illuminate their idea. Both find that it is rarely to be had without research.

C. H. Cooley, as quoted in *The Science of Society*

The world would be a safer place,
    If someone had a plan,
Before exploring Outer space,
    To find the Inner man.

E. Y. Harburg, *Rhymes for the Irreverent*

Existing scientific concepts cover always only a very limited part of reality.

Werner Heisenberg, *Physics and Philosophy*

The human brain is a most unusual instrument of elegant and as yet unknown capacity.

Stuart Luman Seaton, speech to the American Institute of Electrical Engineers, as quoted in *Time*, February 17, 1958

All science is concerned with the relationship of cause and effect. Each scientific discovery increases man's ability to predict the consequences of his actions and thus his ability to control future events.

Laurence J. Peter and Raymond Hull, *The Peter Principle*

The fairest thing we can experience is the mysterious. It is the fundamental emotion which stands at the cradle of true science. He who knows it not, and can no longer wonder, no longer feel amazement, is as good as dead. We all had this priceless talent when we were young. But as time goes by, many of us lose it. The true scientist never loses the faculty of amazement. It is the essence of his being.

Hans Selye, as quoted in *Newsweek*, March 31, 1958

The world cannot endure half-darkness and half-light.

J. Robert Oppenheimer, in the *Journal of the Atomic Scientists*, September 1956

There must be no barriers to freedom of inquiry. There is no place for dogma in science. The scientist is free, and must be free to ask any question, to doubt any assertion, to seek for any evidence, to correct any errors.

J. Robert Oppenheimer, as quoted in *Life*, October 10, 1949

In some sort of crude sense which no vulgarity, no humor, no overstatement can quite extinguish, the physicists have known sin; and this is a knowledge which they cannot lose.

J. Robert Oppenheimer, father of the atomic bomb, as quoted in *Time*, November 8, 1948

Science will never be able to reduce the value of a sunset to arithmetic. Nor can it reduce friendship or statesmanship to a formula. Laughter and love, pain and loneliness, the challenge of accomplishment in living, and the depth of insight into beauty and truth: these will always surpass the scientific mastery of nature.

Dr. Louis Orr, presidential address to the American
Medical Association, June 6, 1960

Go and sit in the lounges of the luxury hotels and on the doorsteps of the flophouses; sit on the Gold Coast settees and in the slum shakedown. . . . In short, gentlemen, go get the seat of your pants dirty in real research.

Robert E. Park, address to a group of graduate sociology
students, 1928

I like people. I like animals, too—whales and quail, dinosaurs and dodos. But I like human beings especially, and I am unhappy that the pool of human germ plasm, which determines the nature of the human race, is deteriorating.

Dr. Linus Pauling, as quoted in TheNew York Times,
October 13, 1963

Let both sides seek to invoke the wonders of science instead of its terrors. Together let us explore the stars, conquer the deserts, eradicate disease, tap the ocean depths and encourage the arts and commerce.

John F. Kennedy, speaking of the Communist and
non-Communist blocs, Inaugural Address, January 20, 1961

Every time you scientists make a major invention, we politicians have to invent a new institution to cope with it—and almost invariably, these days, it must be an international institution.

John F. Kennedy, address to the National Academy of
Sciences, October 30, 1963

Science has never drummed up quite as effective a tranquilizing agent as a sunny spring day.

W. Earl Hall, as quoted in Reader's Digest, April 1959

The voices that comment upon science today carry a number of different messages: two of them imply that science (and technology) are virtually omnipotent, but one ascribes to them omnipotence for good, the other omnipotence for evil. The Voice of Expectation says, "With all our much-vaunted science and technology, we ought to be able to feed all the world's hungry, or cure cancer, or (whatever)"; in other words, science may be adequate in content but it is being misapplied. The Voice of Disillusionment says, "It is science and technology that are responsible for all this pollution, or overpopulation, or war, or (whatever); therefore, let us not support them any longer." A third voice, that of Doom-and-Gloom, opposes both these, saying, "The world is in so desperately bad a state, *no amount* of science or technology can ever prevent the disasters in store for us." There is, alas, a fourth voice. It is not primarily directed against science but against the universities—and thus against intellectual activities in general. What it says is simple enough. It says, "We will destroy you."

Kenneth V. Thimann, editorial in *Science*, August 14, 1970

Research is to see what everybody else has seen, and think what nobody has thought.

Dr. Albert Szent-Cyöryi, as quoted in *Reader's Digest*, February 1958

If the determinist is right, reasoning can prove nothing: it is merely an ingenious method for providing us with apparently rational excuses for believing what in any case we cannot help believing. But if all reasoning is a "pathetic fallacy," then the reasons for believing in Determinism itself are fallacious. . . . Unless reason is that which can *discriminate*, there is no criterion of truth and falsehood, all knowledge collapses; one hypothesis is as good as another, and Science itself is a fairy tale.

Burnett H. Streeter, *Reality*

If the molecules in *one* drop of water could be converted into grains of sand, there would be enough sand to build a concrete highway, half a mile wide and one foot thick, from New York to San Francisco.

Lee Rogers, as quoted in *Reader's Digest*, September 1962   635

Facts do not cease to exist because they are ignored.

Aldous Huxley, *Proper Studies*

We have learnt that nothing is simple and rational except what we ourselves have invented; that God thinks in terms neither of Euclid nor of Riemann; that science has "explained" nothing; that the more we know the more fantastic the world becomes and the profounder the surrounding darkness.

Aldous Huxley, *Views of Holland*

There is no magic formula for achieving creativity—it is simply a way of life in a laboratory dedicated to discovery and invention.

Dr. Paul Salzberg, as quoted in *Think*,
November–December 1962

Science must constantly be reminded that her purposes are not the only purposes and that the order of uniform causation which she has use for, and is therefore right in postulating, may be enveloped in a wider order, on which she has no claim at all.

William James, *The Principles of Psychology*

Its [science's] short way of killing any opinion that it disbelieves is to call it "unscientific."

William James, *The Will to Believe and Other Essays*

Science gives us the low view of man—man as matter, man as animal, at best, man as one of the mass.

F. Sherwood Taylor, *Man and Matter*

Science has taught us how to put the atom to work. But to make it work for good instead of for evil lies in the domain dealing with the principles of human duty. We are now facing a problem more of ethics than [of] physics.

Bernard M. Baruch, address to the United Nations Atomic
Energy Agency, June 14, 1946

Whether in the intellectual pursuits of science or in the mystical pursuits of the spirit, the light beckons ahead and the purpose surging in our natures responds.

Arthur S. Eddington, The Nature of the Physical World

Scientists animated by the purpose of proving that they are purposeless constitute an interesting subject for study.

Alfred North Whitehead, The Function of Reason

Motivation researchers are those harlot social scientists who, in impressive psychoanalytic and/or sociological jargon, tell their clients what their clients want to hear, namely, that appeals to human irrationality are likely to be far more profitable than appeals to rationality.

S. I. Hayakawa, as quoted in Etc., Spring 1958

There is more than a mere suspicion that the scientist who comes to ask metaphysical questions and turns away from metaphysical answers may be afraid of those answers.

Dr. Gregory Zilboor, Faith, Reason and Modern Psychiatry

Science has become too complex to affirm the existence of universal truths, but it strives for nothing else.

Henry Adams, The Education of Henry Adams

Science cannot stop while ethics catches up . . . and nobody should expect scientists to do all the thinking for the country.

Elvin Stackman, as quoted in Life, January 9, 1950

Statistics are like a bikini bathing suit. What they reveal is suggestive, but what they conceal is vital.

Aaron Levenstein, as quoted in Reader's Digest, March 1952

The human body comes in only two shapes and three colors. I don't expect there will be any changes, so what we learn about it now will serve us for a long time to come.

Lieutenant Colonel Paul Shapp, as quoted in *Time*,
September 12, 1955

Mankind may wring her secrets from nature, and use their knowledge to destroy themselves.

R. H. Tawney, *Religion and the Rise of Capitalism*

If we want to heal humanity, science can tell us how; if we want to destroy humanity, science can tell us how; but on what grounds can it tell us which of the two to do?

Gerald Vann, *The Heart of Man*

Modern science is still trying to produce a tranquilizer more effective than a few kind words.

Douglas Meador, as quoted in *Reader's Digest*, January
1967

Worthwhile advances are seldom made without taking risks.

W. I. Beveridge, *The Art of Scientific Investigation*

To say that a man is made up of certain chemical elements is a satisfactory description only for those who intend to use him as a fertilizer.

Herbert J. Muller, *Science and Criticism*

Every sentence I utter must be understood not as an affirmation, but as a question.

Niels Bohr, as quoted in *The New York Times Book
Review*, October 20, 1957

Darwin was as much of an emancipator as was Lincoln.

William Graham Sumner, *Conversations*

A problem is not solved in a laboratory. It is solved in some fellow's head, and what all the apparatus is for is to get his head turned around so he can see the thing right.

Charles F. Kettering, *Prophet of Progress*

America, supremely the land of liberty, is also supremely the land of science. Freedom is the oxygen without which science cannot breathe.

David Sarnoff, *Profile of America*

The world of poetry, mythology, and religion represents the world as man would like to have it, while science represents the world as he gradually comes to discover it.

Joseph Wood Krutch, *The Modern Temper*

Science has always promised two things not necessarily related—an increase first in our powers, second in our happiness or wisdom, and we have come to realize that it is the first and less important of the two promises which it has kept most abundantly.

Joseph Wood Krutch, *The Modern Temper*

Science is a cemetery of dead ideas, even though life may issue from them.

Miguel de Unamuno, *The Tragic Sense of Life*

True science teaches, above all, to doubt and be ignorant.

Miguel de Unamuno, *The Tragic Sense of Life*

Not only will atomic power be released, but someday we will harness the rise and fall of the tides and imprison the rays of the sun.

Thomas A. Edison, in a newspaper interview, August 22, 1921

Science is not a sacred cow. Science is a horse. Don't worship it. Feed it.

Aubrey Eben, as quoted in Reader's Digest, March 1963

Science rests itself not in the *world* the scientist beholds at any particular point in time, but in his mode of *viewing* that world. A man is a scientist not because of what he sees, but because of *how* he sees it.

Theodore Roszak, The Making of a Counter Culture

The scientific mind begins in the spirit of the Cartesian zero, with the doubting away of all inherited knowledge in favor of an entirely new method of knowing, which, whether it proceeds on rationalist or empiricist lines, purports to begin from scratch, free of all homage to authority.

Theodore Roszak, The Making of a Counter Culture

In science, all facts, no matter how trivial or banal, enjoy democratic equality.

Mary McCarthy, On the Contrary

Science is built of facts the way a house is built of bricks; but an accumulation of facts is no more science than a pile of bricks is a house.

Henri Poincaré, La Science et l'hypothèse

In science, the total absorption of the individual event in the generalization is the goal; on the other hand, the humanities are concerned rather with providing for the special meaning of the individual event within an appropriate general system.

Moody E. Prior, Science and the Humanities

Science is a first-rate piece of furniture for a man's upper chamber, if he has common sense on the ground floor.

Oliver Wendell Holmes, as quoted in Reader's Digest,
January 1963

... the systems view: to make a useful computer model of a complicated process at work, one must first gather a mass of facts about that process. About the life cycle of the lobster. About the growth and decay of cities. About the dynamics of the American economy. The finished model should help one decide if one wants more lobsters, or healthier cities, or a healthier economy. Its greatest value, however, lies not in such specific guidance, but in the insight one gains while going after the factors that make up a complicated, everchanging process. In short, the common way of thinking in terms of simple cause and effect—the Newtonian, mechanistic view—is replaced by new awareness: of many causes, constantly producing varied effects, in what really are highly complicated and dynamic systems.

Peter T. White, as quoted in the *National Geographic*,
November 1970

Trying to answer students' questions, I soon learned there were great gaps in our scientific knowledge of sex—plenty of folktales, mythology and misunderstanding, of course, but little of the data we have on other phases of life. I resolved to try and fill the gaps.

Dr. Alfred Kinsey, pioneer sex researcher, recalled in reports
of his death in *The New York Times*, August 26, 1956

We are recorders and reporters of the facts—not judges of the behavior we describe.

Dr. Alfred Kinsey, defending the Kinsey reports, recalled
in reports of his death in *The New York Times*, August 26,
1956

Whenever science makes a discovery, the devil grabs it while the angels are debating the best way to use it.

Alan Valentine, as quoted in *Reader's Digest*, April 1962

Science is nothing but trained and organized common sense.

Thomas Huxley, *The Method of Zadig*

God give me strength to face a fact though it slay me.

Thomas Huxley, as quoted in *Reader's Digest*, October
1940

641

The wallpaper with which the men of science have covered the world of reality is falling to tatters.

Henry Miller, *Tropic of Cancer*

The quick harvest of applied science is the usable process, the medicine, the machine. The shy fruit of pure science is Understanding.

Lincoln Barnett, as quoted in *Life*, January 9, 1950

The means by which we live have outdistanced the ends for which we live. Our scientific power has outrun our spiritual power. We have guided missiles and misguided men.

Rev. Martin Luther King, Jr., *Strength to Love*

Nominally a great age of scientific inquiry, ours has actually become an age of superstition about the infallibility of science; of almost mystical faith in its nonmystical methods; above all . . . of external verities; of traffic-cop morality and rabbit-test truth.

Louis Kronenberger, *Company Manners*

It is the man of science, eager to have his every opinion regenerated, his every idea rationalized, by drinking at the fountain of fact, and devoting all the energies of his life to the cult of truth, not as he understands it, but as he does not yet understand it, that ought properly to be called a philosopher.

Charles S. Peirce, as quoted in *Annual Report*, Smithsonian Institution, June 30, 1900

All life is an experiment.

Justice Oliver Wendell Holmes, Jr., dissenting opinion in
Abrams v. *U. S.* (1919)

There are one-story intellects, two-story intellects, and three-story intellects with skylights. All fact collectors with no aims beyond their

facts are one-story men. Two-story men compare reason and genera-
lize using labors of the fact collectors as well as their own. Three-story
men idealize, imagine, and predict. Their best illuminations come from
above through the skylight.

Justice Oliver Wendell Holmes, Jr., as quoted in Urban
Planning in Transition

What is needed in the present plight of mankind is not more science
but a change of heart that shall move mankind to devote to constructive and peaceful purposes what science there is.

Ralph Barton Perry, The Humanity of Man

Science is an imaginative adventure of the mind seeking truth in a
world of mystery.

Cyril Hinshelwood, address to the Science Masters'
Association, Oxford, England, 1953

Our lives would be exceedingly narrow if we based our thoughts and
actions solely on facts that can be subjected to scientific tests.

Arthur H. Compton, The Freedom of Man

Put three grains of sand inside a vast cathedral, and the cathedral will
be more closely packed with sand than space is with stars.

Sir James Jeans, as quoted in Reader's Digest, September
1960

Science is a little bit like the air you breathe—it is everywhere.

Dwight D. Eisenhower, press comment on the
impracticality of establishing a Department of Science in
the federal government, June 18, 1958

Research is something that tells you that a jackass has two ears.

Albert D. Lasker, as quoted in Taken at the Flood: The
Story of Albert D. Lasker 643

Technology

Applied Science is a conjuror, whose bottomless hat yields impartially the softest of Angora rabbits and the most petrifying of Medusas.

Aldous Huxley, *Tomorrow and Tomorrow and Tomorrow*

A world technology means either a world government or world suicide.

Max Lerner, *Actions and Passions*

There is something abhorrent—something offensive to every instinct of comeliness, order, beauty—in this characteristic of machines: that they will not die. Their angular, rusty, immeasurably ugly skeletons mar our sunny fields, corrupt the shores of peaceful streams, lie ghastly by pleasant roadsides. A man dies, or an animal or a tree, and the willing earth soon takes them to itself, grows a flower where they lie, works over them patterns in moss and lichens. But the dead machine does not die: there it lies, inimical to life, to beauty, to order. Man seems unable to efface the ugliness he has made.

David Grayson, as quoted in *Reader's Digest*, August 1961

You cannot endow even the best machine with initiative; the jolliest steamroller will not plant flowers.

Walter Lippmann, *A Preface to Politics*

The machine does not isolate man from the great problems of nature but plunges him more deeply into them.

Antoine de Saint Exupéry, *Wind, Sand, and Stars*

Thanks to science, you can now fly to almost any place in half the time it will take you to wait for your baggage after you get there.

Bill Vaughan, as quoted in *Reader's Digest*, October 1956

Man is the animal that intends to shoot himself out into interplanetary space, after having given up on the problem of an efficient way to get himself five miles or so to work and back each day.

Bill Vaughan, as quoted in Reader's Digest, January 1956

The airplanes they are making nowadays are so fast they can fly halfway across the country before they're obsolete.

Bill Vaughan, as quoted in Reader's Digest, August 1956

Perhaps we're worrying too much about automation taking our jobs. Whenever a traffic jam gets really bad, they turn off the traffic lights and bring in a policeman.

Bill Vaughan, as quoted in Reader's Digest, April 1963

If a couple are introduced by an electronic matchmaker, do they have to ask the computer to be best man at the wedding?

Bill Vaughan, Half the Battle

Someday I would like to stand on the moon, look down through a quarter of a million miles of space and say, "There certainly is a beautiful earth out tonight."

Lieutenant Colonel William H. Rankin, The Man Who Rode the Thunder

The perfect computer has been developed. You just feed in your problems—and they never come out again.

Al Goodman, as quoted in Reader's Digest, October 1968

The computer is not intelligent at all, but very stupid indeed, and that, in fact, is one of its great values—its blind stupidity.

Sidney Lamb, as quoted in The New York Times, January 23, 1965

Ten years ago the moon was an inspiration to lovers and poets. Ten years from now it will be just another airport.

Earl Wilson, as quoted in *Reader's Digest*, September 1962

The greatest of all modern ideas, in its originality, in its widespread adoption, and in its far-reaching importance, is the idea that man can make his way through all the difficulties and dangers that beset him, by means of applied science or technology.

Ralph Barton Perry, *The Present Conflict of Ideas*

Science can give us only the tools in a box, mechanical miracles that it has already given us. But of what use to us are miraculous tools until we have mastered the human cultural use of them? We do not want to live in a world where the machine has mastered the man; we want to live in a world where man has mastered the machine.

Frank Lloyd Wright, lecture in London, May 1939

If it keeps up, man will atrophy all his limbs but the pushbutton finger.

Frank Lloyd Wright, on automation, as quoted in *The New York Times*, November 27, 1955

The presence of humans, in a system containing high-speed electronic computers and high-speed, accurate communications, is quite inhibiting. Every means possible should be employed to eliminate humans in the data-processing chain.

Stuart Luman Seaton, engineering consultant, as quoted in *Time*, February 17, 1958

I could have gone on flying through space forever.

Major Yuri Gagarin, describing his flight as the first man in space, as quoted in *The New York Times*, April 14, 1961

Technology is the science that produces more and more inventions and less and less mechanics to service them.

Evan Esar, as quoted in *Reader's Digest*, April 1967

This new development [automation] has unbounded possibilities for good and for evil.

Norbert Wiener, Cybernetics

If you put tomfoolery into a computer, nothing comes out but tomfoolery. But this tomfoolery, having passed through a very expensive machine, is somehow ennobled, and no one dares to criticize it.

Pierre Gallois, as quoted in Reader's Digest, April 1973

Only science can hope to keep technology in some sort of moral order.

Edgar Z. Friedenberg, The Vanishing Adolescent

If there is technological advance without social advance, there is, almost automatically, an increase in human misery.

Michael Harrington, The Other America

A Ford will run whenever a quorum of its parts is present.

F. L. Warner, as quoted in Reader's Digest, October 1927

It is nothing new that there should exist anti-rationalist elements in our midst. What *is* new is that a radical rejection of science and technological values should appear so close to the center of our society, rather than on the negligible margins. It is the middle-class young who are conducting this politics of consciousness, and they are doing it boisterously, persistently, and aggressively. . . .

Theodore Roszak, The Making of a Counter Culture

The clock is the paragon of automations. . . . The automation of time, in the clock, is the pattern of all larger systems of automation.

Lewis Mumford, The Myth of the Machine

Our two greatest problems are gravity and paper work. We can lick gravity, but sometimes the paper work is overwhelming.

Dr. Werner von Braun, as quoted in Reader's Digest, July 1959

Gods are born and die, but the atom endures.

Alexander Chase, *Perspectives*

Computing machines perhaps can do the work of a dozen ordinary men, but there is no machine that can do the work of one extraordinary man.

E. B. White, as quoted in *Reader's Digest*, July 1960

A computer with as many vacuum tubes as a man has neurons in his head would require the Pentagon to house it, Niagara's power to run it, and Niagara's waters to cool it.

Warren S. McCulloch, as quoted in *Must You Conform?*

I think one of the things which warmed us most during this flight was the realization that however extraordinary computers may be, we are still ahead of them, and that man is still the most extraordinary computer of all.

John F. Kennedy, May 21, 1963, welcoming astronaut
Gordon Cooper to Washington after a safe splash-down in
the Pacific

There are three kinds of lies: lies, damned lies and statistics.

Benjamin Disraeli, as quoted in *Reader's Digest*, February
1949

More than machinery, we need humanity.

Charlie Chaplin, in the film *Modern Times*

Electric clocks reveal to you
Precisely when your fuses blew.

Leonard K. Schiff, as quoted in *Reader's Digest*, January
1957

Men may use what mechanical instruments they please and be none the worse for their use. What kills their souls is when they allow their instruments to use *them.*

R. H. Tawney, *The Acquisitive Society*

The first real technocrat was the cave man who became disturbed because his neighbor used a crooked stick as a plow. Naturally, he thought it would put hundreds of men out of work.

Senator William E. Borah, as quoted in *Reader's Digest,*
May 1933

Every now and then I come across an ad showing an engineer in a business suit and safety helmet, smiling at me over some heading like: "Meet Bill Williams. He's designing your world of tomorrow." Whenever I do, I wish old Bill would go on a long coffee break—say, for 30 or 40 years. He has already horsed around with all the common household objects—doorknobs, taps, electric plugs—until none of them work as well as they did during the reign of Queen Victoria. . . .

This obsession for changing things that already work is spreading fast. . . . I'll fight this kind of change until the day I die, and if I then find out who a few of the designers are who changed all the things that once worked for me, I'll try to come back.

Robert Thomas Allen, as quoted in *Maclean's,* April 1969

The danger of the past was that men became slaves. The danger of the future is that men may become robots. True enough, robots do not rebel. But given man's nature, robots cannot live and remain sane.

Erich Fromm, as quoted in the New York *Post*, January 15, 1956

The real cause for dread is not a machine turned human, but a human turned machine.

Franz F. Winkler, *Man: The Bridge Between Two Worlds*

In a very short time everyone's history will be available at the flick of a computer button. We may end up with 1984 long before we actually get there.

Professor André Moenssens, as quoted in *Reader's Digest*, October 1970

Automobiles insulate man not only from the environment but from human contact as well. They permit only most limited types of interaction, usually competitive, aggressive, and destructive. If people are to be brought together again, given a chance to get acquainted with each other and involved in nature, some fundamental solutions must be found to the problems posed by the automobile.

Edward T. Hall, as quoted in *The Hidden Dimension*

At the moment of our great victories over many . . . diseases . . . we are now confronted with the realization that the more formidable and pervasive challenges to the well-being of man lie in . . . the hazards man has created for himself in the products, processes, and living patterns of his increasingly technological world.

James A. Shannon, former director of the National Institute of Health, as quoted by Senator Edmund Muskie, January 25, 1967

During my eighty-seven years I have witnessed a whole succession of technological revolutions. But none of them has done away with the need for character in the individual or the ability to think.

Bernard M. Baruch, *Baruch, My Own Story*

FRIENDS AND NEIGHBORS

Friends and Fellowship

No man is the whole of himself; his friends are the rest of him.

Rev. Harry Emerson Fosdick, as quoted in Reader's Digest,
October 1972

On the level of the human spirit an equal, a companion, an understanding heart is one who can share a man's point of view. What this means we all know. Friends, companions, lovers, are those who treat us in terms of our unlimited worth to ourselves. They are closest to us who best understand what life means to us, who feel for us as we feel for ourselves, who are bound to us in triumph and disaster, who break the spell of our loneliness.

Henry Alonzo Myers, Are Men Equal?

A book issued by the Army gives all manner of advice to noncommissioned officers. It even tells how to make men who have quarreled friends again. The men are put to washing the same window, one outside, the other inside. Looking at each other, they soon have to laugh and all is forgotten. It works; I have tried it.

Ludwig Bemelmans, as quoted in Reader's Digest, July
1939

A man of active and resilient mind outwears his friendships just as certainly as he outwears his love affairs, his politics and his epistemology.

H. L. Mencken, as quoted in the Smart Set, July 1919   653

You probably wouldn't worry about what people think of you if you could know how seldom they do.

Olin Miller, as quoted in Reader's Digest, June 1939

A friend is someone who stimulates me and to whom I am stimulated to talk. . . . When the stimulation no longer occurs, it is a spent and exhausted friendship, and continues as a burden and a bore. . . . Unfortunately in a long life one gets barnacled over with the mere shells of friendship and it is difficult without hurting one's self to scrape them off.

Bernard Berenson, Sunset and Twilight

It is well, when one is judging a friend, to remember that he is judging you with the same godlike and superior impartiality.

Arnold Bennett, as quoted in Reader's Digest, January 1939

The primary joy of life is acceptance, approval, the sense of appreciation and companionship of our human comrades. Many men do not understand that the need for fellowship is really as deep as the need for food, and so they go throughout life accepting many substitutes for genuine, warm, simple relatedness.

Joshua Loth Liebman, Peace of Mind

Our opinion of people depends less upon what we see in them than upon what they make us see in ourselves.

Sarah Grand, as quoted in Reader's Digest, December 1946

A friend is a present you give yourself.

Robert Louis Stevenson, as quoted in Reader's Digest,
April 1946

When you are down and out, something always turns up—and it is usually the noses of your friends.

Orson Welles, as quoted in The New York Times, April 1,
1962

Nobody is more infuriating, frustrating and embarrassing than an ally who happens to be on our side for the wrong reasons.

Sydney J. Harris, as quoted in *Reader's Digest*, November 1964

The truest test of independent judgment is being able to dislike someone who admires us, and to admire someone who dislikes us.

Sydney J. Harris, as quoted in *Reader's Digest*, January 1974

People decline invitations when they are "indisposed" physically, and I wish they would do likewise when they feel indisposed emotionally. A person has no more right to attend a party with a head full of venom than with a throat full of virus.

Sydney J. Harris, as quoted in *Reader's Digest*, April 1961

We are none of us all of a piece; more than one person dwells within us, often in uneasy companionship with his fellows.

W. Somerset Maugham, *Great Novelists and Their Novels*

We know our friends by their defects rather than by their merits.

W. Somerset Maugham, *The Summing Up*

It's no good trying to keep up old friendships. It's painful for both sides. The fact is, one grows out of people, and the only thing is to face it.

W. Somerset Maugham, *Cakes and Ale*

The best friends are those who know how to keep the same silences.

Bishop Fulton J. Sheen, as quoted in *Reader's Digest*, July 1972

Almost all of our relationships begin and most of them continue as forms of mutual exploitation, a mental or physical barter, to be terminated when one or both parties run out of goods.

W. H. Auden, *The Dyer's Hand*

One does not make friends; one recongizes them.

Isabel Paterson, as quoted in *Reader's Digest*, July 1941

The secret of a man who is universally interesting is that he is universally interested.

William Dean Howells, as quoted in *Reader's Digest*, January 1974

I cannot give you the formula for success but I can give you the formula for failure—which is: Try to please everybody.

Herbert Bayard Swope, speech, December 20, 1950

How do we become true and good, happy and genuine, joyful and free? Never by magic, never by chance, never by sitting and waiting, but only by getting in touch with good, true, happy, genuine human beings, only by seeking the company of the strong and the free, only by catching spontaneity and freedom from those who are themselves spontaneous and free.

Charles Malik, as quoted in *Reader's Digest*, August 1972

To behave with dignity is nothing less than to allow others freely to be themselves, to delight in them within the framework of such a demanding guarantee. The dignity of others derives less from being themselves than from encouraging you to be yourself.

Sol Chaneles, *The New Civility*

Advice can no more be withheld than can breathing. We advise by example, by preventing someone's misfortune, by giving approbation, or by a display of scorn so timed and delivered that it is instructional rather than disgusting. . . . To seek and give advice are ways of entwining your life with another's, and civility exacts involvement.

Sol Chaneles, The New Civility

The happiest miser on earth—the man who saves up every friend he can make.

Robert E. Sherwood, as quoted in Reader's Digest,
November 1948

If we were all given by magic the power to read each other's thoughts, I suppose the first effect would be to dissolve all friendships. The second effect, however, might be excellent, for the world without friends would be intolerable, and we should learn to like each other without needing a veil of illusion to conceal from ourselves that we did not think our friends absolutely perfect.

Bertrand Russell, as quoted in Reader's Digest, February
1941

Existence warps too much. It sets us so we can only receive certain kinds of opposite numbers. But in the abstract, in essence, any two human beings can find warmth together.

Norman Mailer, Barbary Shore

No one agrees with other people's opinions, he merely agrees with his own opinions expressed by somebody else.

Sydney Tremayne, as quoted in Reader's Digest, January
1949

The opinions which we hold of one another, our relations with friends and kinsfolk are in no sense permanent, save in appearance, but are as eternally fluid as the sea itself.

Marcel Proust, Remembrance of Things Past: The
Guermantes Way 657

A man who trims himself to suit everybody will soon whittle himself away.

Charles Schwab, as quoted in Reader's Digest, May 1955

There is no hope of joy except in human relations.

Antoine de Saint-Exupéry, Wind, Sand, and Stars

Your opinion of others is apt to be their opinion of you.

B. C. Forbes, as quoted in Reader's Digest, September 1947

If it's very painful for you to criticize your friends, you're safe in doing it. But if you take the slightest pleasure in it, that's the time to hold your tongue.

Alice Duer Miller, as quoted in Reader's Digest, August 1947

One of the best ways to persuade others is with your ears—by listening to them.

Dean Rusk, as quoted in Reader's Digest, July 1961

With three or more people there is something bold in the air: direct things get said which would frighten two people alone and conscious of each inch of their nearness to one another. To be three is to be in public, you feel safe.

Elizabeth Bowen, The House in Paris

The heart may think it knows better; the senses know that absence blots people out. We have really no absent friends.

Elizabeth Bowen, The Death of the Heart

Do you wish to find out a man's weak points? Note the failings he has the quickest eye for in others.

J. C. and W. A. Hare, as quoted in Reader's Digest, May 1941

To really know someone is to have loved and hated him in turn.

Marcel Jouhandeau, Défense de l'enfer

He's the kind of man who picks his friends—to pieces.

Mae West, as quoted in Reader's Digest, August 1935

Acquaintance: a person whom we know well enough to borrow from, but not well enough to lend to.

Ambrose Bierce, The Devil's Dictionary

Friendship: n. A ship big enough to carry two in fair weather, but only one in foul.

Ambrose Bierce, The Devil's Dictionary

We like a man to come right out and say what he thinks, if we agree with him.

Mark Twain, as quoted in Reader's Digest, April 1949   659

The proper office of a friend is to side with you when you are in the wrong. Nearly anybody will side with you when you are in the right.

Mark Twain, *Notebook*

The holy passion of Friendship is of so sweet and steady and loyal and enduring a nature that it will last through a whole lifetime, if not asked to lend money.

Mark Twain, *Pudd'nhead Wilson's Calendar*

Anyone can sympathize with the sufferings of a friend, but it requires a very fine nature to sympathize with a friend's success.

Oscar Wilde, as quoted in *Reader's Digest*, June 1945

We need new friends; some of us are cannibals who have eaten their old friends up; others must have ever-renewed audiences before whom to re-enact the ideal version of their lives.

Logan Pearsall Smith, *Afterthoughts*

If we treat people too long with that pretended liking called politeness, we shall find it hard not to like them in the end.

Logan Pearsall Smith, as quoted in *Reader's Digest*, January 1947

There's nothing I'm afraid of like scared people.

Robert Frost, as quoted in *Reader's Digest*, May 1961

Constant use will wear out anything—especially friends.

Warren Hull, as quoted in *Reader's Digest*, December 1957

To cement a new friendship, especially between foreigners or persons of a different social world, a spark with which both were secretly charged must fly from person to person, and cut across the accidents of place and time.

George Santayana, Persons and Places: The Middle Span

Friendship is almost always the union of a part of one mind with a part of another; people are friends in spots.

George Santayana, Soliloquies in England

Charm seems to me to be the ability to captivate other people without doing anything about it. The "charm" of it is that one cannot define its ingredients.

Rudolf Bing, former General Manager of the Metropolitan
Opera, as quoted in Reader's Digest, August 1959

Platonic friendship: the interval between the introduction and the first kiss.

Sophie Irene Loeb, as quoted in Reader's Digest, June 1948

Mixing politics and friends
Is often where the friendship ends.

S. H. Dewhurst, as quoted in Reader's Digest, December
1947

Love demands infinitely less than friendship.

George Jean Nathan, The Autobiography of an Attitude

If you treat people right they will treat you right—90 percent of the time.

Franklin D. Roosevelt, as quoted in Reader's Digest,
October 1947

Sooner or later you've heard all your best friends have to say. Then comes the tolerance of real love.

Ned Rorem, Music from Inside Out   661

The chief lesson I have learned in a long life is that the only way to make a man trustworthy is to trust him; and the surest way to make him untrustworthy is to distrust him and show your mistrust.

> Henry L. Stimson, as quoted in *Reader's Digest*, October
> 1947

With every friend I love who has been taken into the brown bosom of the earth a part of me has been buried there; but their contribution to my being of happiness, strength and understanding remains to sustain me in an altered world.

> Helen Keller, as quoted in *Reader's Digest*, November 1961

There are some people who are very resourceful
At being remorseful,
And who apparently feel that the best way to make friends
Is to do something terrible and then make amends.

> Ogden Nash, as quoted in *Reader's Digest*, May 1974

Half the pleasure of solitude comes from having with us some friend to whom we can say how sweet solitude is.

> William Jay, as quoted in *Reader's Digest*, November 1961

Friends are born, not made.

> Henry Adams, *The Education of Henry Adams*

One friend in a lifetime is much; two are many; three are hardly possible.

> Henry Adams, *The Education of Henry Adams*

Treat a friend as a person who may someday become your enemy; an enemy as a person who may someday become your friend.

> George Bernard Shaw, as quoted in *Reader's Digest*,
> August 1959

The only man who behaves sensibly is my tailor; he takes my measure anew every time he sees me, whilst all the rest go on with their old measurements, and expect them to fit me.

George Bernard Shaw, as quoted in *Reader's Digest*,
September 1938

One measure of friendship consists not in the number of things friends can discuss, but in the number of things they need no longer mention.

Clifton Fadiman, as quoted in *Reader's Digest*, October
1963

Friendship is like money, easier made than kept.

Samuel Butler, *Notebooks*

Rare is the person who can weigh the faults of others without putting his thumb on the scales.

Byron J. Langenfeld, as quoted in *Reader's Digest*, April
1962

No real friendship is ever made without an intial clashing which discloses the metal of each to each.

David Grayson, *Adventures in Contentment*

Friendliness is contagious. The trouble is, many of us wait to catch it from someone else, when we might better be giving them a chance to catch it from us.

Donald A. Laird, as quoted in *Reader's Digest*, May 1961

If you approach each new person you meet in a spirit of adventure, you will find yourself endlessly fascinated by the new channels of thought and experience and personality that you encounter.

Eleanor Roosevelt, as quoted in *Reader's Digest*, January
1961   663

The finest kind of friendship is between people who expect a great deal of each other but never ask it.

Sylvia Bremer, as quoted in Reader's Digest, December
1959

Don't believe your friends when they ask you to be honest with them. All they really want is to be maintained in the good opinion they have of themselves.

Albert Camus, The Fall

Real friends are those who, when you've made a fool of yourself, don't feel that you've done a permanent job.

Erwin T. Randall, as quoted in Reader's Digest, July 1955

Your friend is the man who knows all about you, and still likes you.

Elbert Hubbard, The Note Book

It is very easy to forgive others their mistakes; it takes more grit and gumption to forgive them for having witnessed your own.

Jessamyn West, as quoted in Reader's Digest, April 1974

As we move around this world and as we act with kindness, perhaps, or with indifference or with hostility toward the people we meet, we are setting the great spider web atremble. The life that I touch for good or ill will touch another life, and that in turn another, until who knows where the trembling stops or in what far place my touch will be felt.

Frederick Buechner, The Hungering Dark

The wise thing to do is to divide all people into two classes—friends and strangers. Friends we love too well to gossip about; strangers we know too little.

Heywood Broun, as quoted in Reader's Digest, September
1959

One can never pay in gratitude; one can only pay "in kind" somewhere else in life.

Anne Morrow Lindbergh, *Listen! the Wind*

Nothing spoils friendship so much as an exaggeration of a friend's merits.

Maria Moravsky, as quoted in *Reader's Digest*, February 1947

Silence is the space surrounding every action and every communication of people. Freindship needs no words—it is a loneliness relieved of the anguish of loneliness.

Dag Hammarskjöld, *Road Signs*

The friends who are most stimulating to us are those who disagree with us. It is they whose ideas we should ponder; not that we may be converted by them but that, in the light of their certainties, we may search out the basis of our own. We dignify by the name of beliefs a jumble of traditions and superstitions, and we need to go over them periodically, spurred by some skeptic, to sort out the grain from the chaff.

Cornelia James Cannon, as quoted in *Reader's Digest*, May 1937

In general, American social life constitutes an evasion of talking to people. Most Americans don't, in any vital sense, get together; they only do things together.

Louis Kronenberg, *Company Manners*

In any relationship, we feel an unconscious need to create, as it were, a new picture, a new edition of ourselves to present to the fresh person who claims our interest; for them, we in a strange sense wish to, and do, start life anew.

Ann Bridge, as quoted in *Reader's Digest*, January 1937 **665**

Only the person who has faith in himself is able to be faithful to others.

Erich Fromm, *The Art of Loving*

Few human beings are proof against the implied flattery of rapt attention.

Jack Woodford, as quoted in *Reader's Digest*, March 1936

We must learn to live together as brothers or perish together as fools.

Rev. Martin Luther King, Jr., address in St. Louis, March 23, 1964

Some of my best friends are children. In fact, all of my best friends are children.

J. D. Salinger, as quoted in *Time*, July 16, 1951

What we do, what we are, what we make of ourselves decides not only the quality of our own life but that of those around us. If a man develops his talents, his capacity to use and enjoy the many opportunities for growth within everyone's reach, his family, his environment catch the fire from him. He may seem to himself but a cog in the machine, but he is also a master craftsman and a creator in the greatest of all arts—the art of living.

I. A. R. Wylie, as quoted in *Reader's Digest*, November 1956

It is always well to accept your own shortcomings with candor but to regard those of your friends with polite incredulity.

Russell Lynes, as quoted in *Vogue*, September 1, 1952

The art of acceptance is the art of making someone who has just done you a small favor wish that he might have done you a greater one.

Russell Lynes, as quoted in *Reader's Digest*, December 1954

A true apology is more than just acknowledgment of a mistake. It's recognition that something you have said or done has damaged a relationship—and that you *care* enough about that relationship to want it repaired and restored.

Norman Vincent Peale, as quoted in *Reader's Digest,*
December 1973

If you must tell people what to do, try to tell them by indirection. You will make more friends that way than by giving too much advice!

Harry Simmons, *How to Talk Your Way to Success*

It is more blessed to give than to receive. But the givers who cannot take in return miss one of the finest graces in life, the grace of receiving. To receive gratefully from others is to enhance others' sense of their worth. It puts them on a give-and-take level, the only level on which real fellowship can be sustained. It changes one of the ugliest things in the world, patronage, into one of the richest things in the world, friendship.

Halford E. Luccock, as quoted in *Reader's Digest,* May
1973

How delightful is the company of generous people, who overlook trifles and keep their minds instinctively fixed on whatever is good and positive in the world about them. People of small caliber are always carping. They are bent on showing their own superiority, their knowledge or their prowess or good breeding. But magnanimous people have no vanity, they have no jealousy, they have no reserves, and they feed on the true and the solid wherever they find it. And what is more, they find it everywhere.

Van Wyck Brooks, *From a Writer's Notebook*

You cannot be friends upon any other terms than upon the terms of equality.

Woodrow Wilson, speech, October 27, 1913   667

To go against the dominant thinking of your friends, of most of the people you see every day, is perhaps the most difficult act of heroism you can perform.

Theodore H. White, as quoted in *Reader's Digest*, October
1971

It is in the thirties that we want friends. In the forties we know they won't save us any more than love did.

F. Scott Fitzgerald, *Notebooks*

To speak ill of others is a dishonest way of praising ourselves; let us be above such transparent egotism. . . . If you can't say good and encouraging things, say nothing. Nothing is often a good thing to say, and always a clever thing to say.

Will Durant, as quoted in the New York *World-Telegram
and Sun*, June 6, 1958

We form limited-involvement relationships and easily abandon friendships—it's too difficult keeping in touch when jobs, status, locations change. Compared with previous generations, whose personal ties were relatively few and stable, we deal with many more people in the course of our daily lives and the cast of characters changes frequently. . . . In earlier generations a "best friend" lasted a long time. Today our children, caught up in the rapid pace of our culture, turn over their friendships at a frenetic speed, with staggering results in terms of loneliness, isolation, and loss of deep satisfying emotional involvement.

Alvin Toffler, as quoted in *Reader's Digest*, August 1971

I have had a very varied and interesting life and have met some remarkable people. But now that I have reached "the end game," the figures that still stand out are the people to whom, in different ways and in different degrees, I have been bound by affection. Not only are they the people I most vividly remember, but I realize it is only through them that I have learned anything about life at all. All of my past life that has not faded into mist has passed through the filter, not of my mind, but of my affection.

Iris Origo, as quoted in *Reader's Digest*, October 1972

Sometimes a man's fitness for a post of trust is determined by his associations.

Sidney Hook, as quoted in *The New York Times Magazine*,
July 9, 1950

Seeing ourselves as others see us wouldn't do much good. We wouldn't believe it anyway.

M. Walthall Jackson, as quoted in *Reader's Digest*, April
1951

The Person Next Door

You're never quite sure how you feel about a neighbor until a "For Sale" sign suddenly appears in front of his house.

O. A. Battista, as quoted in *Reader's Digest*, October 1955

As man increases his knowledge of the heavens, why should he fear the unknown on earth? As man draws nearer to the stars, why should he not also draw nearer to his neighbor?

Lyndon B. Johnson, news conference in Johnson City,
Texas, August 29, 1965

There is a Law that man should love his neighbor as himself. In a few hundred years it should be as natural to mankind as breathing or the upright gait; but if he does not learn it he must perish.

Alfred Adler, *Social Interest*

Nothing makes you more tolerant of a neighbor's noisy party than being there.

Franklin P. Jones, as quoted in *Reader's Digest*, January
1953

The Fifth Commandment, which forbids injuries to our neighbors, forbids as well the appalling injuries which our prejudices and acts of discrimination cause whole groups of our neighbors.

Julian J. Reiss, speech, October 11, 1946

Our position (in San Francisco) is that of the Virginia gentleman of long ago who warned his son: "Never ask a man from what state he comes. If he's a Virginian, you'll know it. If he isn't you'll shame him."

Kathleen Norris, as quoted in *Reader's Digest*, January 1933

In the field of world policy, I would like to dedicate this nation to the policy of the good neighbor.

Franklin D. Roosevelt, First Inaugural Address, March 4, 1933

Good fences make good neighbors.

Robert Frost, "The Mending Wall"

The interest I take in my neighbor's nursery,
Would have to grow to be even cursory.

Ogden Nash, as quoted in *Reader's Digest*, December 1933

How often is it true that the ignorant who do not know how to help their neighbor, and the weak who lack the power to help him, nevertheless are the ones who love him, while the learned and strong who could help him, do not because they no longer love him; on the contrary they use their knowledge and their power to rob and enslave him.

W. H. Auden, Karl Shapiro, *et al.*, as quoted in *Poets at Work*

Not many sounds in life, and I include all urban and all rural sounds, exceed in interest a knock at the door.

Charles Lamb, as quoted in *Reader's Digest*, October 1936

The impersonal hand of government can never replace the helping hand of a neighbor.

Hubert H. Humphrey, speech in Washington, D.C.,
February 10, 1965

Sometimes a neighbor whom we have disliked a lifetime for his arrogance and conceit lets fall a single commonplace remark that shows us another side, another man, really; a man uncertain, and puzzled, and in the dark like ourselves.

Willa Cather, *Shadows on the Rock*

Get acquainted with your neighbor; you might like him.

Father H. B. Tierney, as quoted in *Reader's Digest*,
February 1947

Living next to you is in some ways like sleeping with an elephant. No matter how friendly and even-tempered is the beast, one is affected by every twitch and grunt.

Pierre Elliott Trudeau, Canadian Prime Minister,
commenting on Canada's relations with the United States,
March 16, 1969

If you want to know whether you're a welcome visitor to other people's gardens, test your character thus: Can you stand by your neighbor's borders five minutes without saying I—my—me—mine?

Julian R. Meade, as quoted in *Reader's Digest*, July 1947

The good neighbor looks beyond the external accidents and discerns those inner qualities that make all men human and, therefore, brothers.

Rev. Martin Luther King, Jr., *Strength to Love*

Each man is afraid of his neighbor's disapproval—a thing which, to the general run of the race, is more dreaded than wounds and death.

Mark Twain, "The United States of Lyncherdom"

The pioneers didn't brood about life—they lived it. And in the living they learned a priceless lesson: self-preservation goes hand-in-hand with "keeping" your brother. Ironically, on a lonely continent which separated men with alien vastnesses, they discovered that no man is ever alone, and that he dare not be alone, even if he wants to be.

Paul Engle, as quoted in *Reader's Digest*, March 1971

Every man is the architect of his own fortunes, but the neighbors superintend the construction.

George Ade, *Hand-Made Fables*

Probably the most common of all antagonisms arises from a man's taking a seat beside you on a train, a seat to which he is completely entitled.

Robert Benchley, as quoted in *Reader's Digest*, September 1950

If you are already secured in your shelter and others try to break in, they may be treated as unjust aggressors and repelled with whatever means will effectively deter their assault.

L. C. McHugh, S.J., on the ethics of fallout shelters, as quoted in *America*, September 30, 1961

Were it not for the misfortunes of our neighbors, life would be positively unbearable.

C. E. Jerningham, as quoted in *Reader's Digest*, December 1948

Give the neighbors' kids an inch and they'll take a yard.

Helen Castle, as quoted in *Reader's Digest*, November 1950

There is a heaven, for ever, day by day,
The upward longing of my soul doth tell me so.
There is a hell, I'm quite sure; for pray,
If there were not, where would my neighbors go?

Paul Laurence Dunbar, "Theology"

RELIGION AND MORALITY

Religion

The church must be reminded that it is not the master or the servant of the state, but rather the conscience of the state.

Rev. Martin Luther King, Jr., Strength to Love

Science without religion is lame; religion without science is blind.

Albert Einstein, as quoted in Reader's Digest, January 1973

The man who is thoroughly convinced of the universal operation of the law of causation cannot for a moment entertain the idea of a being who interferes in the course of events. . . . He has no use for the religion of fear and equally little for social or moral religion.

Albert Einstein, in The New York Times Magazine,
November 9, 1930

I could prove God statistically. Take the human body alone—the chance that all the functions of the individual would just happen is a statistical monstrosity.

George Gallup, as quoted in Reader's Digest, October 1943

One of the supreme hours of human experience arrives when a man gets his eye on something concerning which he is persuaded that it is the eternal truth.

Rev. Harry Emerson Fosdick, A Great Time to Be Alive   677

The world has forgotten, in its preoccupation with Left and Right, that there is an Above and Below.

Franz Werfel, as quoted in *Reader's Digest*, May 1949

Most of us spend the first six days of each week sowing wild oats; then we go to church on Sunday and pray for a crop failure.

Fred Allen, as quoted in *Reader's Digest*, April 1960

I can't talk religion to a man with bodily hunger in his eyes.

George Bernard Shaw, *Major Barbara*

Christianity can no more escape democracy than democracy can escape socialism.

George Bernard Shaw, preface to *John Bull's Other Island*

Religion is a great force—the only real motive force in the world; but you must get at a man through his own religion, not through yours.

George Bernard Shaw, as quoted in *Reader's Digest*,
August 1961

I always find that statistics are hard to swallow and impossible to digest. The only one I can ever remember is that if all the people who go to sleep in church were laid end to end they would be a lot more comfortable.

Mrs. Robert A. Taft, as quoted in *Reader's Digest*, March
1952

The most prevalent failure of Christian love is the failure to express it.

Rev. Paul E. Johnson, *Christian Love*

Christian love is growing interest in, appreciation of, and responsibility for every person as a member of one family of God.

678

Rev. Paul E. Johnson, *Christian Love*

I once asked a Quaker friend to describe the essence of his faith. "No pomp," he replied, "under any circumstance."

Edward Stevenson, as quoted in *Reader's Digest*, February 1973

Lord, when we are wrong, make us willing to change. And when we are right, make us easy to live with.

Peter Marshall, as quoted in *Reader's Digest*, August 1953

In Cardinal Cushing I felt the kind of thing Christ and the disciple John must have had—simple availability. He exuded absolute confidence in his Church and his priestliness. He never worried about "little things"—like theology. He lived by his basic creed and his inheritance as a worker for God: "Man is sinful. Life is sad. There is something beyond." He was my idea of a saint.

Harry Reasoner, as quoted in *Reader's Digest*, November 1973

To believe in God is to yearn for His existence and, furthermore, it is to act as if He did exist.

Miguel de Unamuno, *The Tragic Sense of Life*

An informal survey shows that what most people wanted for Christmas was two more weeks to prepare for it.

Bob Stanley, as quoted in *Reader's Digest*, January 1968

The ideas I stand for are not mine. I borrowed them from Socrates. I swiped them from Chesterfield. I stole them from Jesus. And I put them in a book. If you don't like their rules, whose would you use?

Dale Carnegie, as quoted in *Newsweek*, August 8, 1955

There are people who say you should read the Bible as literature, for the stories it tells and the history it contains. Don't worry about what it is supposed to mean to religious faith. Read it like any other book.   679

The trouble is that the Bible is not like any other book. To read the Bible as literature is like reading *Moby Dick* as a whaling manual or the Gettysburg Address for its punctuation.

Frederick Buechner, as quoted in *Reader's Digest,*
September 1972

What does it take to be an Archbishop of Canterbury? The strength of a horse—and the ability to be a cart horse one day and a race horse the next.

Geoffrey Fisher, as quoted in *The Hundredth Archbishop
of Canterbury*

When we pray, we link ourselves with the inexhaustible power that spins the universe. We ask that a part of this power be apportioned to our needs. Even in asking, our human deficiencies are filled and we arise strengthened and repaired.

Dr. Alexis Carrel, as quoted in *Reader's Digest,* March 1941

I didn't go to church today,
I trust the Lord to understand.
The surf was swirling blue and white,
The children swirling on the sand.

He knows, He knows how brief my stay,
How brief this spell of summer weather,
He knows when I am said and done
We'll have a plenty of time together.

Ogden Nash, as quoted in *Reader's Digest,* August 1972

The truth is all things seen under the form of eternity.

George Santayana, *The Realm of Truth*

The shell of Christendom is broken. The unconquerable mind of the East, the pagan past, the industrial socialistic future confront it with their equal authority. Our whole life and mind is saturated with the slow upward filtration of a new spirit—that of an emancipated, atheistic, international democracy.

George Santayana, Winds of Doctrine

Jesus is God spelling Himself out in language that man can understand.

S. D. Gordon, as quoted in Reader's Digest, July 1972

Be not afraid of life. Believe that life *is* worth living and your belief will help create the fact.

William James, The Will to Believe and Other Essays

If Christmas didn't already exist, man would have had to invent it. There has to be at least one day in the year to remind us we're here for something else besides our general cussedness.

Eric Sevareid, as quoted in Reader's Digest, December 1971

Most people have some sort of religion—at least they know what church they're staying away from.

John Erskine, as quoted in Reader's Digest, February 1942

No one can worship God or love his neighbor on an empty stomach.

Woodrow Wilson, speech, May 23, 1912

Meditation is not an escape from daily living, but a preparation for it, and what is of surpassing importance is what we bring back from the experience. Like pearl divers, meditators plunge deep into the inner ocean of consciousness and hope to come swimming back to the surface with jewels of great price.

Ardis Whitman, as quoted in Reader's Digest, September
1973

A religion that is small enough for our understanding would not be large enough for our needs.

Arthur Balfour, as quoted in Reader's Digest, June 1958   681

To tip the scales by the will to believe is childish foolishness since things will generally continue to weigh what they do despite this tipping.

Morris R. Cohen, as quoted in the *Journal of Philosophy and Scientific Method*, 1925

The world is equally shocked at hearing Christianity criticized and seeing it practiced.

D. Elton Trueblood, as quoted in *Reader's Digest*, February 1963

Ask any decent person what he thinks matters most in human conduct: five to one his answer will be "kindness."

Lord Kenneth Clark, as quoted in *Reader's Digest*, June 1971

Religion is caught, not taught.

W. R. Inge, as quoted in *Reader's Digest*, February 1935

To sensible men, every day is a day of reckoning.

John W. Gardner, *No Easy Victories*

To me, faith means not worrying.

John Dewey, as quoted in *Reader's Digest*, April 1950

In its last analysis it is not freedom of thought which endangers Jewish values, but the freedom which some people arrogate to themselves not to think at all.

Milton Steinberg, *The Land Question*

Certainly we must do all in our power to bring social justice, to work for peace among nations, to put down poverty. These are proper concerns of the church. But even though you give people the highest standard of living, firm laws that make social and racial justice mandatory, and assign aid by the billions to needy people, your efforts will be largely futile if greed and prejudice and hatred are still there. God alone can remove those elements from human nature. . . .

Rev. Billy Graham, as quoted in Reader's Digest, July 1970

I don't know what the future holds, but I know Who holds the future.

Rev. Billy Graham, as quoted in Reader's Digest, July 1970

God will not look you over for medals, degrees or diplomas, but for scars.

Elbert Hubbard, as quoted in Reader's Digest, May 1960

The submergence of self in the pursuit of an ideal, the readiness to spend oneself without measure, prodigally, almost ecstatically, for something intuitively apprehended as great and noble, spend oneself one knows not why—some of us like to believe that this is what religion means.

Justice Benjamin N. Cardozo, Values

An atheist is a guy who watches a Notre Dame–SMU football game and doesn't care who wins.

Dwight D. Eisenhower, as quoted in news summaries of
November 6, 1954

Doubt isn't the opposite of faith; it is an element of faith

Paul Tillich, as quoted in Reader's Digest, January 1974

From the early centuries of our era, the lone, pathetic figure of Christ's mother has fired the imagination of the believers. Statues of Mary began to grace the crossroads of the world. Pious pilgrimages brought thousands to her shrines. Hymns were sung to her. Cities were named for her. And some of the world's great cathedrals—among them Notre Dame of Paris—were dedicated in her name.

Thus today, as the lofty symbol of eternal motherhood, Mary belongs to all civilization.

Ernest O. Hauser, as quoted in Reader's Digest, December
1971

We may some day catch an abstract truth by the tail, and then we shall have our religion and our immortality.

Henry Adams, as quoted in Henry Adams: The Middle
Years

The only authority that both sides to an argument must necessarily recognize will have to be an authority in the very nature of humanity.

James Bissett Pratt, Religious Liberals Reply

Everywhere, rapt and radiant-faced young people are wading into oceans and lakes for mass baptisms, studying the Bible with feverish intensity, gathering in Christian communes, organizing prayer groups and proclaiming Jesus Christ their Lord and Saviour. . . .

There's no doubt that the Jesus people can and often do shake up the established order of things. But, watching them, I have become convinced that very often they are full of two qualities that all of us need desperately in our lives: love and joy. And I also believe that they stand ready to share these qualities with us, if we will just let them.

Rev. Norman Vincent Peale, as quoted in Reader's Digest,
December 1971

The new emphasis upon service and cooperation has helped precipitate the wide-spread identity crisis of priests, who have discovered that they are less qualified to serve the community than many competent laymen.

Dr. Mary Daly, as quoted in Sisterhood Is Powerful

Religion is behavior and not mere belief.

S. Radhakrishnan, as quoted in Reader's Digest, February
1970

Men like to have things neatly explained and ticketed and systematized. It takes spiritual grandeur to admit that we cannot synthesize the deepest realities of our experience, and yet cling to all of them.

B. Bamberger, *Fallen Angels*

Some people want an affidavit from God that He really exists.

Danny Thomas, as quoted in *Reader's Digest*, July 1955

The belief in a supernatural source of evil is not necessary; men alone are quite capable of every wickedness.

Joseph Conrad, *Under Western Eyes*

Man, even if he does not commit scientific suicide, will perish ultimately through failure of water or air or warmth. It is difficult to believe that Omnipotence needed so vast a setting for so small and transitory a result.

Apart from the minuteness and brevity of the human species, I cannot feel that it is a worthy climax to such an enormous prelude.

Bertrand Russell, in a BBC broadcast, 1953

God is the sum of all possibilities.

Isaac Bashevis Singer, as quoted in *Reader's Digest*, April 1972

I have encountered nothing on Apollo 15 or in this age of space and science that dilutes my faith in God. While I was on the moon, in fact, I felt a sense of inspiration, a feeling that someone was with me and watching over me, protecting me. There were several times when tasks seemed to be impossible—but they worked out all right every time.

Colonel James B. Irwin, as quoted in *The New York Times*, August 13, 1971

The theological problem today is to find the art of drawing religion out of a man, not pumping it into him.

Rev. Karl Rahner, as quoted in *Reader's Digest*, May 1963   685

I think it not improbable that man . . . may have cosmic destinies that he does not understand.

Justice Oliver Wendell Holmes, Jr., as quoted in *An Autobiography of the Supreme Court*

When you come down to it, what is our wondering but worship? To worship is to admit worth. And to wonder at something with open mouth, incredulous eye and awestruck mind is to do the same. It is to get beneath the common husk of things, to get above the plodding levels on which we live. To wonder and to worship is to be ushered into the essence of God. So look up at the sky, look down at the earth, look around at your brothers, and wonder at the kingdom in which we live.

Rev. Weston A. Stevens, as quoted in *Reader's Digest*, October 1971

To admit the unattainableness of the end in a finite world by a finite being is the very condition of our acquiring the conviction that there is an infinite world, and that we . . . are included in it.

Felix Adler, *The Reconstruction of the Spiritual Ideal*

Russia has abolished God, but so far God has been more tolerant.

John Cameron Swayze, as quoted in *Reader's Digest*, July 1959

Deification of accidents serves of course as rationalization for every people that is not master of its own destiny.

Hannah Arendt, *The Origins of Totalitarianism*

Going to church doesn't make you a Christian any more than going to a garage makes you an automobile.

W. A. "Billy" Sunday, as quoted in *Reader's Digest*, May 1955

Pharisaism does not mean wearing a cloak of righteousness; it means sincerely believing that one is more righteous than one really is.

Ralph Barton Perry, *Puritanism and Democracy*

By and with religion the living together of men was made not merely possible, but also desirable. Religion clothed and adorned the cold nakedness of primitive existence with shreds and patches of beauty. All that grace and color which transmutes mere existence into life—in a word, all art—may truly be said to have arisen out of religion. Sculpture had its origin in idol making, architecture in temple building, poetry in prayer writing, music in psalm singing, drama in legend telling and dancing in the seasonal worship of the gods.

Lewis Browne, as quoted in *Reader's Digest*, July 1959

This concern with the immortality of the soul of man, with its survival in a place no one has ever seen, is part ot the wasted energy of the mind.

Ben Hecht, *A Child of the Century*

Most people are akin to the old theologian who said that he was entirely open to conviction, but would like to see anybody who would convince him.

Ernest R. Trattner, as quoted in *Reader's Digest*, June 1938

An atheist is a man who believes himself an accident.

Francis Thompson, *Paganism Old and New*

Who rises from prayer a better man, his prayer is answered.

George Meredith, as quoted in *Reader's Digest*, September 1949

I believe that if we really want human brotherhood to spread and increase until it makes life safe and sane, we must also be certain that there is no one true faith or path by which it may spread.

Adlai E. Stevenson, *This I Believe*

I respect faith, but doubt is what gets you an education.

Wilson Mizner, as quoted in *Reader's Digest*, March 1943

It often happens that I wake at night and begin to think about a serious problem and decide that I must tell the Pope about it. Then I wake up completely and remember that I am the Pope.

Pope John XXIII, as quoted in Time, February 1, 1960

The best of all the preachers are the men who live their creeds.

Edgar A. Guest, Sermons We See

We will not believe that the final truth is not *in* us and that it must come *to* us in a singular, external event in history.

Emil Brunner, The Theology of Crisis

For God's sake, believe in something—even if it is only in the existence of the Devil.

Ramsay MacDonald, as quoted in Reader's Digest, May
1929

Only man, among living things, says prayers. Or needs to.

Peter Bowman, as quoted in *Reader's Digest*, January 1963

No absolute is going to make the lion lie down with the lamb; unless the lamb is inside.

D. H. Lawrence, *The Later D. H. Lawrence*

Religion is what the individual does with his own solitude . . . if you are never solitary you are never religious.

Dean Inge, as quoted in *Reader's Digest*, November 1935

Christianity has not been tried and found wanting; it has been found difficult and not tried.

G. K. Chesterton, as quoted in *Reader's Digest*, June 1941

Moral Living

The fundamental idea of good is thus, that it consists in preserving life, in favoring it, in wanting to bring it to its highest value, and evil consists in destroying life, doing it injury, hindering its development.

Albert Schweitzer, as quoted in the *Saturday Review*, June 13, 1953

One thing I know: the only ones among you who will be really happy are those who will have sought and found how to serve.

Albert Schweitzer, as quoted in *Reader's Digest*, April 1951

A man is ethical only when life, as such, is sacred to him, that of plants and animals as well as that of his fellowman, and when he devotes himself helpfully to all life that is in need of help.

Albert Schweitzer, *Out of My Life and Thoughts* 689

Rightness is a gift. It has nothing to do with experience, or knowledge, or the sort of liberal thinking which comes of contact with many men of many opinions, classes, nations, religions, manners, prejudices and fancy cuts of coats.

Henry I. Brock, Meddlers

We are all actors. We have to be; otherwise people in groups could not exist. Practically no social behavior is "natural." It is natural to rush and grab what we want like a baby or an animal. It is natural to growl and scream when our desire is thwarted, be it for a bone, a rattle or a bishopric. Socially acceptable behavior is a highly unnatural performance, attainable only after considerable training.

Sir Tyrone Guthrie, as quoted in Reader's Digest, March
1972

In our day, to say that a man, or more frequently a woman, lives morally amounts to saying that he or she is chaste. It is seldom intended to affirm that he or she is courageous, or temperate, or prudent, or just, in most of the affairs of life. These qualities seem to have disappeared from our description of the moral life. Morality has become largely a matter of obeying the rules in regard to sexual behavior.

Mortimer Adler, as quoted in Reader's Digest, June 1961

The effect which great beauty has upon us today is in a large measure that of exasperating our nerves, of making us restless and ultimately

690

miserable. For we are paying the penalty for dissociating the beautiful from the moral.

Lawrence Hyde, *The Prospects of Humanism*

The new-morality concept of letting your feelings be your guide would be workable if human beings were merely animals—if they had no conscience or soul. But man is more than animal and he debases himself when he lives on an animalistic level.

Mary Jane Chambers, as quoted in *Reader's Digest*, March 1973

Conscience is the perfect interpreter of life.

Karl Barth, *The Word of God and the Word of Man*

The saints are the sinners who keep on going.

Robert Louis Stevenson, as quoted in *Reader's Digest*, June 1961

If your morals make you dreary, depend on it they are wrong.

Robert Louis Stevenson, as quoted in *Reader's Digest*, May 1942

The civilized man has a moral obligation to be skeptical, to demand credentials of all statements that claim to be facts.

Bergen Evans, *The Natural History of Nonsense*

It was not the apple on the tree, but the pair on the ground, I believe, that caused the trouble in the garden.

M. D. O'Connor, as quoted in *Reader's Digest*, March 1961

Let each of us look for truth where it is most accessible and where it speaks the language he best understands.

L. P. Jacks, *Religious Perplexities*   691

I have a deep-seated bias against hate and intolerance. I have a bias against racial and religious bigotry. I have a bias against war, a bias for peace. I have a bias which leads me to believe that no problem of human relations is ever insoluble.

Ralph J. Bunche, as quoted in Reader's Digest, April 1952

In our world, we should feel nothing but plain, simple, humble reverence for the mystery of misfortune.

John Cowper Powys, The Meaning of Culture

Be unselfish. That is the first and final commandment for those who would be useful, and happy in their usefulness. If you think of yourself only, you cannot develop because you are choking the source of development, which is spiritual expansion through thought for others.

Charles W. Eliot, as quoted in Reader's Digest, November 1947

Sin has always been an ugly word, but it has been made so in a new sense over the last half-century. It has been made not only ugly but passé. People are no longer sinful, they are only immature or under-privileged or frightened or, more particularly, sick.

Phyllis McGinley, The Province of the Heart

Find out where you can render a service, and then render it. The rest is up to the Lord.

S. S. Kresge, as quoted by International News Service, July 31, 1957

The only tyrant I accept in this world is the "still small voice" within me.

Mahatma Gandhi, as quoted in Reader's Digest, March 1963

Both egoism and altruism are necessary to welfare. Both are moral motives. Right living is the right balance between them.

Herbert L. Samuel, Belief and Action

If people fought sin as hard as they do middle age, earth would be a moral paradise.

Hal Boyle, as quoted in *Reader's Digest*, April 1968

What is morality in any given time or place? It is what the majority then and there happen to like and immorality is what they dislike.

Alfred North Whitehead, as quoted in *Dialogues of Alfred North Whitehead*

Mencius enumerated the three "mature virtues" of his "great man" as "wisdom, compassion and courage." I should like to lop off one syllable and regard as the qualities of a great soul passion, wisdom and courage.

Lin Yutang, *The Importance of Living*

I do not believe in a fate that falls on men however they act; but I do believe in a fate that falls on them unless they act.

G. K. Chesterton, as quoted in *Reader's Digest*, February 1967

We think for a landlady considering a lodger it is important to know his income, but still more important to know his philosophy.

G. K. Chesterton, *Heretics*

The state of a man's soul has no necessary connection with the state of his bank account. For the prince in the penthouse can become saintly or satanic—and so can the pauper in the pig pen.

John E. Large, *The Small Needle of Doctor Large*

The tough idealist is nature's noblest creature.

Eli J. Schleifer, as quoted in *Reader's Digest*, December 1965

Between the extremes of despairing pessimism and the belief in imminent deliverance stand all those who see the grave evils and shortcomings of our time, who do not know how they are to be remedied and overcome, but who hope and work, who strive to understand and are ready to bear.

Johan Huizinga, *In the Shadow of Tomorrow*

Don't compromise yourself. You are all you've got.

Janis Joplin, as quoted in *Reader's Digest*, April 1973

To remain neutral, in a situation where the laws of the land virtually criticized God for having created men of color, was the sort of thing I could not, as a Christian, tolerate.

Albert John Luthuli, former Zulu chief, in an address on
receiving the Nobel Peace Prize, as quoted in *Time*,
December 22, 1961

The Lord is Almighty, but don't forget the devil. He can be pretty powerful. I know, because I used to be one of *his* best customers, too! I mean he lost a good bet when he lost me!

Ethel Waters, as quoted in *Reader's Digest*, December 1972

Eternal vigilance is the price, not only of liberty, but of a great many other things. It is the price of everything that is good. It is the price of one's own soul.

Woodrow Wilson, address in Washington, D.C., October
1914

The devil is easy to identify. He appears when you're terribly tired and makes a very reasonable request which you know you shouldn't grant.

Fiorello LaGuardia, as quoted in *Reader's Digest*, May
1962

Conscience is nothing but other people inside you.

694

Luigi Pirandello, *Each in His Own Way*

You know, folks, I've been around this crazy old world of ours and seen so many different hues and cries of people. Well, I've never been a non-believer, but the one thing I really do believe is that there ain't no one religion. That if the theologians would just live by the example of our Saviour, and stop trying to decide on His mode of arrival and departure from this earth, we'd all be a lot better off.

Will Rogers, as quoted in Reader's Digest, June 1972

So far there has been no known human society in which the distinction between right and wrong, and the obligation to do right, have been denied.

Arnold J. Toynbee, A Study of History

The soul is dyed with the color of its leisure thoughts.

Rev. William R. Inge, Recreation

Action is the normal completion of the act of will which begins as prayer. That action is not always external but it is always some kind of effective energy.

Rev. William R. Inge, Speculum Animae

Is any group of human beings organized for a particular purpose exempt from those laws of human behavior and accepted morality which are considered binding on each member as an individual? There is nothing I can find in Old or New Testament which says that the laws of human behavior are any less universal in application than the law of gravity, or that men can with impunity devise a successful means or form for avoiding obedience to either.

J. Irwin Miller, Reader's Digest, April 1972

Morals being mostly only social habits and circumstantial necessities.

George Bernard Shaw, preface to Major Barbara   695

The worst sin toward our fellow creatures is not to hate them but to be indifferent to them; that's the essence of inhumanity.

George Bernard Shaw, as quoted in *Reader's Digest*, March 1943

The golden rule is that there is no golden rule.

George Bernard Shaw, *Maxims for Revolutionists*

The greatness of a man can nearly always be measured by his willingness to be kind.

G. Young, as quoted in *Reader's Digest*, September 1967

I believe that every right implies a responsibility; every opportunity, an obligation; every possession, a duty.

John D. Rockefeller, Jr., speech in New York, July 8, 1941

Moral indignation is jealousy with a halo.

H. G. Wells, as quoted in *Reader's Digest*, February 1949

It is the besetting sin of the idealist to sacrifice reality for his ideals; to reject life because it fails to come up to his ideal; and this vice is just as prevalent among religious idealists as secular ones.

Christopher Dawson, *The Judgment of the Nations*

What is moral is what you feel good after and what is immoral is what you feel bad after.

Ernest Hemingway, *Death in the Afternoon*

Boredom is a vital problem for the moralist, since at least half the sins of mankind are caused by fear of it.

Bertrand Russell, *The Conquest of Happiness*

Once we assuage our conscience by call something a "necessary evil," it begins to look more and more necessary and less and less evil.

Sydney J. Harris, as quoted in Reader's Digest, October 1963

Men, who are driven by their nature as living creatures to act, are also compelled by their nature as free spirits to relate their action to, and bring them into conformity with, some total scheme of meaning.

Reinhold Niebuhr, Religion and the Modern World

Through faith man experiences the meaning of the world; through action he is to give to it a meaning.

Leo Baeck, The Essence of Judaism

The most painful wound in the world is a stab of conscience.

John Ellis Large, as quoted in Reader's Digest, May 1962

Be not content to know the Truth; rouse your heart to love it.

B. W. Martin, Self-Knowledge and Self-Discipline

Religion has always known that lasting guilt can be a deadly poison. Buried or repressed guilt feelings don't just fade away. They stay there, festering. Religion teaches that the only way to deal with a guilt problem is to regret the offense, resolve not to repeat it, make amends if possible, seek forgiveness of the person you have wronged—and then forget it.

Rev. Norman Vincent Peale, as quoted in Reader's Digest, June 1970

No matter what difficulty you're facing, the practice of creative patience is a proven road to solutions.

Rev. Norman Vincent Peale, as quoted in Reader's Digest, April 1972   697

We lie loudest when we lie to ourselves.

Eric Hoffer, The Passionate State of Mind.

Let unswerving integrity ever be your watchword.

Bernard Baruch, in an interview, August 20, 1955

The old view that the principles of right and wrong are immutable and eternal is no longer tenable. The moral world is as little exempt as the physical world from the law of ceaseless change, of perpetual flux.

Sir James Frazer, The Golden Bough

We are all inclined to judge ourselves by our ideals; others by their acts.

Harold Nicholson, as quoted in Reader's Digest, May 1936

It is a sin to believe evil of others, but it is seldom a mistake.

H. L. Mencken, Prejudices

Most of us live our lives the way we watch television. Even though the program isn't as good as we would like it to be, we are too lazy to get up and change it.

Pamela J. Bowlin, as quoted in Reader's Digest, August 1972

It is easy to dodge our responsibilities, but we cannot dodge the consequences of dodging our responsibilities.

Lord Josiah Charles Stamp, as quoted in the English Digest, December 1965

I have often thought what a heaven this world could be, if only we behaved to our fellow men as we do to our dogs.

Albert Guérard, as quoted in Reader's Digest, October 1948

That dull, leaden, soul-depressing sensation known as the sense of duty.

O. Henry, "No Story"

I believe that there is one story in the world and only one. Human beings are caught—in their lives, in their hungers and ambitions, in their avarice and cruelty, and in their kindness and generosity, too—in a net of good and evil. A man, after he has brushed off the dust and chips of his life, will have left only the hard, clean question: Was it good or was it evil? Have I done well, or ill?

John Steinbeck, as quoted in *Reader's Digest*, October 1960

O God, give us serenity to accept what cannot be changed; courage to change what should be changed; and wisdom to distinguish one from the other.

Reinhold Niebuhr, as quoted in *A New Treasury of Words to Live By*

Understanding is often a prelude to forgiveness, but they are not the same, and we often forgive what we cannot understand (seeing nothing else to do) and understand what we cannot pardon.

Mary McCarthy, as quoted in *Reader's Digest*, January 1972

Hope is a necessity for normal life, and the major weapon against the suicide impulse. Hope is not identical with optimism. Optimism is distant from reality; like pessimism, it emphasizes the importance of "I." Hope is modest, humble, selfless; it implies progress; it is an adventure, a going forward—a confident search for a rewarding life.

Dr. Karl Menninger, as quoted in *Quote*, June 19, 1960

Until you know that life is interesting—and find it so—you haven't found your soul. . . . What matters is that we do our best for the Kingdom of God. If we say, we're not doing too badly, we're sunk. But if we say, things are frightful and we'll do our best, we're okay.

Geoffrey Fisher, former Archbishop of Canterbury, as quoted in *Reader's Digest*, October 1955

699

There is no such thing as an evil in itself. Evil is not a thing, but a wrong function; it is the use of a good impulse at the wrong time, in the wrong place, towards a wrong end, that constitutes an evil function.

J. A. Hadfield, Psychology and Morals

I'm living in a house and I know I built it. I work in a workshop which was constructed by me. I speak a language which I developed. And I know I shape my life according to my desires by my own ability. I feel I am safe. I can defend myself. I am not afraid. This is the greatest happiness a man can feel—that he could be a partner with the Lord in creation. This is the real happiness of man—creative life, conquest of nature, and a great purpose.

David Ben-Gurion, former Israeli Prime Minister, on
NBC-TV, September 22, 1957

There is a basic morality to which we owe a supreme loyalty, a morality derived from our common humanity, a morality greatly affected by the conditions under which men work and live.

Norman Thomas, A Socialist's Faith

My philosophy is not that of stones that say you must leave behind your estates and monuments, but of the wind—which says you blow wherever you want and do whatever you want when you want to do it.

Jacques-Yves Cousteau, as quoted in Reader's Digest,
November 1973

My code of life and conduct is simply this: work hard; play to the allowable limit; disregard equally the good and bad opinion of others; never do a friend a dirty trick; . . . never grow indignant over anthing . . . live the moment to the utmost of its possibilities . . . and be satisfied with life always, but never with oneself.

George Jean Nathan, Testament of a Critic

A burning purpose attracts others who are drawn along with it and help fulfill it.

Margaret Bourke-White, *Portrait of Myself*

You must be true to yourself. Strong enough to be true to yourself. Brave enough to be strong enough to be true to yourself. Wise enough to be brave enough, to be strong enough to shape yourself from what you actually are.

Sylvia Ashton-Warner, Myself

Our Founding Fathers had many differences, but they agreed on one thing: Honor. Two hundred years later, we seem to have lost it.

We seldom learn about Honor in school, because it can't be measured in inches or ounces or dollars-and-cents. Honor has become a sucker's game: if Abraham Lincoln were to walk ten miles to return a library book today, he'd be laughed at and labeled a *loser*. Honor is for the naïve, the square, the fool—a childish relic left over from King Arthur and Don Quixote. But is it?

Allan Sherman, as quoted in Reader's Digest, May 1971

Goodness and nobility have an inherent power to attract, whereas self-seeking and evil inevitably repel.

Rev. Francis B. Sayre, as quoted in Reader's Digest, July
1948

Make no little plans; they have no magic to stir men's blood. . . . Make big plans, aim high in hope and work.

Daniel H. Burnham, as quoted in the Christian Science
Monitor, January 18, 1927

Man has wrested from nature the power to make the world a desert or to make the deserts bloom. There is no evil in the atom; only in men's souls.

Adlai E. Stevenson, speech at Hartford, Connecticut,
September 18, 1952

We help or hinder one another, summoning one another to be and grow, or to surrender and retreat, influencing one another as sun and frost "influence" a green field. . . . We live when we are true to

701

ourselves, authentic in our feelings, responsive to our convictions; we live when we love, when we are involved in the lives of others, when we are committed and concerned; we live when we build and create, hope, suffer and rejoice.

Treasure life in yourself and you give it to others; give it to others and it will come back to you. For life, like love, cannot thrive inside its own threshold but is renewed as it offers itself. Life grows as it is spent.

Ardis Whitman, as quoted in Reader's Digest, April 1972

WAR AND PEACE

War

War is both the product of an earlier corruption and a producer of new corruptions.

Lewis Mumford, The Conduct of Life

The quickest way of ending a war is to lose it.

George Orwell, Shooting an Elephant

To delight in war is a merit in the soldier, a dangerous quality in the captain, and a positive crime in the statesman.

George Santayana, The Life of Reason

To call war the soil of courage and virtue is like calling debauchery the soil of love.

George Santayana, The Life of Reason

War. There is no solution for it. There is never a conqueror. The winner generates such hatred that he is ultimately defeated.

Michel Simon, as quoted in The New York Times, March 17, 1968

The butter to be sacrificed because of the war always turns out to be the margarine of the poor.

James Tobin, speech before the Social Sciences Association, Washington, D.C., December 27, 1967

Once we thought a few hundred corpses would be enough
then we saw thousands were still too few
and today we can't even count all the dead
Everywhere you look.

Peter Weiss, Marat/Sade

A political war is one in which everyone shoots from the lip.

Raymond Moley, as quoted in Reader's Digest, September
1946

A guerilla war is an intimate affair, fought not merely with weapons but fought in the minds of the men who live in the villages and in the hills, fought by the spirit and policy of those who run the local government.

W. W. Rostow, as quoted in The Viet-Nam Reader

If nations had any sense, they would begin their wars by sending their oldest men into the trenches. They would not risk the lives of their young men except in the last extremity. In 1914, it was a dreadful thing to see regiments of lads singing "Tipperary" on their way to the slaughterhouse. But the spectacle of regiments of octogenarians hobbling to the front waving their walking sticks and piping up to the tune of "We'll never come back no more, we'll never come back no more"—wouldn't you cheer that enthusiastically? I should.

George Bernard Shaw, as quoted in Reader's Digest,
February 1938

In the past, wars were something that soldiers went off to fight in remote places; today war is something that the people who stay at home have to take with their supper.

Robin Day, as quoted in Encounter (London), May 1970

In time of war, the first casualty is truth.

706

Boake Carter, as quoted in Reader's Digest, January 1938

What difference does it make to the dead, the orphans and the homeless, whether the mad destruction is wrought under the name of totalitarianism or the holy name of liberty or democracy?

Mahatma Gandhi, *Non-Violence in Peace and War*

Morality is contraband in war.

Mahatma Gandhi, *Non-Violence in Peace and War*

War is an unmitigated evil. But it certainly does one good thing. It drives away fear and brings bravery to the surface.

Mahatma Gandhi, *Non-Violence in Peace and War*

During war we imprison the rights of man.

Jean Giraudoux, *Tiger at the Gates*

Everyone, when there's war in the air, learns to live with a new element: falsehood.

Jean Giraudoux, *Tiger at the Gates*

Death and sorrow will be the companions of our journey; hardship our garment; constancy and valor our only shield. We must be united, we must be undaunted, we must be inflexible.

Sir Winston Churchill, report on the war before the House of Commons, October 8, 1940

We will have no truce or parley with you [Hitler], or the grisly gang who work your wicked will. You do your worst—and we will do our best.

Sir Winston Churchill, speech, London County Council, July 14, 1941

Here is the answer which I will give to President Roosevelt. . . . Give us the tools, and we will finish the job.

Sir Winston Churchill, radio broadcast, February 9, 1941

Victory at all costs, victory in spite of all terror, victory however long and hard the road may be; for without victory there is no survival.

Sir Winston Churchill, first statement as Prime Minister before the House of Commons, May 13, 1940

I have watched this famous island descending incontinently, fecklessly, the stairway which leads to a dark gulf. It is a fine broad stairway at the beginning, but after a bit the carpet ends. A little farther on there are only flagstones, and a little farther on still these break beneath your feet.

Sir Winston Churchill, *While England Slept*

The German dictator, instead of snatching the victuals from the table, has been content to have them served to him course by course.

Sir Winston Churchill, speech on the Munich agreement before the House of Commons, October 5, 1938

There is no working middle course in wartime.

Sir Winston Churchill, speech, House of Commons, July 2, 1942

For each and for all, as for the Royal Navy, the watchword should be, "Carry on, and dread nought."

Sir Winston Churchill, speech on traffic at sea before the House of Commons, December 6, 1939

This is not the end. It is not even the beginning of the end. But it is, perhaps, the end of the beginning.

Sir Winston Churchill, speech reporting on the progress of the war, November 10, 1942

The disproportion between the quarrels of nations and the suffering which fighting out those quarrels involves; the poor and barren prizes which reward sublime endeavor on the battlefields; the fleeting triumphs of war; the long, slow rebuilding; the awful risks so hardily run; the doom missed by a hair's breadth, by the spin of a coin, by the accident of an accident—all this should make the prevention of another great war the main preoccupation of mankind.

Sir Winston Churchill, as quoted in *Reader's Digest,* June 1944

One cannot say how many invaders were blocked by the Great Wall. Except for brief periods, China was subject to continual barbarian invasions from the north, and was conquered repeatedly. Today, crumbling in many of its parts, the Wall is a useless, if still awesomely impressive, hulk. Like all barriers that nations raise to keep other people out, and their own people in, it failed.

Lowell Thomas, as quoted in *Reader's Digest,* October 1973

Older men declare war. But it is youth that must fight and die.

Herbert Hoover, speech, Republican National Convention, Chicago, June 27, 1944

War is nothing but a duel on a larger scale.

Karl Von Clausewitz, *War, Politics and Power*

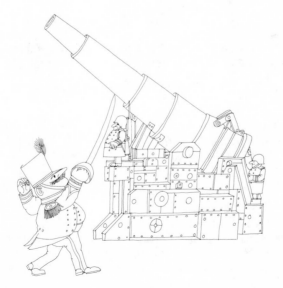

All the gods are dead except the god of war.

Eldridge Cleaver, *Soul on Ice*

The problem of modern civilization is to keep space satellites from turning into shooting stars.

Dan Bennett, as quoted in *Reader's Digest*, August 1960

In the final choice a soldier's pack is not so heavy a burden as a prisoner's chains.

Dwight D. Eisenhower, First Inaugural Address, January 20, 1953

Today the real test of power is not capacity to make war but capacity to prevent it.

Anne O'Hare McCormick, as quoted in *Reader's Digest*, September 1948

Every nation prepares, through its government, to equip itself with the power to hurl death upon its fellow-nations. No people seeks that power; it is governments that seek it.

Harold J. Laski, as quoted in *The Nation*, December 15, 1945

The only war I ever approved of was the Trojan War; it was fought over a woman, and the men knew what they were fighting for.

William Lyon Phelps, as quoted in *Reader's Digest*, May 1961

Computers now do most of the planning for our wars. It would seem only fair to let them do the fighting, too.

Bill Vaughan, *Half the Battle*

Military science: That remarkable art in which the lessons learned in winning one war can, if strictly followed, lose the next.

Bill Vaughan, as quoted in *Reader's Digest*, June 1955

We can lose the world, one parcel of real estate after another, while we wait for a shot that may never be fired.

Arthur W. Radford, as quoted in *Reader's Digest*, March
1962

The most shocking fact about war is that its victims and its instruments are individual human beings, and that these individual beings are condemned by the monstrous conventions of politics to murder or be murdered in quarrels not their own.

Aldous Huxley, *The Olive Tree*

The only monuments to this war will be the dead, the maimed, the despairing and the forlorn.

Letter to President Lyndon Johnson from the International
Voluntary Services Agency about the Vietnam war, as
quoted in *The New York Times*, September 20, 1967

War is the surgery of crime. Bad as it is in itself, it always implies that something worse has gone before.

Oliver Wendell Holmes, as quoted in *Reader's Digest*,
February 1942

Mankind must put an end to war or war will put an end to mankind.

John F. Kennedy, address, United Nations General
Assembly, September 25, 1961

[Man] is, perhaps no more prone to war than he used to be and no more inclined to commit other evil deeds. But a given amount of ill will or folly will go further than it used to.

Joseph Wood Krutch, *The Measure of Man*

After each war there is a little less democracy to save.

Brooks Atkinson, *Once Around the Sun*   711

Youth is the first victim of war; the first fruit of peace. It takes twenty years or more of peace to make a man; it takes only twenty seconds of war to destroy him.

King Baudouin I of Belgium, address to a joint session of
the U.S. Congress, May 12, 1959

The way to prevent war is to bend every energy toward preventing it, not to proceed by the dubious indirection of preparing for it.

Max Lerner, Actions and Passions

One believes in the coming of war if one does not sufficiently abhor it.

Thomas Mann, The Magic Mountain

War can only be abolished through war, and in order to get rid of the gun it is necessary to take up the gun.

Mao Tse-tung, Quotations from Chairman Mao

Despise the enemy strategically, but take him seriously tactically.

Mao Tse-tung, as quoted in Time, March 22, 1963

We used to wonder where war lived, what it was that made it so vile. And now we realize where it lives, that it is inside ourselves.

Albert Camus, Notebooks 1935–1942

Since time began there has never been a conscientious objector in the war between the sexes.

Dorothy Shay, as quoted in Reader's Digest, October 1960

A general and a bit of shooting makes you forget your troubles . . . it takes your mind off the cost of living.

Brendan Behan, The Hostage

We do not fight for the real but for shadows we make.
A flag is a piece of cloth and a word is a sound,
But we make them something neither cloth nor a sound,
Totems of love and hate, black sorcery-stones.

Stephen Vincent Benét, John Brown's Body

Battle: n. A method of untying with the teeth a political knot that would not yield to the tongue.

Ambrose Bierce, The Devil's Dictionary

War is like love, it always finds a way.

Bertolt Brecht, Mother Courage

To be vanquished and yet not surrender, that is victory.

Joseph Pilsudski, as quoted in Reader's Digest, January 1941

I have a rendezvous with Death
At some disputed barricade.

Alan Seeger, "I Have a Rendezvous with Death"

I have seen children starving. I have seen the agony of mothers and wives. I hate war.

Franklin D. Roosevelt, speech, August 14, 1936

Yesterday, December 7, 1941—a date which will live in infamy—the United States of America was suddenly and deliberately attacked by naval and air forces of the Empire of Japan.

Franklin D. Roosevelt, war message to Congress following Pearl Harbor, December 8, 1941

War is a contagion.

Franklin D. Roosevelt, speech, Chicago, October 5, 1937　713

It is the savor of bread broken with comrades that makes us accept the values of war.

Antoine de Saint-Exupéry, Wind, Sand, and Stars

In war nothing is impossible, provided you use audacity.

General George S. Patton, War As I Knew It

A pint of sweat will save a gallon of blood.

General George S. Patton, War As I Knew It

It cost 75 cents to kill a man in Caesar's time. The price rose to about $3000 during the Napoleonic wars; to $5000 in the American Civil War; and then to $21,000 per man in the World War. Estimates for the present war indicate that it may cost the warring countries not less than $50,000 for each man killed.

Senator Homer T. Bone, as quoted in Reader's Digest,
February 1943

Enemy advances, we retreat; enemy halts, we harass; enemy tires, we attack; enemy retreats, we pursue.

Mao Tse-tung, on his war strategy, as quoted in Dwight
Eisenhower's Mandate for Change

They shall not pass.

General Henri Philippe Pétain, at the battle of Verdun,
February 26, 1916

War alone brings up to its highest tension all human energy and puts the stamp of nobility upon the peoples who have the courage to face it.

Benito Mussolini, as quoted in Sawdust Caesar

To make a people great it is necessary to send them to battle even if you have to kick them in the pants.

Benito Mussolini, as quoted in *Ciano Diaries*, April 11,
1940

There are not fifty ways of fighting, there is only one: to be the conqueror.

André Malraux, *L'Espoir*

Well, let's take another look at the newspapers. "Youth for Peace March on Nation's Capitol." Now, I been reading a lot about that lately. Kids don't want us involved there in the Yangtze River and—what is it—the Sino-Japanese War? They been marching to keep from going to war . . . seems to me they must be getting just about the same training they'd be getting in the military.

But the joke's on the kids anyway. We ain't got no war . . . other side says we ain't got no war . . . the League of Nations says we ain't got no war. Course the guys getting shot at say it's the best imitation they've seen yet.

Will Rogers, as quoted in *Reader's Digest*, June 1972

War may make a fool of man, but it by no means degrades him; on the contrary, it tends to exalt him, and its net effects are much like those of motherhood on women.

H. L. Mencken, *Minority Report*

General George Catlett Marshall, one of the finest military leaders the United States ever produced, had a genuine hatred of war. During World War II, he saw to it that President Roosevelt got a casualty chart with the figures marked in *color*. Otherwise, said the general, "You get hardened to these things. You have to be very careful to keep them in the forefront of your mind."

Forest C. Pogue, as quoted in *Reader's Digest*, November
1973   715

A phrase has spread from civilians to soldiers and back again: "This is a phony war."

Edouard Daladier, speech to the French Chamber of Deputies, December 22, 1939

As the bomb fell over Hiroshima and exploded, we saw an entire city disappear. I wrote in my log the words: "My God, what have we done?"

Captain Robert Lewis, co-pilot of the plane that dropped the atomic bomb on Hiroshima, as quoted on NBC-TV, May 19, 1955

This war no longer bears the characteristics of former inter-European conflicts. It is one of those elemental conflicts which usher in a new millennium and which shake the world once in a thousand years.

Adolf Hitler, speech to the Reichstag, April 26, 1942

The field of combat was a long, narrow, green-baize covered table. The weapons were words.

Admiral Turner Joy, commenting on a year of truce talks in Korea, as quoted in news summaries of December 31, 1952

I don't know what will be the most important weapon in the next war, but I know what will be the most important weapon in the war after that—the bow and arrow.

Anonymous World War II remark quoted in Joseph Wood Krutch's The Measure of Man

There are enough targets to aim at without firing at each other.

Theodore Roosevelt, speech to the National Federation of Churches, 1902

Man, biologically considered, and whatever else he may be into the bargain, is the most formidable of all beasts of prey, and, indeed, the only one that preys systematically on his own species.

William James, Memories and Studies

There is no substitute for victory.

General Douglas MacArthur, at a news conference,
October 21, 1954

I've been a little bit disturbed that most everything that the church tried to give up at the Vatican Council has been picked up by the Defense Department—the idea of grace of office, a little hint of infallibility, a kind of revival of the idea of heresy and of holy wars, the Inquisition, a kind of index on publications.

Eugene J. McCarthy, address in Milwaukee,
June 22, 1968

Hitherto man had to live with the idea of his death as an individual; from now onward mankind will have to live with the idea of its death as a species.

Arthur Koestler, as quoted in *The New York Times Magazine*, March 20, 1960

. . . schools are out to teach patriotism; newspapers are out to stir up excitement; and politicians are out to get re-elected. None of the three, therefore, can do anything whatever toward saving the human race from reciprocal suicide.

Bertrand Russell, as quoted in the *Atlantic Monthly*,
January 1952

Air power is like poker. A second-best hand is like none at all—it will cost you dough and win you nothing.

General George Kenney, as quoted in *Reader's Digest*, July 1954

The Hawk and the Dove

The problem of deterrence is novel in the history of military policy. In the past, the military establishment was asked to prepare for war. Its 717 test was combat; its vindication, victory. In the nuclear age, victory has lost its traditional significance. The *outbreak* of war is increasingly considered the worst catastrophe. Henceforth, the adequacy of any military establishment will be tested by its ability to preserve the peace.

> Henry Kissinger, as quoted in *Reader's Digest*, January
> 1974

The grim fact is that we prepare for war like precocious giants and for peace like retarded pygmies.

> Lester Pearson, as quoted in news summaries of March 15,
> 1955

There is only one thing we Americans take more pride in than knocking down an enemy. That is setting him up again.

> Wes Lawrence, as quoted in *Reader's Digest*, May 1952

We think—although of course, now, we very seldom
Clearly think—
That the other side of War is Peace

> Edna St. Vincent Millay, "Make Bright the Arrows"

The good Lord had only ten.

> Georges Clemenceau, in reference to Woodrow Wilson's
> Fourteen Points

Upon this battle [of Britain] depends the survival of Christian civilization. Upon it depends our own British life, and the long continuity of our institutions and our Empire. The whole fury and might of the enemy must very soon be turned on us. Hitler knows that he will have to break us in this island or lose the war. If we can stand up to him, all Europe may be free and the life of the world may move forward into broad, sunlit uplands. But if we fail, then the whole world, including the United States, including all that we have known and cared for, will sink into the abyss of a new Dark Age made more sinister, perhaps more protracted, by the lights of perverted science. Let us therefore brace ourselves to our duties, and so bear ourselves that, if the British Empire and its Commonwealth last for a thousand years, men will still say: "This was their finest hour."

Sir Winston Churchill, speech before the House of
Commons, June 18, 1940

I cannot forecast to you the action of Russia. It is a riddle wrapped in a mystery inside an enigma.

Sir Winston Churchill, radio broadcast on the Nazi–Soviet
nonaggression pact, October 1, 1939

We have not journeyed all this way across the centuries, across the oceans, across the mountains, across the prairies, because we are made of sugar candy.

Sir Winston Churchill, speech to the Canadian Senate and
House of Commons, December 30, 1941

In War: Resolution. In Defeat: Defiance. In Victory: Magnanimity. In Peace: Good Will.

Sir Winston Churchill, *The Second World War: Moral of
the Work*, Vol. I, *The Gathering Storm*

There are those who considered that the atomic bomb should never have been used at all . . . that rather than throw the bomb we should have sacrificed a million American and a quarter of a million British lives in the desperate battles and massacres of an invasion of Japan. Future generations will judge this dire decision, and I believe, if they find themselves in a happier world from which war has been banished and where freedom reigns, they will not condemn those who struggled for their benefit amid the horrors and miseries of this grim and ferocious epoch.

The bomb brought peace, but man alone can keep that peace.

Winston Churchill, as quoted in *Reader's Digest*, October
1945

719

A sentry between the United States and Canada would be about as appropriate as a fire extinguisher on top of the Great Pyramid.

Vincent Massey, first Minister from Canada to the United States, as quoted in Reader's Digest, November 1927

Perhaps there is nothing in the whole of creation that knows the meaning of peace. For is not the soil restless by comparison with the unyielding rock?

Ugo Betti, The Fugitive

People want peace so much that governments had better get out of their way and let them have it.

Dwight D. Eisenhower, as quoted in Reader's Digest, May 1960

1. Open covenants of peace, openly arrived at.
2. Absolute freedom of navigation upon the seas.
5. A free, open-minded, and absolutely impartial adjustment of all colonial claims.
14. A general association of nations must be formed . . . for the purpose of affording mutual guarantees of political independence and territorial integrity to great and small states alike.

Woodrow Wilson, address to Congress (excerpts from the Fourteen Points), January 8, 1918

The world must be made safe for democracy.

Woodrow Wilson, address to Congress for a declaration of war, April 2, 1917

Armed neutrality is ineffectual enough at best.

Woodrow Wilson, address to Congress asking for a declaration of war, April 2, 1917

It must be a peace without victory. . . . Victory would mean peace
720 forced upon the loser, a victor's terms imposed upon the vanquished. It

would be accepted in humiliation, under duress, at an intolerable sacrifice, and would leave a sting, a resentment, a bitter memory upon which terms of peace would rest, not permanently, but only as upon quicksand. Only a peace between equals can last.

Woodrow Wilson, address to the U.S. Senate, January 22, 1917

The United States must be neutral in fact as well as in name. . . . We must be impartial in thought as well as in action.

Woodrow Wilson, message to the U.S. Senate, August 19, 1914

There is a price which is too great to pay for peace, and that price can be put in one word. One cannot pay the price of self-respect.

Woodrow Wilson, speech, February 1, 1916

About all the United States is getting to see of the dove of peace is the bill.

Alex Dreier, as quoted in *Reader's Digest,* July 1960

The fight for freedom is an endless battle. Its victories are never final, its defeats are never permanent. Each generation must defend its heritage, for each seeming conquest gives rise to new forces that will

721

attempt to substitute fresh means of oppression for the old. There can be no peace in a world of life and growth—every battle the fathers thought finished will have to be fought anew by their children if they wish to preserve and extend their freedom.

Philip Van Doren Stern, as quoted in *Reader's Digest*,
October 1942

Just as dueling was stopped by public opinion, so, when we are really resolved to stop war, wars will cease.

Lord Hugh Richard Heatcote Cecil, as quoted in *Reader's Digest*, October 1927

We must establish the respectability of peace and get rid of the false glamour surrounding war.

Rev. Frederick Norwood, as quoted in *Reader's Digest*,
February 1929

It is not atomic bombs that we need fear, but atomic men—the men who have built a civilization in which bombs might be used.

Bishop Fulton J. Sheen, *The Way to Happiness*

In a world that sits not on a powder keg but on a hydrogen bomb, one begins to suspect that the technician who rules our world is not the master magician he thinks he is but only a sorcerer's apprentice who does not know how to turn off what he has turned on—or even how to avoid blowing himself up.

Joseph Wood Krutch, as quoted in the *Saturday Review*,
June 8, 1963

Even better than disarmament as a step toward permanent peace might be some sort of international law that no new war could be started until all the books about the last one had been published.

722 Bill Vaughan, as quoted in *Reader's Digest*, April 1960

It wasn't too long ago that you could finance a pretty good war for what six months of peace costs today.

Bill Vaughan, as quoted in *Reader's Digest*, June 1958

Make love, not war.

Popular slogan of the Vietnam antiwar movement

Hell no, we won't go.

Popular slogan of the Vietnam antiwar movement

If the League of Nations succeeds, civilization is safe; if it fails, civilization is doomed. I have seen the horrors of war, and they have made me vow to concentrate my remaining energy to making it impossible for humanity to pass through the fire, the torment, the cruelty, the horror and the squalor of war.

David Lloyd George, as quoted in *Reader's Digest*, October 1922

And while I am talking to you mothers and fathers, I give you one more assurance. I have said this before, but I shall say it again and again and again: Your boys are not going to be sent into any foreign wars.

Franklin D. Roosevelt, campaign speech, Boston, October 30, 1940

Peace, like charity, begins at home.

Franklin D. Roosevelt, speech, August 14, 1936

We can destroy ourselves by cynicism and disillusion, just as effectively as by bombs.

Lord Kenneth Clark, as quoted in *Reader's Digest*, August 1971

Strengthen the international framework that we have already forged in war and we can have a great and lasting peace.

Walter Lippmann, as quoted in Reader's Digest, September 1944

War makes rattling good history; but Peace is poor reading.

Thomas Hardy, The Dynasts

Arms alone are not enough to keep the peace. It must be kept by men.

John F. Kennedy, State of the Union message, January 11, 1962

The mere absence of war is not peace.

John F. Kennedy, State of the Union message, January 14, 1963

A man may build himself a throne of bayonets, but he cannot sit on it.

Dean Inge, as quoted in Reader's Digest, June 1942

We tell ourselves that we have emerged from this war the most powerful nation in the world—the most powerful nation, perhaps, in all history. That is true, but not in the sense some of us believe it to be true.

The war has shown us that we have tremendous resources to make all the materials for war. It has shown us that we have skillful workers and managers and able generals, and a brave people capable of bearing arms. All these things we knew before.

The new thing—the thing we had not known—the thing we have learned now and should never forget, is this: that a society of self-governing men is more powerful, more enduring, more creative than any other kind of society, however disciplined, however centralized. We know now that the basic proposition of the worth and dignity of man is not a sentimental aspiration or a vain hope or a piece of rhetoric. It is the strongest, the most creative force now present in the world.

Now let us use that force and all our resources and all our skills in the great cause of a just and lasting peace.

Harry S. Truman, address on returning from Potsdam, as
quoted in *Reader's Digest,* November 1945

Since wars begin in the minds of men, it is in the minds of men that the defenses of peace must be constructed.

UNESCO constitution

Peace is a virtual, mute, sustained victory of potential powers against probable greeds.

Paul Valéry, *Réflections sur le monde actuel*

The only way to win a war is to prevent it.

George C. Marshall, as quoted in *Reader's Digest,* January
1948

If in this troubled world we can produce enough properly guided men, we won't need guided missiles.

General David M. Shoup, as quoted in *Reader's Digest,*
May 1963

When you have lived for a long time in close contact with the loss and grief which today pervade the world, any personal sorrow seems to be lost in the general sadness of humanity. For a long time all hearts have been heavy for every service man sacrificed in the war. There is only one way in which those of us who live can repay the dead who have given their utmost for the cause of liberty and justice. They died in the hope that, through their sacrifice, an enduring peace would be built and a more just world would emerge for humanity.

Eleanor Roosevelt, message on the death of her husband,
as quoted in *Reader's Digest,* June 1945   725

The last sound on the worthless earth will be two human beings trying to launch a homemade space-ship and already quarreling about where they are going next.

> William Faulkner, address to a UNESCO meeting, as quoted
> in *The New York Times*, October 3, 1959

We Jews have a secret weapon in our struggle with the Arabs—we have no place to go.

> Golda Meir, as quoted in *Reader's Digest*, July 1971

Mankind has grown strong in eternal struggles and it will only perish through eternal peace.

> Adolf Hitler, *Mein Kampf*

If we are to live together in peace, we must come to know each other better.

> Lyndon B. Johnson, State of the Union message, January 4,
> 1965

Let no one think that retreat from Vietnam would bring an end to conflict. The battle would be renewed in one country and then another. The central lesson of our time is that the appetite of aggression is never satisfied. To withdraw from one battlefield means only to prepare for the next. We must say in Southeast Asia—as we did in Europe—in the words of the Bible: "Hitherto shall thou come, but no further."

> Lyndon B. Johnson, speech at Johns Hopkins University,
> April 7, 1965

Anybody who feels at ease in the world today is a fool.

> Robert M. Hutchins, address on receiving the Sidney
> Hillman Award, New York, January 21, 1959

I believe that the vital condition of coexistence will have been fulfilled when the nations that now view each other with such suspicion can approach one another instead in something of the spirit of Pope John's words to Khrushchev's son-in-law: "They tell me you are an atheist. But you will not refuse an old man's blessing for your children."

Senator J. William Fulbright, as quoted in *Report,* Center for the Study of Democratic Institutions, August 1973

We are in Viet-Nam because our own security and the security of the entire free world demands that a firm line be drawn against the further advance of Communist imperialism—in Asia, in Africa, in Latin America, and in Europe.

We are in Viet-Nam because it is our national interest to assist every nation, large and small, which is seeking to defend itself against Communist subversion, infiltration, and aggression. There is nothing new about this policy; it is a policy, in fact, to which every administration has adhered since the proclamation of the Truman Doctrine.

Senator Thomas J. Dodd, as quoted in *The Viet-Nam Reader*

We need a world in which it is safe to be human.

Arthur J. Goldberg, as quoted in *Reader's Digest,* October 1968

What man most needs now is to apply his conversion skills to those things that are essential for his survival. He needs to convert facts into logic, free will into purpose, conscience into decision. He needs to convert historical experience into a design for a sane world.

Norman Cousins, *In Place of Folly*

. . . what the world needs today are two billion angry men who will make it clear to their national leaders that the earth does not exist for the purpose of being a stage for the total destruction of man.

Norman Cousins, as quoted in the *Saturday Review,* February 1, 1958

The world has achieved brilliance without conscience. Ours is a world of nuclear giants and ethical infants.

General Omar Bradley, address on Armistice Day, 1948

Eternal vigilance is the condition, not only of liberty, but of everything which as civilized men we hold dear.

August Heckscher, speech at Kenyon College, April 4, 1957

The human race has today the means for annihilating itself—either in a fit of complete lunacy, i.e., in a big war, by a brief fit of destruction, or by a careless handling of atomic technology, through a slow process of poisoning and of deterioration in its genetic structure.

Max Born, Nobel laureate in physics, as quoted in the
Bulletin of the Atomic Scientists, June 1957

The Military

The soldier, above all other people, prays for peace, for he must suffer and bear the deepest wounds and scars of war.

General Douglas MacArthur, address at West Point, May 12,
1962

Duty, honor, country: Those three hallowed words reverently dictate what you ought to be, what you can be, what you will be. They are your rallying point to build courage when courage seems to fail, to regain faith when there seems to be little cause for faith, to create hope when hope becomes forlorn.

General Douglas MacArthur, address at West Point, May 12,
1962

The world has turned over many times since I took the oath on the plain at West Point, and the hopes and dreams have long since vanished; but I still remember the refrain of one of the most popular barracks ballads of that day which proclaimed most proudly that old soldiers never die; they just fade away. And like the old soldier in that ballad, I now close my military career and just fade away, an old

728

soldier who tried to do his duty as God gave him the sight to see that duty.

General Douglas MacArthur, address to Congress after being relieved of duties by President Truman, April 19, 1951

The military caste did not originate as a party of patriots, but as a party of bandits.

H. L. Mencken, *Minority Report*

We want to get rid of the militarist not simply because he hurts and kills, but because he is an intolerable thick-voiced blockhead who stands hectoring and blustering in our way to achievement.

H. G. Wells, *The Outline of History*

There are so many women in the army now that when a soldier sees a uniform coming down the street he has to wait till it gets within twenty feet before he knows whether to salute or whistle.

Bob Hope, as quoted in *Reader's Digest*, September 1943   **729**

One tends to forget that conscription entails the suspension of any. number of basic human rights; conscription, for example, allows the government to exact involuntary servitude, and to curtail essential civil liberties.

William F. Buckley, Jr., *Quotations from Chairman Bill*

The sword is the axis of the world, and grandeur is indivisible.

Charles de Gaulle, *The Sword's Edge*

We would never do for infantrymen, but if you armor-plated some of us we might do as tanks.

J. B. Priestley, registering with other forty-seven-year-olds
for military service, as quoted in *Reader's Digest*, October
1942

To be a successful soldier you must know history. . . . What you must know is how man reacts. Weapons change but man who uses them changes not at all. To win battles you do not beat weapons—you beat the soul of the enemy man.

General George S. Patton, letter to his son, June 6, 1944

How different the new order would be if we could consult the veteran instead of the politician.

Henry Miller, *The Wisdom of the Heart*

It takes the wool of twenty sheep to clothe a U.S. soldier—and the hides of ten taxpayers.

Charles A. Knouse, as quoted in *Reader's Digest*,
December 1954

Militarism is the great preserver of our ideals of hardihood, and human life with no use of hardihood would be contemptible.

William James, *The Moral Equivalent of War*

It is characteristic of the military mentality that non-human factors ... are held essential, while the human being, his desires and thoughts—in short, the psychological factors—are considered as unimportant and secondary.

Albert Einstein, Out of my Later Life

It is essential to persuade the soldier that those he is being urged to massacre are bandits who do not deserve to live; before killing other good, decent fellows like himself, his gun would fall from his hands.

André Gide, as quoted in Journals, February 10, 1943

A ship is always referred to as a "she" because it costs so much to keep one in paint and powder.

Rear Admiral Chester W. Nimitz, as quoted in Reader's
Digest, April 1940

In Europe, the ubiquitous G.I., with his camera like a third eye, created wherever he went a little America, air-conditioned, steam-heated and neon-lighted. In American eyes, he was a liberator and defender of freedom. In other eyes he often seemed part of an American army of occupation. To all he symbolized Europe's enfeeblement, and the shift of world power and wealth across the Atlantic.

Malcolm Muggeridge, as quoted on BBC-TV, January 16,
1962

The Marine Corps is the Navy's police force and as long as I am President that is what it will remain. They have a propaganda machine that is almost equal to Stalin's. . . .

Harry S. Truman, as quoted in Time, September 18, 1950

I rose by sheer military ability to the rank of corporal.

Thornton Wilder, on his World War I army service, as
quoted in news summaries of January 12, 1953   731

HABITAT

Conservation

It is essential to realize that man and his environment, all life, all natural beauty, were created in wildness by a wisdom that preceded the human mind's impact on evolution. Compare these miraculous accomplishments with creations of the intellect that is so worshiped by modern man: our population explosion, our genetic deficiencies, our nuclear weapons, the breaking-down environment with which life now intertwines. How can one avoid the conclusion that, to date, the mind of man has selected for life a negative evolution?

Charles A. Lindbergh, as quoted in *Reader's Digest*, November 1971

We haven't too much time left to ensure that the government of the earth, by the earth, for the earth, shall not perish from the people.

C. P. Snow and Philip Snow, as quoted in *Reader's Digest*, March 1972

Do no dishonor to the earth lest you dishonor the spirit of man.

Henry Beston, *The Outermost House*

Our ideals, laws and customs should be based on the proposition that each generation in turn becomes the custodian rather than the absolute owner of our resources—and each generation has the obligation to pass this inheritance on to the future.

Alden Whitman, as quoted in *Reader's Digest*, September 1971

735

The most unhappy thing about conservation is that it is never permanent. Save a priceless woodland or an irreplaceable mountain today, and tomorrow it is threatened from another quarter. Man, our most ingenious predator, sometimes seems determined to destroy the precious treasures of his own environment.

Hal Borland, as quoted in *The New York Times Book Review*, February 25, 1964

Though a number of states and localities still assiduously seek new industry, many others are becoming flatly hostile to growth. "Welcome, stranger," the typical American attitude, is fast changing to that of "Stranger, get lost." . . .

In large part, ecology and pollution are the driving forces behind the new regional exclusionism. . . . [But] in a good many parts of the country, people are fighting simply to keep their elbowroom, to defend their turf against growing pressure from the teeming, troubled parts of the country. Don't crowd us, they're saying. Thus, even tourism, once considered the ideal "clean" industry, has run afoul of the no-trespassing mood in places.

Forbes essay, as quoted in *Reader's Digest*, September 1971

I recognize the right and duty of this generation to develop and use our natural resources, but I do not recognize the right to waste them, or to rob by wasteful use, the generations that come after us.

Theodore Roosevelt, speech on conservation, Washington, D.C., 1900

Remember, this *planet* is also disposable.

Paul Palmer, as quoted in *Reader's Digest*, May 1972

Industrialism is the systematic exploitation of wasting assets . . . progress is merely an acceleration in the rate of that exploitation. Such prosperity as we have known up to the present is the consequence of rapidly spending the planet's irreplaceable capital.

Aldous Huxley, *Themes and Variations*

We are choking on the fumes of our own exhaust. We are spending literally millions of unproductive hours examining the bumpers of our neighbors' cars, and we stand immobilized, waiting for trains that never arrive. The time has come to say "Enough!"

William Cahill, as quoted in Reader's Digest, January 1973

The automobile and the American public are locked in a life and death struggle. The car is robbing the American people of their land, air, minds and their very lives.

Kenneth P. Cantor, The Environment Handbook

The common justification of the environmentalists' technique of deliberate exaggeration is the claim that it is necessary to stir people up to get things done. But Aesop knew what happened to shepherd boys who cried wolf too often. People are easily anesthetized by overstatement, and there is a danger that the environmental movement will fall flat on its face when it is most needed, simply because it has pitched its tale too strongly.

John Maddox, as quoted in Reader's Digest, February 1973

Here then is the terrible dilemma. The lands we shred for needed minerals are the same lands that feed, clothe and shelter us. When we dig, we shrink our farms. There is no land to spare.

Harry M. Caudill, as quoted in Reader's Digest, December 1973

Perhaps our age will be known to the future historian as the age of the bulldozer and the exterminator; and in many parts of the country the building of a highway has about the same result upon vegetation and human structures as the passage of a tornado or the blast of an atom bomb.

Lewis Mumford, The Highway and the City

Is it only nostalgia that makes me and millions of other Americans hope for a more modest technology? I do not think so. The issue is nobler than survival. It is whether we can equip ourselves to live truly decent lives. If we are to meet this challenge, our inventors and technicians will have . . . to build us machines that use, not abuse, the unearned gifts of nature.

Steward L. Udall, as quoted in Reader's Digest, May 1971

America today stands poised on a pinnacle of wealth and power, yet we live in a land of vanishing beauty, of increasing ugliness, of shrinking open spaces, and of an over-all environment that is diminished daily by pollution and noise and blight. This, in brief, is the quiet conservation crisis of the 1960's.

Stewart L. Udall, The Quiet Crisis

Man will survive as a species for one reason: He can adapt to the destructive effects of our power-intoxicated technology and of our ungoverned population growth, to the dirt, pollution and noise of a New York or Tokyo. And that is the tragedy. It is not man the ecological crisis threatens to destroy but the quality of human life. . . .

Human beings can survive in the polluted cage of technological civilization, but in adapting to such conditions, we may sacrifice much of our humanness. . . . Man can improve the quality of his life, not by imposing himself on nature as a conqueror, but by participating in the continuous act of creation in which all living things are engaged. Otherwise, he may be doomed to survive as something less than human.

René Dubos, as quoted in Life, July 28, 1970

Shall we surrender to our surroundings or shall we make peace with nature and begin to make reparations for the damage we have done to our air, to our land, and to our water?

Richard M. Nixon, State of the Union message, January 22, 1970

Instead of worrying about deadlines for man's extinction, we should give immediate thought to a closer danger: adaptation. The horror is not only that we are killing the land and possibly ourselves, but that we calmly *adapt* to it, often without even a fight. . . . Because adaptation to pollution is made in small fits, we see each giving-in as only a minor loss. Why sweat the penny-ante stuff? But in the end we find our fortune—our environment—taken away.

Colman McCarthy, as quoted in *Reader's Digest,* August
1972

We read of industrial vapors, automobile and jet-plane exhausts that contaminate the air. We never hear of the millions of *human* exhausts expelling tobacco smoke.

Dr. Harry Swartz, as quoted in *Reader's Digest*, November
1972

Man is a complex being: he makes deserts bloom—and lakes die.

Gil Stern, as quoted in the Chicago *Sun-Times,* October 10,
1970

Man alone of all Creation has the power of rational thought; yet he has consistently used this power to advance his own short-term interests.   739

The crucial test is whether he will gain the wisdom to take the longer view; whether he will ever appreciate that ecological anarchy is likely to be as disastrous to the human race as to other life forms.

Noel M. Simon and Paul Geroudet, as quoted in *Reader's Digest*, April 1972

Man comes again and again into the position of being able to preserve his own life and life generally only at the cost of other life.

Albert Schweitzer, *Memories of Childhood and Youth*

The environmental crisis is the result of success—success in cutting down the mortality of infants (which has given us the population explosion), success in raising farm output sufficiently to prevent mass famine (which has given us contamination by pesticides and chemical fertilizers), success in getting people out of the noisome tenements of the 19th-century city and into the greenery and privacy of the single-family home in the suburbs (which has given us urban sprawl and traffic jams). The environmental crisis, in other words, is largely the result of doing too much of the right sort of thing.

Peter F. Drucker, as quoted in *Reader's Digest*, March 1972

Nature may be a thing of beauty and is indeed a symphony, but above and below and within its own immutable essences, its distances, its apparent quietness and changelessness, it is an active, purposeful, coordinated machine. Each part is dependent upon another, all are related to the movement of the whole. Parts of the earth, once living and productive, have died at the hand of man. Others are now dying. If we cause more to die, Nature will compensate for this in her own way, inexorably, as already she has begun to do.

Fairfield Osborn, *Our Plundered Planet*

We Americans had better wake up and realize that an ever larger population in our country is bound to make everyday living more difficult and undesirable. The idea that population growth guarantees a

740

better life—financially or otherwise—is a myth that only those who sell diapers, baby carriages and the like have any right to believe.

Fairfield Osborn, as quoted in Reader's Digest, October
1972

My special plea is that we do not, out of a combination of emotional zeal and ecological ignorance, hastily substitute environmental tragedy for existing environmental deterioration. Let's not replace known devils with insufficiently understood unknown devils.

Dr. Philip Handler, as quoted in Reader's Digest, January
1972

The environment is a complex, subtly balanced system, and it is this integrated whole which received the impact of all the separate insults inflicted by the pollutants. Never before in the history of this planet has its thin life-supporting surface been subjected to such diverse, novel, and potent agents. I believe the cumulative effects of these pollutants, their interactions and amplifications, can be fatal to the complex fabric of the biosphere.

Dr. Barry Commoner, Science and Survival

When you fully understand the situation it is worse than you think.

Dr. Barry Commoner, TV comment during Earth Week,
1970

Western man labors under the infinitely satisfying and destructive delusion that there's something special about him that makes him independent of his environment. What he must come to realize is that—contrary to all the teachings about his "divine right" and his unique place in the cosmos—he is just a parasite. Man is totally dependent on his environment.

Ian L. MacHarg, as quoted in Reader's Digest,
August 1970   741

Many tiger experts feel that man himself, by killing off the tiger's natural prey and destroying its normal habitats, is chiefly responsible for the creation of man-eating tigers.

Leland Stowe, as quoted in *Outdoor World,* July–August
1970

In one respect every natural area has a common uniqueness—it takes everyone forever to preserve it, but one person and one time to destroy it.

E. J. Koestner, as quoted in *Reader's Digest,* August 1970

I think that I shall never see
A billboard lovely as a tree.
Perhaps, unless the billboards fall,
I'll never see a tree at all.

Ogden Nash, as quoted in *Reader's Digest,* September 1937

The reversal of birth figures in the United States may loom even larger in history books than the turnabout in our China policy.

Max Lerner, as quoted in *Reader's Digest,* June 1972

Only a few human beings should grow to the square mile. They commonly are planted too close.

William T. Davis, as quoted in *North with the Spring*

One of the best things people could do for their descendants would be to sharply limit the number of them.

Olin Miller, as quoted in *Reader's Digest,* November 1971

America's energy binge is over.

Hollis M. Dole, Assistant Secretary of the Interior for
Mineral Resources, as quoted in *Reader's Digest,* January

1973

Conservation in America is rather a force than a political movement.

William F. Buckley, Jr., *Quotations from Chairman Bill*

Those who warn of a population explosion picture a world of too many people and not enough food—sort of like the average cocktail party.

Bill Vaughan, as quoted in *Reader's Digest*, September 1967

Since man is an animal savage from birth,
We'll never improve our condition
Until we have posted a warning on Earth:
"NO HUNTIN', NO SHOOTIN', NO FISSION!"

Norman R. Jaffray, as quoted in *Reader's Digest*, May 1949

There is an old saying here that a man must do three things during life: plant trees, write books and have sons. I wish they would plant more trees and write more books.

Luis Muñoz Marin, former governor of Puerto Rico, as quoted in *Time*, June 23, 1958

Whenever I hear people discussing birth control, I always remember that I was the fifth.

Clarence Darrow, as quoted in *Reader's Digest*, June 1934

A society which practices death control must at the same time practice birth control.

John Rock, *The Time Has Come*

Our task is not to create an idyllic environment peopled by the poor. Our task is to create a decent environment peopled by the proud.

Robert S. McNamara, as quoted in *Reader's Digest*, March 1973

743

As the sales curve of automobiles goes up, the curve of births goes down. It costs no more to rear a child than to maintain an automobile, but the preference of the American people is clear.

Professor Oliver E. Baker, predicting a decline in the birth
rate during the postwar industrial boom, as quoted in
Reader's Digest, January 1947

Nature

In a lightning flash, coming in the deep hush after thunder, lies terror; such unthinkably swift and formless motion, instantaneously bridging the abyss of space without a sound, is like some fearful portent.

Mary Webb, The Spring of Joy

Are our senses undeveloped, since the dramas of dawn and moonrise have for us no chorus; the wind steals by invisible; the stars go through their stately ritual with silent tread, weaving their radiant dances to no murmur of music?

Mary Webb, The Spring of Joy

Color, like fragrance, is intimately connected with light; and between the different rays of the spectrum and the color cells of plants there is a strange telepathy. These processes, so little explored, seem in their deep secrecy and earthly spirituality more marvelous than the most radiant visions of the mystics.

Mary Webb, The Spring of Joy

Nature sets her dances to every rhythm, from slow undulations to the swift, dangerous rushes that bring wild exhilaration. . . . In the same way a poised mind sweeps out to all new ideas, but is not torn from its place because of its roots.

Mary Webb, The Spring of Joy

Science cannot solve the ultimate mystery of nature. And that is because, in the last analysis, we ourselves are part of nature and therefore part of the mystery that we are trying to solve.

Max Planck, as quoted in Reader's Digest, December 1962

It is simply that in all life on earth as in all good agriculture there are no short-cuts that by-pass Nature and the nature of man himself and animals, trees, rocks and streams. Every attempt at a formula, a short-cut, a panacea, always ends in negation and destruction.

Louis Bromfield, Malabar Farm

Spring, once announced by the first bare toes in the schoolroom, is now heralded by the first bare midriff in the supermarket.

Bill Vaughan, as quoted in Reader's Digest, May 1961

The man around the corner keeps experimenting with new flowers every year, and now has quite an extensive list of things he can't grow.

Bill Vaughan, as quoted in Reader's Digest, August 1961

Nothing in nature is more beautiful than one snowflake, but unfortunately they seldom come that way.

Bill Vaughan, as quoted in Reader's Digest, December 1961

Among famous traitors of history one might mention the weather.

Ilka Chase, The Varied Airs of Spring

The Weather Bureau has changed its name to Environmental Science Services Administration—and we still get six inches of snow when the forecast says partly cloudly.

Jack Wilson, as quoted in Reader's Digest, February 1967

To the laborer in the sweat of his labor, the raw stuff on his anvil is an adversary to be conquered. So was wilderness an adversary to the   745 pioneer. But to the laborer in repose, able for the moment to cast a philosophical eye on his world, that same raw stuff is something to be loved and cherished, because it gives definition and meaning to his life.

Aldo Leopold, *A Sand County Almanac*

Lawn: A place where hardy grasses, that flourish in empty lots and grow between the cracks in sidewalks, wither and die from the householder's tender care.

Burton Hillis, as quoted in *Reader's Digest*, June 1955

I can never lose the feeling, when I spread plant food on the lawn each spring, that somehow I am working against myself.

Burton Hillis, as quoted in *Reader's Digest*, April 1953

Rachel Carson, author of *Silent Spring*, watched a fall migration of monarch butterflies with a friend in Maine one day toward the end of her life, when she was aware that she had cancer and would probably not return to that spot. That evening she wrote: "It occurred to me this afternoon, remembering, that it had been a happy spectacle, that we had felt no sadness when we spoke of the fact that there would be no return. And rightly—for when any living thing has come to the end of its cycle we accept that end as natural. For the monarch butterfly, that cycle is measured in a known span of months. For ourselves, the measure is something else, the span of which we cannot know. But the thought is the same: when that intangible cycle has run its course, it is a natural and not unhappy thing that a life comes to its end."

Paul Brooks, *House of Life: Rachel Carson at Work*

I have no patience with people who say they love nature and go out to look at a field on Sunday afternoon. Our families, the way we live with our fellowmen, are part of nature, too.

Thornton Wilder, as quoted in *The New York Times Magazine*, April 15, 1962

What would you not pay to see the moon rise, if Nature had not improvidently made it a free entertainment!

Richard Le Gallienne, as quoted in *Reader's Digest,*
November 1948

Hills may exalt the spirit; rivers cleanse and soothe it. Seas and forests awe men by their vastness; rivers are informal and companionable. One part of a woodland is pretty much like the rest of it; dozens of mountains resemble each other; no single acre of ocean, lake or pond differs perceptibly from the remainder. No one has ever seen two rivers that were identical for a furlong. No one ever will.

Frederic F. Van de Water, *In Defense of Worms*

... rivers are the most vital of all inanimate things and, in their substance, not too remotely the kin of all living beings. Rivers have voice and strength and mobility. They lack only the personal essence of sentient things, and of this deficiency neither the ancients nor I ever have been quite certain. Rivers are quick and bright and volatile, gay in their rapids, soberly contemplative in their shining, slow reaches, forever moving on yet everlastingly here.

Frederic F. Van de Water, *In Defense of Worms*

It's time we stopped turning up our noses at the nation's garbage dumps and started appreciating them for what they really are—the municipal mines, forests, oil wells and energy sources of the future!

Max Spendlove, as quoted in *Reader's Digest,* March 1972

Like life she [Nature] strips men of their pretentions and vanities, exposes the weakness of the weak and the folly of the fool.

W. Macneile Dixon, *The Human Situation*

Oh, leaf, that yesterday was green
But now is blushing rosy red,

747

What happened to you overnight?
Why not to me, instead?

Doris Black, as quoted in *Reader's Digest*, November 1940

What a man needs in gardening is a cast-iron back, with a hinge in it.

Charles Dudley Warner, as quoted in *Reader's Digest*, July 1947

We have no cause to regret the youth of the world, if indeed the world were ever young. When we imagine in our cities that the wind no longer calls us to such things, it is only our reading that blinds us, and the picture of satiety which our reading breeds is wholly false. Any man today may go out and take his pleasure with the wind upon the high seas. He will also make his landfalls today, or in a thousand years, and the sight is always the same, and the appetite for such discoveries is wholly satisfied, even though he be only sailing, as I have sailed, over seas that he has known from childhood, and come upon an island far away, mapped and well known, and visited for the hundredth time.

Hilaire Belloc, *First and Last*

The child of civilization, remote from wild nature and her ways, is more susceptible to her grandeur than is her untutored son who has looked at her and lived close to her from childhood up, on terms of prosaic familiarity.

Thomas Mann, *The Magic Mountain*

Trees will come down to the shore of a lake and grow there, and sometimes they will lean out over the water. It was in that way that I first discovered that trees are vain. I saw them standing by the hour looking at themselves. A lake is the vanity case of a tree.

Charles E. Jefferson, as quoted in *Reader's Digest*, January 1935

A river has no politics.

David E. Lilienthal, during his directorship of the Tennesse Valley Authority

Wilderness is a bench mark, a touchstone. In wilderness we can see where we have come from, where we are going, how far we've gone. In wilderness is the only unsullied earth sample of the forces generally at work in the universe.

Kenneth Bower, The Environmental Handbook

The mastery of nature is vainly believed to be an adequate substitute for self-mastery.

Reinhold Niebuhr, as quoted in Christian Century, April 22,
1926

God made the grass, the air and the rain; and the grass, the air and the rain made the Irish, and the Irish turned the grass, the air and the rain back into God.

Sean O'Faolain, as quoted in Holiday, June 1958

The sort of man who likes to spend his time watching a cage of monkeys chase one another, or a lion gnaw its tail, or a lizard catch flies, is precisely the sort of man whose mental weakness should be combatted at the public expense, and not fostered.

H. L. Mencken, as quoted in the New York Evening Mail,
February 2, 1918

All they [zoos] actually offer to the public in return for the taxes spent upon them is a form of idle and witless amusement, compared to which a visit to a penitentiary, or even to a State Legislature in session, is informing, stimulating and ennobling.

H. L. Mencken, as quoted in the New York Evening Mail,
February 2, 1918

Animals reflect their surroundings: their faces grow refined or stupid according to the people with whom they live. A domestic animal will become good or bad, frank or sly, sensitive or stupid, not only   749 according to what its master teaches it, but according to what its master is.

Romain Rolland, as quoted in Reader's Digest, January 1941

Every lover of beauty becomes over-soon aware of that tragic shadow, the destruction of beauty; the destruction of joy which is in itself a kind of beauty—the fallen tree, the fire-scarred mountain-side, the disease-stricken body.

Ella Young, Flowering Dusk

April prepares her green traffic light, and the world thinks *Go!*

Christopher Morley, John Mistletoe

The birds have a harder life than we do except for the robber birds and the heavy strong ones. Why did they make birds so delicate and fine as those sea swallows when the ocean can be so cruel? She is kind and very beautiful. But she can be so cruel and it comes so suddenly and such birds that fly, dipping and hunting, with their small sad voices are made too delicately for the sea.

Ernest Hemingway, The Old Man and the Sea

Do you know the sin it would be to ruffle the arrangement of feathers on a hawk's neck if they could never be replaced as they were?

Ernest Hemingway, as quoted in Reader's Digest, January 1935

No matter how often
I level this weed,
It returns after rain
As if there is no need
To remind men who sever
Life's delicate string
That destruction is never
A permanent thing.

Mark Soifer, as quoted in Reader's Digest, June 1961

Many observers have commented on what seems to be the fact that fear plays a much smaller part than we should think it must in the life of an animal who lives dangerously. Terror he can know, and perhaps he knows it frequently. But it seems to last only a little longer than the immediate danger it helps him to avoid, instead of lingering, as in the human being it does, until it becomes a burden and a threat. The frightened bird resumes his song as soon as danger has passed, and so does the frightened rabbit his game. It is almost as though they knew that "Cowards die many times before their deaths; the valiant never taste of death but once."

Joseph Wood Krutch, The Twelve Seasons

I wish a month like April were more aware of what we expect from it.

Beryl Pfizer, as quoted in Reader's Digest, April 1972

The ant is knowing and wise; but he doesn't know enough to take a vacation. The worshiper of energy is too physically energetic to see that he cannot explore certain higher fields until he is still.

Clarence Day, This Simian World

If we had been as strong as the elephant, we might have been kinder. When great power comes naturally to people, it is used more urbanely. We use it as parvenus do, because that's what we are. The elephant, being born to it, is easy-going, confident, tolerant. He would have been a more humane king.

Clarence Day, This Simian World

That wonderful world of high mountains, dazzling in their rock and ice, acts as a catalyst. It suggests the infinite but it is not the infinite. The heights only give us what we ourselves bring to them. Climbing is a means of self-expression.

Lucien Devies, preface to Annapurna

With the warmth of embers in my face, a black night around me and a star-pierced sky above, I feel transposed to an ancestor in a primitive   751 age. This, I think, is my normal way of life; anything else has been a dream.

Charles A. Lindbergh, on campfires, as quoted in *Reader's Digest*, July 1972

When all has been said, the adventure of the sun is the great natural drama by which we live, and not to have joy in it and awe of it, not to share in it, is to close a dull door on nature's sustaining and poetic spirit.

Henry Beston, *The Outermost House*

When the great earth, abandoning the day, rolls up the deeps of the heavens and the universe, a new door opens for the human spirit, and there are few so clownish that some awareness of the mystery of being does not touch them as they gaze.

Henry Beston, *The Outermost House*

The sea has many voices. Listen to the surf, really lend it to your ears, and you will hear in it a world of sound; hollow boomings and heavy roarings, great watery tumblings and tramplings, long hissing seethes, sharp, rifle-shot reports, splashes, whispers, the grinding undertone of the half-heard talk of people in the sea.

Henry Beston, *The Outermost House*

The three great elemental sounds in nature are the sound of rain, the sound of wind in a primeval wood, and the sound of outer ocean on a beach. I have heard them all, and of the three elemental voices, that of ocean is the most awesome, beautiful and varied.

Henry Beston, *The Outermost House*

Those manuals of make-believe, the seed catalogues, have one weakness: they don't tell me how to sustain my April gardening enthusiasm through the heat of late July.

Oren Arnold, as quoted in *Reader's Digest*, July 1953

Man is constantly needing to be reminded of the rest of animate nature and the earth from which he in common came. Smile if you like, but something deep in him is answered when he watches the cows slowly crossing the field, coming up from pasture, imperturbable, and, if you insist, dumb. A little of his fretfulness, at least, slips away.

J. Donald Adams, *Literary Frontiers*

It's spring! Again life focuses
On grasses and on crocuses,
On rows of deep-blue irises
And one or two new viruses.

Philene Hammer, as quoted in *Reader's Digest,* April 1956

Every man reaps what he sows—except the amateur gardener.

Cholly Knickerbocker, as quoted in *Reader's Digest,*
September 1960

The oldest voice in the world is the wind. When it murmurs in summer's leaves, it seems an idle trifler. When in the night it goes wandering by, setting the old house faintly to groaning, it sounds like a pilgrim that has lost the road. When you see it fitfully turning the blades of a mill lazily to draw water, you think of it as an unreliable servant of man. But in truth it is one of our masters, obedient only to the lord sun and the whirling of the great globe itself.

Donald Culross Peattie, *A Cup of Sky*

The summer world is the insect world. Like it or not, that is how it is. There are few insects that ever find the day too hot.

Donald Culross Peattie, *An Almanac for Moderns*

The earth holds a silver treasure, cupped between ocean bed and tenting sky. Forever the heavens spend it, in the showers that refresh our temperate lands, the torrents that sluice the tropics. Every suckling root absorbs it, the very soil drains it down; the rivers run unceasing to the sea, the mountains yield it endlessly, in bubbling spring and far last   753 slim cascade that flings away forever its bright similitude of life. Yet none is lost; in vast convection our water is returned, for soil to sky, and sky to soil, and back again, to fall as pure as blessing. There was never less; there could never be more. A mighty mercy on which life depends, for all its glittering shifts water is constant.

Donald Culross Peattie, A Cup of Sky

Now that sweet unwritten moment when all things are possible has just begun. The little tree has not quite leafed. The mate is not yet chosen. To the rambler in the woods all that he can find in heavy books will be of less worth than what he learns by sitting on a log and listening to the first quiver of sound from the marshes, or by prodding with a stick at the soil and turning out the sluggish beetles. It is good enough just to sit still and hold your palm out to the sunlight, like a leaf, and turn it over slowly, wondering: What is light? What is flesh? What is it to be alive?

Donald Culross Peattie, An Almanac for Moderns

Man feels himself an infinity above those creatures who stand, zoologically, only one step below him, but every human being looks up to the birds. They suit the fancy of us all. What they feel they can voice, as we try to; they court and nest, they battle with the elements, they are torn by two opposing impulses, a love of home and a passion for far places. Only with birds do we share so much emotion.

Donald Culross Peattie, as quoted in Reader's Digest, April
1937

Winter is fury—and white silence. It can freeze a blade of grass with a glance. It's a lake with an opaque monocle, a garbage can with an ermine hat. Winter is the jealous season; it demands two distinct years for a single appearance. Mercilessly, it strips the orange and russet from autumn and looks defiantly ahead for spring to step onstage.

Jim Bishop, as quoted in Reader's Digest, January 1970

Everybody should own a tree at this time of year. Or a valley full of trees, or a whole hillside. Not legally, not in the formal way . . . but in

754

the way that one comes to own a tree by seeing it at the turn of the road, or down the street, or in a park, and watching it day after day, and seeing color come to its leaves. That way it is your tree whenever you choose to pass that way, and neither fence nor title can take it from you. And it will be your tree as long as you remember.

Hal Borland, as quoted in *Reader's Digest,* October 1972

May I still, when I can count my hairs, be given grace and fortitude in the chill spring weather to say when first I see the wild spiral of the swallow that winter is over and done.

Donald Culross Peattie, *An Almanac for Moderns*

You can't be suspicious of a tree, or accuse a bird or a squirrel of subversion or challenge the ideology of a violet.

Hal Borland, *Sundial of the Seasons*

How little do we know of the business of the earth, not to speak of the universe; of time, not to speak of eternity. It was not by taking thought 755 that man survived the mastodon. The acts and thoughts that will save the race, that will profit this commonwealth of things that live in the sun, the air, the earth, the sea, now and through all time, are not known and never will be known. The rumor of much toil and scheming and triumph may never teach the stars, and what we value not at all, are not conscious of, may break the surface of eternity with endless ripples of good. We know not by what we survive.

Edward Thomas, *The South Country*

The splendor of furrowed fields is this: that like all grave things they are made straight, and therefore they bend. In everything that bows gracefully there must be an effort at stiffness. Bows are beautiful when they bend only because they try to remain rigid, and sword-blades can curl like silver ribbons only because they are certain to spring straight again. But the same is true of every tough curve of the tree trunk, of every strong-backed bend of the bough; there is hardly any such thing in Nature as a mere droop of weakness. Rigidity yielding a little, like justice swayed by mercy, is the whole beauty of the earth.

G. K. Chesterton, *Alarms and Discussions*

I am free to admit that I am the kind of man who would never notice an oriole building a nest unless it came and built it in my hat in the hat room of the club.

Stephen Leacock, as quoted in *Reader's Digest*, May 1965

Spring being a tough act to follow, God created June.

Al Bernstein, as quoted in *Reader's Digest*, May 1968

. . . the waves, as they hasten toward the pebbled shore, remind me, as they have reminded others, of our own moments hastening to their end.

Logan Pearsall Smith, *All Trivia*

Roses are red, violets are blue;
But they don't get around like the
    dandelions do.

Slim Acres, as quoted in *Reader's Digest*, August 1946

I think one reason we admire cats, those of us who do, is their proficiency in one-upmanship. They always seem to come out on top, no matter what they are doing—or pretend they do. Rarely do you see a cat discomfited. They have no conscience, and they never regret. Maybe we secretly envy them.

Barbara Webster, Creatures and Contentments

One can live in the center of the world, in a complicated web of social relations, and remain as invisible as a grasshopper in a spring meadow.

Van Wyck Brooks, Notes from a Journal

Man has been so noisy about the way he has "conquered nature," and Nature has been so silent in her persistent influence over man, that the geographic factor in the equation of human development has been overlooked.

Ellen Semple, Influences of Geographic Environment on the Basis of Ratzel's System of Anthropo-geography

To enter the Sahara is like passing into a vast chamber that earth has surreptitiously held in trust. Instinctively one moves as in a cathedral—with respect and constant awe. The Tuareg, the tall, blue-robed nomads who for thousands of years have made the free sands their home, believe that from the beginning Allah intended the desert to be earth's finest hall, into whose peace he could retire from the pressures of the world. Their reasoning is instantly clear, for even at high noon the Sahara is quieter than any midnight elsewhere.

Imagine then the thralldom of Saharan midnight itself! Under tightly packed stars winking in the glittering sky, no one remains untouched by the utter silence. It seems as varied as sound itself: a composition of subtly changing levels, one moment close, then spacious, sometimes so intense that it seems to hum and vibrate. I found myself miraculously refreshed, as though purified by the mysterious energy of that powerful, palpitating soundlessness.

Noel Mostert, as quoted in Reader's Digest, November
1972

In winter, the male cardinal will not permit the female on a feeder with him. Then suddenly, in early March, they appear together, heralding 757 the rites of spring. And when, a few weeks later, he places a seed in her bill, the wildflowers are not far away.

Jean George, as quoted in Reader's Digest, March 1973

The sea is not always blue. Sometimes it is stained with a dull red that shrimp fishermen compare with tobacco juice and tourists with tomato soup. In the evening a much more dazzling color may emerge. A wave that feels the bottom, crests, and topples will release a phosphorescent surf of pale green or red hue. This glowing, advancing surf can be stunning, like lambent lightning across the sky or a rainbow on the horizon. Once, while viewing this radiance from a Malibu beach, I happened to glance back over my shoulder and noticed that my footprints also glowed for an instant in the wet sand.

Wesley Marx, The Frail Ocean

First, it's a shy gleam of crocus against melting March snow, then a yellow blaze of daffodil. The heart begins to sing, the step to lighten, because spring is just up ahead. But when dogwood white and dogwood pink burst into radiant chorus along the greening hillsides— then, then at last, you know that spring is really here, and here to stay.

Robert O'Brien, as quoted in Reader's Digest, May 1973

I never saw a wild thing sorry for itself.

D. H. Lawrence, Self-Pity

Repetition is the only form of permanence that nature can achieve.

George Santayana, as quoted in Reader's Digest, April 1972

Winter's first fall of snow is not only an event; it is a magical event. You go to bed in one world and wake up in another, and if this is not enchantment, then where is it to be found? The very stealth, the eerie quietness, of the thing makes it more magical. If all the snow fell in one shattering crash, awakening us in the night, the event would be robbed of its wonder. But it flutters down, soundlessly, hour after hour while we are asleep. Outside, a vast transformation is taking place, just as if myriad elves and brownies were at work, and we turn and yawn and stretch and know nothing about it. And then, what an extraordinary change it is! It is as if the house you are in had been dropped down in another continent. Even the inside seems different, every room appearing smaller and cozier. . . .

Nobody can resist the windows. It is not the snow itself, the sight of the blanketed world, that is so enchanting, but the first coming of the snow, that sudden and silent change, a magical event.

J. B. Priestley, *Essays of Five Decades*

It is enough for me to contemplate the mystery of conscious life perpetuating itself through all eternity, which we dimly perceive, and to try humbly to comprehend even an infinitesimal part of the intelligence manifested in nature.

Albert Einstein, as quoted in *Living Philosophies*

Nature thrives on patience; man on impatience.

Paul Boese, as quoted in *Reader's Digest*, September 1968

It increases our weight, diminishes our height, lengthens our lives. It prevents us from whirling off the surface of a globe which spins, at the equator, at 1000 miles an hour. It holds air to the earth, enabling us to breathe. It draws rain from the clouds, then pulls the water down through streams, lakes and rivers to the ocean in a never-ending cycle on which all living things depend. Yet it can also cause death and destruction, bringing disabled airplanes crashing to earth, toppling buildings during earthquakes. There is no other force in the universe remotely like the fantastic force of gravity.

Ronald Schiller, as quoted in *Reader's Digest*, July 1971

One of the healthiest ways to gamble is with a spade and a package of garden seeds.

Dan Bennett, as quoted in *Reader's Digest*, April 1972

A garden is a lovely thing
That must be spaded in the spring
Weeded when the summer's searing
Mulched in fall when winter's nearing.

Of all the seasons, do you wonder
I like it best when it's snowed under?

Glen Lorang, as quoted in *Reader's Digest*, January 1957

Winter is not a season, it's an occupation.

Sinclair Lewis, as quoted in *Reader's Digest*, January 1952

It is only now and then, in a jungle, or amidst the towering white menace of a burnt or burning Australian forest, that Nature strips the moral veils from vegetation and we apprehend its stark ferocity.

H. G. Wells, *The Happy Turning*

Urban Life

Great cities are not like towns, only larger. They differ from towns and suburbs in basic ways, and one of these is that cities are, by definition, full of strangers.

Jane Jacobs, *The Death and Life of Great American Cities*

A neighborhood is where, when you go out of it, you get beat up.

Murray Kempton, quoting Puerto Rican labor office worker, *America Comes of Middle Age*

The trouble with New York is it's so convenient to everything I can't afford.

Jack Barry, as quoted in *Reader's Digest*, December 1952

In great cities men are like a lot of stones thrown together in a bag; their jagged corners are rubbed off till in the end they are as smooth as marbles.

W. Somerset Maugham, *The Summing Up*

The city man, in his neon-and-mazda glare, knows nothing of nature's midnight. His electric lamps surround him with synthetic sunshine. They push back the dark. They defend him from the realities of the age-old night.

Edwin Way Teale, North with the Spring

Commuters give the city its tidal restlessness; natives give it solidity and continuity; but the settlers give it passion.

E. B. White, as quoted in Holiday, April 1949

A twofold national problem is how to preserve the wilderness in the country and get rid of the jungle in the cities.

Bill Vaughan, as quoted in Reader's Digest, October 1963

We will neglect our cities to our peril, for in neglecting them we neglect the nation.

John F. Kennedy, message to Congress, January 30, 1962

The city is squalid and sinister,
With the silver-barred street in the midst,
Slow-moving,
A river leading nowhere.

Amy Lowell, Sword Blades and Poppy Seeds

American city: A place where by the time you've finished paying for your home in the suburbs, the suburbs have moved 20 miles farther out.

Earl Wilson, as quoted in Reader's Digest, June 1956

Coming to New York from the muted mistiness of London, as I regularly do, is like traveling from a monochrome antique shop to a Technicolor bazaar.

Kenneth Tynan, as quoted in Holiday, December 1960　761

The pneumatic noisemaker is becoming the emblematic Sound of New York, the way the bells of Big Ben are the Sound of London.

Horace Sutton, as quoted in the *Saturday Evening Post*, March 11, 1961

Cities are growing so fast their arteries are showing through their outskirts.

Clyde Moore, as quoted in *Reader's Digest*, November 1963

Many times have I consulted them as one consults an oracle. If we are to believe the ancients, the voice of the people must be taken very seriously indeed.

Sir Gladwyn Jebb, British ambassador to the United Nations, on Manhattan cab drivers, as quoted in news summaries of February 24, 1954

A pedestrian is a man in danger of his life; a walker is a man in possession of his soul.

David McCord, as quoted in *Reader's Digest*, July 1949

He speaks English with the flawless imperfection of a New Yorker.

Gilbert Millstein, on restaurant owner André Surmain, as quoted in *Esquire*, January 1962

Take a good deep breath of filth.

Alan Steiger and Stanton Burnett, program on air pollution
in New York, NBC-TV, December 3, 1962

New York is a different country. Maybe it ought to have a separate government. Everybody thinks differently, acts differently—they just don't know what the hell the rest of the United States is.

Henry Ford, as quoted in *Reader's Digest*, October 1973

Who the hell looks up in this town? Who has time?

David Zickerman, New York cab driver, when asked if he
had noticed a reproduction of the Statue of Liberty atop a
West Side warehouse, as quoted in *The New York Times*,
October 2, 1960

Slums may well be breeding-grounds of crime, but middle-class suburbs are incubators of apathy and delirium.

Cyril Connolly, *The Unquiet Grave*

Suburbs are things to come into the city from.

Art Linkletter, *A Child's Garden of Misinformation*

The greatest crime committed in American cities may not be murder, rape or robbery, but rather the wholesale and constant exposure of children to noise, ugliness and garbage in the street, thereby conditioning them to accept public squalor as the normal state of affairs and diminishing their future enjoyment of life.

René Dubos, as quoted in *Reader's Digest*, March 1972

A ghetto can be improved in one way only: out of existence.

James Baldwin, *Nobody Knows My Name*

A quiet city is a contradiction in terms. It is a thing uncanny, spectral.

Max Beerbohm, *Mainly on the Air*

Vandalism is rebellion with a cause. To prevent it, we must combat the cause itself—social indifference, apathy, the loss of community, neighborhood and family values.

Philip G. Zimbardo, as quoted in Reader's Digest, May 1973

The silence of a shut park does not sound like the country silence: it is tense and confined.

Elizabeth Bowen, The Death of the Heart

The real illness of the American city today, and especially of the deprived groups within it, is voicelessness.

Harvey Cox, The Secular City

What is needed to deal effectively with the twin problems of urban overcrowding and rural blight is a comprehensive national population resettlement plan that will enable us to *design* our future instead of resigning ourselves to it.

Ronald Schiller, as quoted in Reader's Digest, July 1972

The city roared with life, traffic sped up the Outer Drive, trucks rumbled down Western Avenue, and elevated trains roared by overhead on the wondrous El, reared against the sky. Randolph Street in the theatrical district blazed with light all night long. . . . And always there was the wonderful lake, a limitless inland sea. It was all rather innocent foolishness. Today the El no longer seems romantic to me, just an obsolete nuisance. The slums are not picturesque, just appalling; Randolph Street and Rush Street not glamorous, just tinsel cheap; gangsterism not exciting, just dreary and dangerous. But this change is in me, not in the city, and I have no doubt that only yesterday some other young man got off a train from Indiana, longing for excitement and opportunity, and found it here.

John Bartlow Martin, on Chicago, as quoted in the
Saturday Evening Post, October 15, 1960

The only real advantage of New York is that all its inhabitants ascend to heaven right after their deaths, having served their full term in hell right on Manhattan Island.

Barnard Bulletin, September 22, 1967

Melting pot Harlem—Harlem of honey and chocolate and caramel and rum and vinegar and lemon and lime and gall. Dusky dream Harlem rumbling into a nightmare tunnel where the subway from the Bronx keeps right on downtown.

Langston Hughes, as quoted in *Freedomways*, Summer 1963

What poor as well as rich families leave on the sidewalks these days for the Sanitation Department to cart away looks to me like the stuff people used to load on moving vans, not on dump trucks. I see lamps, umbrellas, TV sets, playpens, baby carriages, bicycles, tables, refrigerators—all cut down in the prime of life.

We have been educated to use; we shall now have to be reeducated to reuse, restore, renew and conserve.

Sam Levenson, as quoted in *Reader's Digest*, June 1972

What we get in the city is not life, but what someone else tells us about life.

David Grayson, *Adventures in Contentment*

In the Big City a man will disappear with the suddenness and completeness of a candle that is blown out.

O. Henry, *Sixes and Sevens*

Already, within the main centers of change, in California and Cambridge, Mass., in New York and London and Tokyo, millions are living the life of the future. What makes them different? Certainly they are richer, better educated, more mobile. But what specifically marks them is the fact that they "live faster."

To survive in such communities, however, the individual must come infinitely more adaptable than ever before. Above all he must understand *transience*. Transience is the new "temporariness" in everyday life. It can be defined as the rate at which our relationships—with things, places, people and information—turn over.

Alvin Toffler, as quoted in Reader's Digest, August 1971

Teen-agers in the ghetto see the hell caught by their parents struggling to get somewhere. They make up their own minds they would rather be like the hustlers whom they see dressed "sharp" and flashing money. So the ghetto youth become attracted to the hustler worlds of dope, thievery, prostitution, general crime and immorality.

Malcolm X, Autobiography of Malcolm X

Hardly a day goes by, you know, that some innocent bystander ain't shot in New York City. All you got to do is be innocent and stand by and they're gonna shoot you. The other day, there was four people shot in one day—four innocent people—in New York City. Amazing. It's kind of hard to *find* four innocent people in New York. That's why a policeman don't have to aim. He just shoots anywhere. Whoever he hits, that's the right one.

Will Rogers, as quoted in Reader's Digest, June 1972

You find it driving to work, alongside all those other people, but alone with your thoughts. The car has become a secular sanctuary for the individual, his shrine to the self, his mobile Walden Pond.

Edward McDonagh, as quoted in Time, May 10, 1963

We ought to learn from biology and go underground. In biology, the circulation systems are always on the inside. The idea in our cities is to take all things that have to do with machines and put them underground. This would leave the area above the ground to the walking people. Eventually, all urban transit would have to go underground, no matter what the cost.

Constantinos A. Doxiadis, as quoted in Reader's Digest,
March 1972

The modern town-dweller has no God and No Devil; he lives without awe, without admiration, without fear.

William Ralph Inge, *Outspoken Essays; First Series*

So our cities are dying. And they will go on dying until the federal income tax is used to pay for the solutions to national problems. . . . More than money is needed, however. The creativity of the nation is necessary; the United States has to figure out how to make an urban society work.

Richard Reeves, as quoted in *Reader's Digest*,
August 1971

When we come to a large urban area, we forget to bring with us the most precious ingredient of life in a small place—humanness. . . .

It's an old saying that what is everybody's business is nobody's business. City officials, the police, clubs, churches, schools and newspapers can't do all that's needed to make a town livable. They can help, but it is we ordinary citizens—all of us together—who create the spirit of a community, whether it be New York or Eastport, Maine.

David Dunn, *Try Giving Yourself Away*

It does not take 20-20 vision to see that our big cities are not merely in a state of crisis. They are dying. Inevitably.

They are physically obsolete, financially unworkable, crime-ridden, garbage-strewn, polluted, torn by racial conflicts, wallowing in welfare, unemployment, despair and official corruption. As they exist at present they are unsalvageable, destined to join the dinosaur in deserved extinction. . . .

Eugene Raskin, as quoted in *Reader's Digest*,
August 1971

We shape our buildings; thereafter they shape us.

Sir Winston Churchill, as quoted in *Time*, August 8, 1954

[New York] is the place where all the aspirations of the Western World meet to form one vast master aspiration, as powerful as the action of a steam dredge. It is the icing on the pie called Christian civilization.

H. L. Mencken, Prejudices: Sixth Series

Made by General Motors, on order from Sears Roebuck.

Richard Condon, on American cities, as quoted in
Newsweek, February 11, 1963

We are, in effect, returning to the Middle Ages, when men wouldn't dare venture out without their armor. The modern American puts on his car in the morning, thereby changing from a soft-skinned target for autos into a missile himself.

Robert Rodale, as quoted in Reader's Digest, March 1973

No more fiendish punishment could be devised, were such a thing physically possible, than that one should be turned loose in society and remain absolutely unnoticed by all the members thereof.

William James, The Principles of Psychology

Any fool can stand upon a hill in the country and be aware that grass is up and trees have begun to bud; but in the city spring is served a la carte rather than in heaping portions. Back on my farm lie heavy woods, yet none of these trees appeals to me so deeply as a scrubby sapling which grew in the back yard of my house in New York—when a tree digs its roots down among water pipes and gas mains and thrusts its way up through dust and cinders, that's something. I sometimes think that never blooms a tulip quite so red as that which shows its head in a Park Avenue flower bed between the traffic. We Manhattan nature lovers love her best because we know so little about her.

Heywood Broun, as quoted in Reader's Digest, April 1938

I doubt if there is anything in the world uglier than a midwestern city.

Frank Lloyd Wright, address in Evanston, Illinois, August 8,
1954

Clear out eight hundred thousand people and preserve it as a museum piece.

> Frank Lloyd Wright, suggesting how to dispose of Boston,
> as quoted in *The New York Times*, November 27, 1955

A hundred times have I thought New York is a catastrophe and fifty times: It is a beautiful catastrophe.

> Le Corbusier, as quoted in the New York *Herald Tribune*,
> August 6, 1961

Our national flower is the concrete overleaf.

> Lewis Mumford, on the proliferation of superhighways, as
> quoted in *Quote*, October 8, 1961

Boston is a moral and intellectual nursery always busy applying first principles to trifles.

> George Santayana, *Santayana: The Later Years*

The name of the subspecies, then, is Exurbanite; its habitat, the Exurbs. The exurb is generally further from New York than the suburb on the same railway line. Its houses are more widely spaced and generally more various and more expensive. The town center tends to quaintness and class, rather than modernity and glass, and the further one lives from the station the better.

> A. C. Spectorsky, *The Exurbanites*

With progress in roads came more cars, more roads for the cars, and more cars for the roads that had been built to accommodate more cars.

> "One for the Roads," report on U. S. highways and
> superhighways, as quoted in *Time*, October 6, 1961

After 20 annual visits, I am still surprised each time I return to see this giant asparagus bed of alabaster and rose and green skyscrapers.

> Cecil Beaton, on New York, *It Gives Me Great Pleasure*   769

Source Index

776

777

778

781

Moses, Grandma, 18
Moses, Robert, 20–21
Mosley, Jean Bell, 11
Mostert, Noel, 757
Motherwell, Robert, 13, 20
Motley, Arthur H., 215
Moynihan, Daniel P., 327
Mue, Edwin, 147
Mueller, Robert, 408
Muggeridge, Malcolm, 61, 423, 510, 731
Muhammad Ali, 557
Muldoon, Mary, 407
Muller, Herbert J., 638
Mumford, Lewis, 23, 117, 174, 319, 461, 544, 647, 705, 737, 769
Munn, Charles Clark, 513
Muñoz Marin, Luis, 743
Munthe, Axel, 464
Murchison, Clint, Jr., 192
Murray, Dave, 208
Murray, James D. C., 353
Murray, Ken, 540
Murrow, Edward R., 368
Murry, John Middleton, 464
Musselman, M. M., 89
Mussolini, Benito, 714–15
Myers, Henry Alonzo, 653
Myrdal, Gunnar, 324

Nabrit, James J., Jr., 353
Nader, Ralph, 592
Nash, Ogden, 41, 75, 103, 112, 125, 148, 255, 505–06, 516, 563–64, 662, 670, 680, 742
Nathan, George Jean, 5–6, 52, 63, 138, 384, 399–400, 452, 564, 597, 661, 700
Nathan, Robert, 376
National (Wickersham) Commission on Law Observance and Law Enforcement (*Report*), 337
Neely, Luke, 48, 547
Nehru, Jawaharlal, 204, 313, 574
Nelson, John Kirk, 543
Nevill, Dorothy, 147
Newman, Jon O., 138
Newman, Mildred, 470
Newman, Paul, 52
Newton, A. Edward, 186
Newton, Howard W., 173, 315
Newton, Joseph Fort, 450, 474
New York Times, 274
New York *World*, 59
Nichols, Beverley, 327
Nicolson, Harold, 101, 187–88, 621, 698
Nicolson, Marjorie, 404
Niebuhr, Reinhold, 287, 597, 697, 699, 749
Nielsen, Helen, 511
Nimitz, Chester W., 731
Nin, Anais, 467
Nixon, Richard M., 67, 185, 221–22, 335, 352, 480, 559, 573, 610–11, 738
Nizer, Louis, 151, 174, 447, 513
Nock, Albert Jay, 155, 458, 526

Noland, Felix, 474
Nolen, William A., 561
Nordell, Roderick, 156
Norman, Jean Mary, 7
Norris, Kathleen, 89, 670
Norwood, Frederick, 722
Novalis, M., 320
Nungesser, Charles, 485
Nyerere, Julius K., 602

O'Brien, Edna, 413
O'Brien, Robert, 758
O'Casey, Sean, 523
O'Connor, Frank, 398
O'Connor, M. D., 691
O'Faolain, Sean, 749
O'Hara, Neal, 176, 197
Olinghouse, Lane, 90
Oliver, Vic, 193
Olivier, Laurence, 50
O'Malley, Pat, 148
O'Neal, Paul, 336
O'Neill, Eugene, 358
Oppenheimer, J. Robert, 7, 633
Orben, Robert, 185, 605–06
Origo, Iris, 668
Orr, Louis, 634
Ortega y Gasset, José, 438
Orton, William A., 150
Orwell, George, 176, 194, 295, 298, 310, 619, 705
Osborn, Fairfield, 740–41
Oursler, Fulton, 468
Overstreet, Bonaro W., 116
Overstreet, Harry, 29, 477
O'Walsh, Francis, 267
Owen, Jean, 470
Owens, Jesse, 303

Packard, Vance, 193
Paddleford, Clementine, 119
Pagnol, Marcel, 497
Paige, Satchel, 180
Pain, Barry, 81
Paley, Grace, 408
Palmer, Cecil, 594
Palmer, George Herbert, 241
Palmer, Paul, 736
Pankhurst, Christabel, 415
Papadakis, Angie, 75
Papashvily, George, 492
Park, Robert E., 634
Parker, Dorothy, 59, 79, 388, 407, 471, 523, 530
Parker, John F., 618
Parrish, Mary, 380
Parsons, Geoffrey, 484
Pasternak, Boris, 278, 282
Paterson, Isabel, 656
Patterson, Grove, 483
Patterson, Norman, 403
Patton, George S., 480, 714, 730
Paul, Art, 212

786

Subject Index

795

ice cream, 565–66
idealism, idealists, 325, 501, 693, 696
  definitions of, 507, 617
  power and, 307
ideals, 447, 698
  vs. possible, 432
ideas, 281, 449, 489, 499
  action and, 438
  books and, 36, 37, 155
  fear of, 239, 299, 431
  new, 145, 242, 443, 450, 452, 455, 506
  power of, 309
  transplanted, 437
identity, memory as core of, 459
"I don't know," 521
ignorance, 247–50, 439
  advantages of, 248
illness, 262–69
illusions, 457, 458
imagination, 413, 446, 454, 489, 550
  child's, 76, 77, 78, 79
  vs. knowledge, 249
  realization and, 179
imbeciles, 344
immorality, definition of, 696
immortality, 537, 684, 687
  deserving of, 446
  love and, 390
  meaning of, 449
immortals, 23
impartiality, 333
impatience, 492, 506, 759
  as sin, 448
impeachment proceedings, 603–04
Impossible, vs. "Difficult," 518
impulses, 441
incompetence:
  law and, 347
  level of, 170, 208
"in" crowds, 116
India, 313
Indians, American, 300
indifference:
  love and, 380, 399
  as sin, 696
"indispensable man," 579
individuality, 314, 323, 450, 458, 461
industrialism, 736
infidelity, 418, 423
inflation, definition of, 217
injustice (see also justice), 341, 348, 597
  sense of, 346
insects, 753
  takeover by, 299
insincerity, 465
inspiration, 481
instincts:
  aggressiveness and, 389
  civilization vs., 315
  of women, 397
insults, 495, 523
integrity, 698
intellectuals, 635, 642
  types of, 431
intelligence, 187, 458

  vs. sense, 515
  signs and tests of, 446, 480
intelligentsia, glibness in, 152
intimacy, communication and, 158, 159
intolerance, 468, 692
  age and, 118
inventions, 202, 280
investments, 519
  in land, 197
  in stock, 200, 203, 207
invocations, 151
Iron Curtain, 602
irrationality, 637
irreverent observations, 489–511
isms, 460
Israel, 315, 726
Italy, Italians, 535
  women and, 403, 415

Jacob and the angel, 346
jazz, 32
jealousy, 696
  in marriage, 103, 375
Jefferson, Thomas, 504, 615
Jesus Christ, 469, 681, 684
Jews:
  vs. Arabs, 726
  historic sense of, 314
  Israel and, 315
John XXIII, Pope, 726–27
jokes, 530
journalism, vs. fiction, 161
joy, 477, 479, 654, 658, 684
  sharing of, 478
joys, small, 484
Judeo-Christian ethic, 322–23
judges, 333–40
  decisions of, 333, 334, 337, 338
  English, 334
  types of, 339–40
jukeboxes, 119
jury service, 337
justice (see also courts), 301, 311, 331–70,
    597
  for accuser, 335
  as fairness, 349
  institution and, 342
  miscarriages of, 345
juvenile delinquency, 75, 83, 107, 353

kindness, 259, 379, 482, 664, 682, 696
kissing, 394, 396, 418, 419, 425
  making up and, 392
  among women, 391
knowledge, 247–50, 461
  humbleness and, 248, 249
  incompleteness of, 449
  vs. understanding, 249
  use of, 248
"Know Thyself," 150, 260
Korea, invasion of, 583

labor (see also work), 198–207
  demands of, 202–03, 207
  machines vs., 208

799

803